THE INVINCIBLE
ARMOUR WARS

East Riding of Yorkshire
Library and Information Service

The Invincible Iron Man: Armour Wars

The Invincible Iron Man: Armour Wars. Marvel Pocketbook Vol. 4. Contains material originally published in magazine form as The Invincible Iron Man (Vol 1) #225-232. First printing 2013. Published by Panini Publishing, a division of Panini UK Limited. Mike Riddell, Managing Director. Alan O'Keefe, Managing Editor. Mark Irvine, Production Manager. Marco M. Lupoi, Publishing Director Europe. Ed Hammond, Reprint Editor. Sam Taylor, Editorial Assistant, Eddie Jones, Designer. Office of publication: Brockbourne House, 77 Mount Ephraim, Tunbridge Wells, Kent TN4 8BS. Licensed by Marvel Characters B.V. www.marvel.com. All rights reserved. No similarity between any of the names, characters, persons and/or institutions in this edition with those of any living or dead person or institution is intended, and any such similarity which may exist is purely coincidental. This publication may not be sold, except by authorised dealers, and is sold subject to the condition that it shall not be sold or distributed with any part of its cover or markings removed, nor in a mutilated condition.

Printed in the UK.

ISBN: 978-1-84653-180-4

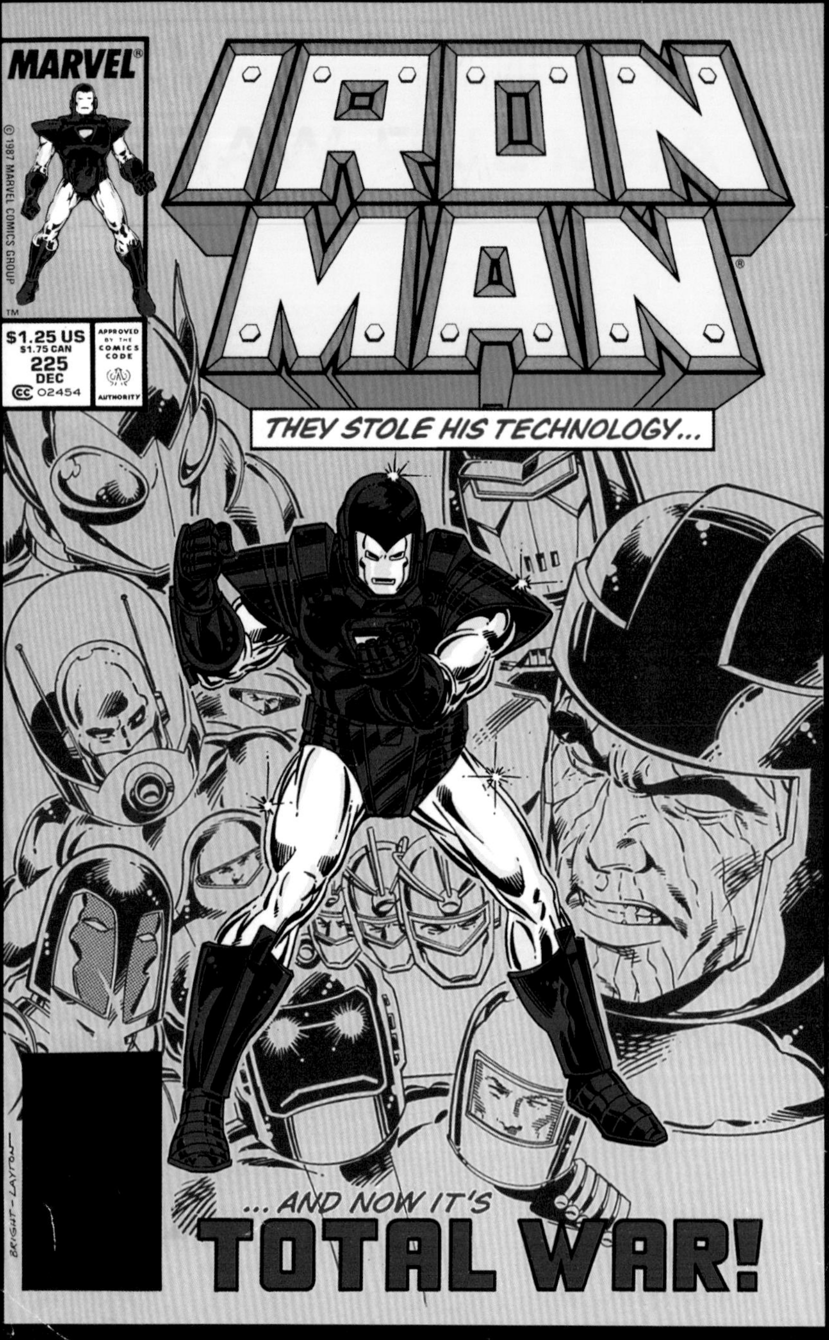
MARVEL®
IRON MAN®
© 1987 MARVEL COMICS GROUP
$1.25 US
$1.75 CAN
225
DEC
CC 02454
APPROVED BY THE COMICS CODE AUTHORITY
THEY STOLE HIS TECHNOLOGY...
... AND NOW IT'S
TOTAL WAR!
BRIGHT–LAYTON

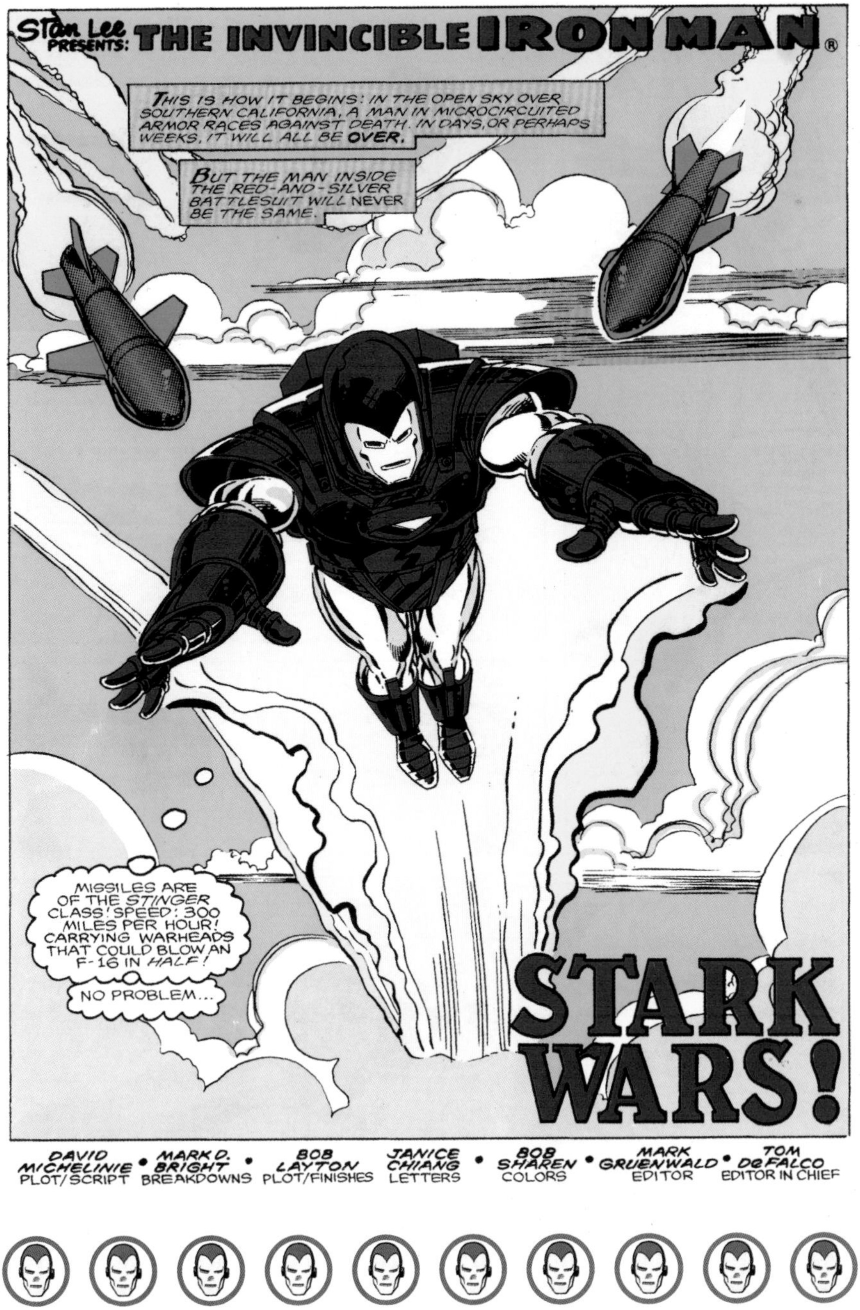
Stan Lee PRESENTS: THE INVINCIBLE IRON MAN®
THIS IS HOW IT BEGINS: IN THE OPEN SKY OVER SOUTHERN CALIFORNIA, A MAN IN MICROCIRCUITED ARMOR RACES AGAINST DEATH. IN DAYS, OR PERHAPS WEEKS, IT WILL ALL BE OVER.
BUT THE MAN INSIDE THE RED-AND-SILVER BATTLESUIT WILL NEVER BE THE SAME.
MISSILES ARE OF THE STINGER CLASS! SPEED: 300 MILES PER HOUR! CARRYING WARHEADS THAT COULD BLOW AN F-16 IN HALF!
NO PROBLEM...
STARK WARS!

DAVID MICHELINIE PLOT/SCRIPT • MARK D. BRIGHT BREAKDOWNS • BOB LAYTON PLOT/FINISHES • JANICE CHIANG LETTERS • BOB SHAREN COLORS • MARK GRUENWALD EDITOR • TOM DeFALCO EDITOR IN CHIEF

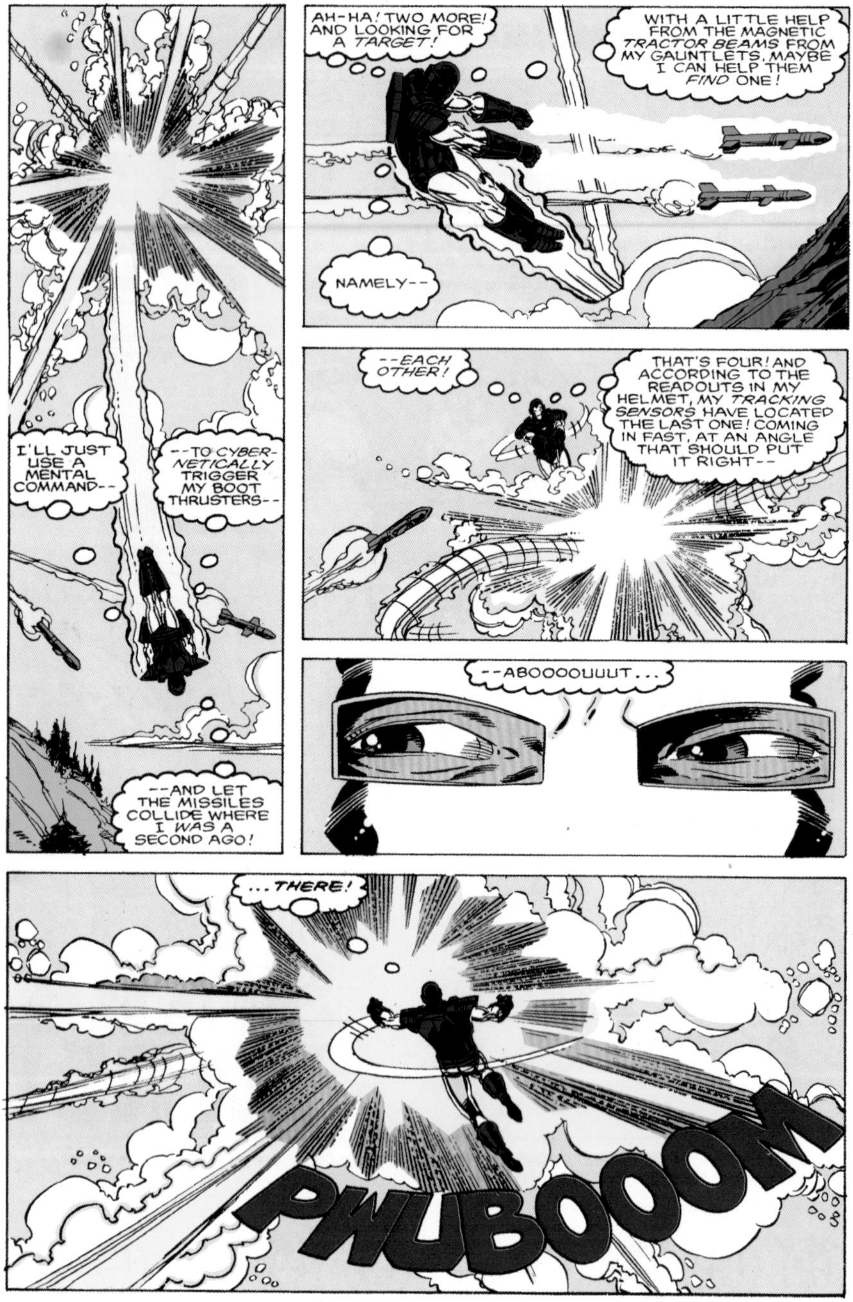

I'LL JUST USE A MENTAL COMMAND--
--TO CYBERNETICALLY TRIGGER MY BOOT THRUSTERS--
--AND LET THE MISSILES COLLIDE WHERE I WAS A SECOND AGO!
AH-HA! TWO MORE! AND LOOKING FOR A TARGET!
WITH A LITTLE HELP FROM THE MAGNETIC TRACTOR BEAMS FROM MY GAUNTLETS, MAYBE I CAN HELP THEM FIND ONE!
NAMELY--
--EACH OTHER!
THAT'S FOUR! AND ACCORDING TO THE READOUTS IN MY HELMET, MY TRACKING SENSORS HAVE LOCATED THE LAST ONE! COMING IN FAST, AT AN ANGLE THAT SHOULD PUT IT RIGHT--
--ABOOOOUUUT...
...THERE!
PWUBOOOM

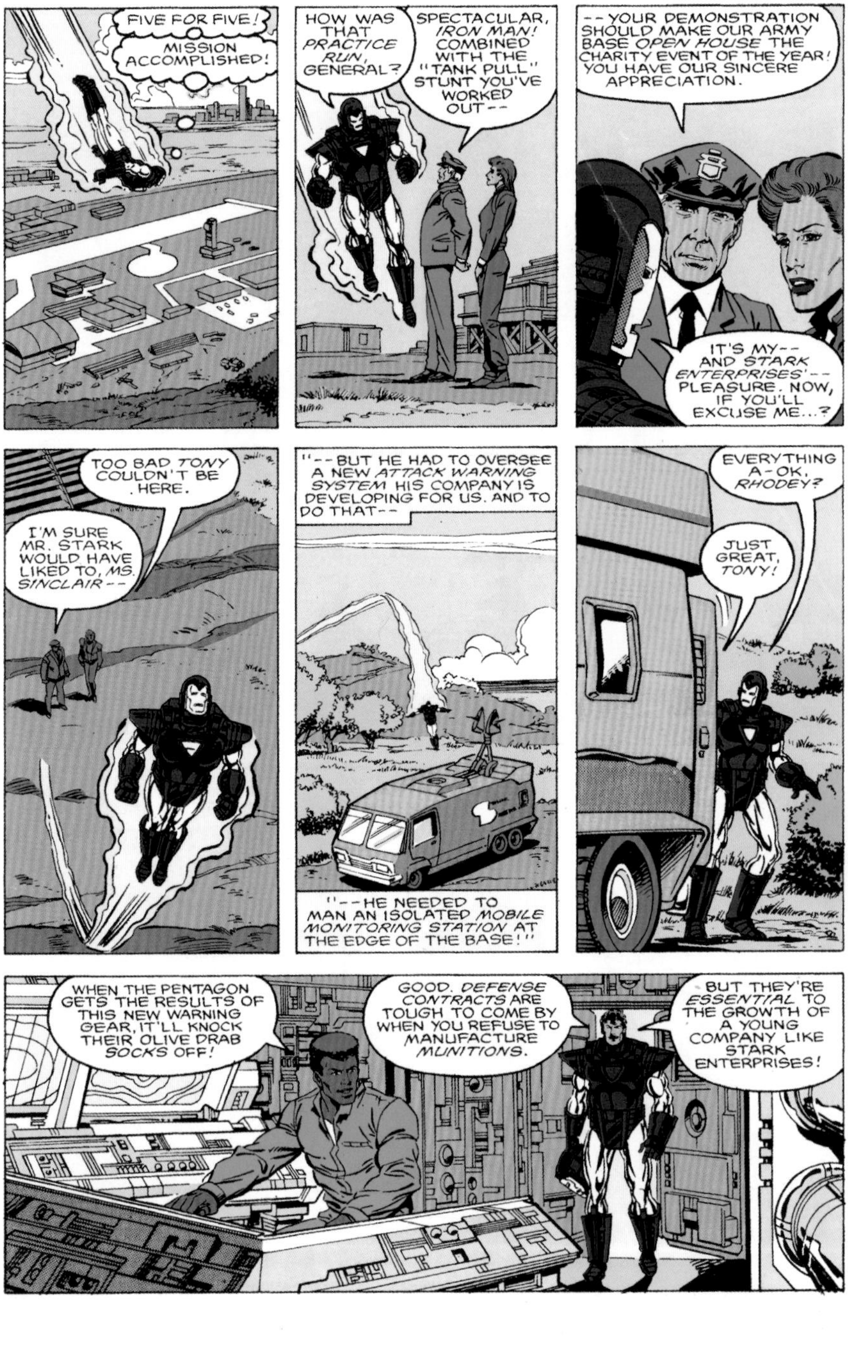
FIVE FOR FIVE!
MISSION ACCOMPLISHED!
HOW WAS THAT PRACTICE RUN, GENERAL?
SPECTACULAR, IRON MAN! COMBINED WITH THE "TANK PULL" STUNT YOU'VE WORKED OUT--
--YOUR DEMONSTRATION SHOULD MAKE OUR ARMY BASE OPEN HOUSE THE CHARITY EVENT OF THE YEAR! YOU HAVE OUR SINCERE APPRECIATION.
IT'S MY-- AND STARK ENTERPRISES'-- PLEASURE. NOW, IF YOU'LL EXCUSE ME...?
TOO BAD TONY COULDN'T BE HERE.
I'M SURE MR. STARK WOULD HAVE LIKED TO, MS. SINCLAIR--
"--BUT HE HAD TO OVERSEE A NEW ATTACK WARNING SYSTEM HIS COMPANY IS DEVELOPING FOR US. AND TO DO THAT--
"--HE NEEDED TO MAN AN ISOLATED MOBILE MONITORING STATION AT THE EDGE OF THE BASE!"
EVERYTHING A-OK, RHODEY?
JUST GREAT, TONY!
WHEN THE PENTAGON GETS THE RESULTS OF THIS NEW WARNING GEAR, IT'LL KNOCK THEIR OLIVE DRAB SOCKS OFF!
GOOD. DEFENSE CONTRACTS ARE TOUGH TO COME BY WHEN YOU REFUSE TO MANUFACTURE MUNITIONS.
BUT THEY'RE ESSENTIAL TO THE GROWTH OF A YOUNG COMPANY LIKE STARK ENTERPRISES!

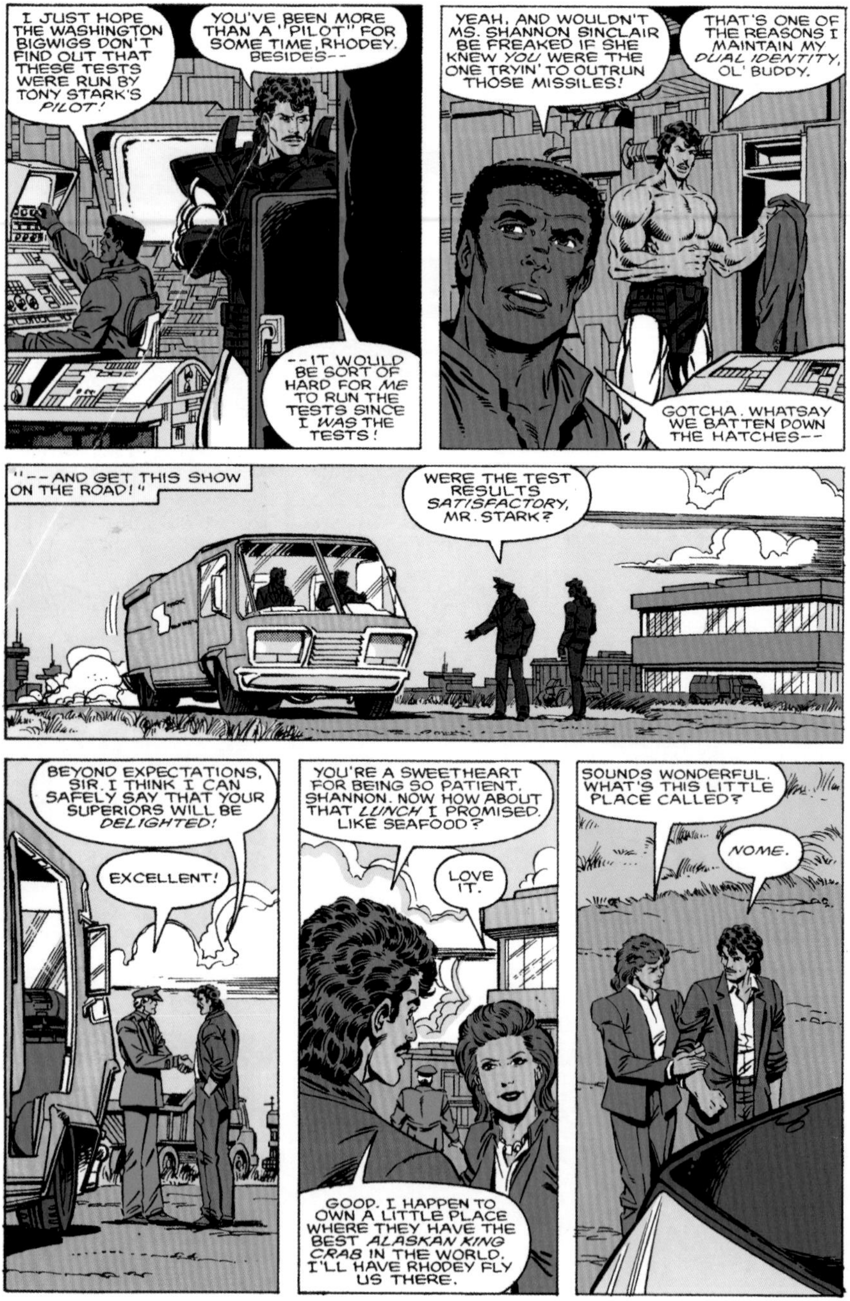
I JUST HOPE THE WASHINGTON BIGWIGS DON'T FIND OUT THAT THESE TESTS WERE RUN BY TONY STARK'S PILOT!
YOU'VE BEEN MORE THAN A "PILOT" FOR SOME TIME, RHODEY. BESIDES--
--IT WOULD BE SORT OF HARD FOR ME TO RUN THE TESTS SINCE I WAS THE TESTS!
YEAH, AND WOULDN'T MS. SHANNON SINCLAIR BE FREAKED IF SHE KNEW YOU WERE THE ONE TRYIN' TO OUTRUN THOSE MISSILES!
THAT'S ONE OF THE REASONS I MAINTAIN MY DUAL IDENTITY, OL' BUDDY.
GOTCHA. WHATSAY WE BATTEN DOWN THE HATCHES--
"--AND GET THIS SHOW ON THE ROAD!"
WERE THE TEST RESULTS SATISFACTORY, MR. STARK?
BEYOND EXPECTATIONS, SIR. I THINK I CAN SAFELY SAY THAT YOUR SUPERIORS WILL BE DELIGHTED!
EXCELLENT!
YOU'RE A SWEETHEART FOR BEING SO PATIENT, SHANNON. NOW HOW ABOUT THAT LUNCH I PROMISED. LIKE SEAFOOD?
LOVE IT.
GOOD. I HAPPEN TO OWN A LITTLE PLACE WHERE THEY HAVE THE BEST ALASKAN KING CRAB IN THE WORLD. I'LL HAVE RHODEY FLY US THERE.
SOUNDS WONDERFUL. WHAT'S THIS LITTLE PLACE CALLED?
NOME.

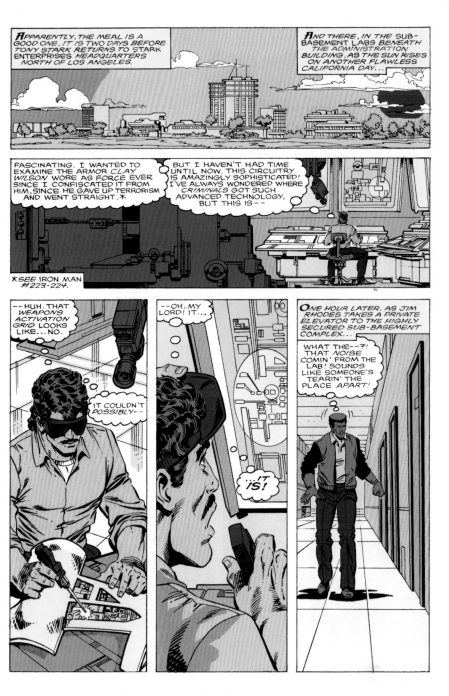

APPARENTLY, THE MEAL IS A GOOD ONE. IT IS TWO DAYS BEFORE TONY STARK RETURNS TO STARK ENTERPRISES HEADQUARTERS NORTH OF LOS ANGELES.

AND THERE, IN THE SUB-BASEMENT LABS BENEATH THE ADMINISTRATION BUILDING, AS THE SUN RISES ON ANOTHER FLAWLESS CALIFORNIA DAY...

FASCINATING. I WANTED TO EXAMINE THE ARMOR CLAY WILSON WORE AS FORCE EVER SINCE I CONFISCATED IT FROM HIM, SINCE HE GAVE UP TERRORISM AND WENT STRAIGHT.*

BUT I HAVEN'T HAD TIME UNTIL NOW. THIS CIRCUITRY IS AMAZINGLY SOPHISTICATED! I'VE ALWAYS WONDERED WHERE CRIMINALS GOT SUCH ADVANCED TECHNOLOGY, BUT THIS IS --

*SEE IRON MAN #223-224.

--HUH. THAT WEAPONS ACTIVATION GRID LOOKS LIKE... NO.

IT COULDN'T POSSIBLY--

--OH, MY LORD! IT...

...IT IS!

ONE HOUR LATER, AS JIM RHODES TAKES A PRIVATE ELEVATOR TO THE HIGHLY SECURED SUB-BASEMENT COMPLEX...

WHAT THE--?! THAT NOISE COMIN' FROM THE LAB! SOUNDS LIKE SOMEONE'S TEARIN' THE PLACE APART!

[9]

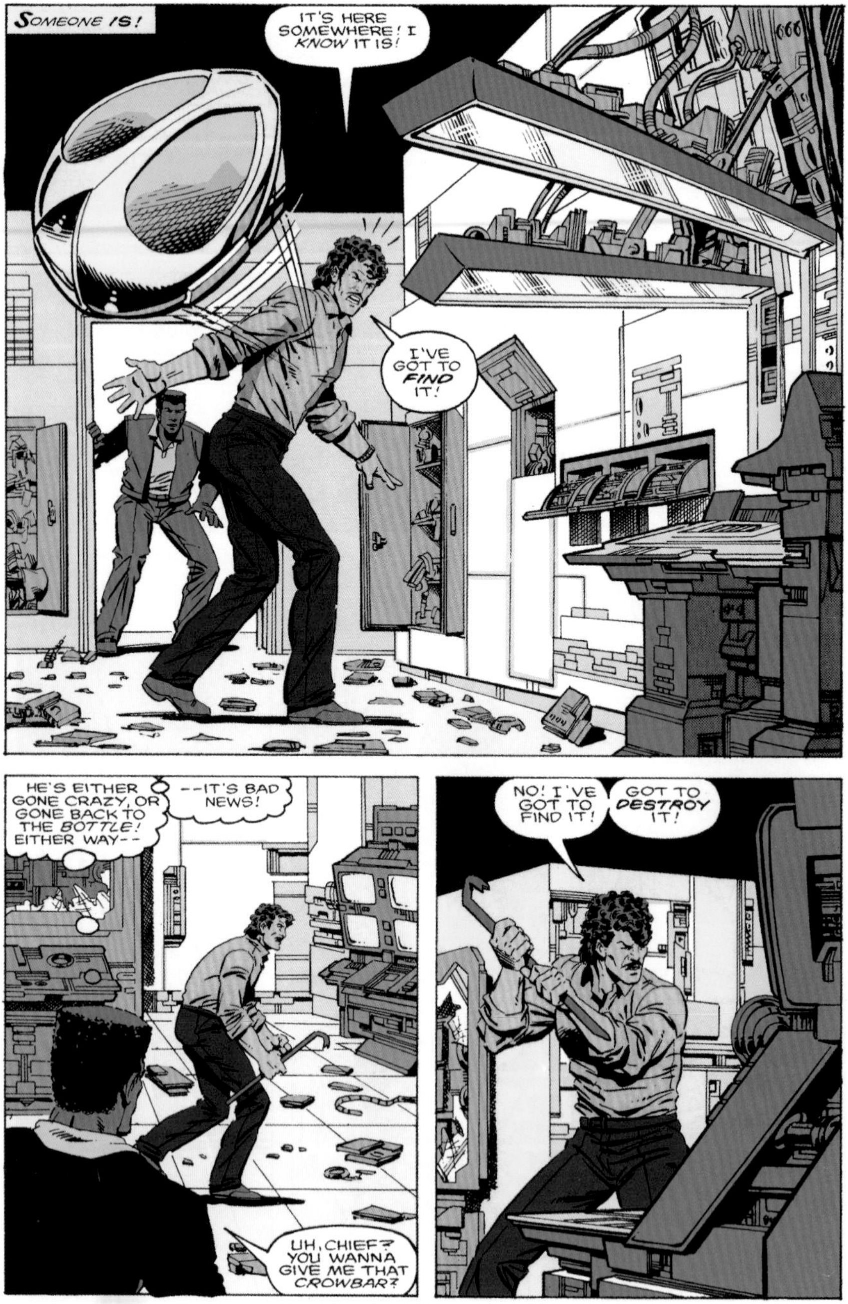
SOMEONE IS!
IT'S HERE SOMEWHERE! I KNOW IT IS!
I'VE GOT TO FIND IT!
HE'S EITHER GONE CRAZY, OR GONE BACK TO THE BOTTLE! EITHER WAY--
--IT'S BAD NEWS!
UH, CHIEF? YOU WANNA GIVE ME THAT CROWBAR?
NO! I'VE GOT TO FIND IT!
GOT TO DESTROY IT!

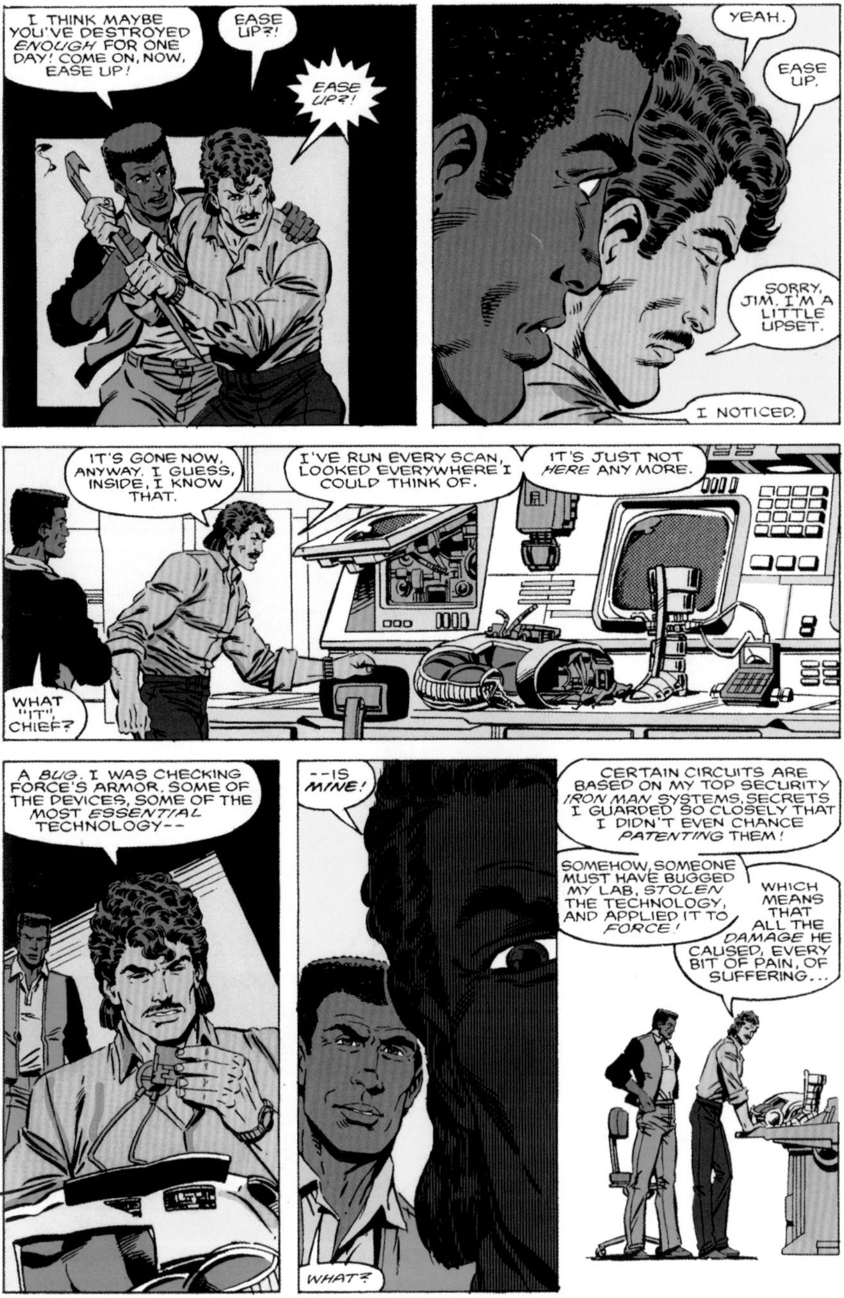
I THINK MAYBE YOU'VE DESTROYED *ENOUGH* FOR ONE DAY! COME ON, NOW, EASE UP!
EASE UP?!
EASE UP?!
YEAH.
EASE UP.
SORRY, JIM. I'M A LITTLE UPSET.
I NOTICED.
IT'S GONE NOW, ANYWAY. I GUESS, INSIDE, I KNOW THAT.
I'VE RUN EVERY SCAN, LOOKED EVERYWHERE I COULD THINK OF.
IT'S JUST NOT *HERE* ANY MORE.
WHAT "IT", CHIEF?
A *BUG*. I WAS CHECKING FORCE'S ARMOR. SOME OF THE DEVICES, SOME OF THE MOST *ESSENTIAL* TECHNOLOGY--
--IS *MINE!*
WHAT?
CERTAIN CIRCUITS ARE BASED ON MY TOP SECURITY *IRON MAN* SYSTEMS, SECRETS I GUARDED SO CLOSELY THAT I DIDN'T EVEN CHANCE *PATENTING* THEM!
SOMEHOW, SOMEONE MUST HAVE BUGGED MY LAB, *STOLEN* THE TECHNOLOGY, AND APPLIED IT TO *FORCE!*
WHICH MEANS THAT ALL THE *DAMAGE* HE CAUSED, EVERY BIT OF PAIN, OF SUFFERING...

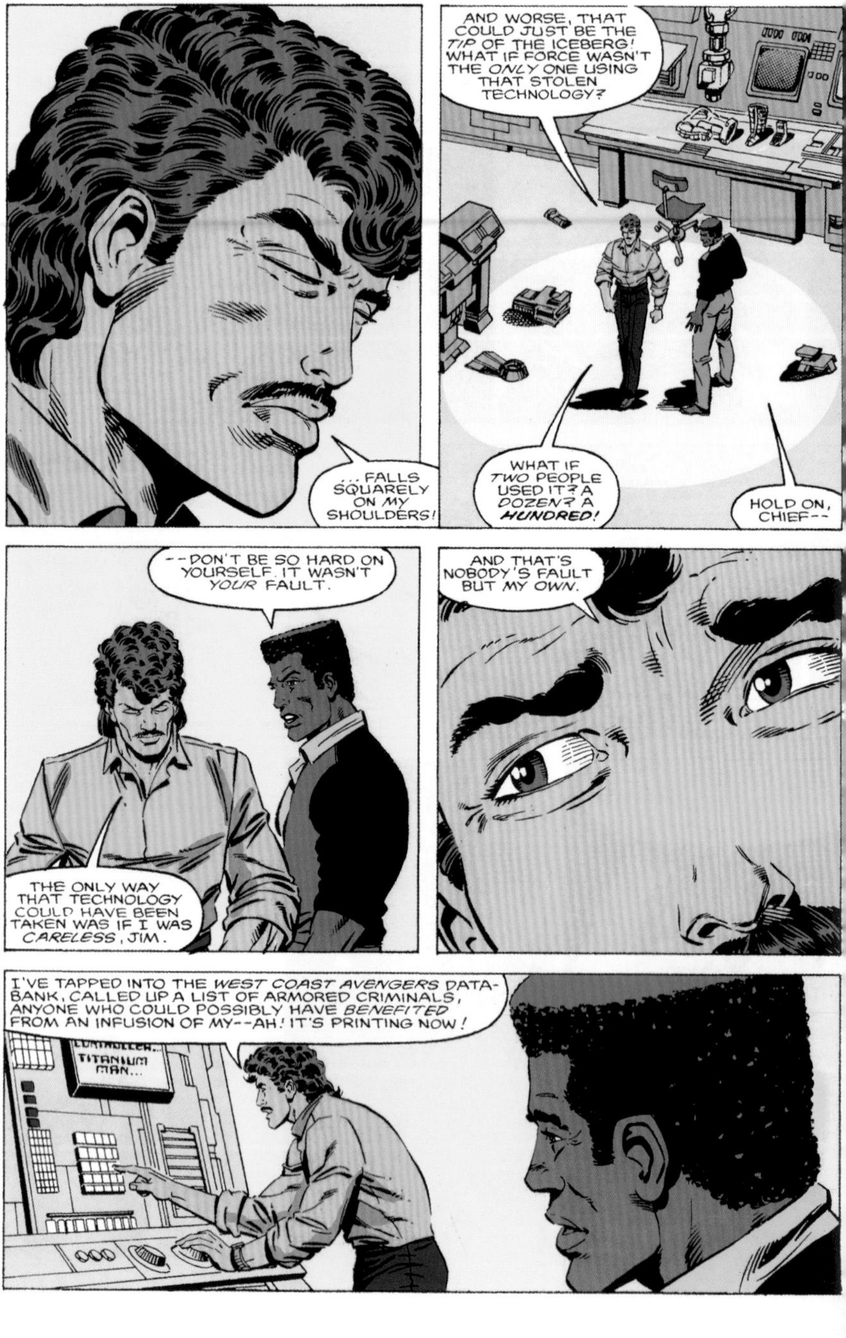
...FALLS SQUARELY ON MY SHOULDERS!
AND WORSE, THAT COULD JUST BE THE TIP OF THE ICEBERG! WHAT IF FORCE WASN'T THE ONLY ONE USING THAT STOLEN TECHNOLOGY?
WHAT IF TWO PEOPLE USED IT? A DOZEN? A HUNDRED!
HOLD ON, CHIEF--
--DON'T BE SO HARD ON YOURSELF. IT WASN'T YOUR FAULT.
THE ONLY WAY THAT TECHNOLOGY COULD HAVE BEEN TAKEN WAS IF I WAS CARELESS, JIM.
AND THAT'S NOBODY'S FAULT BUT MY OWN.
I'VE TAPPED INTO THE WEST COAST AVENGERS DATA-BANK, CALLED UP A LIST OF ARMORED CRIMINALS, ANYONE WHO COULD POSSIBLY HAVE BENEFITED FROM AN INFUSION OF MY--AH! IT'S PRINTING NOW!
TITANIUM MAN...

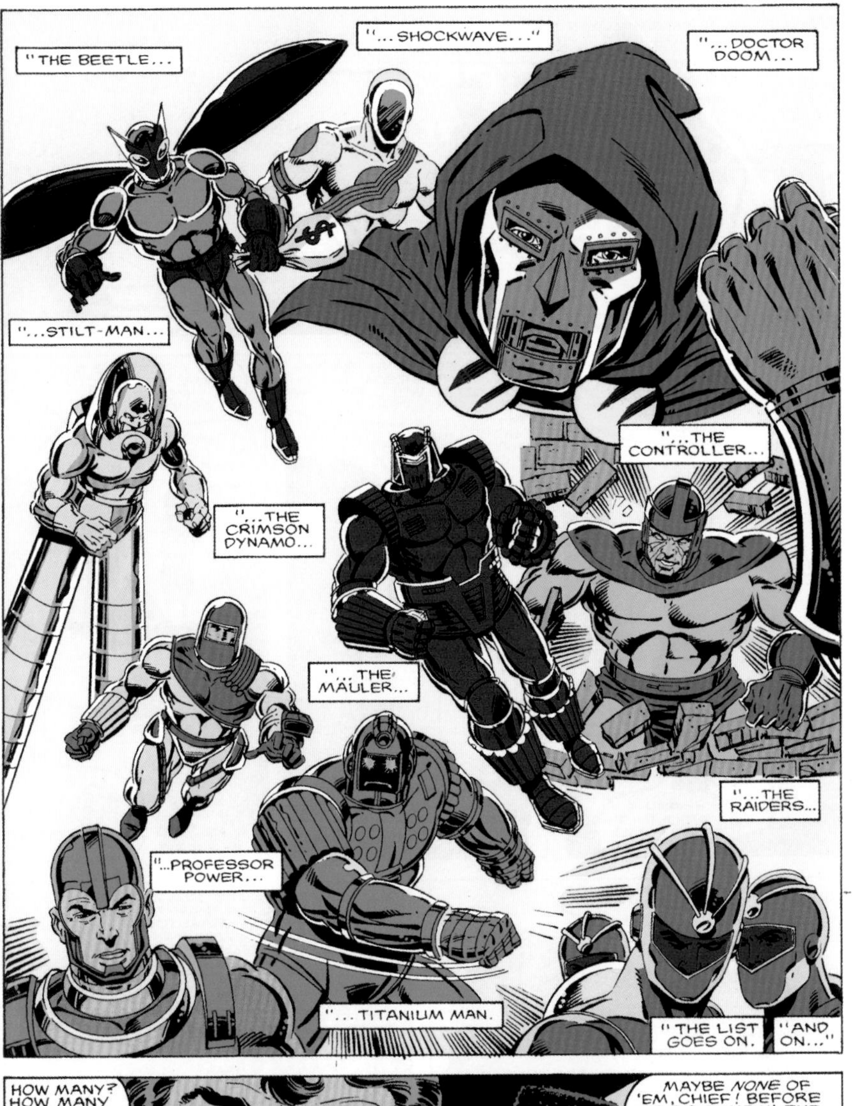
"THE BEETLE...
"...SHOCKWAVE..."
"...DOCTOR DOOM...
"...STILT-MAN...
"...THE CRIMSON DYNAMO...
"...THE CONTROLLER...
"...THE MAULER...
"...THE RAIDERS...
"...PROFESSOR POWER...
"...TITANIUM MAN.
"THE LIST GOES ON.
"AND ON..."

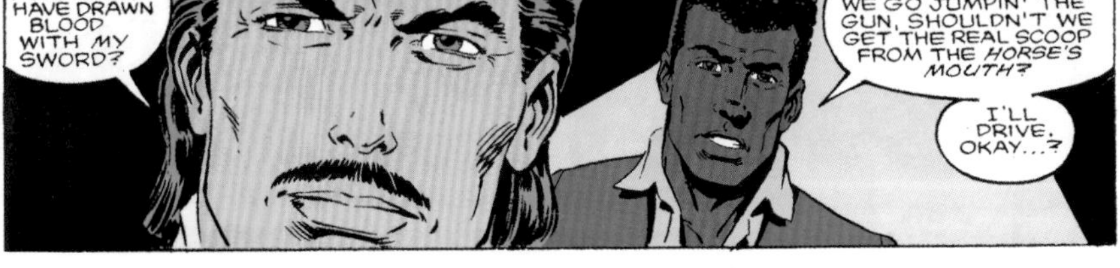
HOW MANY? HOW MANY HAVE DRAWN BLOOD WITH MY SWORD?
MAYBE NONE OF 'EM, CHIEF! BEFORE WE GO JUMPIN' THE GUN, SHOULDN'T WE GET THE REAL SCOOP FROM THE HORSE'S MOUTH?
I'LL DRIVE. OKAY...?

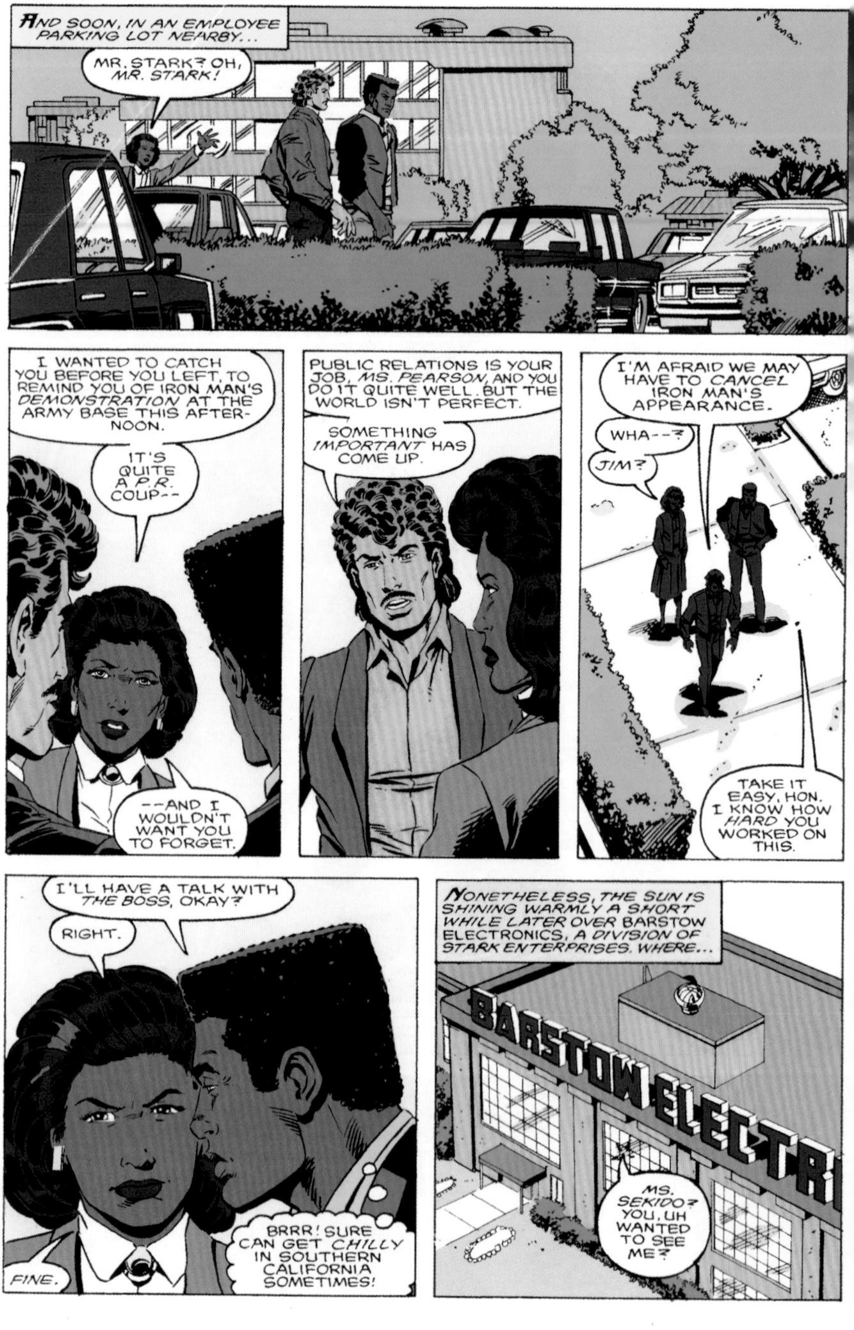
AND SOON, IN AN EMPLOYEE PARKING LOT NEARBY...
MR. STARK? OH, MR. STARK!
I WANTED TO CATCH YOU BEFORE YOU LEFT, TO REMIND YOU OF IRON MAN'S DEMONSTRATION AT THE ARMY BASE THIS AFTER-NOON.
IT'S QUITE A P.R. COUP--
--AND I WOULDN'T WANT YOU TO FORGET.
PUBLIC RELATIONS IS YOUR JOB, MS. PEARSON, AND YOU DO IT QUITE WELL. BUT THE WORLD ISN'T PERFECT.
SOMETHING IMPORTANT HAS COME UP.
I'M AFRAID WE MAY HAVE TO CANCEL IRON MAN'S APPEARANCE.
WHA--?
JIM?
TAKE IT EASY, HON. I KNOW HOW HARD YOU WORKED ON THIS.
I'LL HAVE A TALK WITH THE BOSS, OKAY?
RIGHT.
BRRR! SURE CAN GET CHILLY IN SOUTHERN CALIFORNIA SOMETIMES!
FINE.
NONETHELESS, THE SUN IS SHINING WARMLY A SHORT WHILE LATER OVER BARSTOW ELECTRONICS, A DIVISION OF STARK ENTERPRISES. WHERE...
BARSTOW ELECTR
MS. SEKIDO? YOU, UH WANTED TO SEE ME?

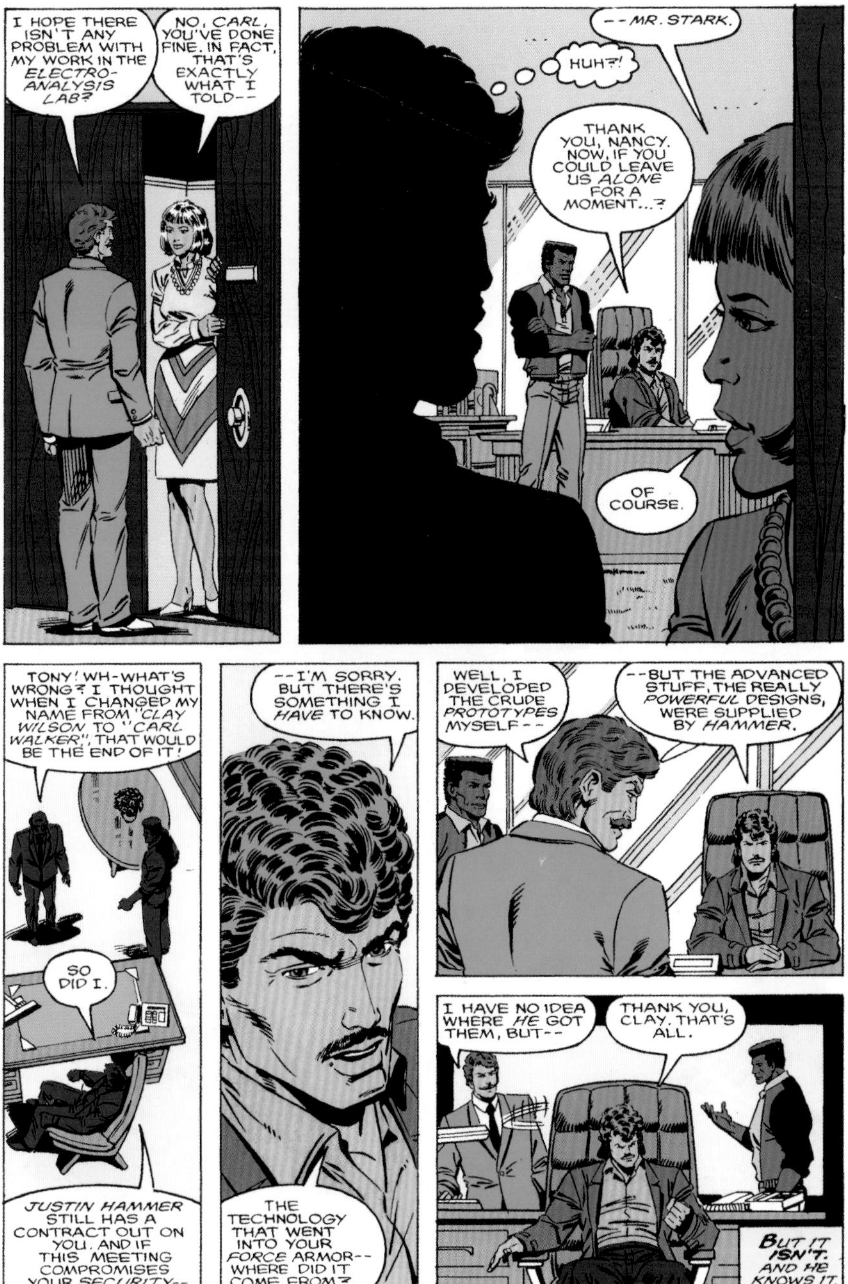
I HOPE THERE ISN'T ANY PROBLEM WITH MY WORK IN THE ELECTRO-ANALYSIS LAB?
NO, CARL, YOU'VE DONE FINE. IN FACT, THAT'S EXACTLY WHAT I TOLD--
--MR. STARK.
HUH?!
THANK YOU, NANCY. NOW, IF YOU COULD LEAVE US ALONE FOR A MOMENT...?
OF COURSE.
TONY! WH-WHAT'S WRONG? I THOUGHT WHEN I CHANGED MY NAME FROM "CLAY WILSON" TO "CARL WALKER", THAT WOULD BE THE END OF IT!
SO DID I.
JUSTIN HAMMER STILL HAS A CONTRACT OUT ON YOU. AND IF THIS MEETING COMPROMISES YOUR SECURITY--
--I'M SORRY. BUT THERE'S SOMETHING I HAVE TO KNOW.
THE TECHNOLOGY THAT WENT INTO YOUR FORCE ARMOR-- WHERE DID IT COME FROM?
WELL, I DEVELOPED THE CRUDE PROTOTYPES MYSELF--
--BUT THE ADVANCED STUFF, THE REALLY POWERFUL DESIGNS, WERE SUPPLIED BY HAMMER.
I HAVE NO IDEA WHERE HE GOT THEM, BUT--
THANK YOU, CLAY. THAT'S ALL.
BUT IT ISN'T. AND HE KNOWS IT.

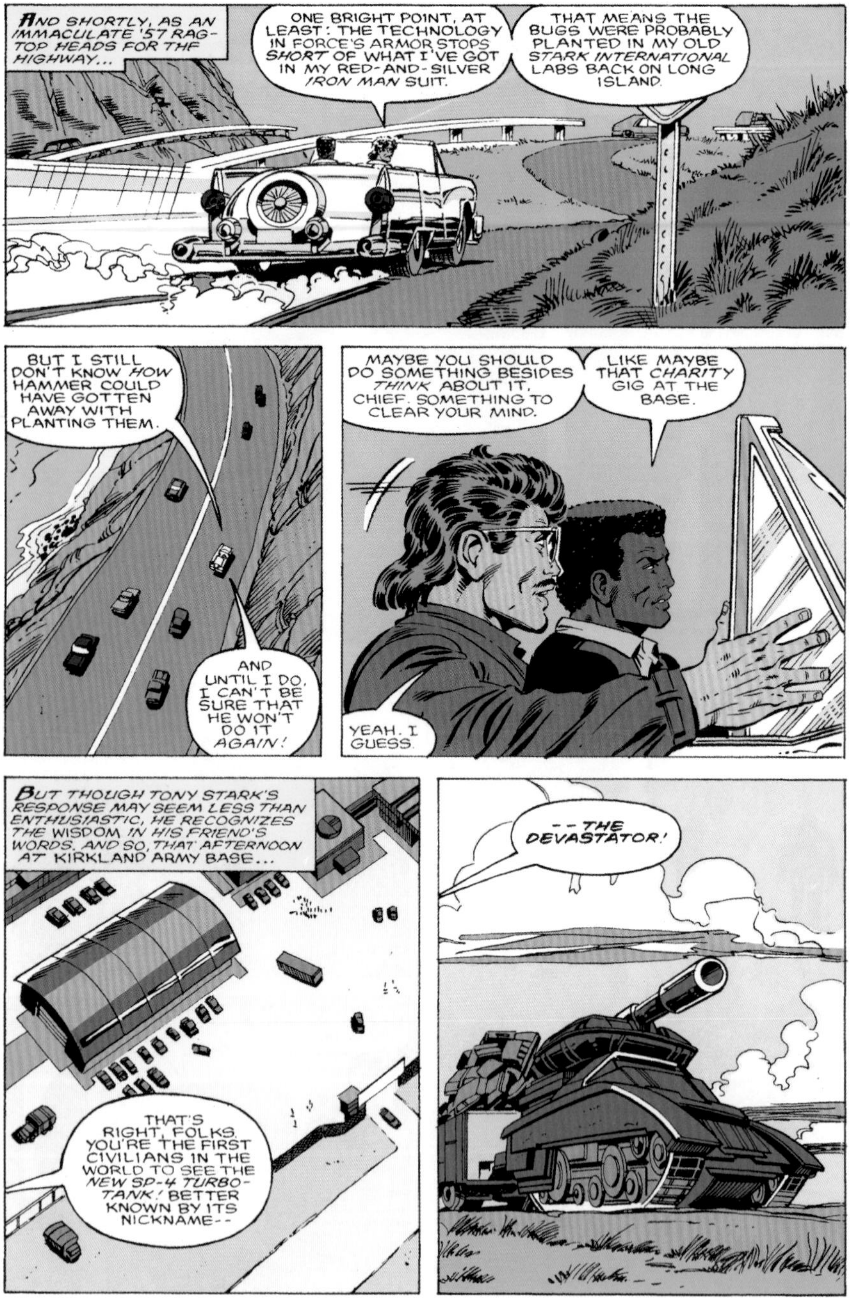
AND SHORTLY, AS AN IMMACULATE '57 RAG-TOP HEADS FOR THE HIGHWAY...
ONE BRIGHT POINT, AT LEAST: THE TECHNOLOGY IN FORCE'S ARMOR STOPS SHORT OF WHAT I'VE GOT IN MY RED-AND-SILVER IRON MAN SUIT.
THAT MEANS THE BUGS WERE PROBABLY PLANTED IN MY OLD STARK INTERNATIONAL LABS BACK ON LONG ISLAND.
BUT I STILL DON'T KNOW HOW HAMMER COULD HAVE GOTTEN AWAY WITH PLANTING THEM.
AND UNTIL I DO, I CAN'T BE SURE THAT HE WON'T DO IT AGAIN!
MAYBE YOU SHOULD DO SOMETHING BESIDES THINK ABOUT IT, CHIEF. SOMETHING TO CLEAR YOUR MIND.
LIKE MAYBE THAT CHARITY GIG AT THE BASE.
YEAH. I GUESS.
BUT THOUGH TONY STARK'S RESPONSE MAY SEEM LESS THAN ENTHUSIASTIC, HE RECOGNIZES THE WISDOM IN HIS FRIEND'S WORDS. AND SO, THAT AFTERNOON AT KIRKLAND ARMY BASE...
THAT'S RIGHT, FOLKS. YOU'RE THE FIRST CIVILIANS IN THE WORLD TO SEE THE NEW SP-4 TURBO-TANK! BETTER KNOWN BY ITS NICKNAME--
--THE DEVASTATOR!

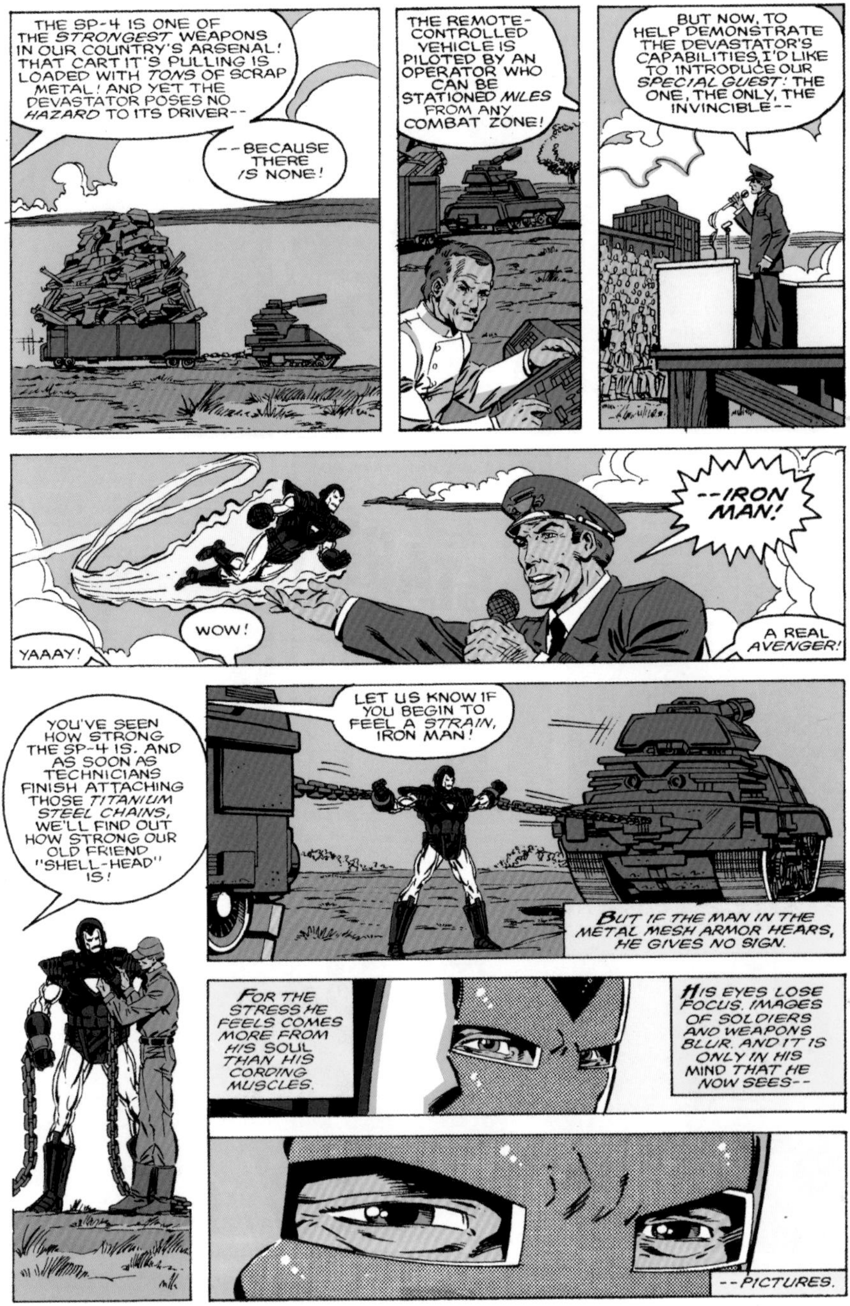
THE SP-4 IS ONE OF THE STRONGEST WEAPONS IN OUR COUNTRY'S ARSENAL! THAT CART IT'S PULLING IS LOADED WITH TONS OF SCRAP METAL! AND YET THE DEVASTATOR POSES NO HAZARD TO ITS DRIVER--
--BECAUSE THERE IS NONE!
THE REMOTE-CONTROLLED VEHICLE IS PILOTED BY AN OPERATOR WHO CAN BE STATIONED MILES FROM ANY COMBAT ZONE!
BUT NOW, TO HELP DEMONSTRATE THE DEVASTATOR'S CAPABILITIES, I'D LIKE TO INTRODUCE OUR SPECIAL GUEST: THE ONE, THE ONLY, THE INVINCIBLE--
--IRON MAN!
YAAAY!
WOW!
A REAL AVENGER!
YOU'VE SEEN HOW STRONG THE SP-4 IS. AND AS SOON AS TECHNICIANS FINISH ATTACHING THOSE TITANIUM STEEL CHAINS, WE'LL FIND OUT HOW STRONG OUR OLD FRIEND "SHELL-HEAD" IS!
LET US KNOW IF YOU BEGIN TO FEEL A STRAIN, IRON MAN!
BUT IF THE MAN IN THE METAL MESH ARMOR HEARS, HE GIVES NO SIGN.
FOR THE STRESS HE FEELS COMES MORE FROM HIS SOUL THAN HIS CORDING MUSCLES.
HIS EYES LOSE FOCUS. IMAGES OF SOLDIERS AND WEAPONS BLUR. AND IT IS ONLY IN HIS MIND THAT HE NOW SEES--
--PICTURES.

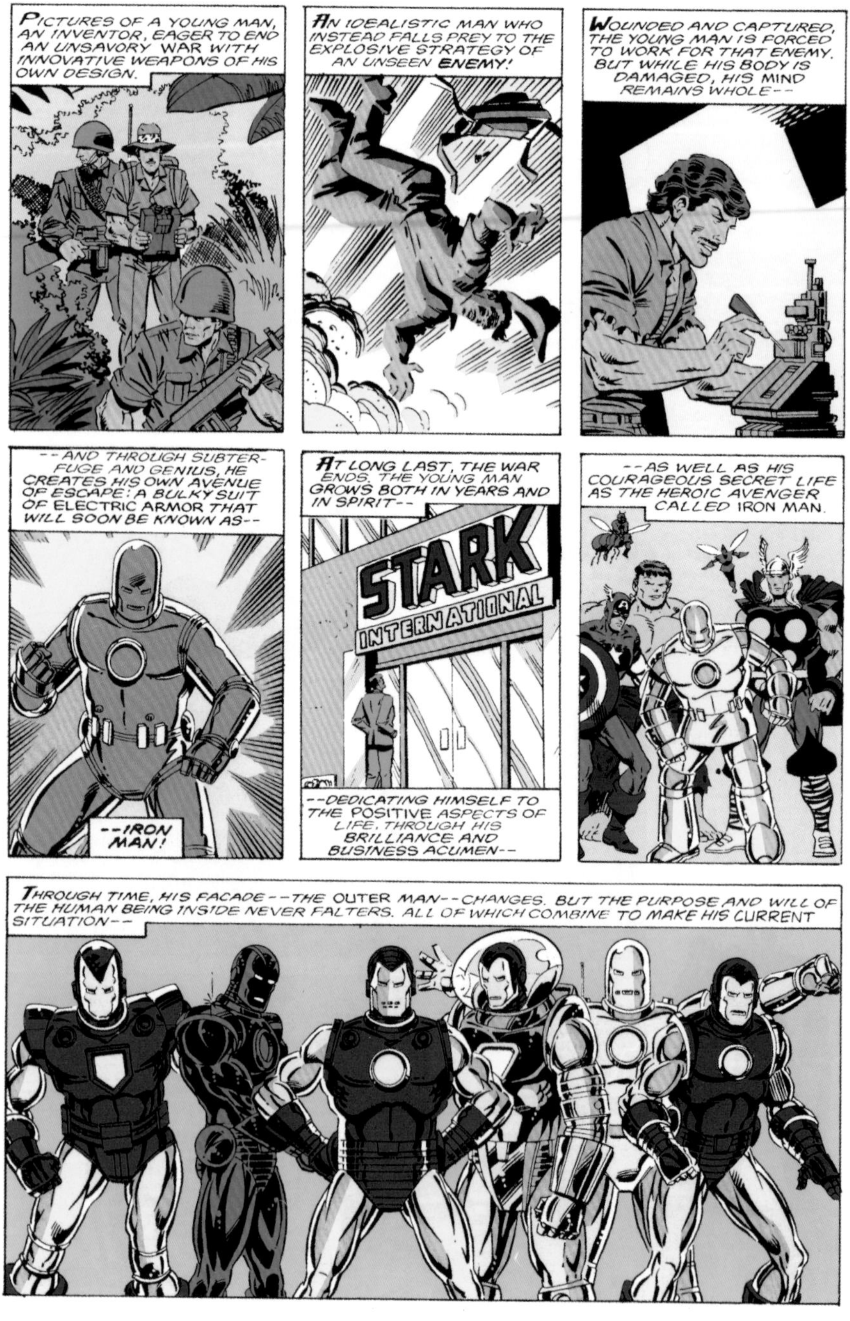
PICTURES OF A YOUNG MAN, AN INVENTOR, EAGER TO END AN UNSAVORY WAR WITH INNOVATIVE WEAPONS OF HIS OWN DESIGN.
AN IDEALISTIC MAN WHO INSTEAD FALLS PREY TO THE EXPLOSIVE STRATEGY OF AN UNSEEN ENEMY!
WOUNDED AND CAPTURED, THE YOUNG MAN IS FORCED TO WORK FOR THAT ENEMY. BUT WHILE HIS BODY IS DAMAGED, HIS MIND REMAINS WHOLE--
--AND THROUGH SUBTERFUGE AND GENIUS, HE CREATES HIS OWN AVENUE OF ESCAPE: A BULKY SUIT OF ELECTRIC ARMOR THAT WILL SOON BE KNOWN AS--
--IRON MAN!
AT LONG LAST, THE WAR ENDS. THE YOUNG MAN GROWS BOTH IN YEARS AND IN SPIRIT--
STARK
INTERNATIONAL
--DEDICATING HIMSELF TO THE POSITIVE ASPECTS OF LIFE. THROUGH HIS BRILLIANCE AND BUSINESS ACUMEN--
--AS WELL AS HIS COURAGEOUS SECRET LIFE AS THE HEROIC AVENGER CALLED IRON MAN.
THROUGH TIME, HIS FACADE--THE OUTER MAN--CHANGES. BUT THE PURPOSE AND WILL OF THE HUMAN BEING INSIDE NEVER FALTERS. ALL OF WHICH COMBINE TO MAKE HIS CURRENT SITUATION--

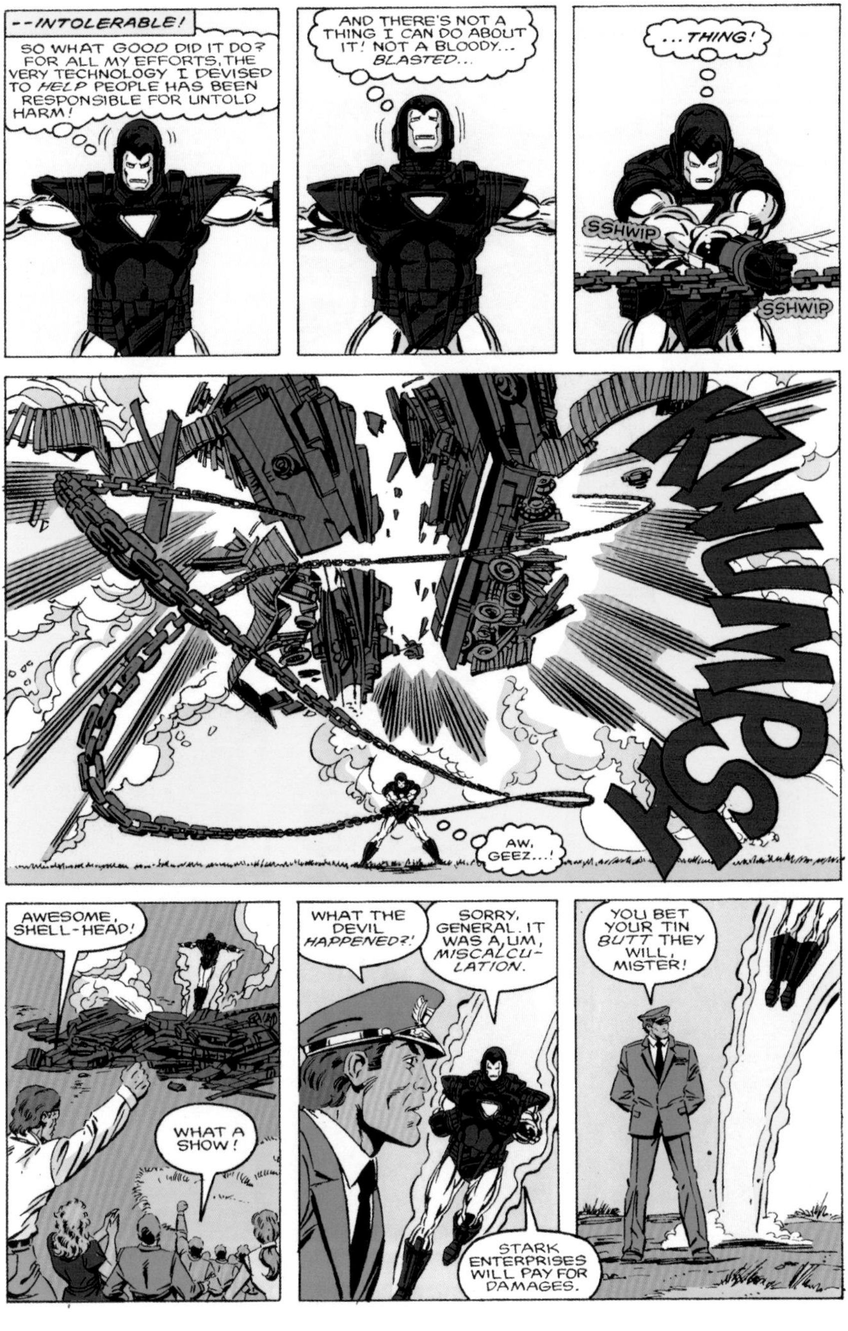
--INTOLERABLE!
SO WHAT GOOD DID IT DO? FOR ALL MY EFFORTS, THE VERY TECHNOLOGY I DEVISED TO HELP PEOPLE HAS BEEN RESPONSIBLE FOR UNTOLD HARM!
AND THERE'S NOT A THING I CAN DO ABOUT IT! NOT A BLOODY... BLASTED...
...THING!
SSHWIP
SSHWIP
KWUMPSH
AW, GEEZ...!
AWESOME, SHELL-HEAD!
WHAT A SHOW!
WHAT THE DEVIL HAPPENED?!
SORRY, GENERAL. IT WAS A, UM, MISCALCU-LATION.
STARK ENTERPRISES WILL PAY FOR DAMAGES.
YOU BET YOUR TIN BUTT THEY WILL, MISTER!

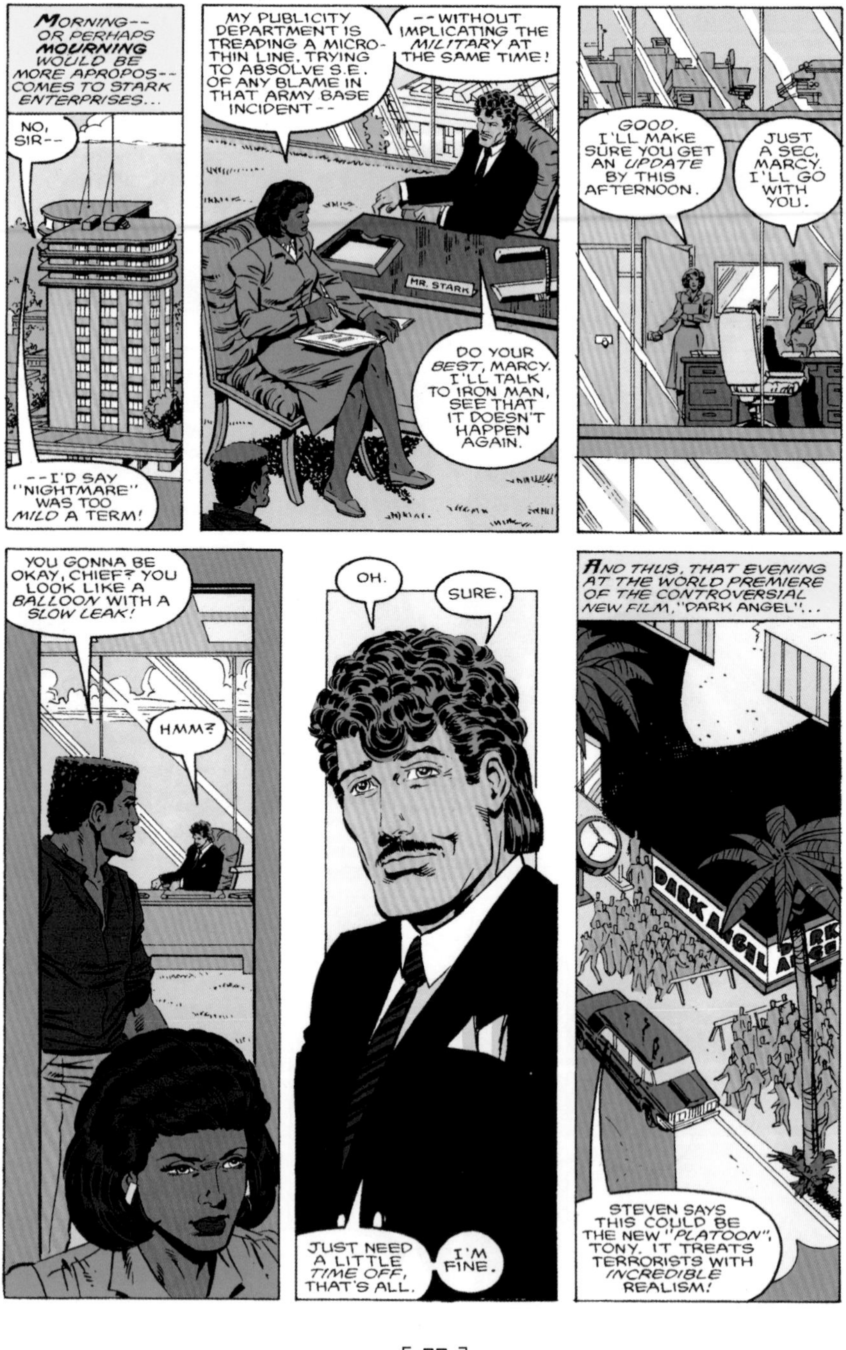
MORNING-- OR PERHAPS MOURNING WOULD BE MORE APROPOS-- COMES TO STARK ENTERPRISES...
NO, SIR--
--I'D SAY "NIGHTMARE" WAS TOO MILD A TERM!
MY PUBLICITY DEPARTMENT IS TREADING A MICRO-THIN LINE, TRYING TO ABSOLVE S.E. OF ANY BLAME IN THAT ARMY BASE INCIDENT--
--WITHOUT IMPLICATING THE MILITARY AT THE SAME TIME!
MR. STARK
DO YOUR BEST, MARCY. I'LL TALK TO IRON MAN, SEE THAT IT DOESN'T HAPPEN AGAIN.
GOOD. I'LL MAKE SURE YOU GET AN UPDATE BY THIS AFTERNOON.
JUST A SEC, MARCY. I'LL GO WITH YOU.
YOU GONNA BE OKAY, CHIEF? YOU LOOK LIKE A BALLOON WITH A SLOW LEAK!
HMM?
OH.
SURE.
I'M FINE.
JUST NEED A LITTLE TIME OFF, THAT'S ALL.
AND THUS, THAT EVENING AT THE WORLD PREMIERE OF THE CONTROVERSIAL NEW FILM, "DARK ANGEL"...
DARK ANGEL
STEVEN SAYS THIS COULD BE THE NEW "PLATOON", TONY. IT TREATS TERRORISTS WITH INCREDIBLE REALISM!

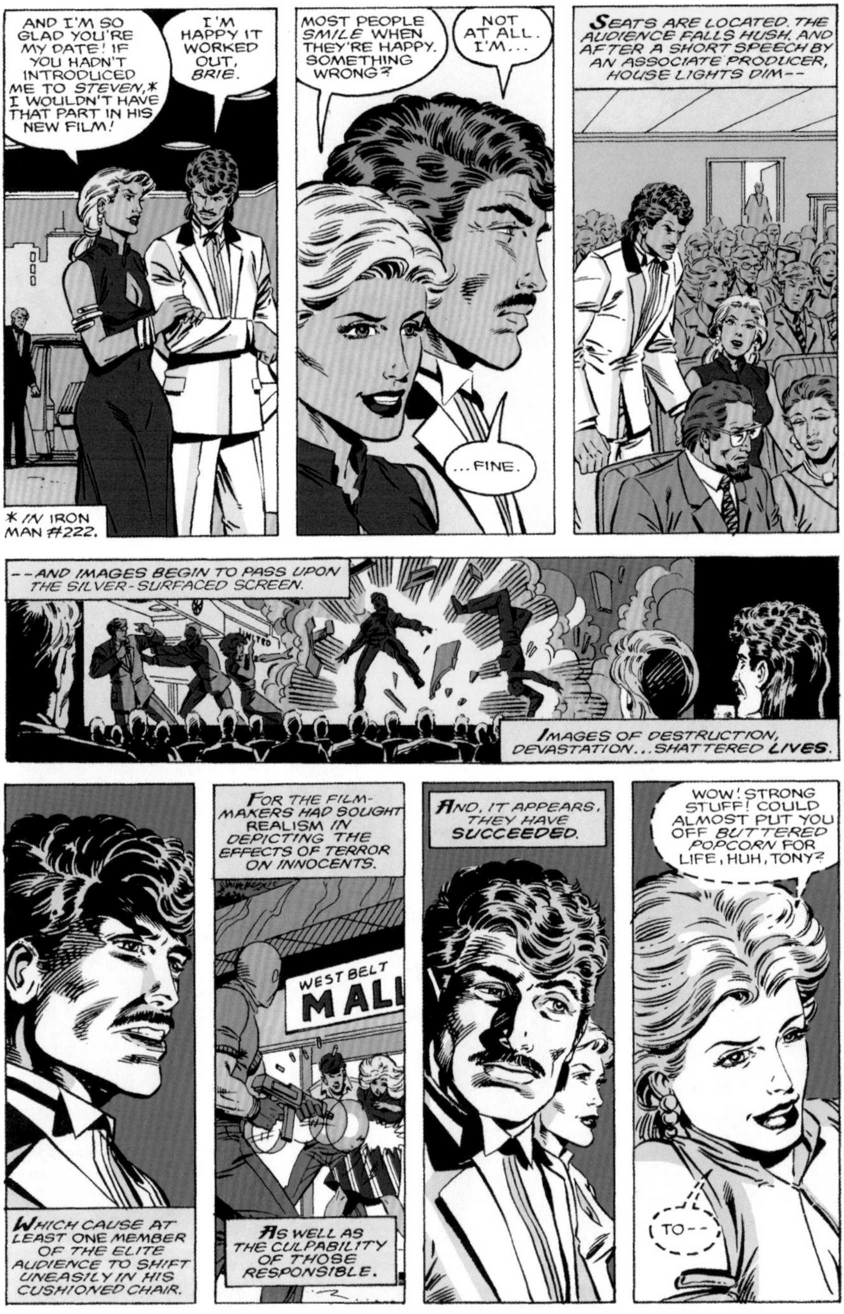
AND I'M SO GLAD YOU'RE MY DATE! IF YOU HADN'T INTRODUCED ME TO STEVEN,* I WOULDN'T HAVE THAT PART IN HIS NEW FILM!
I'M HAPPY IT WORKED OUT, BRIE.
* IN IRON MAN #222.
MOST PEOPLE SMILE WHEN THEY'RE HAPPY. SOMETHING WRONG?
NOT AT ALL. I'M...
...FINE.
SEATS ARE LOCATED. THE AUDIENCE FALLS HUSH. AND AFTER A SHORT SPEECH BY AN ASSOCIATE PRODUCER, HOUSE LIGHTS DIM--
--AND IMAGES BEGIN TO PASS UPON THE SILVER-SURFACED SCREEN.
IMAGES OF DESTRUCTION, DEVASTATION...SHATTERED LIVES.
WHICH CAUSE AT LEAST ONE MEMBER OF THE ELITE AUDIENCE TO SHIFT UNEASILY IN HIS CUSHIONED CHAIR.
FOR THE FILM-MAKERS HAD SOUGHT REALISM IN DEPICTING THE EFFECTS OF TERROR ON INNOCENTS.
WEST BELT MALL
AS WELL AS THE CULPABILITY OF THOSE RESPONSIBLE.
AND, IT APPEARS, THEY HAVE SUCCEEDED.
WOW! STRONG STUFF! COULD ALMOST PUT YOU OFF BUTTERED POPCORN FOR LIFE, HUH, TONY?
TO--

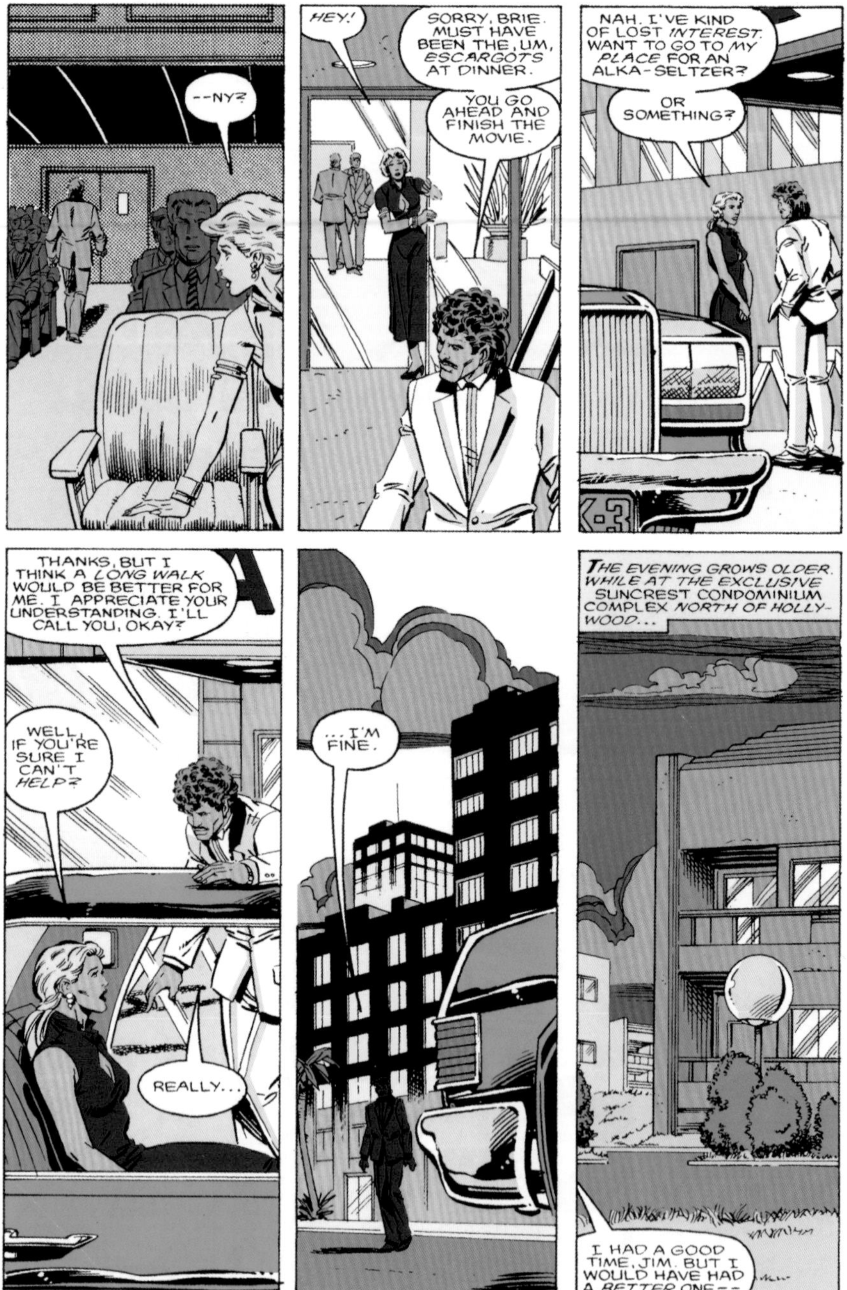
--NY?
HEY!
SORRY, BRIE. MUST HAVE BEEN THE, UM, ESCARGOTS AT DINNER.
YOU GO AHEAD AND FINISH THE MOVIE.
NAH. I'VE KIND OF LOST INTEREST. WANT TO GO TO MY PLACE FOR AN ALKA-SELTZER?
OR SOMETHING?
THANKS, BUT I THINK A LONG WALK WOULD BE BETTER FOR ME. I APPRECIATE YOUR UNDERSTANDING. I'LL CALL YOU, OKAY?
WELL, IF YOU'RE SURE I CAN'T HELP?
REALLY...
...I'M FINE.
THE EVENING GROWS OLDER. WHILE AT THE EXCLUSIVE SUNCREST CONDOMINIUM COMPLEX NORTH OF HOLLYWOOD...
I HAD A GOOD TIME, JIM. BUT I WOULD HAVE HAD A BETTER ONE--

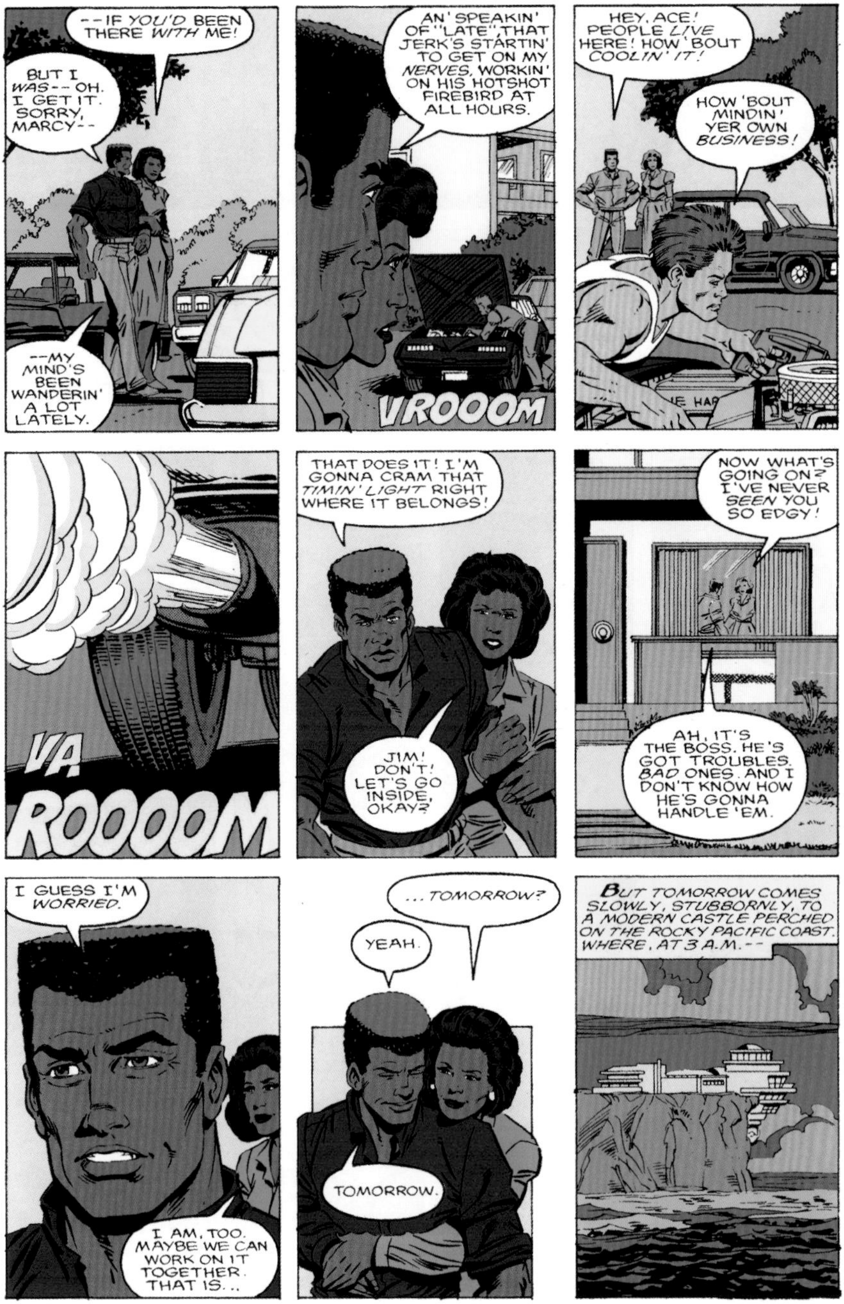
--IF YOU'D BEEN THERE WITH ME!
BUT I WAS-- OH. I GET IT. SORRY, MARCY--
--MY MIND'S BEEN WANDERIN' A LOT LATELY.
AN' SPEAKIN' OF "LATE", THAT JERK'S STARTIN' TO GET ON MY NERVES, WORKIN' ON HIS HOTSHOT FIREBIRD AT ALL HOURS.
VROOOM
HEY, ACE! PEOPLE LIVE HERE! HOW 'BOUT COOLIN' IT!
HOW 'BOUT MINDIN' YER OWN BUSINESS!
VA ROOOOM
THAT DOES IT! I'M GONNA CRAM THAT TIMIN' LIGHT RIGHT WHERE IT BELONGS!
JIM! DON'T! LET'S GO INSIDE, OKAY?
NOW WHAT'S GOING ON? I'VE NEVER SEEN YOU SO EDGY!
AH, IT'S THE BOSS. HE'S GOT TROUBLES. BAD ONES. AND I DON'T KNOW HOW HE'S GONNA HANDLE 'EM.
I GUESS I'M WORRIED.
I AM, TOO. MAYBE WE CAN WORK ON IT TOGETHER. THAT IS...
...TOMORROW?
YEAH.
TOMORROW.
BUT TOMORROW COMES SLOWLY, STUBBORNLY, TO A MODERN CASTLE PERCHED ON THE ROCKY PACIFIC COAST. WHERE, AT 3 A.M.--

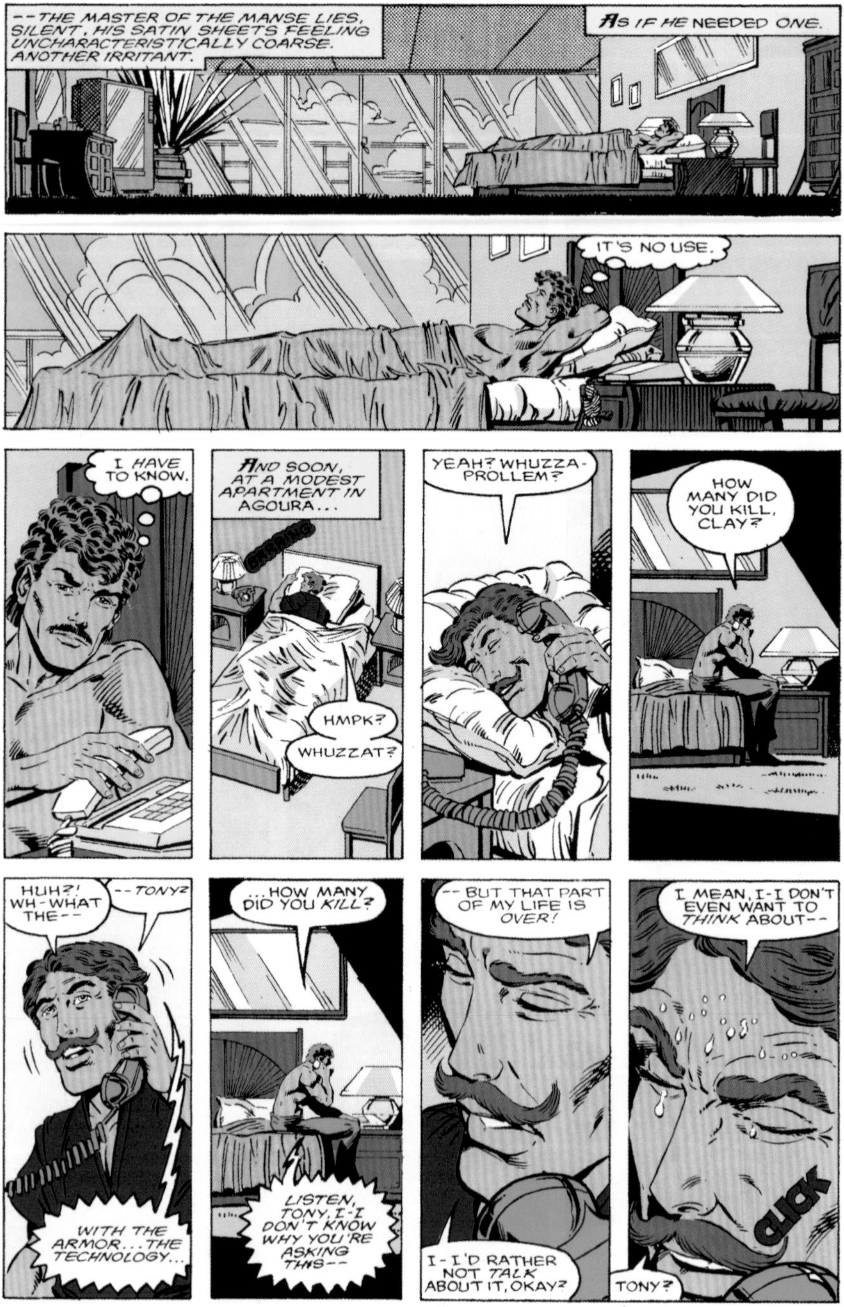
--THE MASTER OF THE MANSE LIES, SILENT, HIS SATIN SHEETS FEELING UNCHARACTERISTICALLY COARSE. ANOTHER IRRITANT.
AS IF HE NEEDED ONE.
IT'S NO USE.
I HAVE TO KNOW.
AND SOON, AT A MODEST APARTMENT IN AGOURA...
HMPK?
WHUZZAT?
YEAH? WHUZZA-PROLLEM?
HOW MANY DID YOU KILL, CLAY?
HUH?! WH-WHAT THE--
--TONY?
WITH THE ARMOR... THE TECHNOLOGY...
...HOW MANY DID YOU KILL?
LISTEN, TONY, I-I DON'T KNOW WHY YOU'RE ASKING THIS--
--BUT THAT PART OF MY LIFE IS OVER!
I-I'D RATHER NOT TALK ABOUT IT, OKAY?
I MEAN, I-I DON'T EVEN WANT TO THINK ABOUT--
CLICK
TONY?

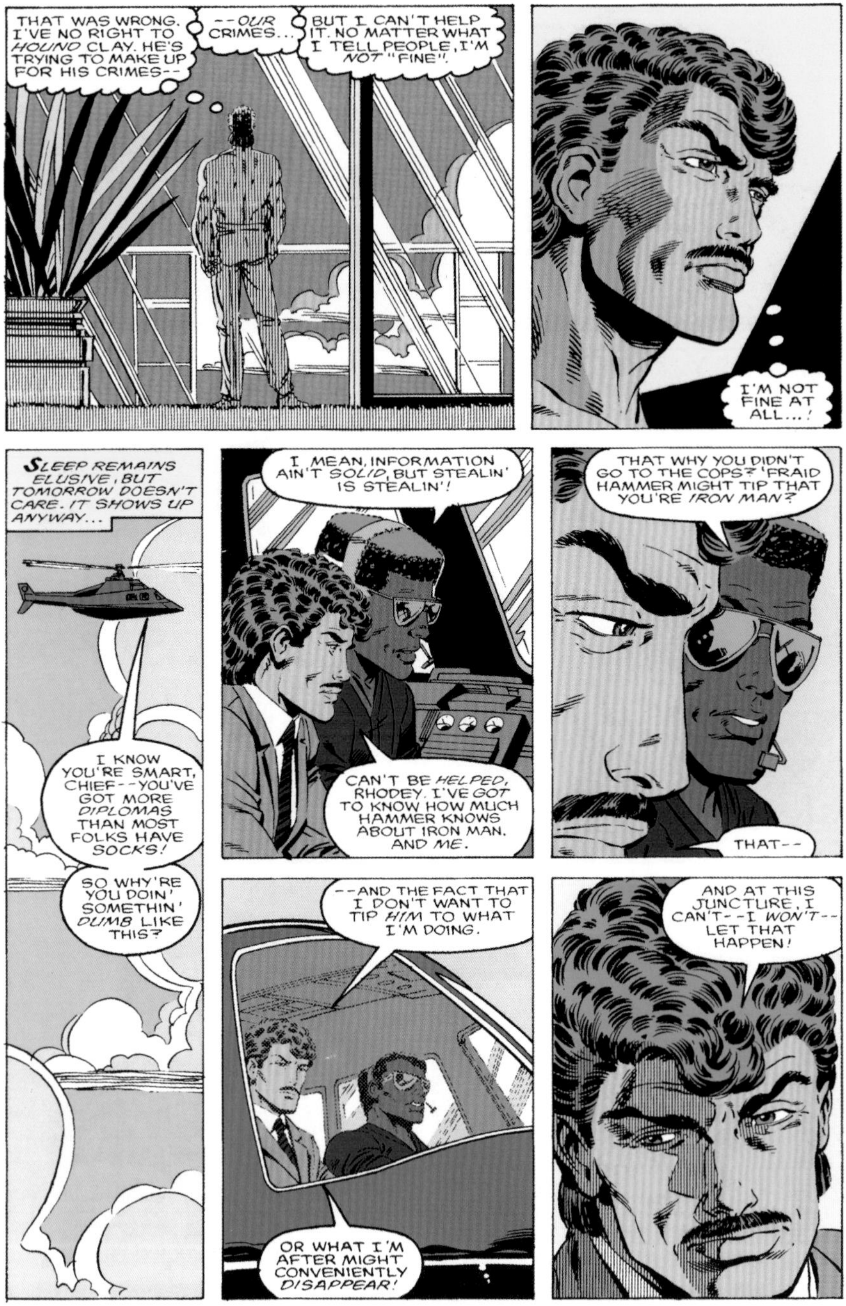
THAT WAS WRONG. I'VE NO RIGHT TO HOUND CLAY. HE'S TRYING TO MAKE UP FOR HIS CRIMES--
--OUR CRIMES...
BUT I CAN'T HELP IT. NO MATTER WHAT I TELL PEOPLE, I'M NOT "FINE".
I'M NOT FINE AT ALL...!
SLEEP REMAINS ELUSIVE, BUT TOMORROW DOESN'T CARE. IT SHOWS UP ANYWAY...
I KNOW YOU'RE SMART, CHIEF--YOU'VE GOT MORE DIPLOMAS THAN MOST FOLKS HAVE SOCKS!
SO WHY'RE YOU DOIN' SOMETHIN' DUMB LIKE THIS?
I MEAN, INFORMATION AIN'T SOLID, BUT STEALIN' IS STEALIN'!
CAN'T BE HELPED, RHODEY. I'VE GOT TO KNOW HOW MUCH HAMMER KNOWS ABOUT IRON MAN. AND ME.
THAT WHY YOU DIDN'T GO TO THE COPS? 'FRAID HAMMER MIGHT TIP THAT YOU'RE IRON MAN?
THAT--
--AND THE FACT THAT I DON'T WANT TO TIP HIM TO WHAT I'M DOING.
OR WHAT I'M AFTER MIGHT CONVENIENTLY DISAPPEAR!
AND AT THIS JUNCTURE, I CAN'T--I WON'T--LET THAT HAPPEN!

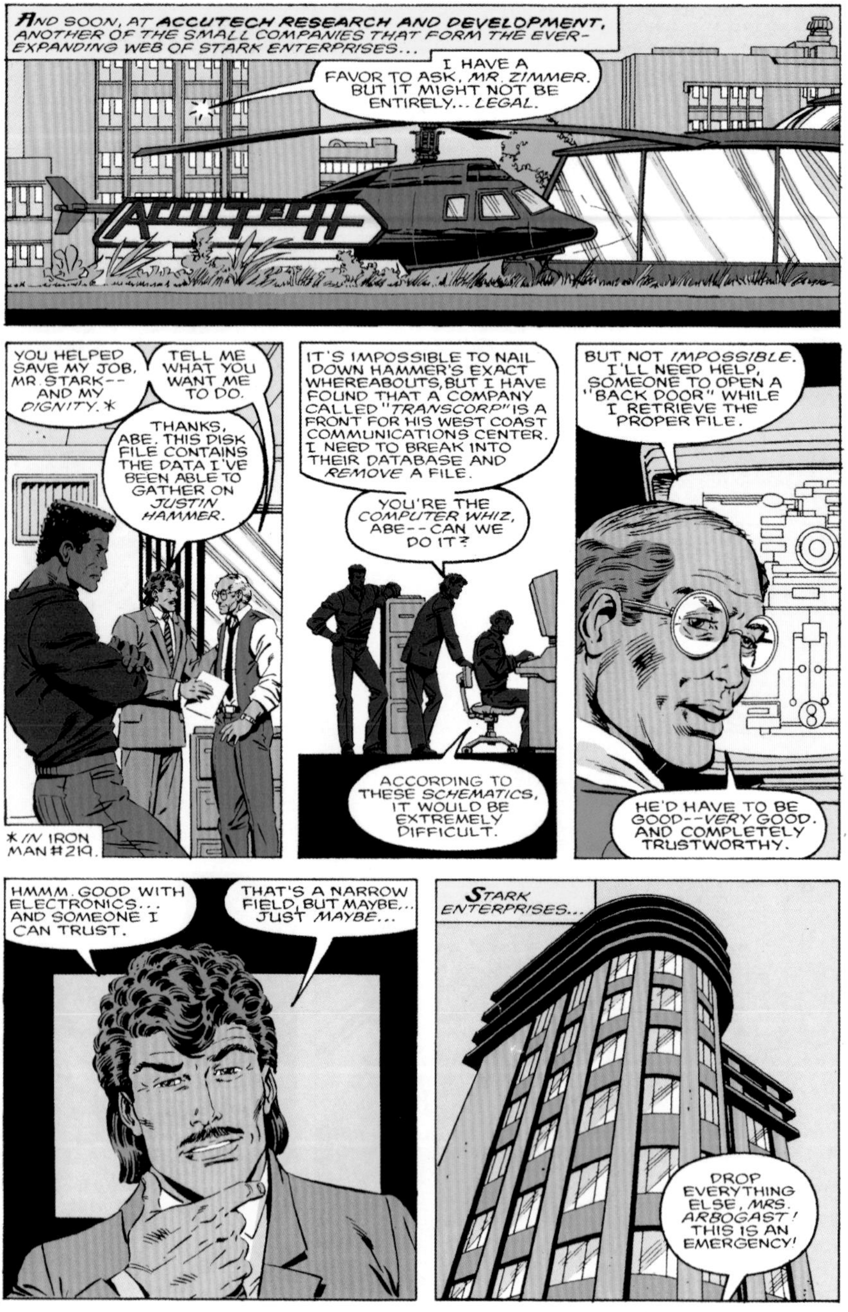
AND SOON, AT ACCUTECH RESEARCH AND DEVELOPMENT, ANOTHER OF THE SMALL COMPANIES THAT FORM THE EVER-EXPANDING WEB OF STARK ENTERPRISES...
I HAVE A FAVOR TO ASK, MR. ZIMMER. BUT IT MIGHT NOT BE ENTIRELY... LEGAL.
ACCUTECH
YOU HELPED SAVE MY JOB, MR. STARK-- AND MY DIGNITY.*
TELL ME WHAT YOU WANT ME TO DO.
THANKS, ABE. THIS DISK FILE CONTAINS THE DATA I'VE BEEN ABLE TO GATHER ON JUSTIN HAMMER.
*IN IRON MAN #219.
IT'S IMPOSSIBLE TO NAIL DOWN HAMMER'S EXACT WHEREABOUTS, BUT I HAVE FOUND THAT A COMPANY CALLED "TRANSCORP" IS A FRONT FOR HIS WEST COAST COMMUNICATIONS CENTER. I NEED TO BREAK INTO THEIR DATABASE AND REMOVE A FILE.
YOU'RE THE COMPUTER WHIZ, ABE--CAN WE DO IT?
ACCORDING TO THESE SCHEMATICS, IT WOULD BE EXTREMELY DIFFICULT.
BUT NOT IMPOSSIBLE. I'LL NEED HELP, SOMEONE TO OPEN A "BACK DOOR" WHILE I RETRIEVE THE PROPER FILE.
HE'D HAVE TO BE GOOD--VERY GOOD. AND COMPLETELY TRUSTWORTHY.
HMMM. GOOD WITH ELECTRONICS... AND SOMEONE I CAN TRUST.
THAT'S A NARROW FIELD, BUT MAYBE... JUST MAYBE...
STARK ENTERPRISES...
DROP EVERYTHING ELSE, MRS. ARBOGAST! THIS IS AN EMERGENCY!

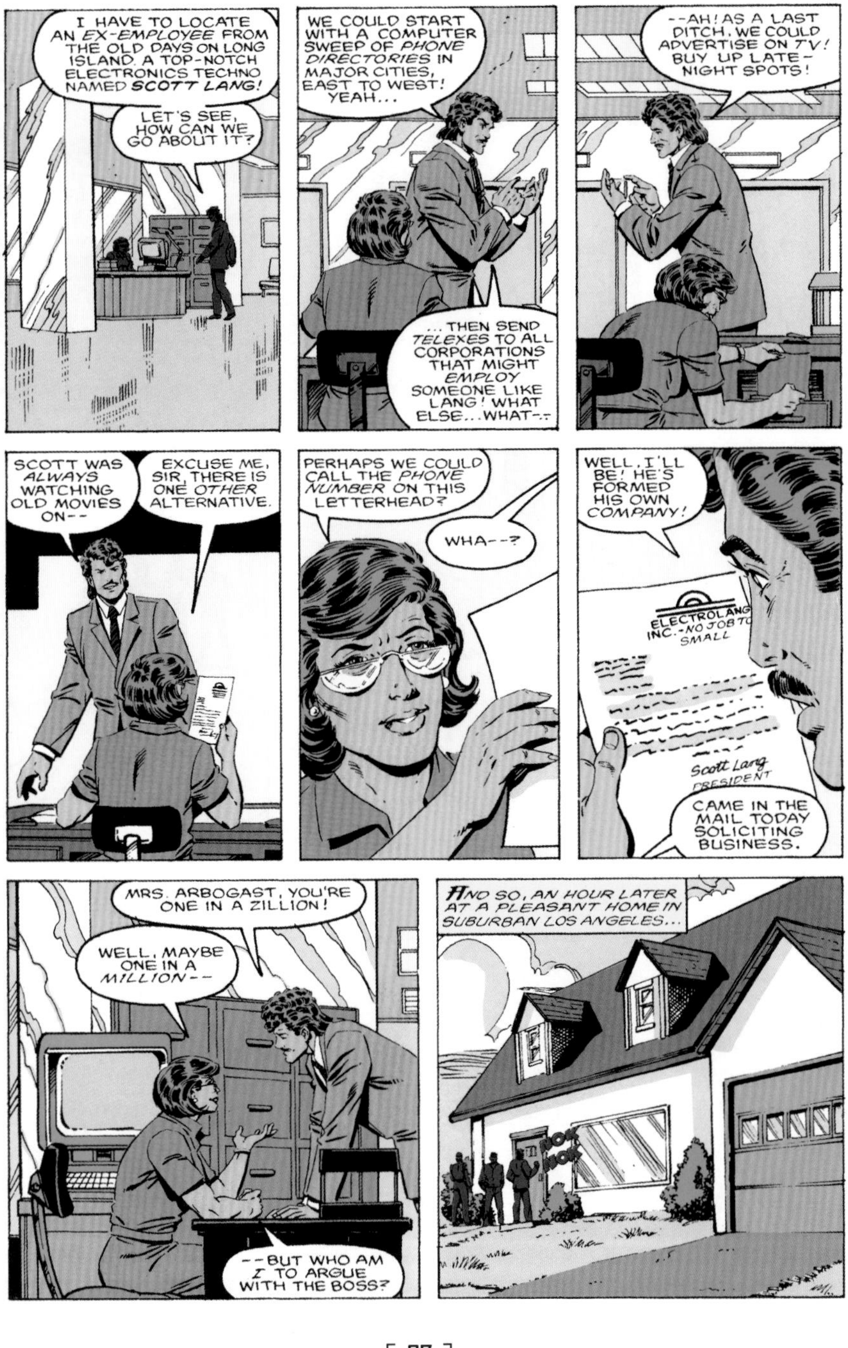
I HAVE TO LOCATE AN EX-EMPLOYEE FROM THE OLD DAYS ON LONG ISLAND. A TOP-NOTCH ELECTRONICS TECHNO NAMED SCOTT LANG!
LET'S SEE, HOW CAN WE GO ABOUT IT?
WE COULD START WITH A COMPUTER SWEEP OF PHONE DIRECTORIES IN MAJOR CITIES, EAST TO WEST! YEAH...
...THEN SEND TELEXES TO ALL CORPORATIONS THAT MIGHT EMPLOY SOMEONE LIKE LANG! WHAT ELSE...WHAT--
--AH! AS A LAST DITCH, WE COULD ADVERTISE ON TV! BUY UP LATE-NIGHT SPOTS!
SCOTT WAS ALWAYS WATCHING OLD MOVIES ON--
EXCUSE ME, SIR, THERE IS ONE OTHER ALTERNATIVE.
PERHAPS WE COULD CALL THE PHONE NUMBER ON THIS LETTERHEAD?
WHA--?
WELL, I'LL BE! HE'S FORMED HIS OWN COMPANY!
ELECTROLANG INC.-NO JOB TO SMALL
Scott Lang
PRESIDENT
CAME IN THE MAIL TODAY SOLICITING BUSINESS.
MRS. ARBOGAST, YOU'RE ONE IN A ZILLION!
WELL, MAYBE ONE IN A MILLION--
--BUT WHO AM I TO ARGUE WITH THE BOSS?
AND SO, AN HOUR LATER AT A PLEASANT HOME IN SUBURBAN LOS ANGELES...
NOK NOK

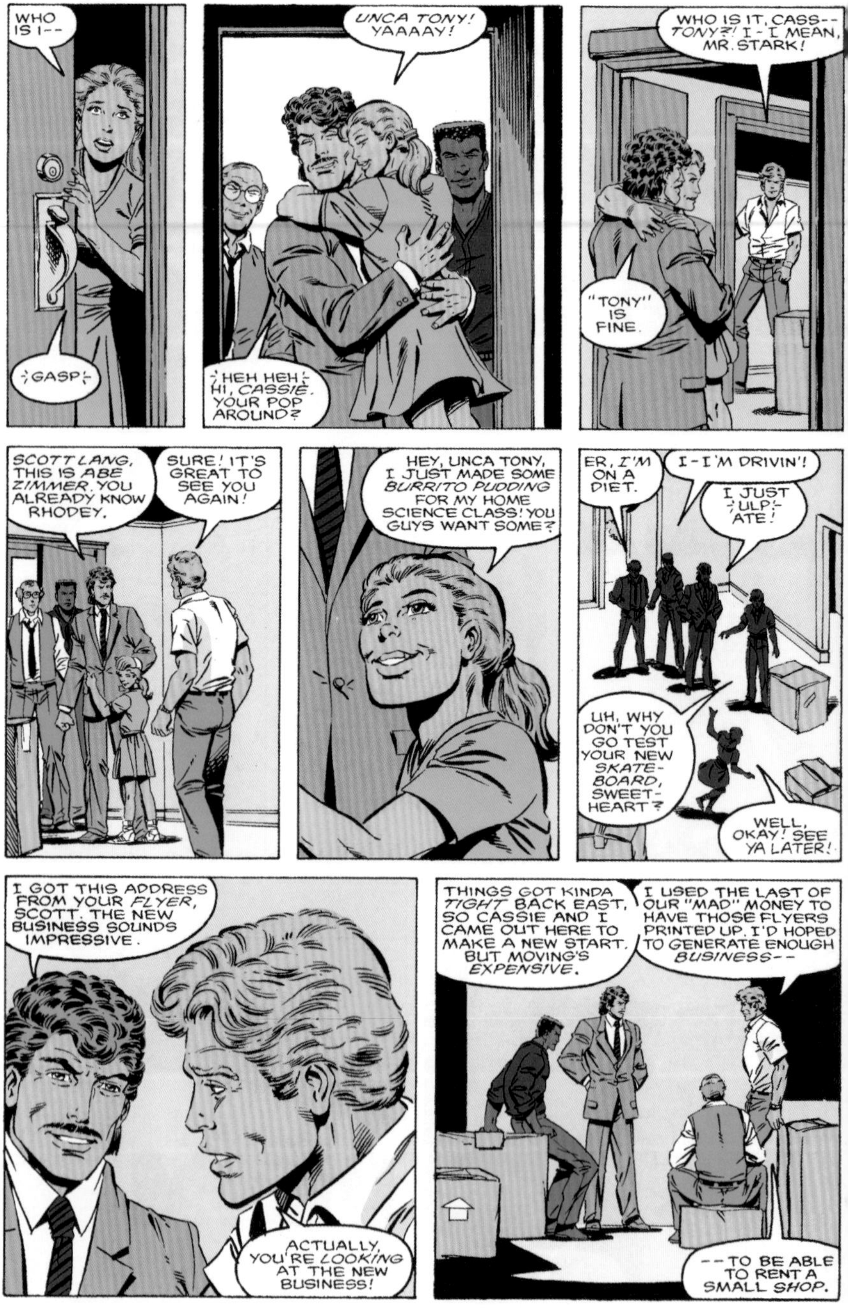
WHO IS I--
¬GASP¬
UNCA TONY! YAAAAY!
¬HEH HEH¬ HI, CASSIE. YOUR POP AROUND?
WHO IS IT, CASS-- TONY?! I-I MEAN, MR. STARK!
"TONY" IS FINE.
SCOTT LANG, THIS IS ABE ZIMMER. YOU ALREADY KNOW RHODEY.
SURE! IT'S GREAT TO SEE YOU AGAIN!
HEY, UNCA TONY, I JUST MADE SOME BURRITO PUDDING FOR MY HOME SCIENCE CLASS! YOU GUYS WANT SOME?
ER, I'M ON A DIET.
I-I'M DRIVIN'!
I JUST ¬ULP¬ ATE!
UH, WHY DON'T YOU GO TEST YOUR NEW SKATE-BOARD, SWEET-HEART?
WELL, OKAY! SEE YA LATER!
I GOT THIS ADDRESS FROM YOUR FLYER, SCOTT. THE NEW BUSINESS SOUNDS IMPRESSIVE.
ACTUALLY, YOU'RE LOOKING AT THE NEW BUSINESS!
THINGS GOT KINDA TIGHT BACK EAST, SO CASSIE AND I CAME OUT HERE TO MAKE A NEW START. BUT MOVING'S EXPENSIVE.
I USED THE LAST OF OUR "MAD" MONEY TO HAVE THOSE FLYERS PRINTED UP. I'D HOPED TO GENERATE ENOUGH BUSINESS--
--TO BE ABLE TO RENT A SMALL SHOP.

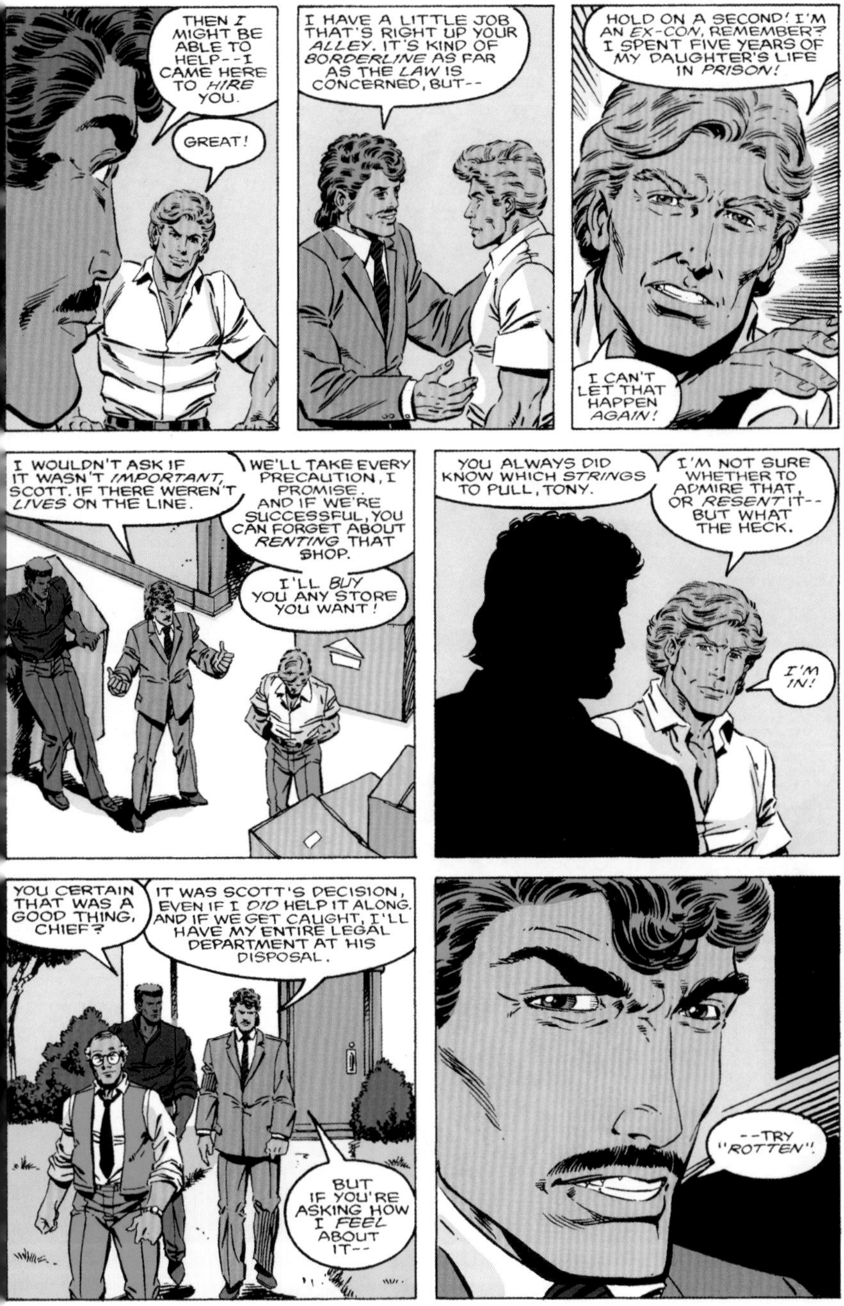
THEN I MIGHT BE ABLE TO HELP--I CAME HERE TO HIRE YOU.
GREAT!
I HAVE A LITTLE JOB THAT'S RIGHT UP YOUR ALLEY. IT'S KIND OF BORDERLINE AS FAR AS THE LAW IS CONCERNED, BUT--
HOLD ON A SECOND! I'M AN EX-CON, REMEMBER? I SPENT FIVE YEARS OF MY DAUGHTER'S LIFE IN PRISON!
I CAN'T LET THAT HAPPEN AGAIN!
I WOULDN'T ASK IF IT WASN'T IMPORTANT, SCOTT. IF THERE WEREN'T LIVES ON THE LINE.
WE'LL TAKE EVERY PRECAUTION, I PROMISE. AND IF WE'RE SUCCESSFUL, YOU CAN FORGET ABOUT RENTING THAT SHOP.
I'LL BUY YOU ANY STORE YOU WANT!
YOU ALWAYS DID KNOW WHICH STRINGS TO PULL, TONY.
I'M NOT SURE WHETHER TO ADMIRE THAT, OR RESENT IT--BUT WHAT THE HECK.
I'M IN!
YOU CERTAIN THAT WAS A GOOD THING, CHIEF?
IT WAS SCOTT'S DECISION, EVEN IF I DID HELP IT ALONG. AND IF WE GET CAUGHT, I'LL HAVE MY ENTIRE LEGAL DEPARTMENT AT HIS DISPOSAL.
BUT IF YOU'RE ASKING HOW I FEEL ABOUT IT--
--TRY "ROTTEN".

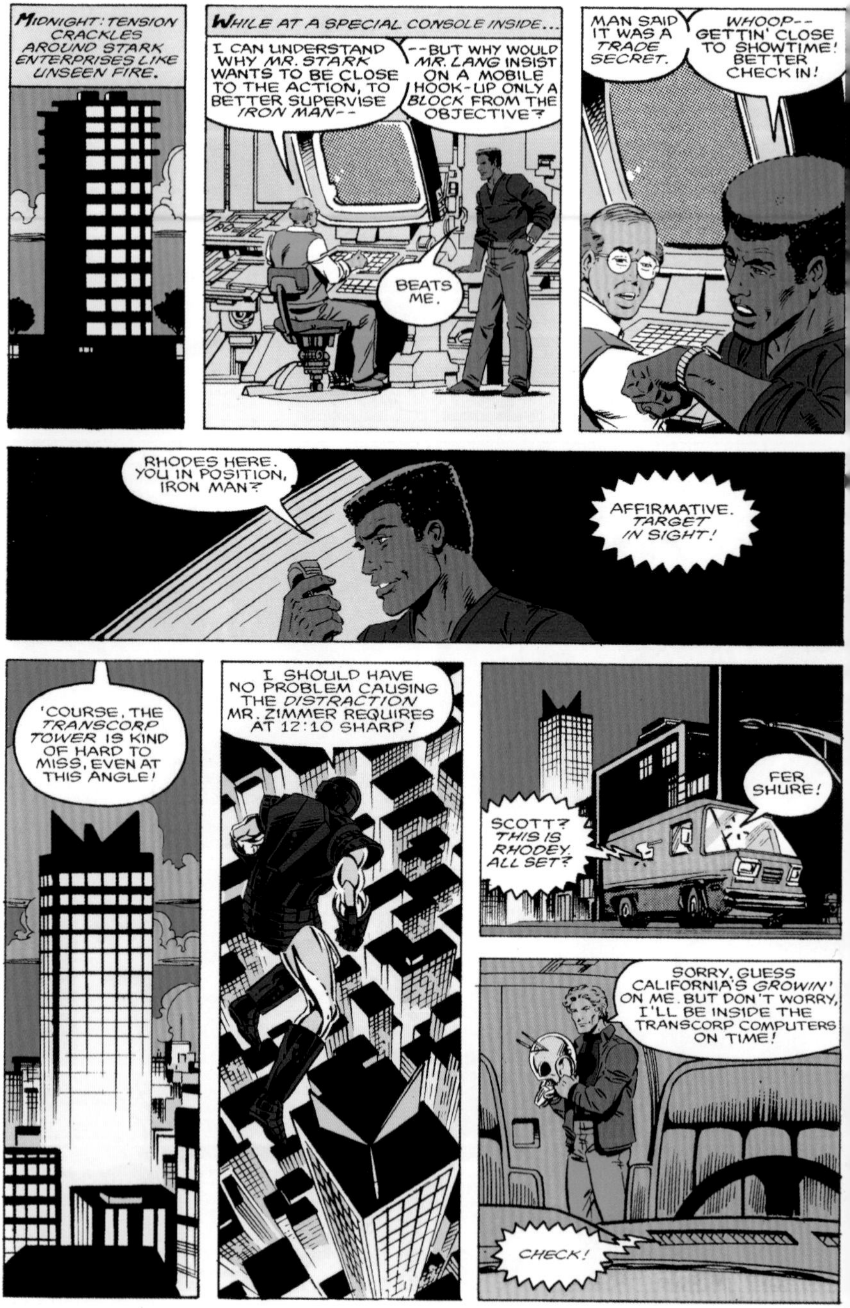
MIDNIGHT: TENSION CRACKLES AROUND STARK ENTERPRISES LIKE UNSEEN FIRE.
WHILE AT A SPECIAL CONSOLE INSIDE...
I CAN UNDERSTAND WHY MR. STARK WANTS TO BE CLOSE TO THE ACTION, TO BETTER SUPERVISE IRON MAN--
--BUT WHY WOULD MR. LANG INSIST ON A MOBILE HOOK-UP ONLY A BLOCK FROM THE OBJECTIVE?
BEATS ME.
MAN SAID IT WAS A TRADE SECRET.
WHOOP-- GETTIN' CLOSE TO SHOWTIME! BETTER CHECK IN!
RHODES HERE. YOU IN POSITION, IRON MAN?
AFFIRMATIVE. TARGET IN SIGHT!
'COURSE, THE TRANSCORP TOWER IS KIND OF HARD TO MISS, EVEN AT THIS ANGLE!
I SHOULD HAVE NO PROBLEM CAUSING THE DISTRACTION MR. ZIMMER REQUIRES AT 12:10 SHARP!
SCOTT? THIS IS RHODEY. ALL SET?
FER SHURE!
SORRY. GUESS CALIFORNIA'S GROWIN' ON ME. BUT DON'T WORRY, I'LL BE INSIDE THE TRANSCORP COMPUTERS ON TIME!
CHECK!

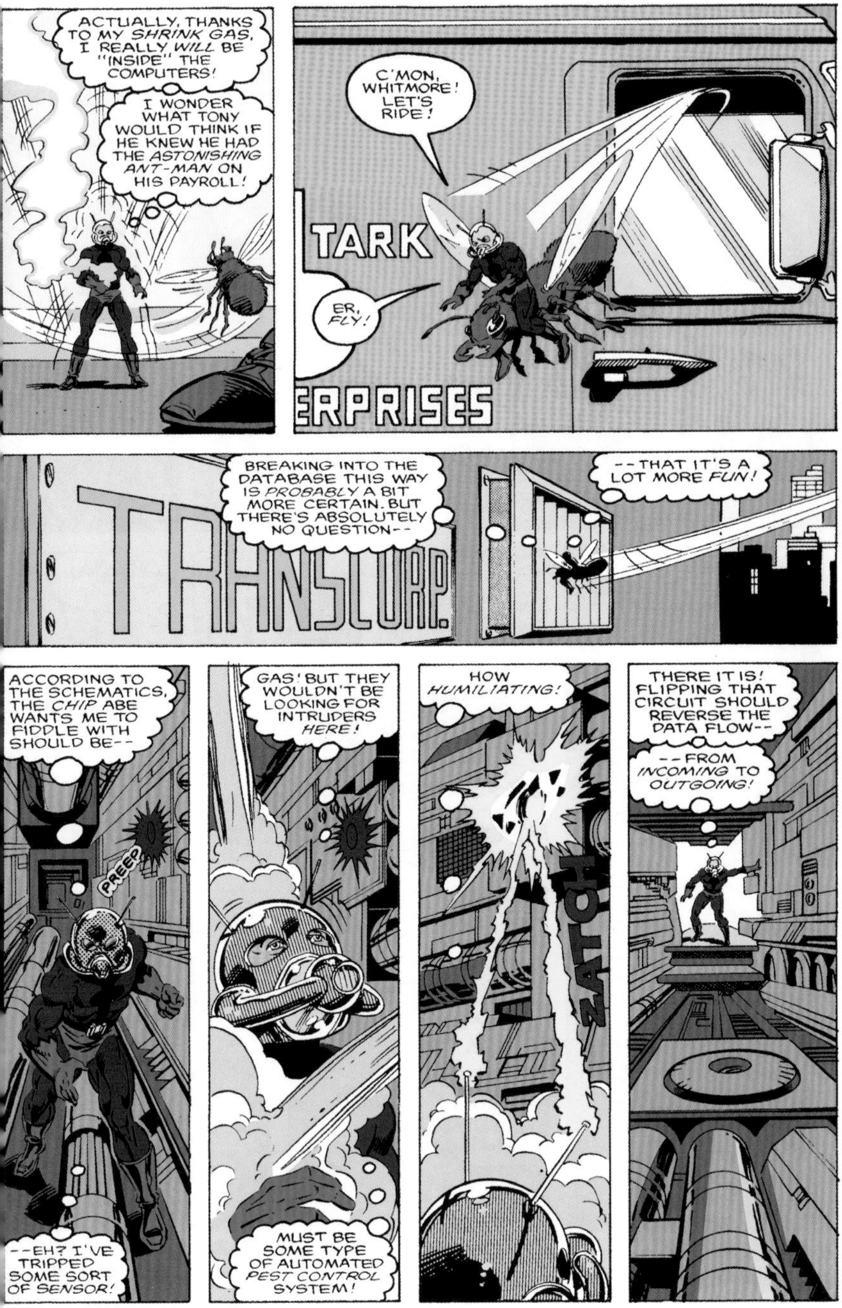
ACTUALLY, THANKS TO MY SHRINK GAS, I REALLY WILL BE "INSIDE" THE COMPUTERS!
I WONDER WHAT TONY WOULD THINK IF HE KNEW HE HAD THE ASTONISHING ANT-MAN ON HIS PAYROLL!
C'MON, WHITMORE! LET'S RIDE!
ER, FLY!
TARK
ERPRISES
BREAKING INTO THE DATABASE THIS WAY IS PROBABLY A BIT MORE CERTAIN. BUT THERE'S ABSOLUTELY NO QUESTION--
--THAT IT'S A LOT MORE FUN!
TRANSCORP.
ACCORDING TO THE SCHEMATICS, THE CHIP ABE WANTS ME TO FIDDLE WITH SHOULD BE--
PREEP
--EH? I'VE TRIPPED SOME SORT OF SENSOR!
GAS! BUT THEY WOULDN'T BE LOOKING FOR INTRUDERS HERE!
MUST BE SOME TYPE OF AUTOMATED PEST CONTROL SYSTEM!
HOW HUMILIATING!
ZATCH
THERE IT IS! FLIPPING THAT CIRCUIT SHOULD REVERSE THE DATA FLOW--
--FROM INCOMING TO OUTGOING!

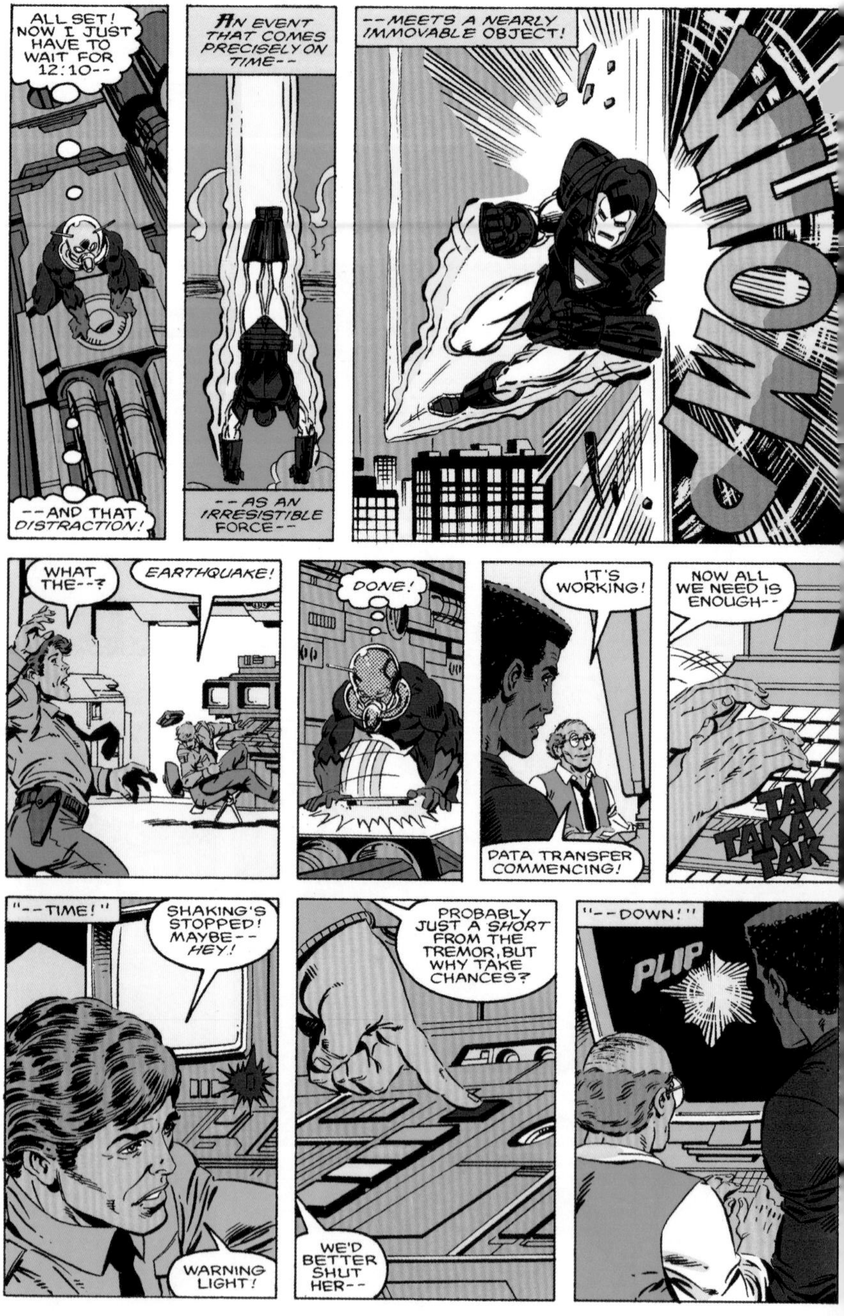
ALL SET! NOW I JUST HAVE TO WAIT FOR 12:10--
--AND THAT DISTRACTION!
AN EVENT THAT COMES PRECISELY ON TIME--
--AS AN IRRESISTIBLE FORCE--
--MEETS A NEARLY IMMOVABLE OBJECT!
WHOOM
WHAT THE--?
EARTHQUAKE!
DONE!
IT'S WORKING!
DATA TRANSFER COMMENCING!
NOW ALL WE NEED IS ENOUGH--
TAK TAKA TAK
"--TIME!"
SHAKING'S STOPPED! MAYBE-- HEY!
WARNING LIGHT!
PROBABLY JUST A SHORT FROM THE TREMOR, BUT WHY TAKE CHANCES?
WE'D BETTER SHUT HER--
"--DOWN!"
PLIP

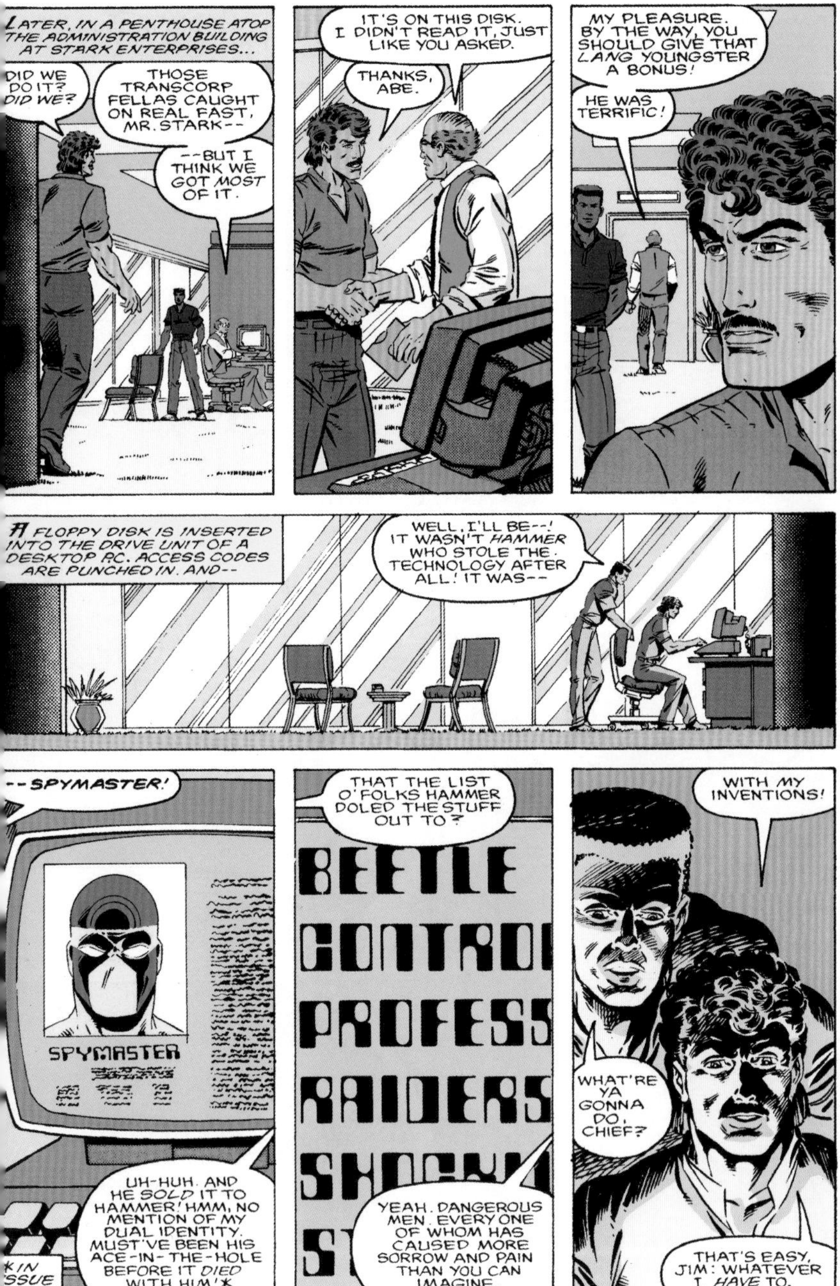
LATER, IN A PENTHOUSE ATOP THE ADMINISTRATION BUILDING AT STARK ENTERPRISES...
DID WE DO IT? DID WE?
THOSE TRANSCORP FELLAS CAUGHT ON REAL FAST, MR. STARK--
--BUT I THINK WE GOT MOST OF IT.
IT'S ON THIS DISK. I DIDN'T READ IT, JUST LIKE YOU ASKED.
THANKS, ABE.
MY PLEASURE. BY THE WAY, YOU SHOULD GIVE THAT LANG YOUNGSTER A BONUS!
HE WAS TERRIFIC!
A FLOPPY DISK IS INSERTED INTO THE DRIVE UNIT OF A DESKTOP PC. ACCESS CODES ARE PUNCHED IN. AND--
WELL, I'LL BE--! IT WASN'T HAMMER WHO STOLE THE TECHNOLOGY AFTER ALL! IT WAS--
--SPYMASTER!
SPYMASTER
UH-HUH. AND HE SOLD IT TO HAMMER! HMM, NO MENTION OF MY DUAL IDENTITY. MUST'VE BEEN HIS ACE-IN-THE-HOLE BEFORE IT DIED WITH HIM!*
*IN ISSUE #220.
THAT THE LIST O' FOLKS HAMMER DOLED THE STUFF OUT TO?
BEETLE
CONTRO
PROFESS
RAIDERS
YEAH. DANGEROUS MEN. EVERY ONE OF WHOM HAS CAUSED MORE SORROW AND PAIN THAN YOU CAN IMAGINE.
WITH MY INVENTIONS!
WHAT'RE YA GONNA DO, CHIEF?
THAT'S EASY, JIM: WHATEVER I HAVE TO.

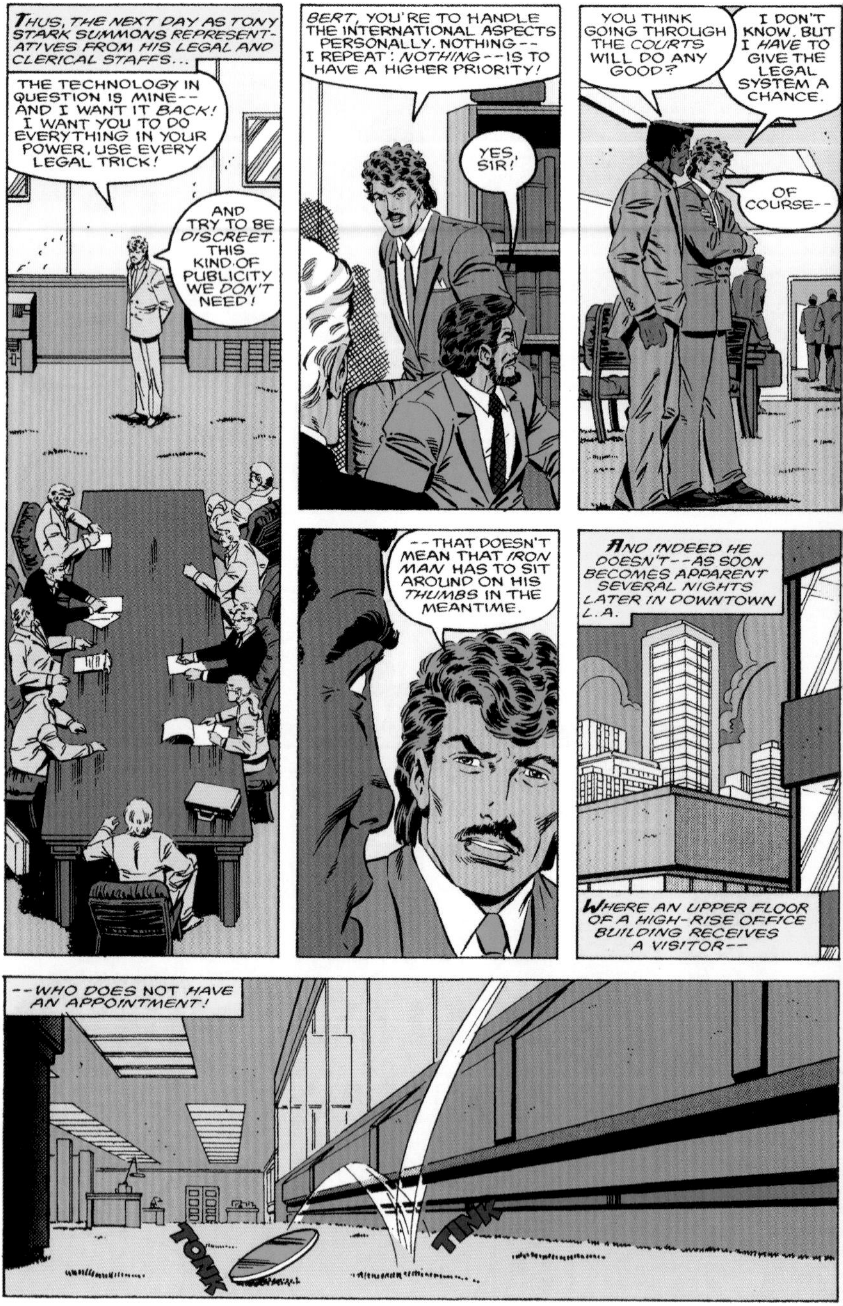
THUS, THE NEXT DAY AS TONY STARK SUMMONS REPRESENTATIVES FROM HIS LEGAL AND CLERICAL STAFFS...
THE TECHNOLOGY IN QUESTION IS MINE-- AND I WANT IT BACK! I WANT YOU TO DO EVERYTHING IN YOUR POWER, USE EVERY LEGAL TRICK!
AND TRY TO BE DISCREET. THIS KIND OF PUBLICITY WE DON'T NEED!
BERT, YOU'RE TO HANDLE THE INTERNATIONAL ASPECTS PERSONALLY. NOTHING-- I REPEAT: NOTHING--IS TO HAVE A HIGHER PRIORITY!
YES, SIR!
YOU THINK GOING THROUGH THE COURTS WILL DO ANY GOOD?
I DON'T KNOW. BUT I HAVE TO GIVE THE LEGAL SYSTEM A CHANCE.
OF COURSE--
--THAT DOESN'T MEAN THAT IRON MAN HAS TO SIT AROUND ON HIS THUMBS IN THE MEANTIME.
AND INDEED HE DOESN'T--AS SOON BECOMES APPARENT SEVERAL NIGHTS LATER IN DOWNTOWN L.A.
WHERE AN UPPER FLOOR OF A HIGH-RISE OFFICE BUILDING RECEIVES A VISITOR--
--WHO DOES NOT HAVE AN APPOINTMENT!
TONK
TINK

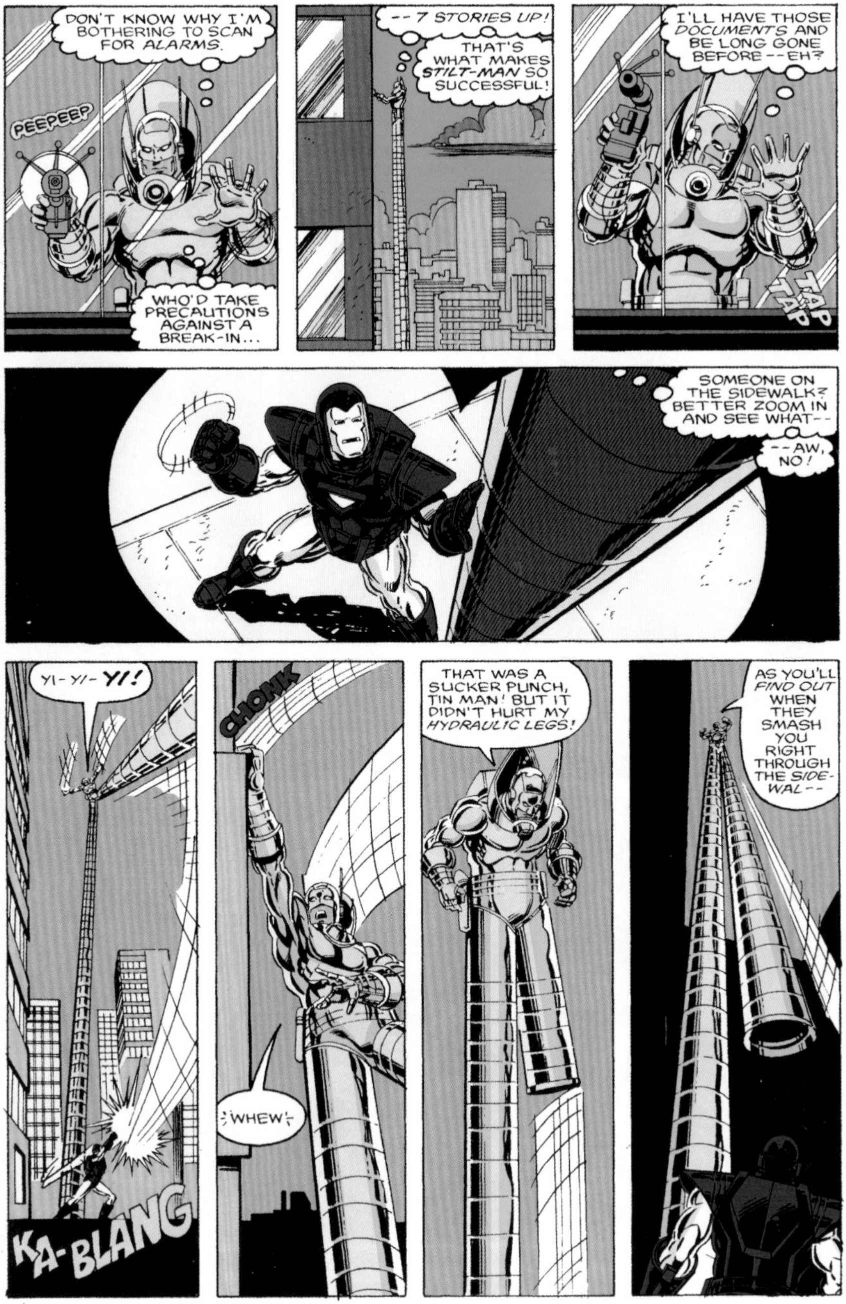
DON'T KNOW WHY I'M BOTHERING TO SCAN FOR ALARMS.
PEEPEEP
WHO'D TAKE PRECAUTIONS AGAINST A BREAK-IN...
--7 STORIES UP!
THAT'S WHAT MAKES STILT-MAN SO SUCCESSFUL!
I'LL HAVE THOSE DOCUMENTS AND BE LONG GONE BEFORE--EH?
TAP TAP
SOMEONE ON THE SIDEWALK? BETTER ZOOM IN AND SEE WHAT--
--AW, NO!
YI-YI-YI!
KA-BLANG
CHONK
WHEW
THAT WAS A SUCKER PUNCH, TIN MAN! BUT IT DIDN'T HURT MY HYDRAULIC LEGS!
AS YOU'LL FIND OUT WHEN THEY SMASH YOU RIGHT THROUGH THE SIDE-WAL--

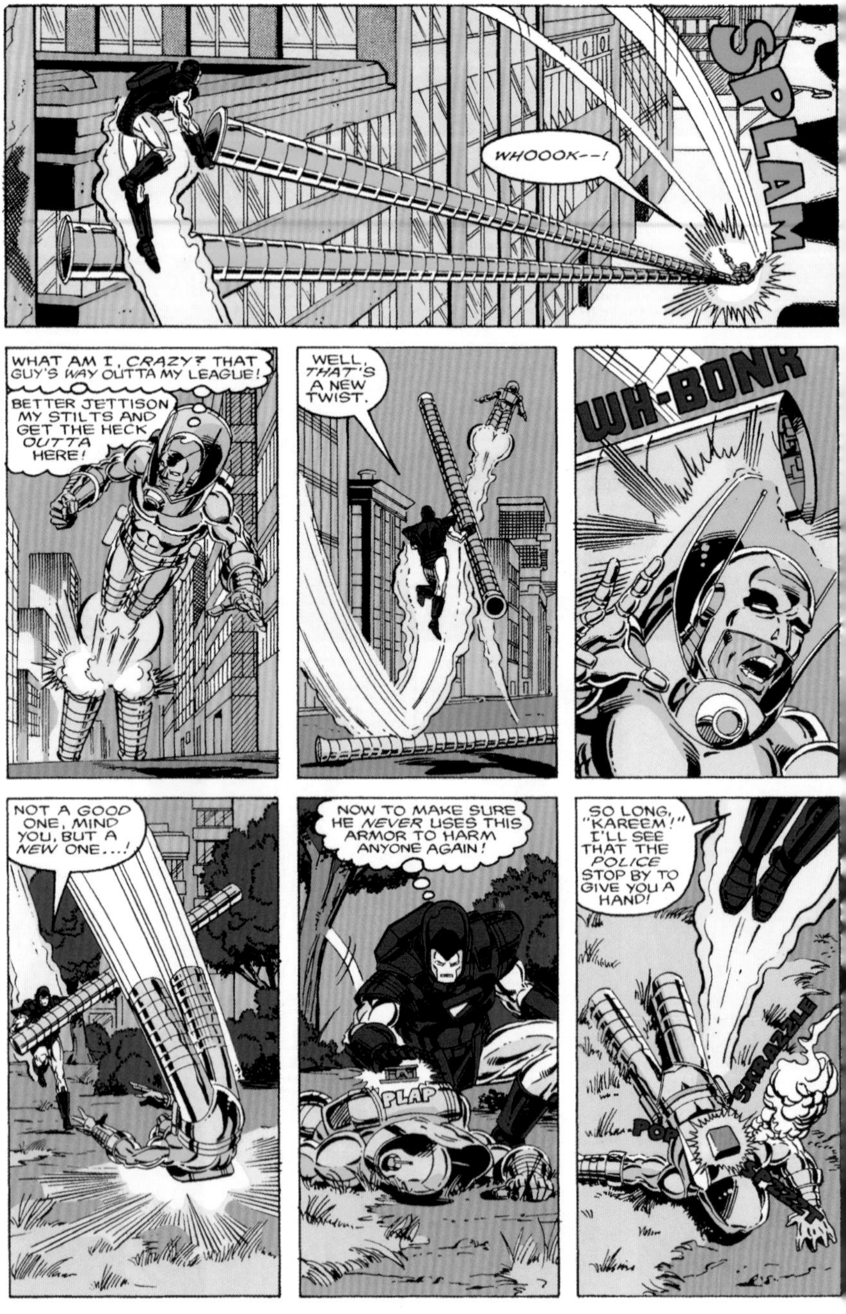

WHOOOK--!
SPLAM
WHAT AM I, CRAZY? THAT GUY'S WAY OUTTA MY LEAGUE!
BETTER JETTISON MY STILTS AND GET THE HECK OUTTA HERE!
WELL, THAT'S A NEW TWIST.
WH-BONK
NOT A GOOD ONE, MIND YOU, BUT A NEW ONE...!
NOW TO MAKE SURE HE NEVER USES THIS ARMOR TO HARM ANYONE AGAIN!
PLAP
SO LONG, "KAREEM!" I'LL SEE THAT THE POLICE STOP BY TO GIVE YOU A HAND!
SKRAZZLE
POP

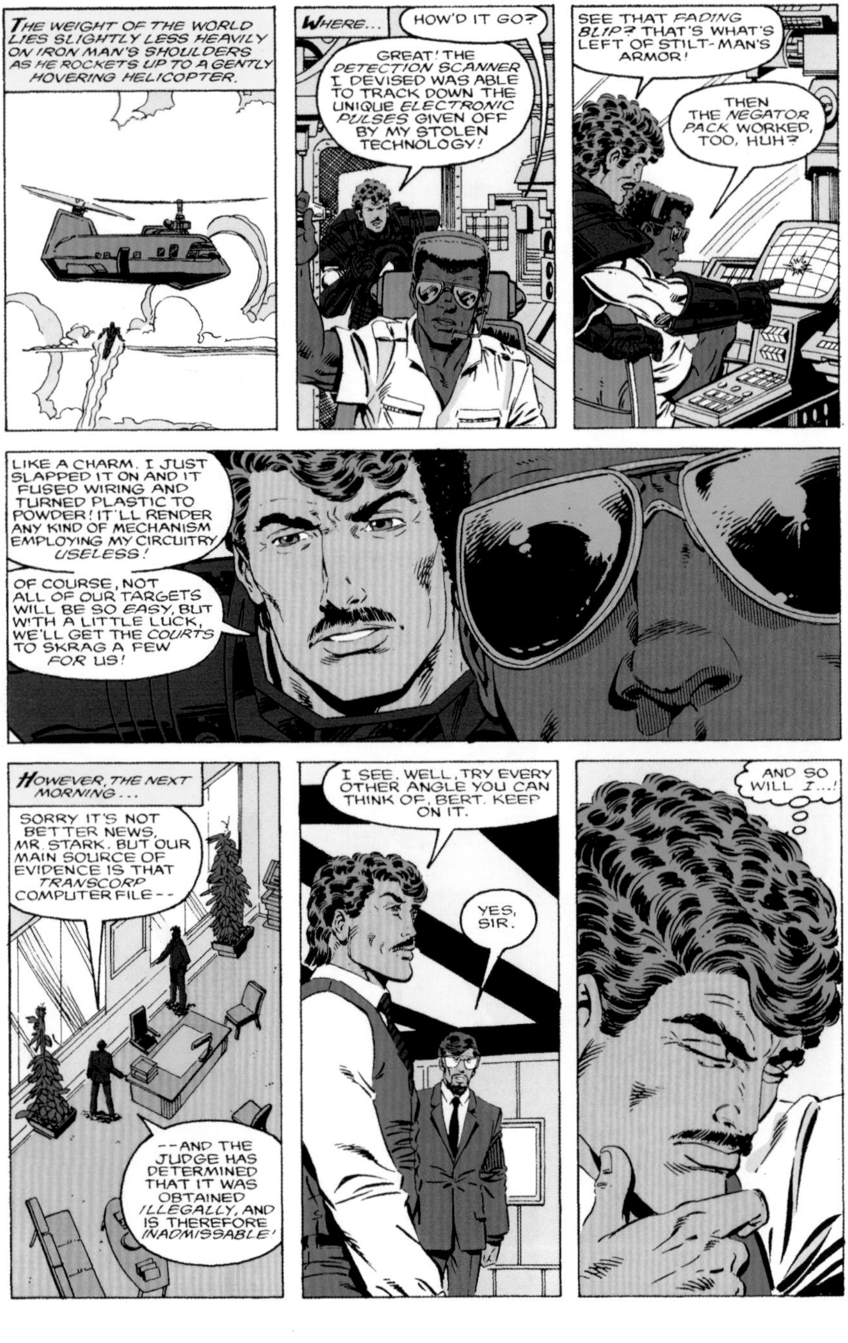
THE WEIGHT OF THE WORLD LIES SLIGHTLY LESS HEAVILY ON IRON MAN'S SHOULDERS AS HE ROCKETS UP TO A GENTLY HOVERING HELICOPTER.
WHERE...
HOW'D IT GO?
GREAT! THE DETECTION SCANNER I DEVISED WAS ABLE TO TRACK DOWN THE UNIQUE ELECTRONIC PULSES GIVEN OFF BY MY STOLEN TECHNOLOGY!
SEE THAT FADING BLIP? THAT'S WHAT'S LEFT OF STILT-MAN'S ARMOR!
THEN THE NEGATOR PACK WORKED, TOO, HUH?
LIKE A CHARM. I JUST SLAPPED IT ON AND IT FUSED WIRING AND TURNED PLASTIC TO POWDER! IT'LL RENDER ANY KIND OF MECHANISM EMPLOYING MY CIRCUITRY USELESS!
OF COURSE, NOT ALL OF OUR TARGETS WILL BE SO EASY, BUT WITH A LITTLE LUCK, WE'LL GET THE COURTS TO SKRAG A FEW FOR US!
HOWEVER, THE NEXT MORNING...
SORRY IT'S NOT BETTER NEWS, MR. STARK. BUT OUR MAIN SOURCE OF EVIDENCE IS THAT TRANSCORP COMPUTER FILE--
--AND THE JUDGE HAS DETERMINED THAT IT WAS OBTAINED ILLEGALLY, AND IS THEREFORE INADMISSABLE!
I SEE. WELL, TRY EVERY OTHER ANGLE YOU CAN THINK OF, BERT. KEEP ON IT.
YES, SIR.
AND SO WILL I...!

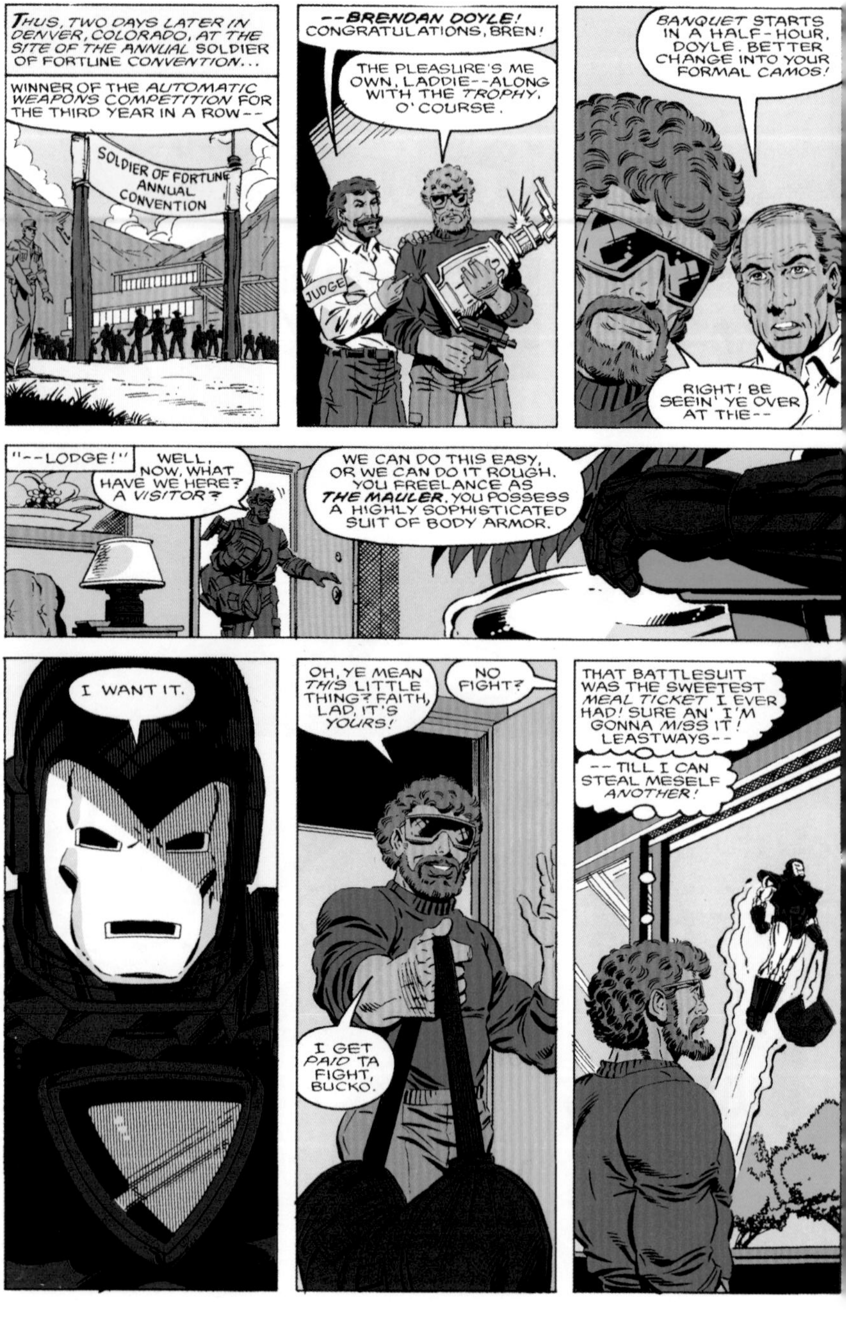

THUS, TWO DAYS LATER IN DENVER, COLORADO, AT THE SITE OF THE ANNUAL SOLDIER OF FORTUNE CONVENTION...
WINNER OF THE AUTOMATIC WEAPONS COMPETITION FOR THE THIRD YEAR IN A ROW--
SOLDIER OF FORTUNE ANNUAL CONVENTION
--BRENDAN DOYLE! CONGRATULATIONS, BREN!
THE PLEASURE'S ME OWN, LADDIE--ALONG WITH THE TROPHY, O' COURSE.
JUDGE
BANQUET STARTS IN A HALF-HOUR, DOYLE. BETTER CHANGE INTO YOUR FORMAL CAMOS!
RIGHT! BE SEEIN' YE OVER AT THE--
"--LODGE!"
WELL, NOW, WHAT HAVE WE HERE? A VISITOR?
WE CAN DO THIS EASY, OR WE CAN DO IT ROUGH. YOU FREELANCE AS THE MAULER. YOU POSSESS A HIGHLY SOPHISTICATED SUIT OF BODY ARMOR.
I WANT IT.
OH, YE MEAN THIS LITTLE THING? FAITH, LAD, IT'S YOURS!
NO FIGHT?
I GET PAID TA FIGHT, BUCKO.
THAT BATTLESUIT WAS THE SWEETEST MEAL TICKET I EVER HAD! SURE AN' I'M GONNA MISS IT! LEASTWAYS--
--TILL I CAN STEAL MESELF ANOTHER!

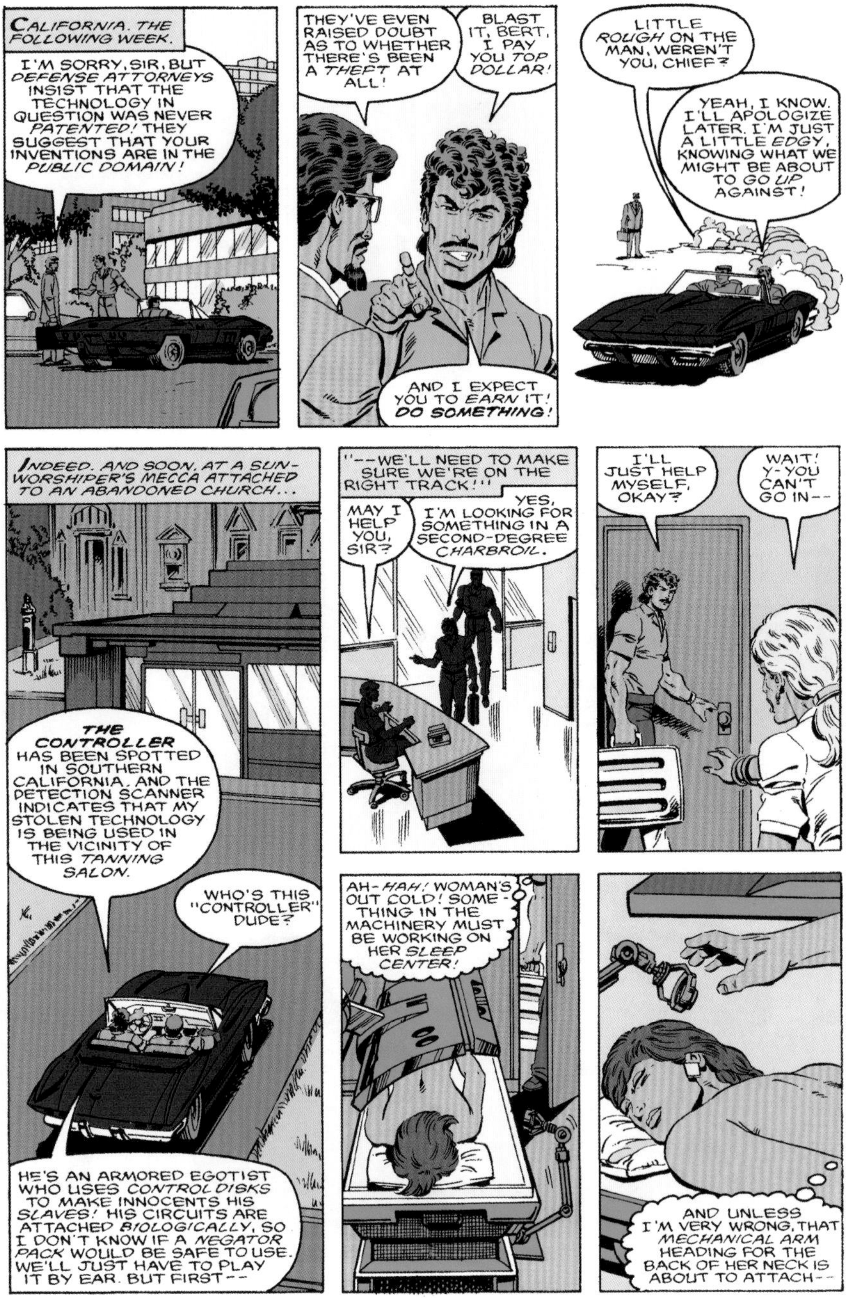
CALIFORNIA. THE FOLLOWING WEEK.
I'M SORRY, SIR, BUT DEFENSE ATTORNEYS INSIST THAT THE TECHNOLOGY IN QUESTION WAS NEVER PATENTED! THEY SUGGEST THAT YOUR INVENTIONS ARE IN THE PUBLIC DOMAIN!
THEY'VE EVEN RAISED DOUBT AS TO WHETHER THERE'S BEEN A THEFT AT ALL!
BLAST IT, BERT, I PAY YOU TOP DOLLAR!
AND I EXPECT YOU TO EARN IT! DO SOMETHING!
LITTLE ROUGH ON THE MAN, WEREN'T YOU, CHIEF?
YEAH, I KNOW. I'LL APOLOGIZE LATER. I'M JUST A LITTLE EDGY, KNOWING WHAT WE MIGHT BE ABOUT TO GO UP AGAINST!
INDEED. AND SOON, AT A SUN-WORSHIPER'S MECCA ATTACHED TO AN ABANDONED CHURCH...
THE CONTROLLER HAS BEEN SPOTTED IN SOUTHERN CALIFORNIA, AND THE DETECTION SCANNER INDICATES THAT MY STOLEN TECHNOLOGY IS BEING USED IN THE VICINITY OF THIS TANNING SALON.
WHO'S THIS "CONTROLLER" DUDE?
HE'S AN ARMORED EGOTIST WHO USES CONTROL DISKS TO MAKE INNOCENTS HIS SLAVES! HIS CIRCUITS ARE ATTACHED BIOLOGICALLY, SO I DON'T KNOW IF A NEGATOR PACK WOULD BE SAFE TO USE. WE'LL JUST HAVE TO PLAY IT BY EAR. BUT FIRST--
"--WE'LL NEED TO MAKE SURE WE'RE ON THE RIGHT TRACK!"
MAY I HELP YOU, SIR?
YES, I'M LOOKING FOR SOMETHING IN A SECOND-DEGREE CHARBROIL.
I'LL JUST HELP MYSELF, OKAY?
WAIT! Y-YOU CAN'T GO IN--
AH-HAH! WOMAN'S OUT COLD! SOMETHING IN THE MACHINERY MUST BE WORKING ON HER SLEEP CENTER!
AND UNLESS I'M VERY WRONG, THAT MECHANICAL ARM HEADING FOR THE BACK OF HER NECK IS ABOUT TO ATTACH--

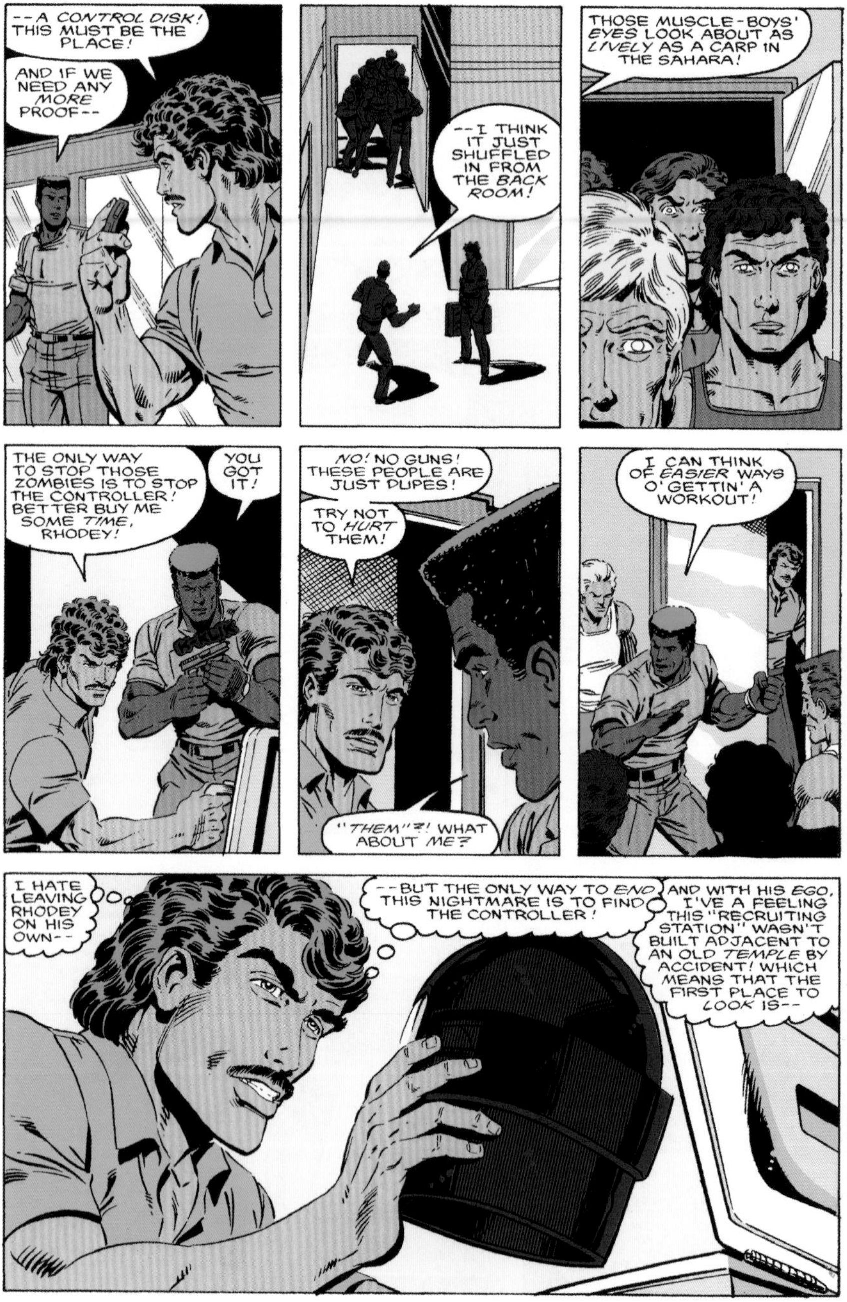
--A CONTROL DISK! THIS MUST BE THE PLACE!
AND IF WE NEED ANY MORE PROOF--
--I THINK IT JUST SHUFFLED IN FROM THE BACK ROOM!
THOSE MUSCLE-BOYS' EYES LOOK ABOUT AS LIVELY AS A CARP IN THE SAHARA!
THE ONLY WAY TO STOP THOSE ZOMBIES IS TO STOP THE CONTROLLER! BETTER BUY ME SOME TIME, RHODEY!
YOU GOT IT!
NO! NO GUNS! THESE PEOPLE ARE JUST DUPES!
TRY NOT TO HURT THEM!
"THEM"?! WHAT ABOUT ME?
I CAN THINK OF EASIER WAYS O' GETTIN' A WORKOUT!
I HATE LEAVING RHODEY ON HIS OWN--
--BUT THE ONLY WAY TO END THIS NIGHTMARE IS TO FIND THE CONTROLLER!
AND WITH HIS EGO, I'VE A FEELING THIS "RECRUITING STATION" WASN'T BUILT ADJACENT TO AN OLD TEMPLE BY ACCIDENT! WHICH MEANS THAT THE FIRST PLACE TO LOOK IS--

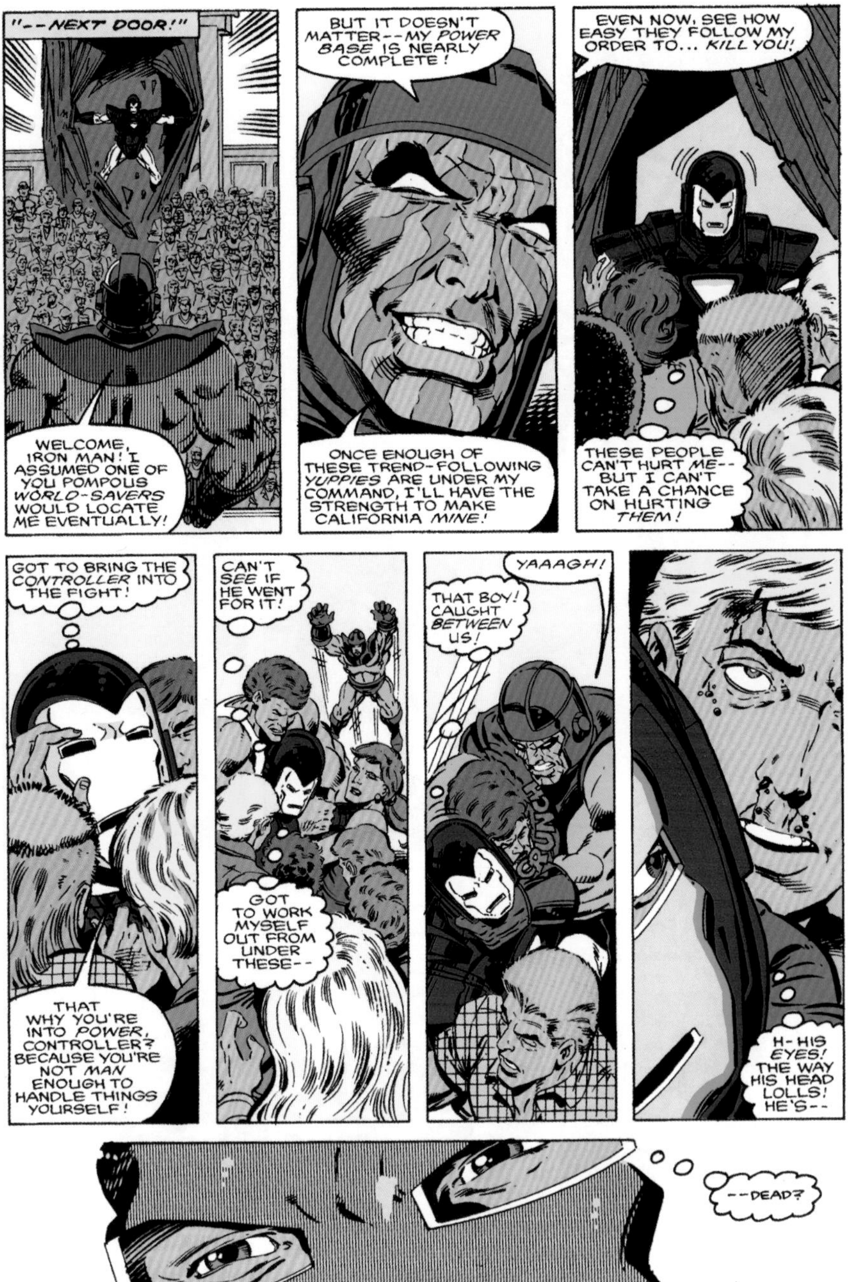

"--NEXT DOOR!"
WELCOME, IRON MAN! I ASSUMED ONE OF YOU POMPOUS WORLD-SAVERS WOULD LOCATE ME EVENTUALLY!
BUT IT DOESN'T MATTER--MY POWER BASE IS NEARLY COMPLETE!
ONCE ENOUGH OF THESE TREND-FOLLOWING YUPPIES ARE UNDER MY COMMAND, I'LL HAVE THE STRENGTH TO MAKE CALIFORNIA MINE!
EVEN NOW, SEE HOW EASY THEY FOLLOW MY ORDER TO... KILL YOU!
THESE PEOPLE CAN'T HURT ME--BUT I CAN'T TAKE A CHANCE ON HURTING THEM!
GOT TO BRING THE CONTROLLER INTO THE FIGHT!
THAT WHY YOU'RE INTO POWER, CONTROLLER? BECAUSE YOU'RE NOT MAN ENOUGH TO HANDLE THINGS YOURSELF!
CAN'T SEE IF HE WENT FOR IT!
GOT TO WORK MYSELF OUT FROM UNDER THESE--
YAAAGH!
THAT BOY! CAUGHT BETWEEN US!
H-HIS EYES! THE WAY HIS HEAD LOLLS! HE'S--
--DEAD?

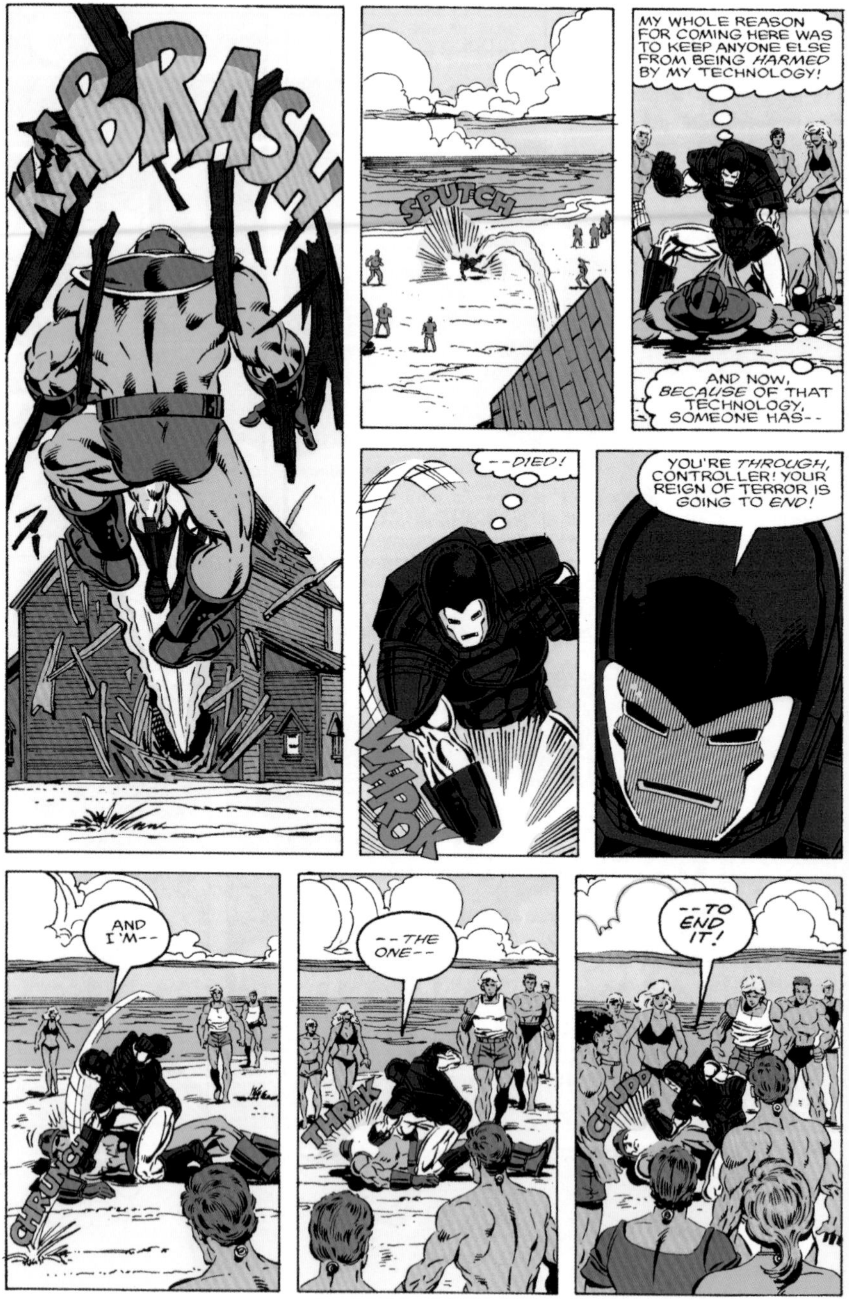
KABRASH
SPUTCH
MY WHOLE REASON FOR COMING HERE WAS TO KEEP ANYONE ELSE FROM BEING *HARMED* BY MY TECHNOLOGY!
AND NOW, *BECAUSE* OF THAT TECHNOLOGY, SOMEONE HAS--
--*DIED*!
WHROK
YOU'RE *THROUGH*, CONTROLLER! YOUR REIGN OF TERROR IS GOING TO *END*!
AND I'M--
CHRUNCH
--THE ONE--
THRAK
--TO *END* IT!
CHUDD

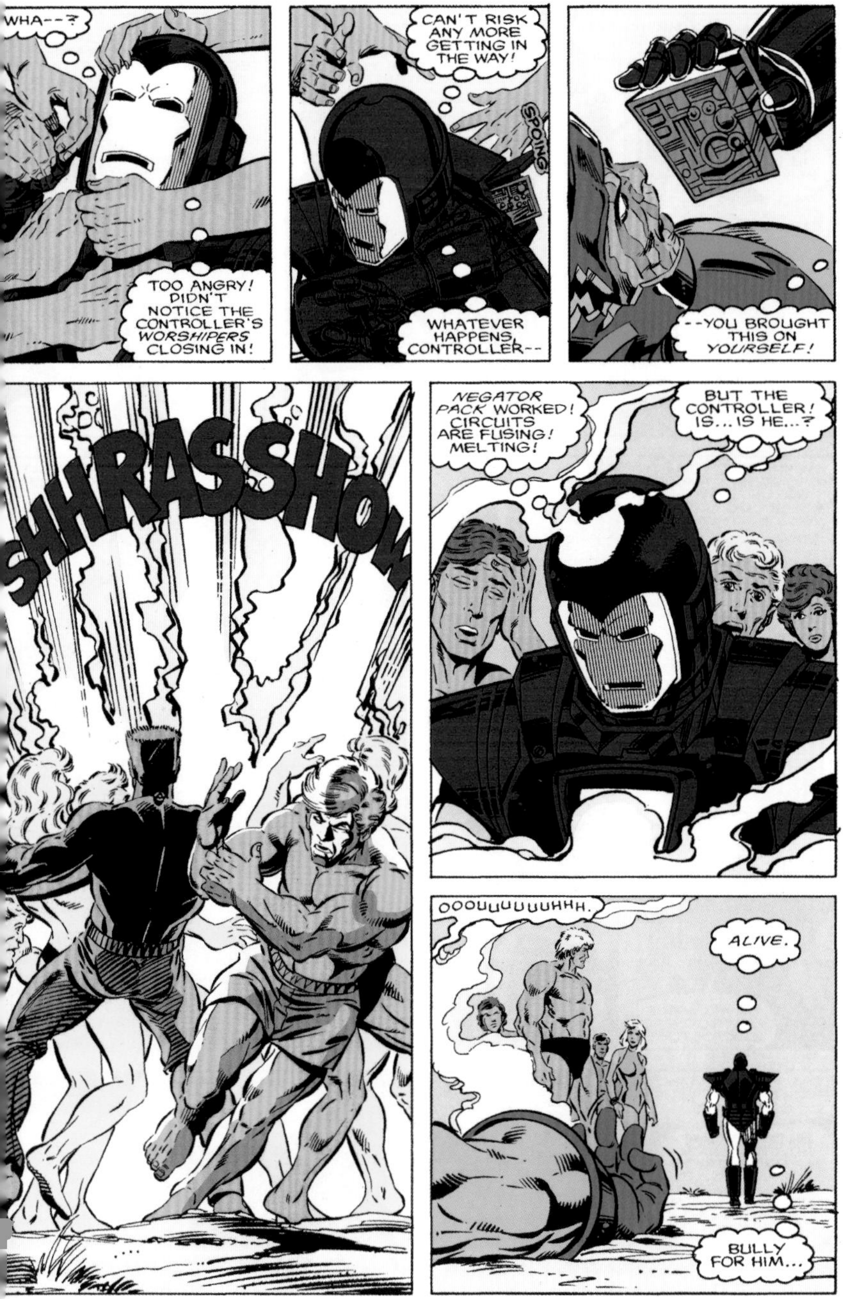
WHA--?
TOO ANGRY! DIDN'T NOTICE THE CONTROLLER'S WORSHIPERS CLOSING IN!
CAN'T RISK ANY MORE GETTING IN THE WAY!
SPOING
WHATEVER HAPPENS, CONTROLLER--
--YOU BROUGHT THIS ON YOURSELF!
SHHRASSHOW
NEGATOR PACK WORKED! CIRCUITS ARE FUSING! MELTING!
BUT THE CONTROLLER! IS... IS HE...?
OOOUUUUUUUHHH.
ALIVE.
BULLY FOR HIM...

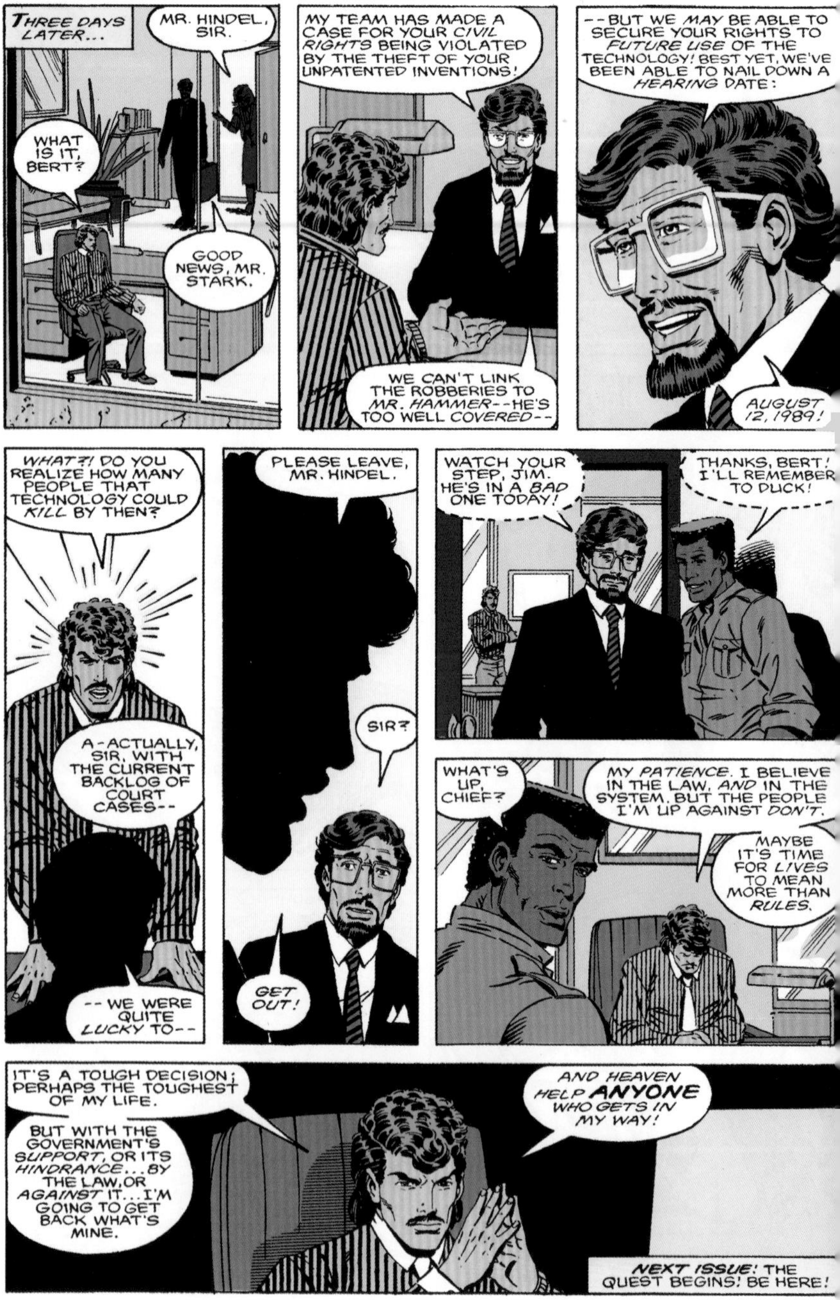
THREE DAYS LATER...
MR. HINDEL, SIR.
WHAT IS IT, BERT?
GOOD NEWS, MR. STARK.
MY TEAM HAS MADE A CASE FOR YOUR CIVIL RIGHTS BEING VIOLATED BY THE THEFT OF YOUR UNPATENTED INVENTIONS!
WE CAN'T LINK THE ROBBERIES TO MR. HAMMER--HE'S TOO WELL COVERED--
--BUT WE MAY BE ABLE TO SECURE YOUR RIGHTS TO FUTURE USE OF THE TECHNOLOGY! BEST YET, WE'VE BEEN ABLE TO NAIL DOWN A HEARING DATE:
AUGUST 12, 1989!
WHAT?! DO YOU REALIZE HOW MANY PEOPLE THAT TECHNOLOGY COULD KILL BY THEN?
A-ACTUALLY, SIR, WITH THE CURRENT BACKLOG OF COURT CASES--
--WE WERE QUITE LUCKY TO--
PLEASE LEAVE, MR. HINDEL.
SIR?
GET OUT!
WATCH YOUR STEP, JIM. HE'S IN A BAD ONE TODAY!
THANKS, BERT! I'LL REMEMBER TO DUCK!
WHAT'S UP, CHIEF?
MY PATIENCE. I BELIEVE IN THE LAW, AND IN THE SYSTEM. BUT THE PEOPLE I'M UP AGAINST DON'T.
MAYBE IT'S TIME FOR LIVES TO MEAN MORE THAN RULES.
IT'S A TOUGH DECISION; PERHAPS THE TOUGHEST OF MY LIFE.
BUT WITH THE GOVERNMENT'S SUPPORT, OR ITS HINDRANCE...BY THE LAW, OR AGAINST IT...I'M GOING TO GET BACK WHAT'S MINE.
AND HEAVEN HELP ANYONE WHO GETS IN MY WAY!
NEXT ISSUE! THE QUEST BEGINS! BE HERE!

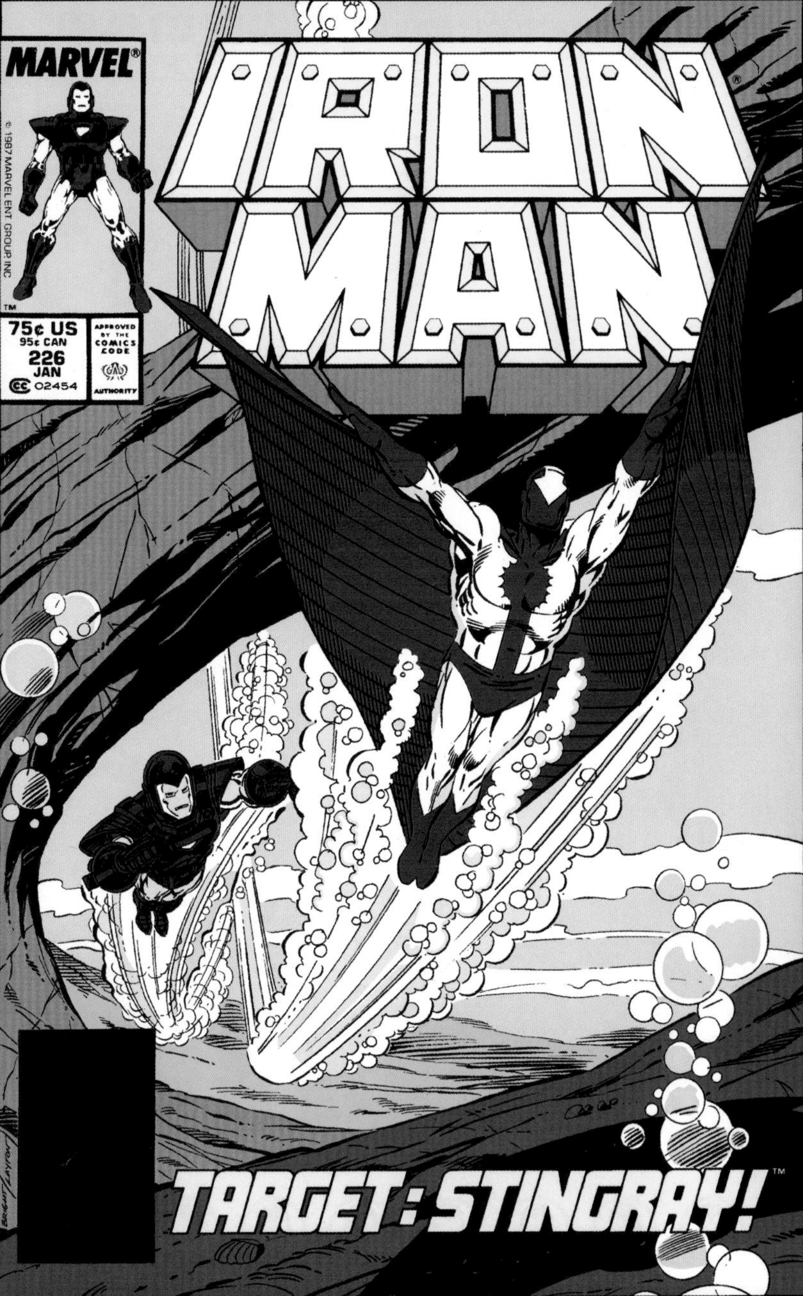
MARVEL®
IRON MAN
© 1987 MARVEL ENT GROUP, INC
TM
75¢ US
95¢ CAN
226
JAN
02454
APPROVED BY THE COMICS CODE AUTHORITY
TARGET: STINGRAY!
TM

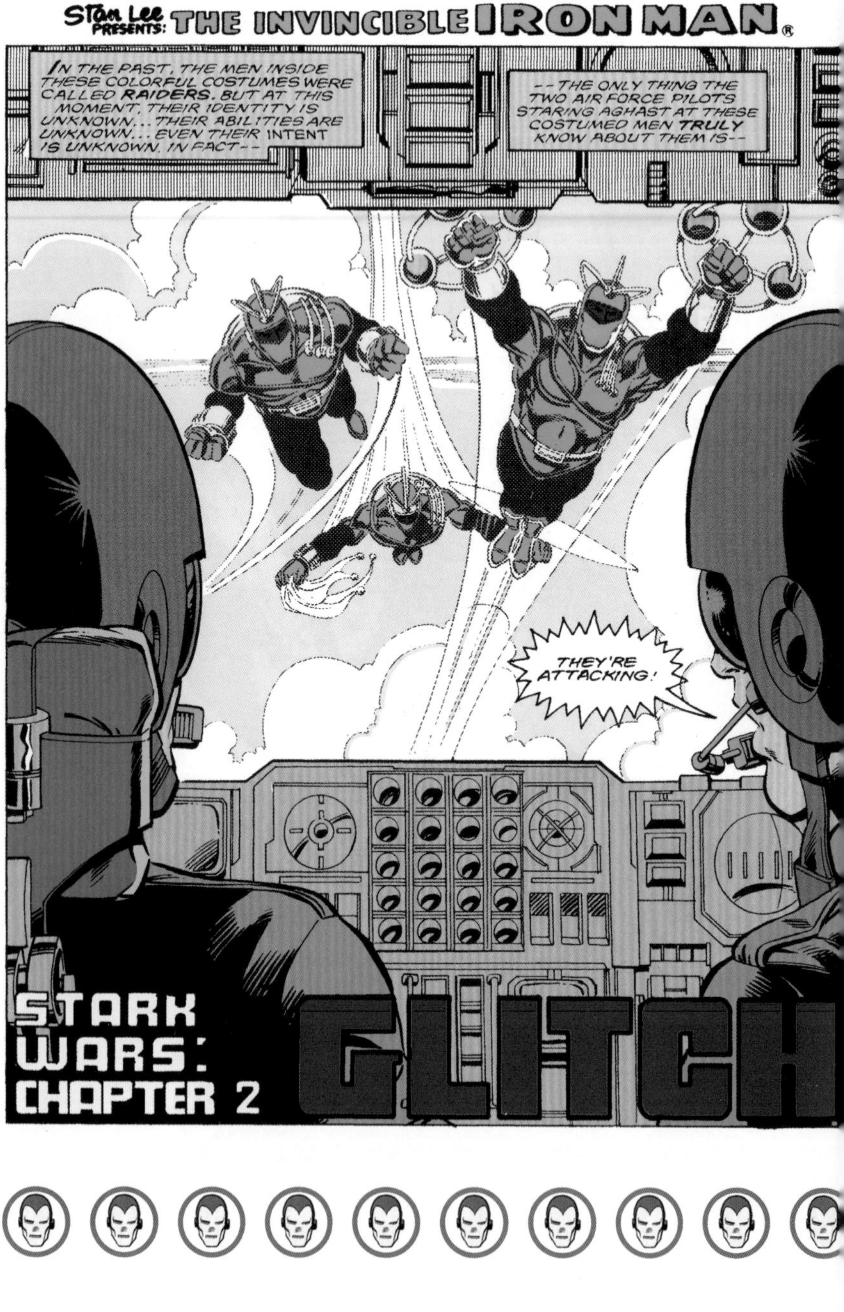
STAN LEE PRESENTS: THE INVINCIBLE IRON MAN®
IN THE PAST, THE MEN INSIDE THESE COLORFUL COSTUMES WERE CALLED RAIDERS. BUT AT THIS MOMENT, THEIR IDENTITY IS UNKNOWN... THEIR ABILITIES ARE UNKNOWN... EVEN THEIR INTENT IS UNKNOWN. IN FACT--
--THE ONLY THING THE TWO AIR FORCE PILOTS STARING AGHAST AT THESE COSTUMED MEN TRULY KNOW ABOUT THEM IS--
THEY'RE ATTACKING!
STARK WARS: CHAPTER 2
GLITCH

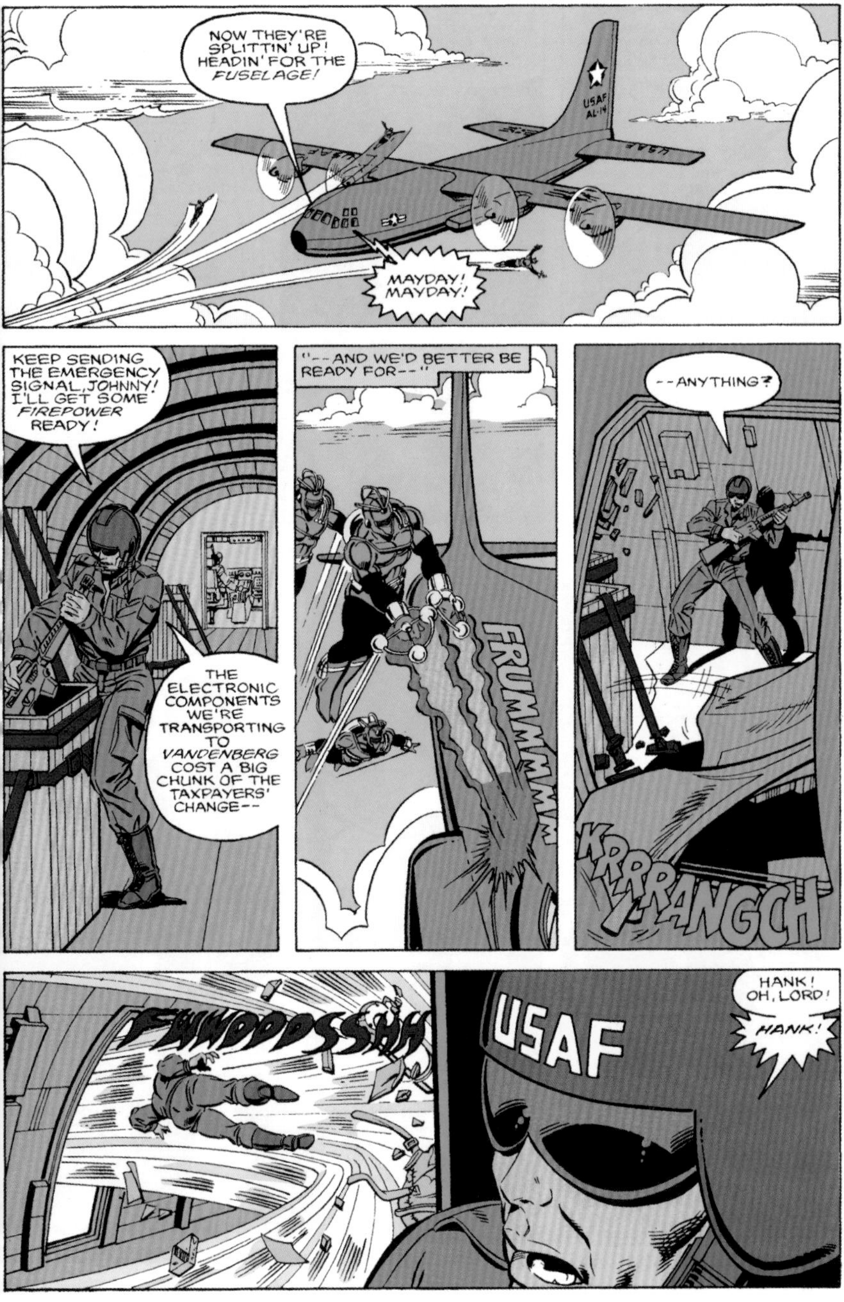
NOW THEY'RE SPLITTIN' UP! HEADIN' FOR THE FUSELAGE!
USAF AL-14
MAYDAY! MAYDAY!
KEEP SENDING THE EMERGENCY SIGNAL, JOHNNY! I'LL GET SOME FIREPOWER READY!
THE ELECTRONIC COMPONENTS WE'RE TRANSPORTING TO VANDENBERG COST A BIG CHUNK OF THE TAXPAYERS' CHANGE--
"--AND WE'D BETTER BE READY FOR--"
FRUMMMMM
--ANYTHING?
KRRRANGCH
FWWOOOSSHH
USAF
HANK! OH, LORD!
HANK!

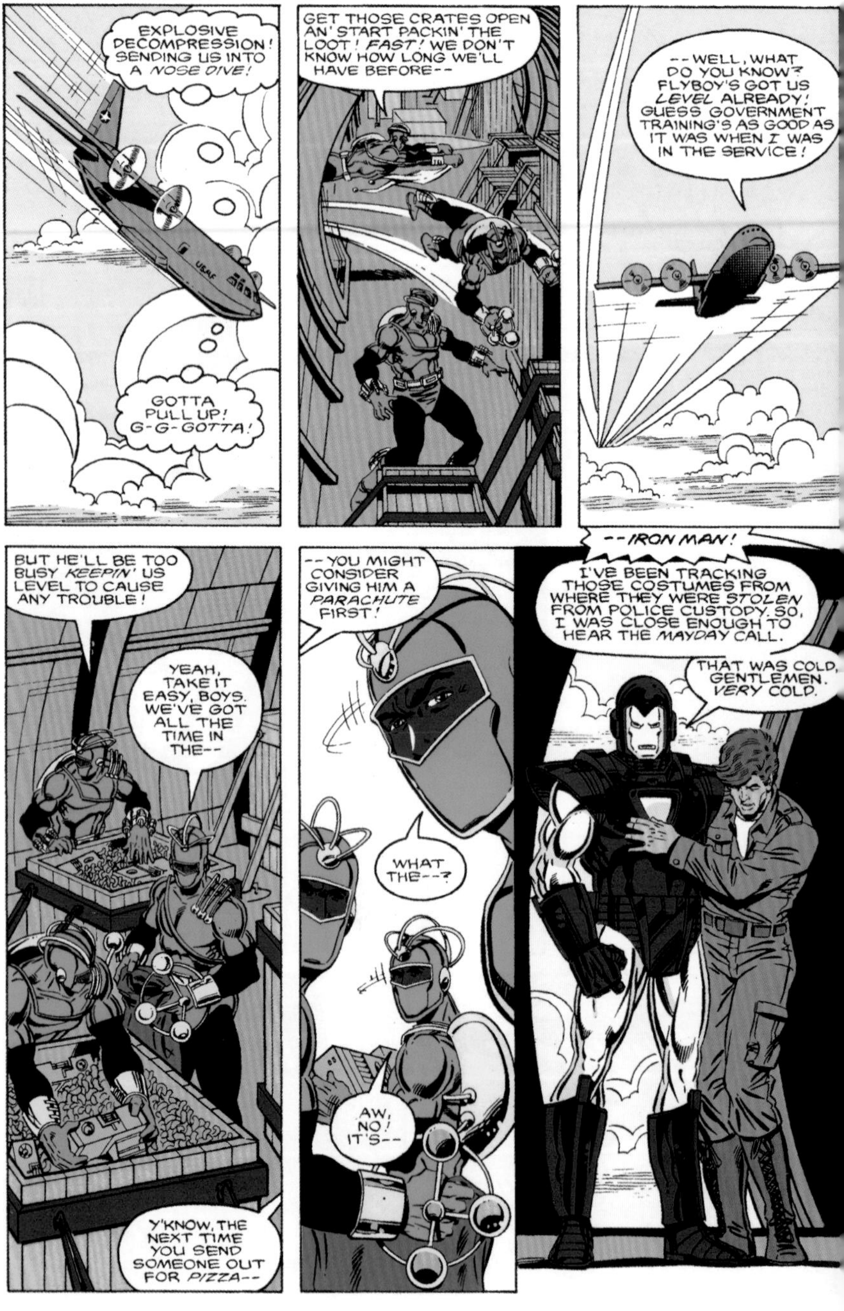
EXPLOSIVE DECOMPRESSION! SENDING US INTO A NOSE DIVE!
GOTTA PULL UP! G-G-GOTTA!
GET THOSE CRATES OPEN AN' START PACKIN' THE LOOT! FAST! WE DON'T KNOW HOW LONG WE'LL HAVE BEFORE--
--WELL, WHAT DO YOU KNOW? FLYBOY'S GOT US LEVEL ALREADY! GUESS GOVERNMENT TRAINING'S AS GOOD AS IT WAS WHEN I WAS IN THE SERVICE!
BUT HE'LL BE TOO BUSY KEEPIN' US LEVEL TO CAUSE ANY TROUBLE!
YEAH, TAKE IT EASY, BOYS. WE'VE GOT ALL THE TIME IN THE--
Y'KNOW, THE NEXT TIME YOU SEND SOMEONE OUT FOR PIZZA--
--YOU MIGHT CONSIDER GIVING HIM A PARACHUTE FIRST!
WHAT THE--?
AW, NO! IT'S--
--IRON MAN!
I'VE BEEN TRACKING THOSE COSTUMES FROM WHERE THEY WERE STOLEN FROM POLICE CUSTODY. SO, I WAS CLOSE ENOUGH TO HEAR THE MAYDAY CALL.
THAT WAS COLD, GENTLEMEN. VERY COLD.

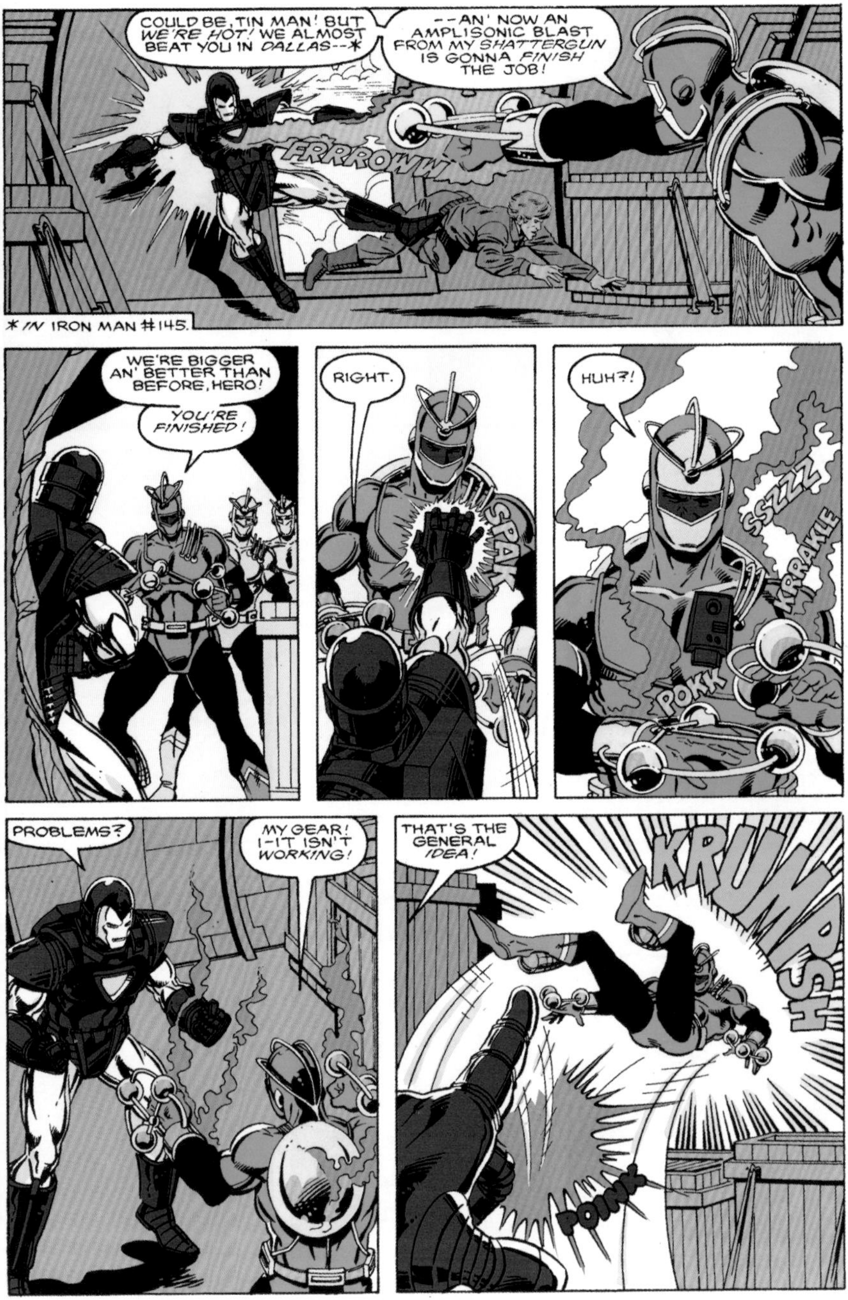
COULD BE, TIN MAN! BUT WE'RE HOT! WE ALMOST BEAT YOU IN DALLAS--*
--AN' NOW AN AMPLISONIC BLAST FROM MY SHATTERGUN IS GONNA FINISH THE JOB!
FRRROWW
*IN IRON MAN #145.
WE'RE BIGGER AN' BETTER THAN BEFORE, HERO!
YOU'RE FINISHED!
RIGHT.
SPAK
HUH?!
SSZZZ
KRRAKLE
POKK
PROBLEMS?
MY GEAR! I-IT ISN'T WORKING!
THAT'S THE GENERAL IDEA!
KRUMPSH
POINK

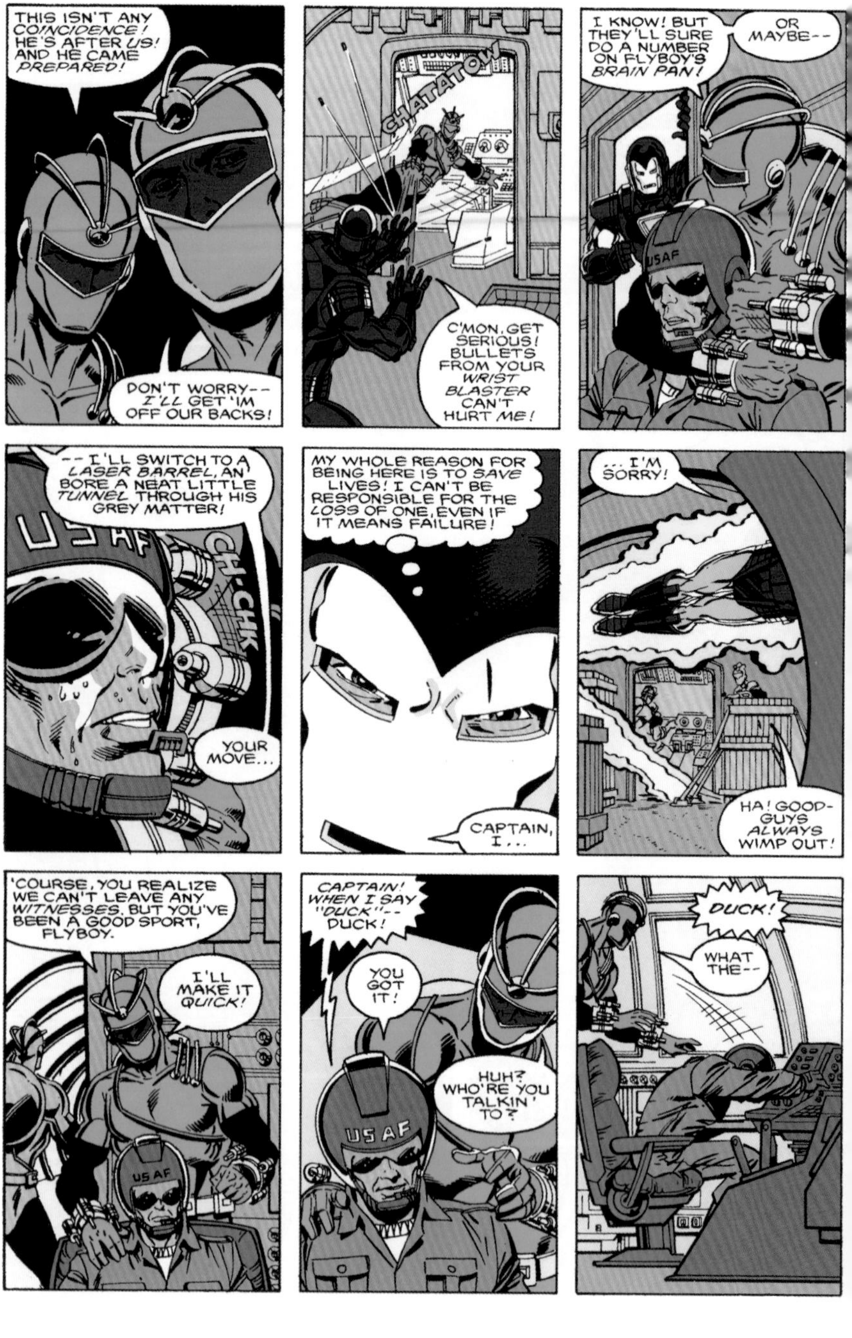
THIS ISN'T ANY COINCIDENCE! HE'S AFTER US! AND HE CAME PREPARED!
DON'T WORRY-- I'LL GET 'IM OFF OUR BACKS!
CHATATOW
C'MON, GET SERIOUS! BULLETS FROM YOUR WRIST BLASTER CAN'T HURT ME!
I KNOW! BUT THEY'LL SURE DO A NUMBER ON FLYBOY'S BRAIN PAN!
OR MAYBE--
-- I'LL SWITCH TO A LASER BARREL, AN' BORE A NEAT LITTLE TUNNEL THROUGH HIS GREY MATTER!
CH-CHK
YOUR MOVE...
MY WHOLE REASON FOR BEING HERE IS TO SAVE LIVES! I CAN'T BE RESPONSIBLE FOR THE LOSS OF ONE, EVEN IF IT MEANS FAILURE!
CAPTAIN, I...
... I'M SORRY!
HA! GOOD-GUYS ALWAYS WIMP OUT!
'COURSE, YOU REALIZE WE CAN'T LEAVE ANY WITNESSES. BUT YOU'VE BEEN A GOOD SPORT, FLYBOY.
I'LL MAKE IT QUICK!
CAPTAIN! WHEN I SAY "DUCK"-- DUCK!
YOU GOT IT!
HUH? WHO'RE YOU TALKIN' TO?
DUCK!
WHAT THE--

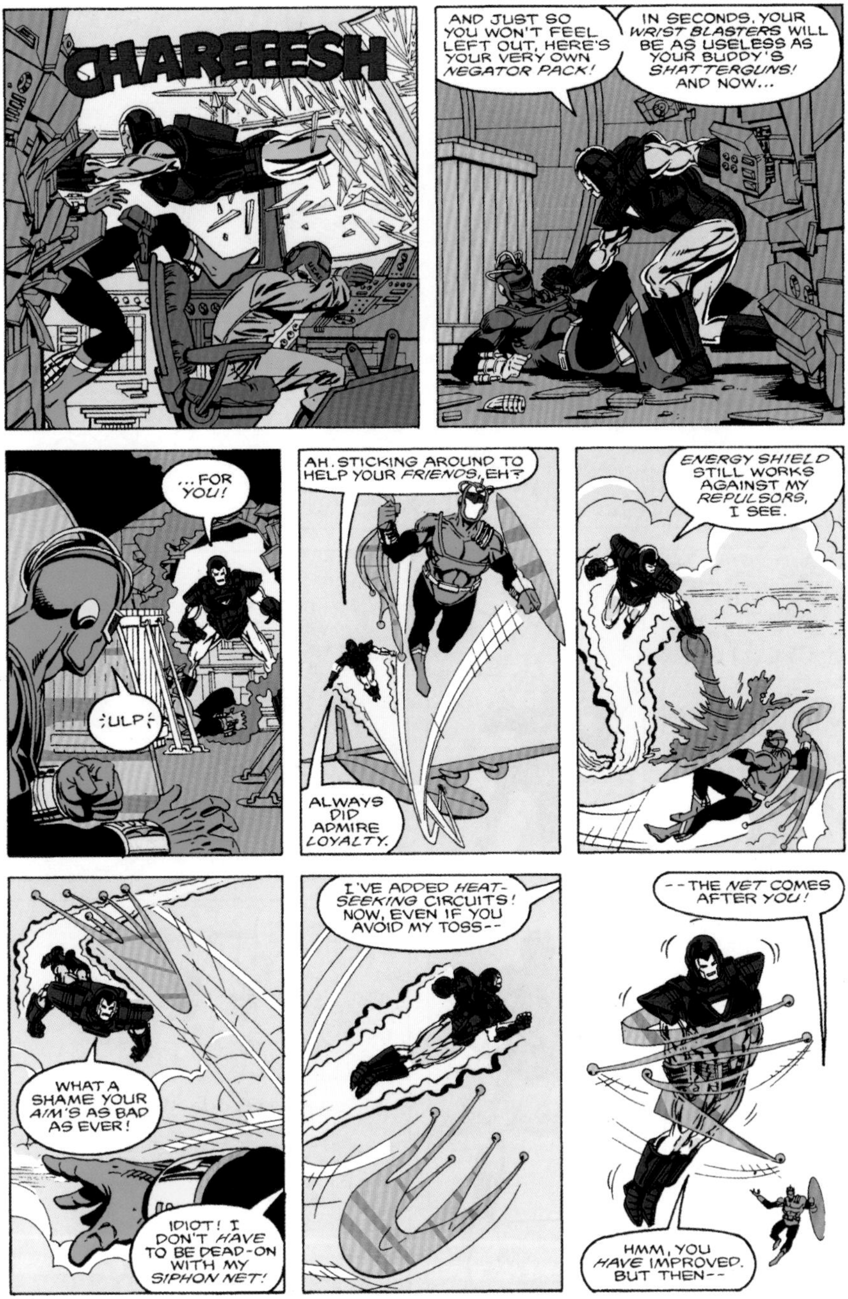
CHAREEESH
AND JUST SO YOU WON'T FEEL LEFT OUT, HERE'S YOUR VERY OWN NEGATOR PACK!
IN SECONDS, YOUR WRIST BLASTERS WILL BE AS USELESS AS YOUR BUDDY'S SHATTERGUNS! AND NOW...
...FOR YOU!
ULP
AH. STICKING AROUND TO HELP YOUR FRIENDS, EH?
ALWAYS DID ADMIRE LOYALTY.
ENERGY SHIELD STILL WORKS AGAINST MY REPULSORS, I SEE.
WHAT A SHAME YOUR AIM'S AS BAD AS EVER!
IDIOT! I DON'T HAVE TO BE DEAD-ON WITH MY SIPHON NET!
I'VE ADDED HEAT-SEEKING CIRCUITS! NOW, EVEN IF YOU AVOID MY TOSS--
--THE NET COMES AFTER YOU!
HMM, YOU HAVE IMPROVED. BUT THEN--

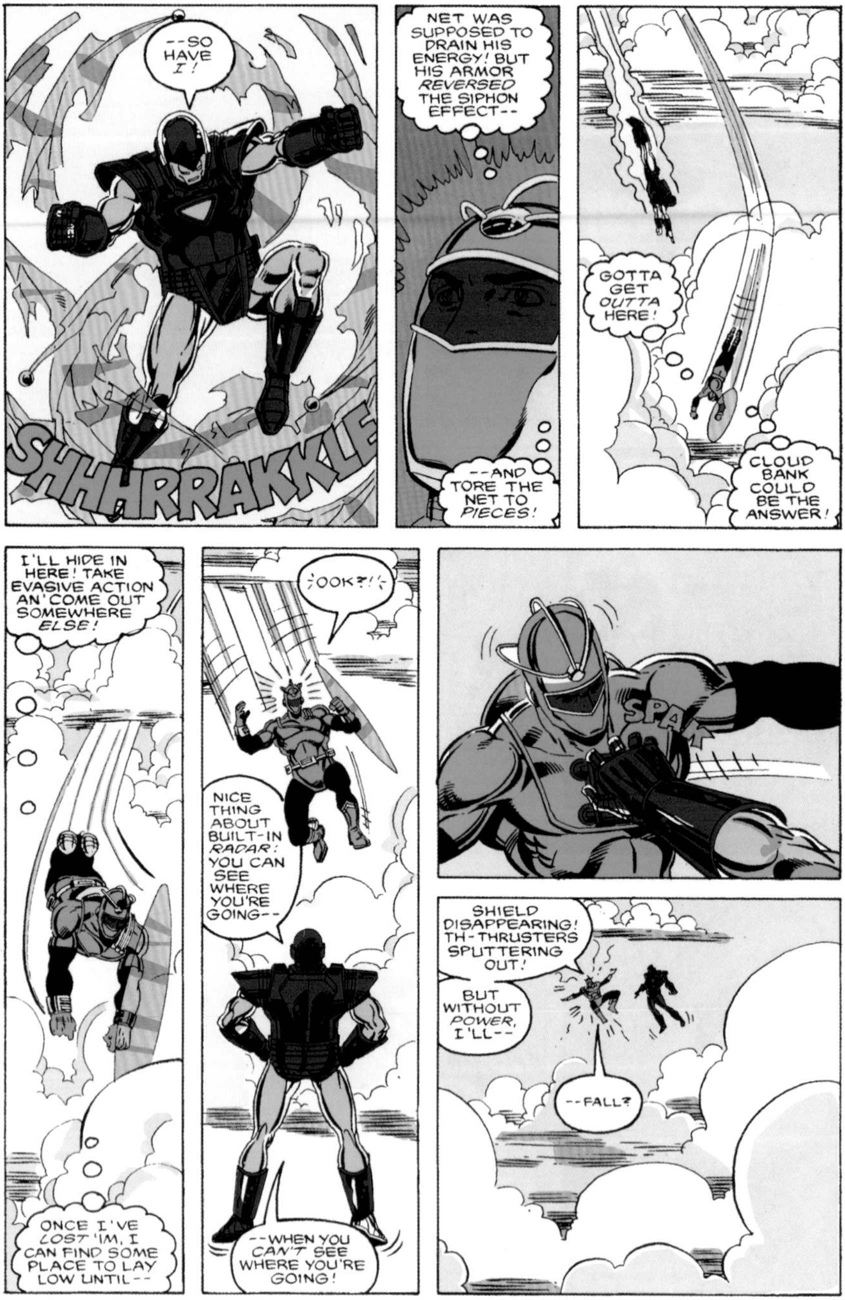
--SO HAVE I!
SHHRRAKKLE
NET WAS SUPPOSED TO DRAIN HIS ENERGY! BUT HIS ARMOR REVERSED THE SIPHON EFFECT--
--AND TORE THE NET TO PIECES!
GOTTA GET OUTTA HERE!
CLOUD BANK COULD BE THE ANSWER!
I'LL HIDE IN HERE! TAKE EVASIVE ACTION AN' COME OUT SOMEWHERE ELSE!
ONCE I'VE LOST 'IM, I CAN FIND SOME PLACE TO LAY LOW UNTIL--
OOK?!
NICE THING ABOUT BUILT-IN RADAR: YOU CAN SEE WHERE YOU'RE GOING--
--WHEN YOU CAN'T SEE WHERE YOU'RE GOING!
SPA
SHIELD DISAPPEARING! TH-THRUSTERS SPUTTERING OUT!
BUT WITHOUT POWER, I'LL--
--FALL?

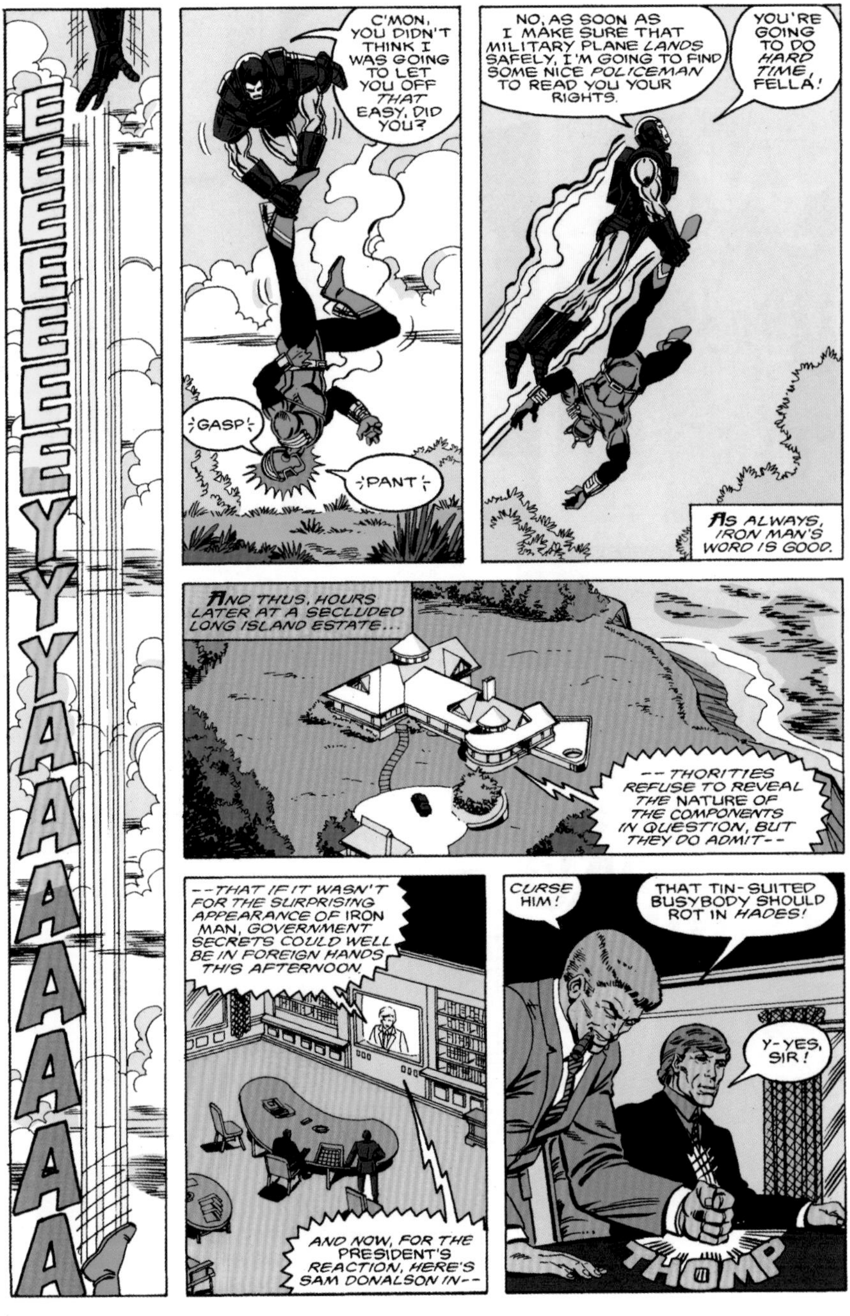
EEEEEEEEEEYYYAAAAAAAA
C'MON, YOU DIDN'T THINK I WAS GOING TO LET YOU OFF *THAT* EASY, DID YOU?
GASP
PANT
NO, AS SOON AS I MAKE SURE THAT MILITARY PLANE *LANDS* SAFELY, I'M GOING TO FIND SOME NICE *POLICEMAN* TO READ YOU YOUR RIGHTS.
YOU'RE GOING TO DO *HARD TIME*, FELLA!
AS ALWAYS, IRON MAN'S WORD IS GOOD.
AND THUS, HOURS LATER AT A SECLUDED LONG ISLAND ESTATE...
--THORITIES REFUSE TO REVEAL THE NATURE OF THE COMPONENTS IN QUESTION, BUT THEY DO ADMIT--
--THAT IF IT WASN'T FOR THE SURPRISING APPEARANCE OF IRON MAN, GOVERNMENT SECRETS COULD WELL BE IN FOREIGN HANDS THIS AFTERNOON.
AND NOW, FOR THE PRESIDENT'S REACTION, HERE'S SAM DONALSON IN--
CURSE HIM!
THAT TIN-SUITED BUSYBODY SHOULD ROT IN *HADES*!
Y-YES, SIR!
THOMP

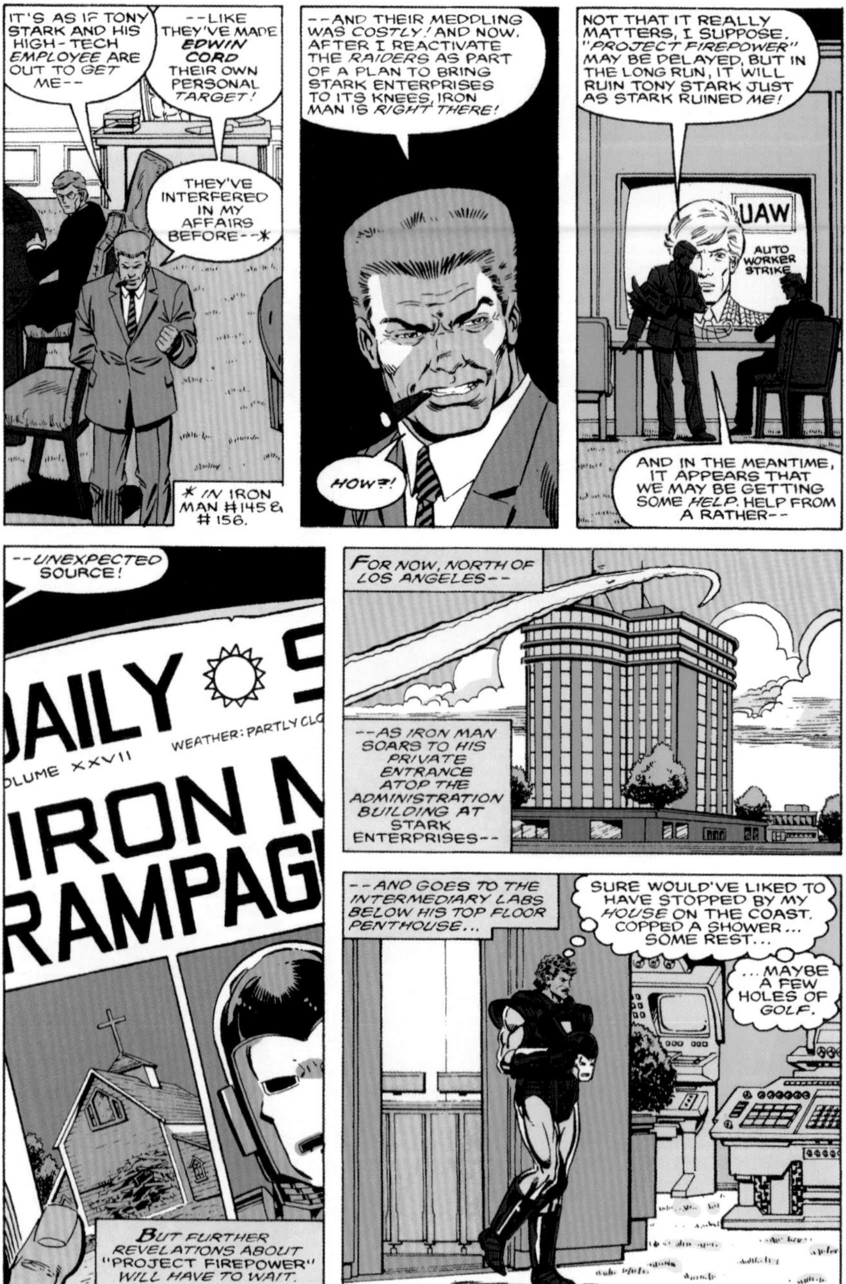
IT'S AS IF TONY STARK AND HIS HIGH-TECH EMPLOYEE ARE OUT TO GET ME--
--LIKE THEY'VE MADE EDWIN CORD THEIR OWN PERSONAL TARGET!
THEY'VE INTERFERED IN MY AFFAIRS BEFORE--*
* IN IRON MAN #145 & #156.
--AND THEIR MEDDLING WAS COSTLY! AND NOW, AFTER I REACTIVATE THE RAIDERS AS PART OF A PLAN TO BRING STARK ENTERPRISES TO ITS KNEES, IRON MAN IS RIGHT THERE!
HOW?!
NOT THAT IT REALLY MATTERS, I SUPPOSE. "PROJECT FIREPOWER" MAY BE DELAYED, BUT IN THE LONG RUN, IT WILL RUIN TONY STARK JUST AS STARK RUINED ME!
UAW
AUTO WORKER STRIKE
AND IN THE MEANTIME, IT APPEARS THAT WE MAY BE GETTING SOME HELP. HELP FROM A RATHER--
--UNEXPECTED SOURCE!
DAILY
WEATHER: PARTLY CLO
OLUME XXVII
IRON M
RAMPAG
BUT FURTHER REVELATIONS ABOUT "PROJECT FIREPOWER" WILL HAVE TO WAIT.
FOR NOW, NORTH OF LOS ANGELES--
--AS IRON MAN SOARS TO HIS PRIVATE ENTRANCE ATOP THE ADMINISTRATION BUILDING AT STARK ENTERPRISES--
--AND GOES TO THE INTERMEDIARY LABS BELOW HIS TOP FLOOR PENTHOUSE...
SURE WOULD'VE LIKED TO HAVE STOPPED BY MY HOUSE ON THE COAST. COPPED A SHOWER... SOME REST...
...MAYBE A FEW HOLES OF GOLF.

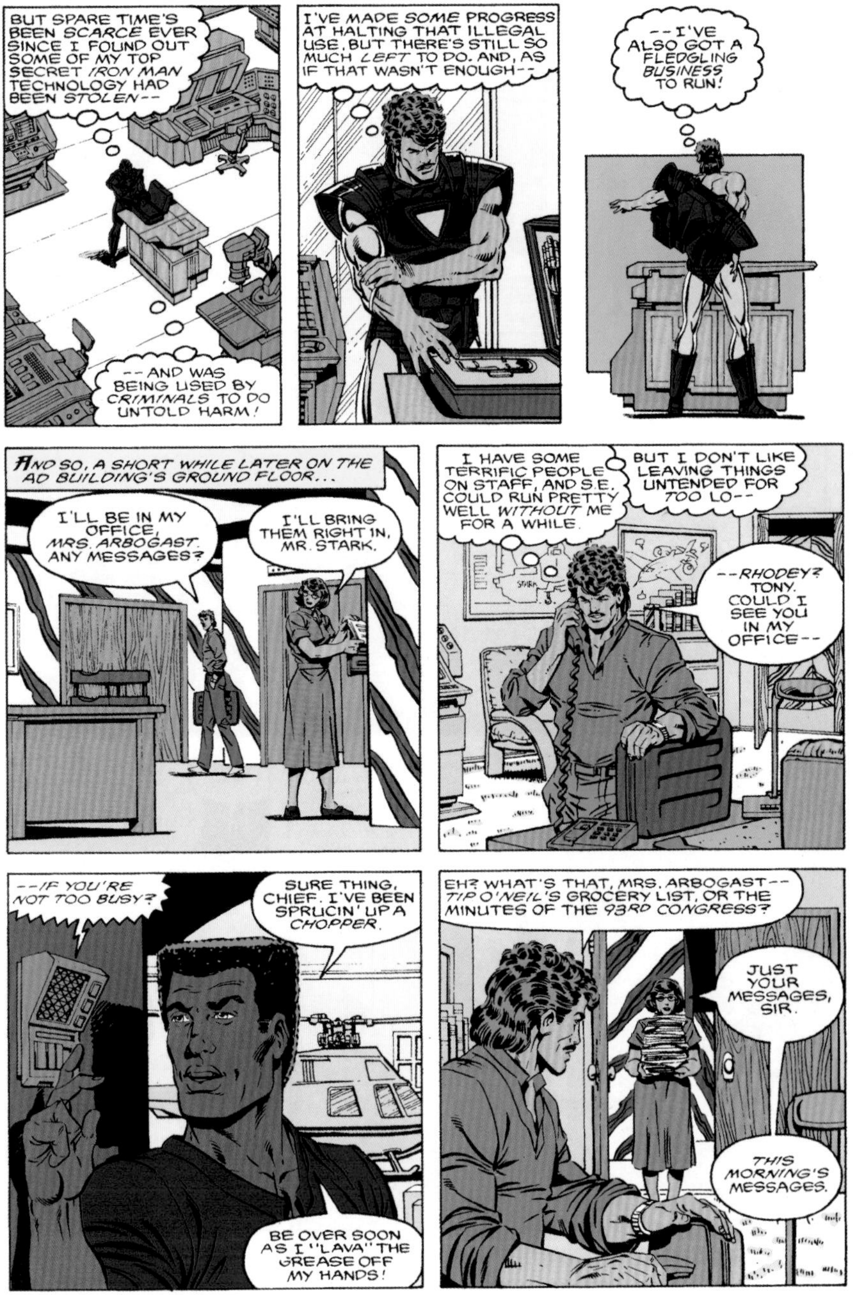
BUT SPARE TIME'S BEEN SCARCE EVER SINCE I FOUND OUT SOME OF MY TOP SECRET IRON MAN TECHNOLOGY HAD BEEN STOLEN--
--AND WAS BEING USED BY CRIMINALS TO DO UNTOLD HARM!
I'VE MADE SOME PROGRESS AT HALTING THAT ILLEGAL USE, BUT THERE'S STILL SO MUCH LEFT TO DO. AND, AS IF THAT WASN'T ENOUGH--
--I'VE ALSO GOT A FLEDGLING BUSINESS TO RUN!
AND SO, A SHORT WHILE LATER ON THE AD BUILDING'S GROUND FLOOR...
I'LL BE IN MY OFFICE, MRS. ARBOGAST. ANY MESSAGES?
I'LL BRING THEM RIGHT IN, MR. STARK.
I HAVE SOME TERRIFIC PEOPLE ON STAFF, AND S.E. COULD RUN PRETTY WELL WITHOUT ME FOR A WHILE.
BUT I DON'T LIKE LEAVING THINGS UNTENDED FOR TOO LO--
--RHODEY? TONY. COULD I SEE YOU IN MY OFFICE--
--IF YOU'RE NOT TOO BUSY?
SURE THING, CHIEF. I'VE BEEN SPRUCIN' UP A CHOPPER.
BE OVER SOON AS I "LAVA" THE GREASE OFF MY HANDS!
EH? WHAT'S THAT, MRS. ARBOGAST-- TIP O'NEIL'S GROCERY LIST, OR THE MINUTES OF THE 93RD CONGRESS?
JUST YOUR MESSAGES, SIR.
THIS MORNING'S MESSAGES.

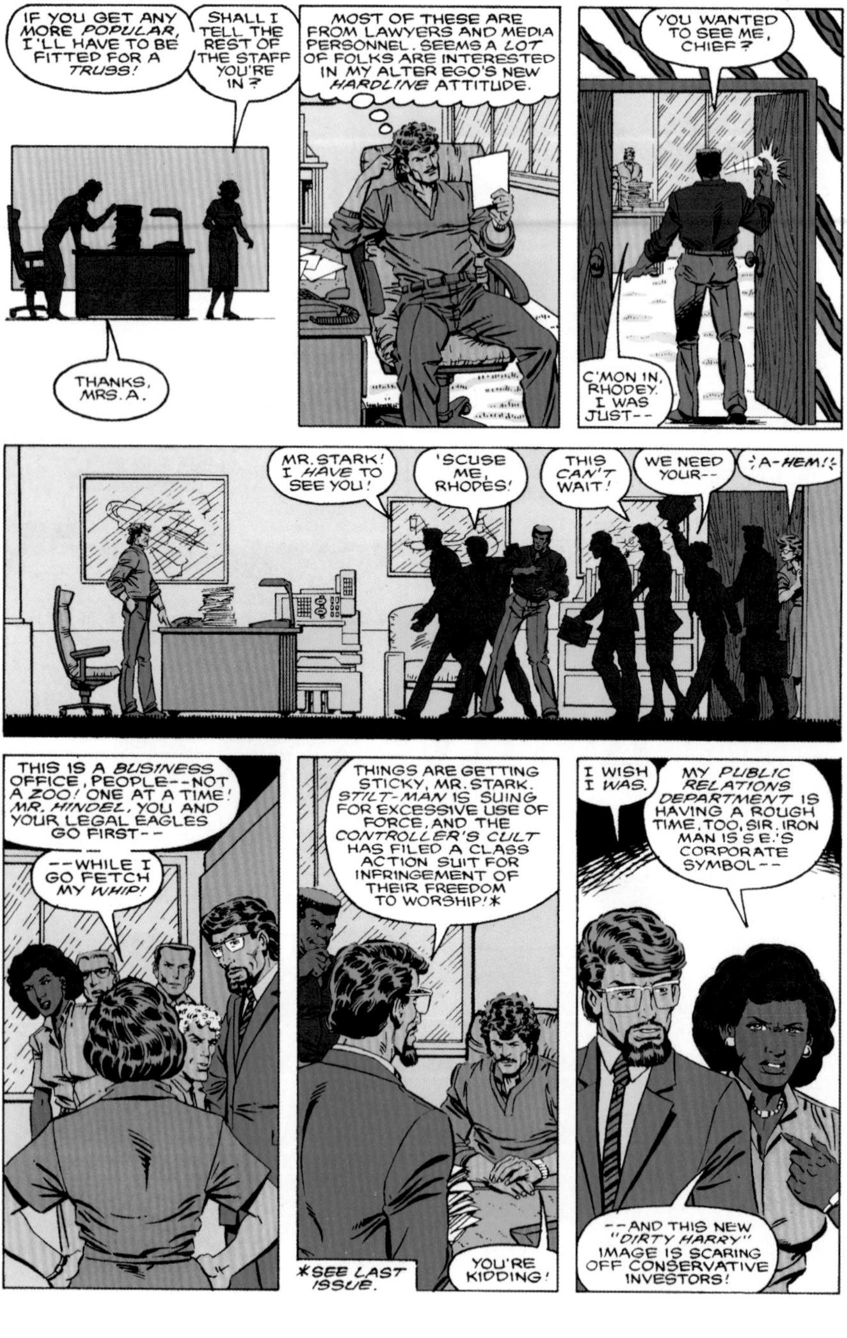
IF YOU GET ANY MORE *POPULAR*, I'LL HAVE TO BE FITTED FOR A *TRUSS!*
SHALL I TELL THE REST OF THE STAFF YOU'RE IN?
THANKS, MRS. A.
MOST OF THESE ARE FROM LAWYERS AND MEDIA PERSONNEL. SEEMS A *LOT* OF FOLKS ARE INTERESTED IN MY ALTER EGO'S NEW *HARDLINE* ATTITUDE.
YOU WANTED TO SEE ME, CHIEF?
C'MON IN, RHODEY. I WAS JUST--
MR. STARK! I *HAVE* TO SEE YOU!
'SCUSE ME, RHODES!
THIS *CAN'T* WAIT!
WE NEED YOUR--
A-*HEM!*
THIS IS A *BUSINESS* OFFICE, PEOPLE--NOT A *ZOO!* ONE AT A TIME! *MR. HINDEL,* YOU AND YOUR LEGAL EAGLES GO FIRST--
--WHILE I GO FETCH MY *WHIP!*
THINGS ARE GETTING STICKY, MR. STARK. *STILT-MAN* IS SUING FOR EXCESSIVE USE OF FORCE, AND THE *CONTROLLER'S CULT* HAS FILED A CLASS ACTION SUIT FOR INFRINGEMENT OF THEIR FREEDOM TO WORSHIP!*
YOU'RE KIDDING!
*SEE LAST ISSUE.
I WISH I *WAS.*
MY *PUBLIC RELATIONS DEPARTMENT* IS HAVING A ROUGH TIME, TOO, SIR. IRON MAN IS S.E.'S CORPORATE SYMBOL--
--AND THIS NEW *"DIRTY HARRY"* IMAGE IS SCARING OFF CONSERVATIVE INVESTORS!

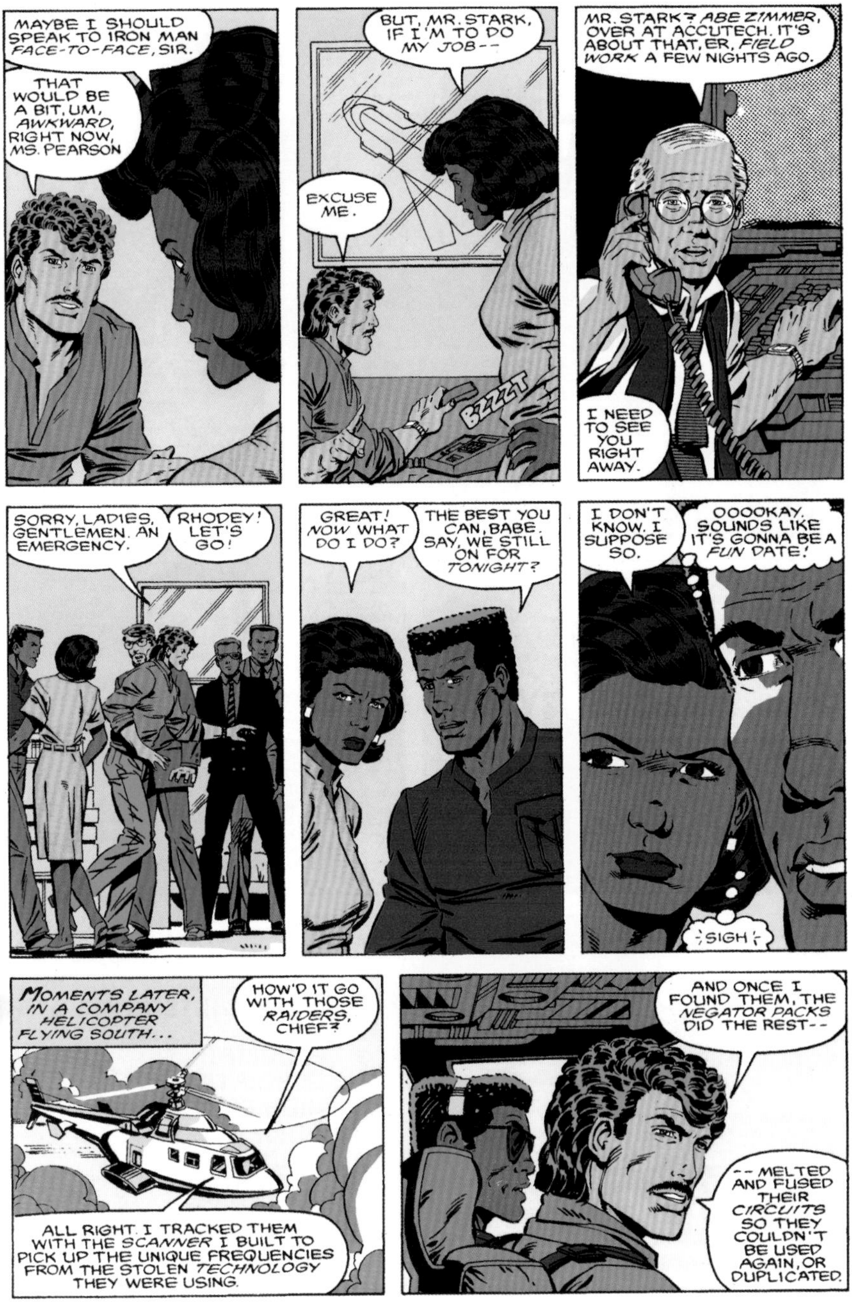
MAYBE I SHOULD SPEAK TO IRON MAN FACE-TO-FACE, SIR.
THAT WOULD BE A BIT, UM, AWKWARD, RIGHT NOW, MS. PEARSON
BUT, MR. STARK, IF I'M TO DO MY JOB--
EXCUSE ME.
BZZZZT
MR. STARK? ABE ZIMMER, OVER AT ACCUTECH. IT'S ABOUT THAT, ER, FIELD WORK A FEW NIGHTS AGO.
I NEED TO SEE YOU RIGHT AWAY.
SORRY, LADIES, GENTLEMEN. AN EMERGENCY.
RHODEY! LET'S GO!
GREAT! NOW WHAT DO I DO?
THE BEST YOU CAN, BABE. SAY, WE STILL ON FOR TONIGHT?
I DON'T KNOW. I SUPPOSE SO.
OOOOKAY. SOUNDS LIKE IT'S GONNA BE A FUN DATE!
SIGH
MOMENTS LATER, IN A COMPANY HELICOPTER FLYING SOUTH...
HOW'D IT GO WITH THOSE RAIDERS, CHIEF?
ALL RIGHT. I TRACKED THEM WITH THE SCANNER I BUILT TO PICK UP THE UNIQUE FREQUENCIES FROM THE STOLEN TECHNOLOGY THEY WERE USING.
AND ONCE I FOUND THEM, THE NEGATOR PACKS DID THE REST--
--MELTED AND FUSED THEIR CIRCUITS SO THEY COULDN'T BE USED AGAIN, OR DUPLICATED.

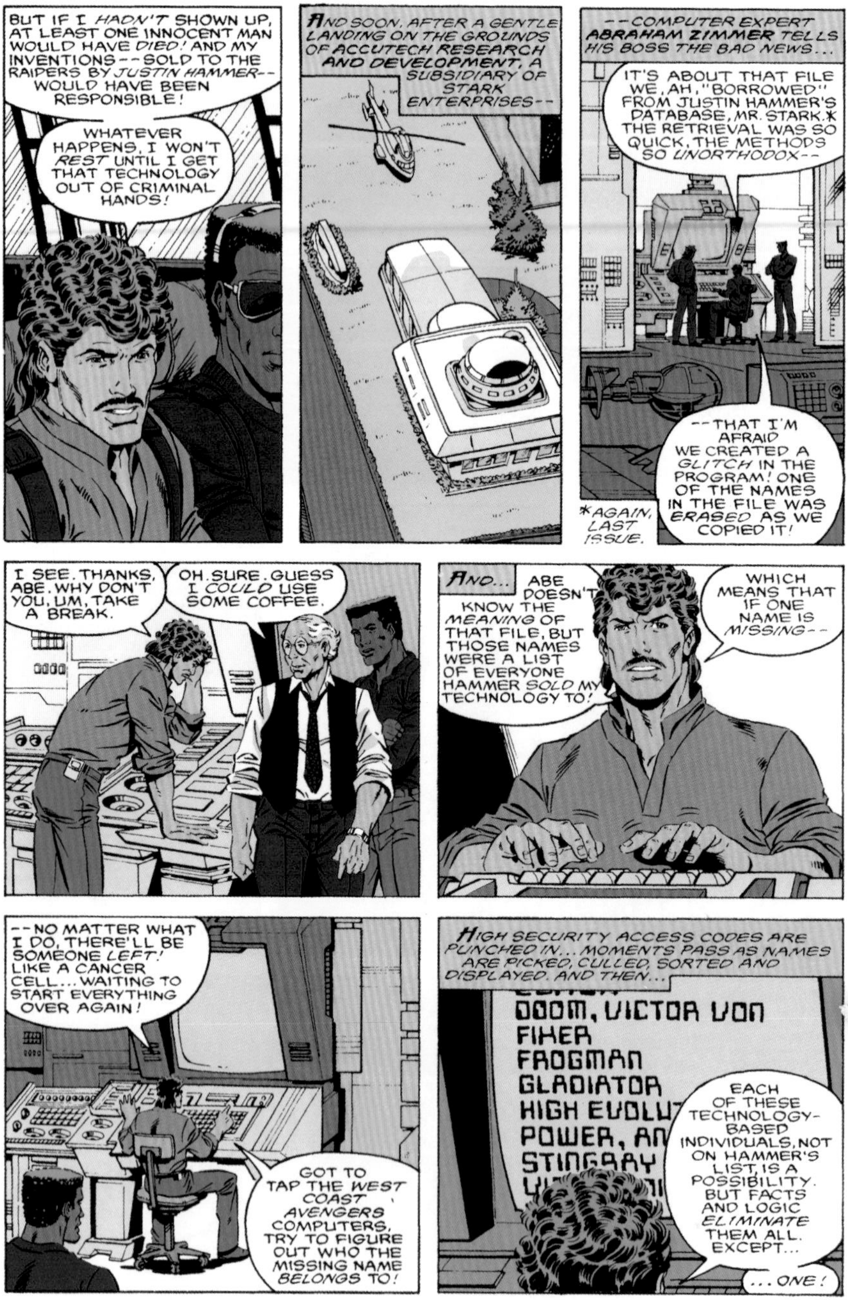

BUT IF I HADN'T SHOWN UP, AT LEAST ONE INNOCENT MAN WOULD HAVE DIED! AND MY INVENTIONS--SOLD TO THE RAIDERS BY JUSTIN HAMMER--WOULD HAVE BEEN RESPONSIBLE!
WHATEVER HAPPENS, I WON'T REST UNTIL I GET THAT TECHNOLOGY OUT OF CRIMINAL HANDS!
AND SOON, AFTER A GENTLE LANDING ON THE GROUNDS OF ACCUTECH RESEARCH AND DEVELOPMENT, A SUBSIDIARY OF STARK ENTERPRISES--
--COMPUTER EXPERT ABRAHAM ZIMMER TELLS HIS BOSS THE BAD NEWS...
IT'S ABOUT THAT FILE WE, AH, "BORROWED" FROM JUSTIN HAMMER'S DATABASE, MR. STARK.* THE RETRIEVAL WAS SO QUICK, THE METHODS SO UNORTHODOX--
--THAT I'M AFRAID WE CREATED A GLITCH IN THE PROGRAM! ONE OF THE NAMES IN THE FILE WAS ERASED AS WE COPIED IT!
*AGAIN, LAST ISSUE.
I SEE. THANKS, ABE. WHY DON'T YOU, UM, TAKE A BREAK.
OH. SURE. GUESS I COULD USE SOME COFFEE.
AND... ABE DOESN'T KNOW THE MEANING OF THAT FILE, BUT THOSE NAMES WERE A LIST OF EVERYONE HAMMER SOLD MY TECHNOLOGY TO!
WHICH MEANS THAT IF ONE NAME IS MISSING--
--NO MATTER WHAT I DO, THERE'LL BE SOMEONE LEFT! LIKE A CANCER CELL... WAITING TO START EVERYTHING OVER AGAIN!
GOT TO TAP THE WEST COAST AVENGERS COMPUTERS, TRY TO FIGURE OUT WHO THE MISSING NAME BELONGS TO!
HIGH SECURITY ACCESS CODES ARE PUNCHED IN... MOMENTS PASS AS NAMES ARE PICKED, CULLED, SORTED AND DISPLAYED. AND THEN...
DOOM, VICTOR VON
FIXER
FROGMAN
GLADIATOR
EACH OF THESE TECHNOLOGY-BASED INDIVIDUALS, NOT ON HAMMER'S LIST, IS A POSSIBILITY. BUT FACTS AND LOGIC ELIMINATE THEM ALL. EXCEPT...
...ONE!

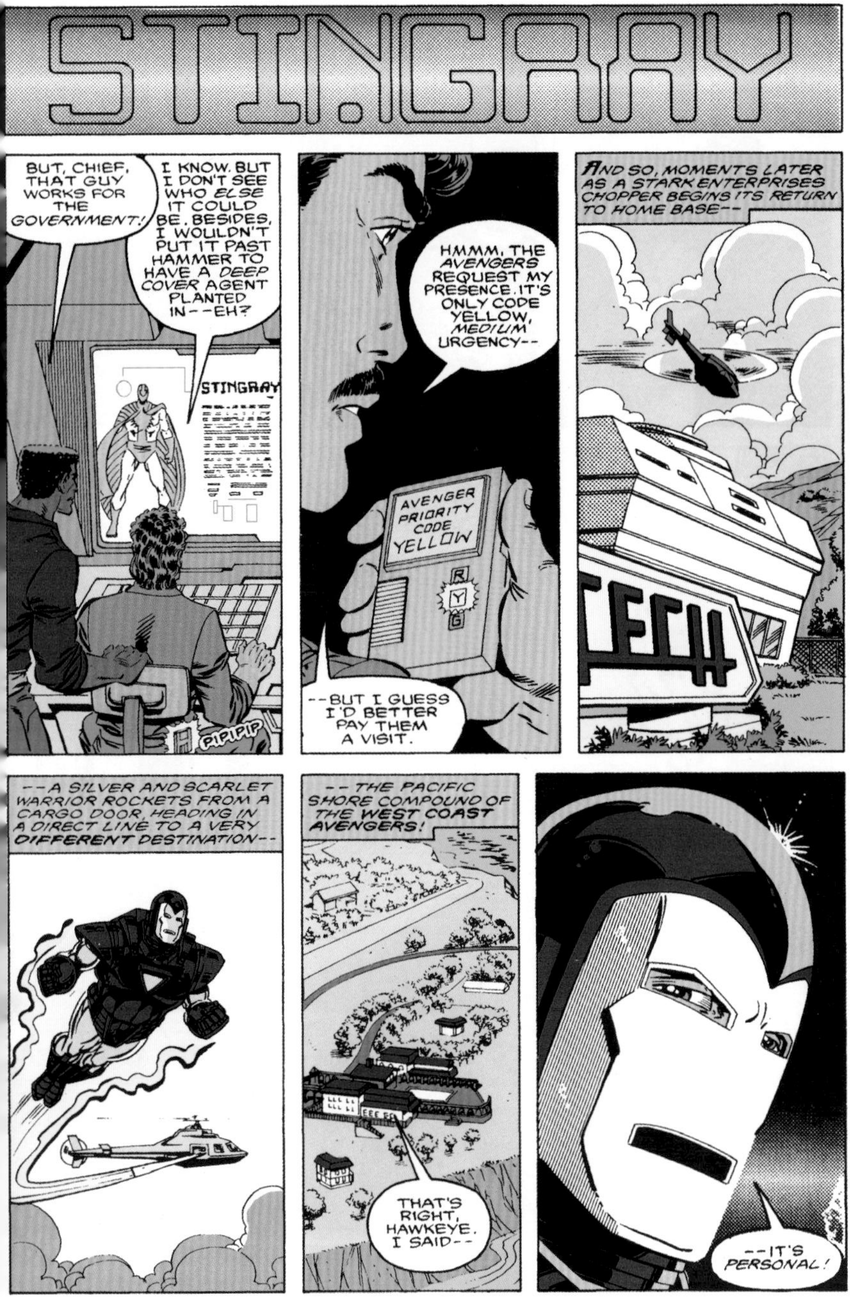
STINGRAY
BUT, CHIEF, THAT GUY WORKS FOR THE GOVERNMENT!
I KNOW. BUT I DON'T SEE WHO ELSE IT COULD BE. BESIDES, I WOULDN'T PUT IT PAST HAMMER TO HAVE A DEEP COVER AGENT PLANTED IN--EH?
STINGRAY
PIPIPIP
HMMM, THE AVENGERS REQUEST MY PRESENCE. IT'S ONLY CODE YELLOW, MEDIUM URGENCY--
AVENGER PRIORITY CODE YELLOW
R
Y
G
--BUT I GUESS I'D BETTER PAY THEM A VISIT.
AND SO, MOMENTS LATER AS A STARK ENTERPRISES CHOPPER BEGINS ITS RETURN TO HOME BASE--
TECH
--A SILVER AND SCARLET WARRIOR ROCKETS FROM A CARGO DOOR, HEADING IN A DIRECT LINE TO A VERY DIFFERENT DESTINATION--
--THE PACIFIC SHORE COMPOUND OF THE WEST COAST AVENGERS!
THAT'S RIGHT, HAWKEYE. I SAID--
--IT'S PERSONAL!

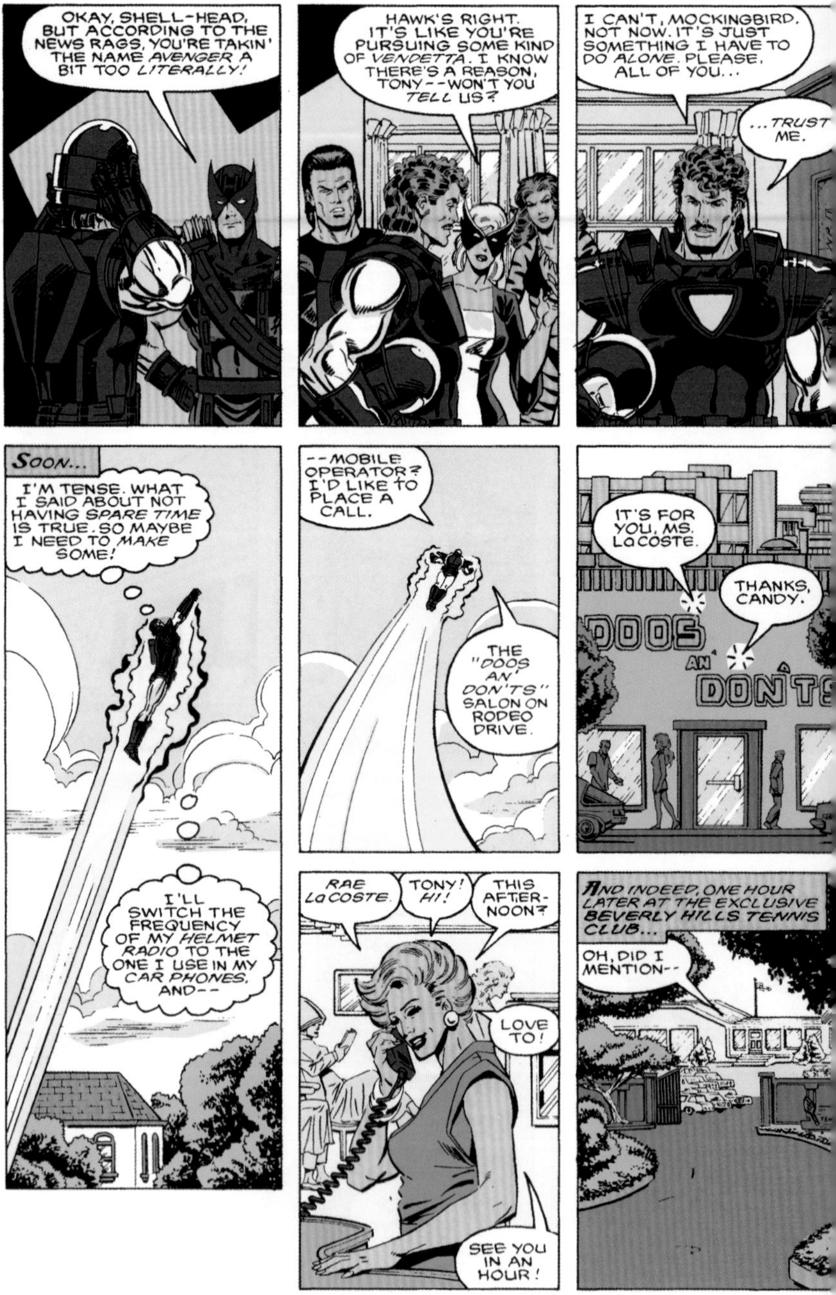

OKAY, SHELL-HEAD, BUT ACCORDING TO THE NEWS RAGS, YOU'RE TAKIN' THE NAME *AVENGER* A BIT TOO *LITERALLY!*
HAWK'S RIGHT. IT'S LIKE YOU'RE PURSUING SOME KIND OF *VENDETTA*. I KNOW THERE'S A REASON, TONY--WON'T YOU *TELL* US?
I CAN'T, MOCKINGBIRD. NOT NOW. IT'S JUST SOMETHING I HAVE TO DO *ALONE*. PLEASE, ALL OF YOU...
...*TRUST* ME.
SOON...
I'M TENSE. WHAT I SAID ABOUT NOT HAVING *SPARE TIME* IS TRUE. SO MAYBE I NEED TO *MAKE* SOME!
I'LL SWITCH THE FREQUENCY OF MY *HELMET RADIO* TO THE ONE I USE IN MY *CAR PHONES*, AND--
--MOBILE OPERATOR? I'D LIKE TO PLACE A CALL.
THE "*DOOS AN' DON'TS*" SALON ON RODEO DRIVE.
IT'S FOR YOU, MS. LaCOSTE.
THANKS, CANDY.
DOOS AN' DON'TS
RAE LaCOSTE.
TONY! *HI!*
THIS AFTER-NOON?
LOVE TO!
SEE YOU IN AN HOUR!
AND INDEED, ONE HOUR LATER AT THE EXCLUSIVE BEVERLY HILLS TENNIS CLUB...
OH, DID I MENTION--

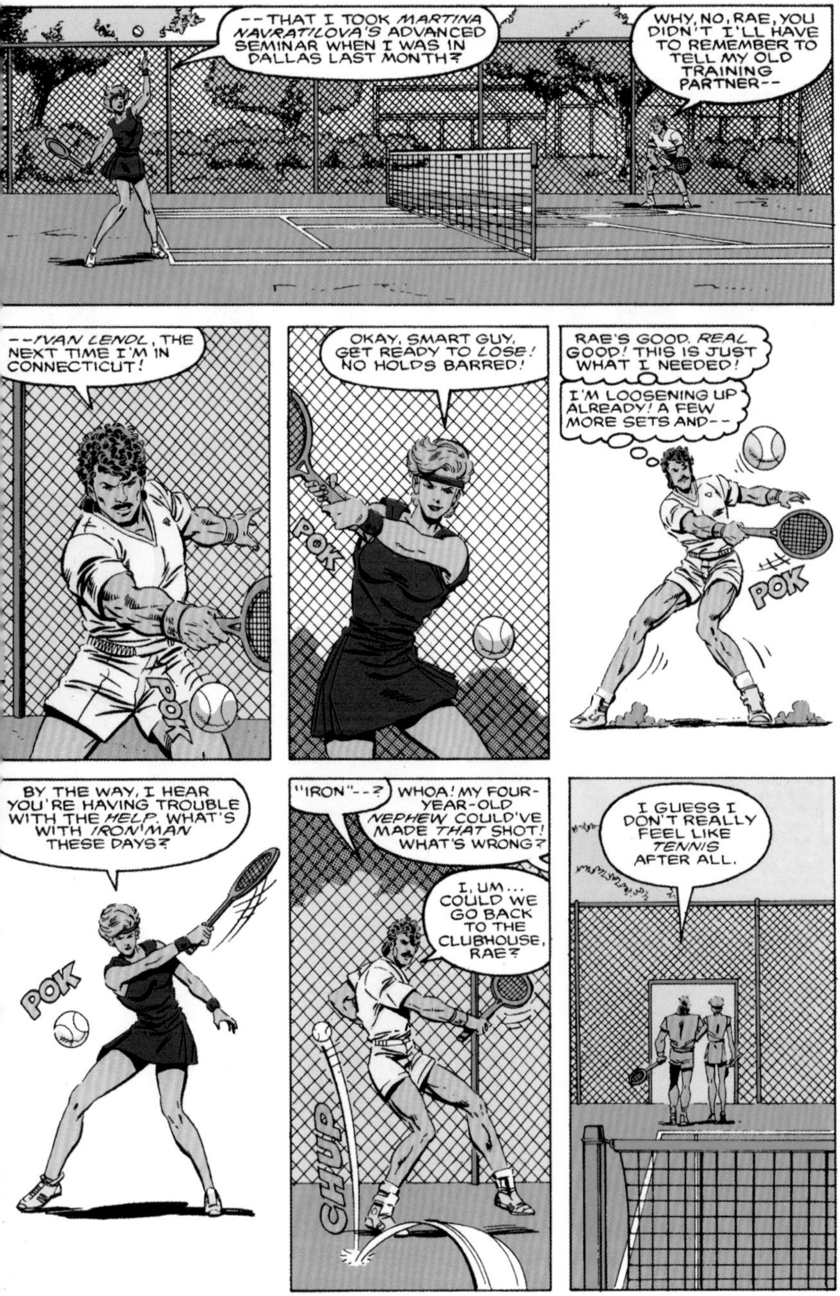
--THAT I TOOK MARTINA NAVRATILOVA'S ADVANCED SEMINAR WHEN I WAS IN DALLAS LAST MONTH?
WHY, NO, RAE, YOU DIDN'T I'LL HAVE TO REMEMBER TO TELL MY OLD TRAINING PARTNER--
--IVAN LENOL, THE NEXT TIME I'M IN CONNECTICUT!
POK
OKAY, SMART GUY, GET READY TO LOSE! NO HOLDS BARRED!
POK
RAE'S GOOD. REAL GOOD! THIS IS JUST WHAT I NEEDED!
I'M LOOSENING UP ALREADY! A FEW MORE SETS AND--
POK
BY THE WAY, I HEAR YOU'RE HAVING TROUBLE WITH THE HELP. WHAT'S WITH IRON MAN THESE DAYS?
POK
"IRON"--?
WHOA! MY FOUR-YEAR-OLD NEPHEW COULD'VE MADE THAT SHOT! WHAT'S WRONG?
I, UM... COULD WE GO BACK TO THE CLUBHOUSE, RAE?
CHUP
I GUESS I DON'T REALLY FEEL LIKE TENNIS AFTER ALL.

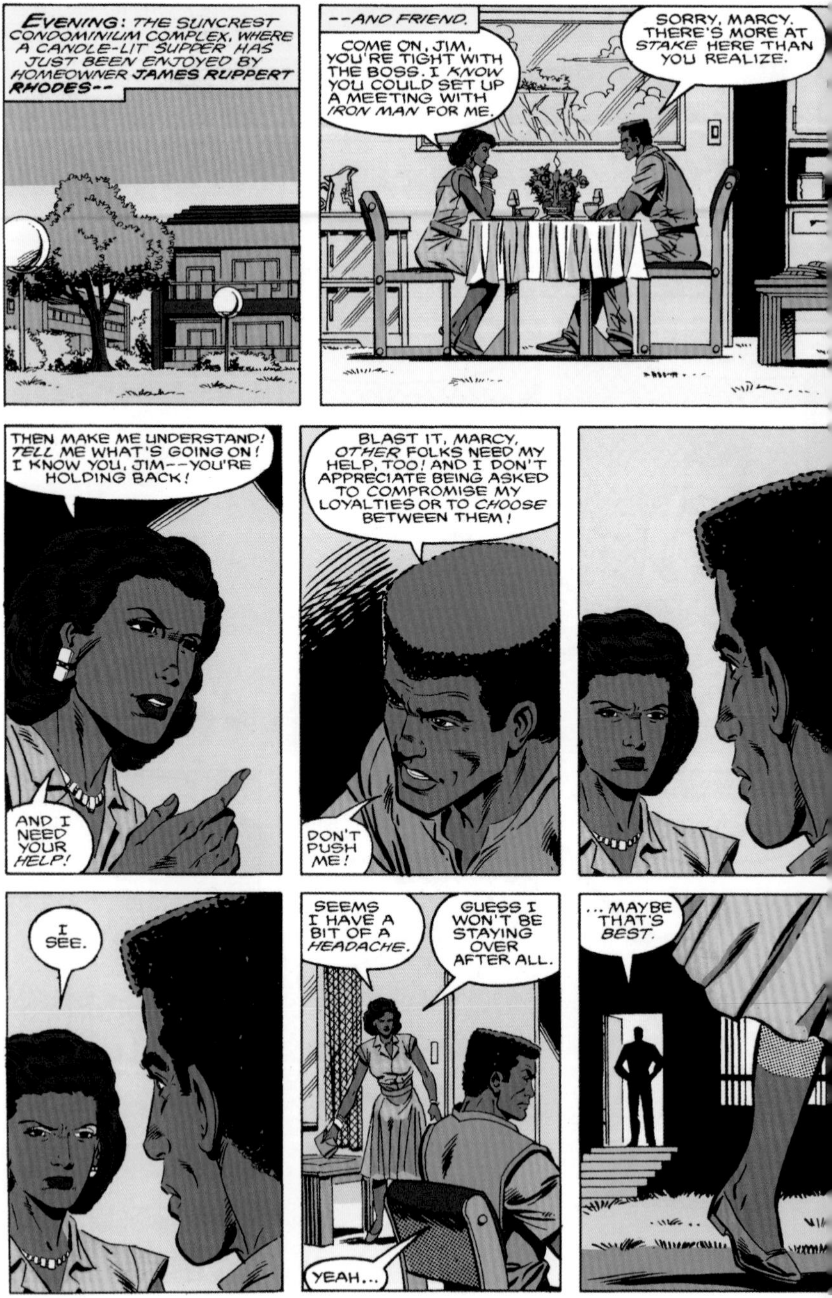
EVENING: THE SUNCREST CONDOMINIUM COMPLEX, WHERE A CANDLE-LIT SUPPER HAS JUST BEEN ENJOYED BY HOMEOWNER JAMES RUPPERT RHODES--
--AND FRIEND.
COME ON, JIM, YOU'RE TIGHT WITH THE BOSS. I KNOW YOU COULD SET UP A MEETING WITH IRON MAN FOR ME.
SORRY, MARCY. THERE'S MORE AT STAKE HERE THAN YOU REALIZE.
THEN MAKE ME UNDERSTAND! TELL ME WHAT'S GOING ON! I KNOW YOU, JIM--YOU'RE HOLDING BACK!
AND I NEED YOUR HELP!
BLAST IT, MARCY, OTHER FOLKS NEED MY HELP, TOO! AND I DON'T APPRECIATE BEING ASKED TO COMPROMISE MY LOYALTIES OR TO CHOOSE BETWEEN THEM!
DON'T PUSH ME!
I SEE.
SEEMS I HAVE A BIT OF A HEADACHE.
GUESS I WON'T BE STAYING OVER AFTER ALL.
YEAH...
...MAYBE THAT'S BEST.

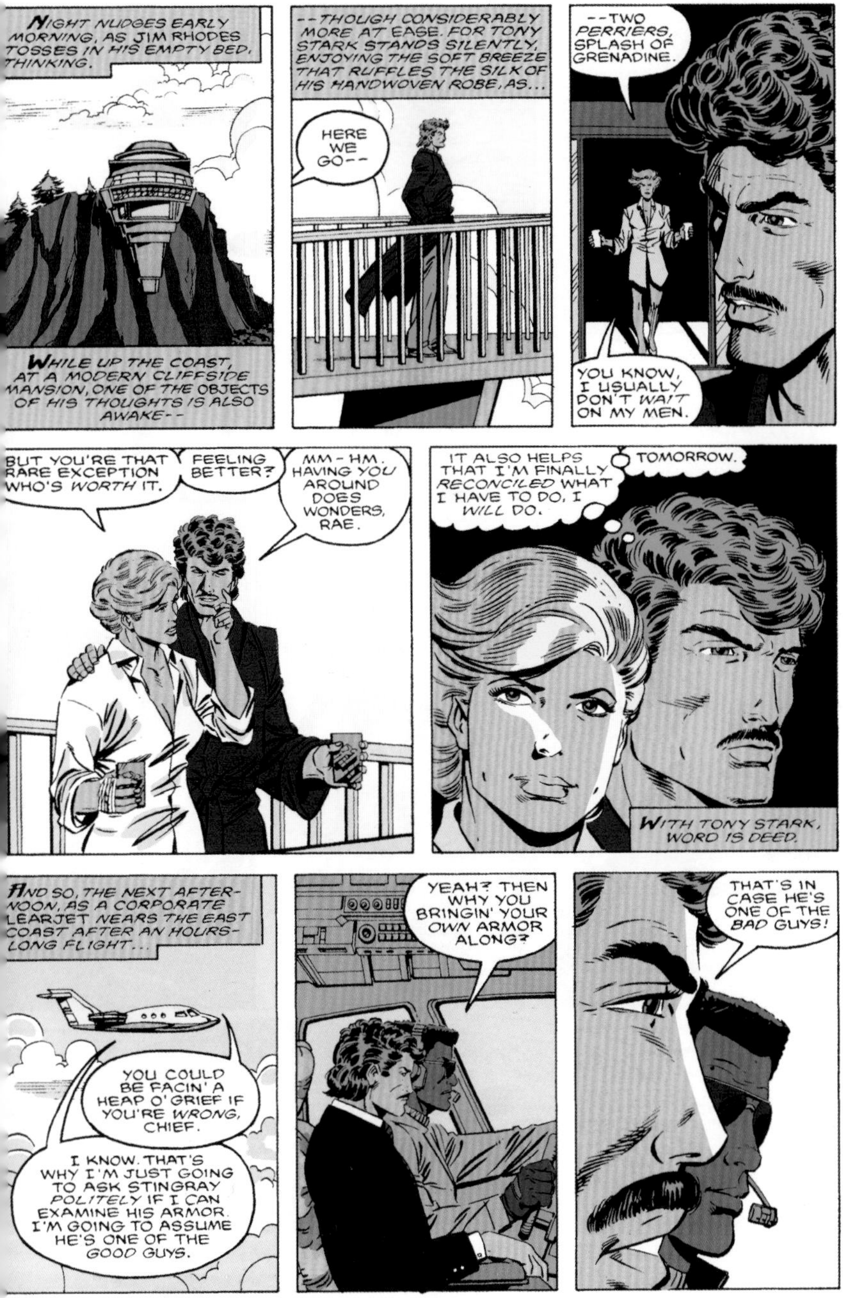
NIGHT NUDGES EARLY MORNING, AS JIM RHODES TOSSES IN HIS EMPTY BED, THINKING.
WHILE UP THE COAST, AT A MODERN CLIFFSIDE MANSION, ONE OF THE OBJECTS OF HIS THOUGHTS IS ALSO AWAKE--
--THOUGH CONSIDERABLY MORE AT EASE. FOR TONY STARK STANDS SILENTLY, ENJOYING THE SOFT BREEZE THAT RUFFLES THE SILK OF HIS HANDWOVEN ROBE, AS...
HERE WE GO--
--TWO PERRIERS, SPLASH OF GRENADINE.
YOU KNOW, I USUALLY DON'T WAIT ON MY MEN.
BUT YOU'RE THAT RARE EXCEPTION WHO'S WORTH IT.
FEELING BETTER?
MM-HM. HAVING YOU AROUND DOES WONDERS, RAE.
IT ALSO HELPS THAT I'M FINALLY RECONCILED WHAT I HAVE TO DO, I WILL DO.
TOMORROW.
WITH TONY STARK, WORD IS DEED.
AND SO, THE NEXT AFTERNOON, AS A CORPORATE LEARJET NEARS THE EAST COAST AFTER AN HOURS-LONG FLIGHT...
YOU COULD BE FACIN' A HEAP O' GRIEF IF YOU'RE WRONG, CHIEF.
I KNOW. THAT'S WHY I'M JUST GOING TO ASK STINGRAY POLITELY IF I CAN EXAMINE HIS ARMOR. I'M GOING TO ASSUME HE'S ONE OF THE GOOD GUYS.
YEAH? THEN WHY YOU BRINGIN' YOUR OWN ARMOR ALONG?
THAT'S IN CASE HE'S ONE OF THE BAD GUYS!

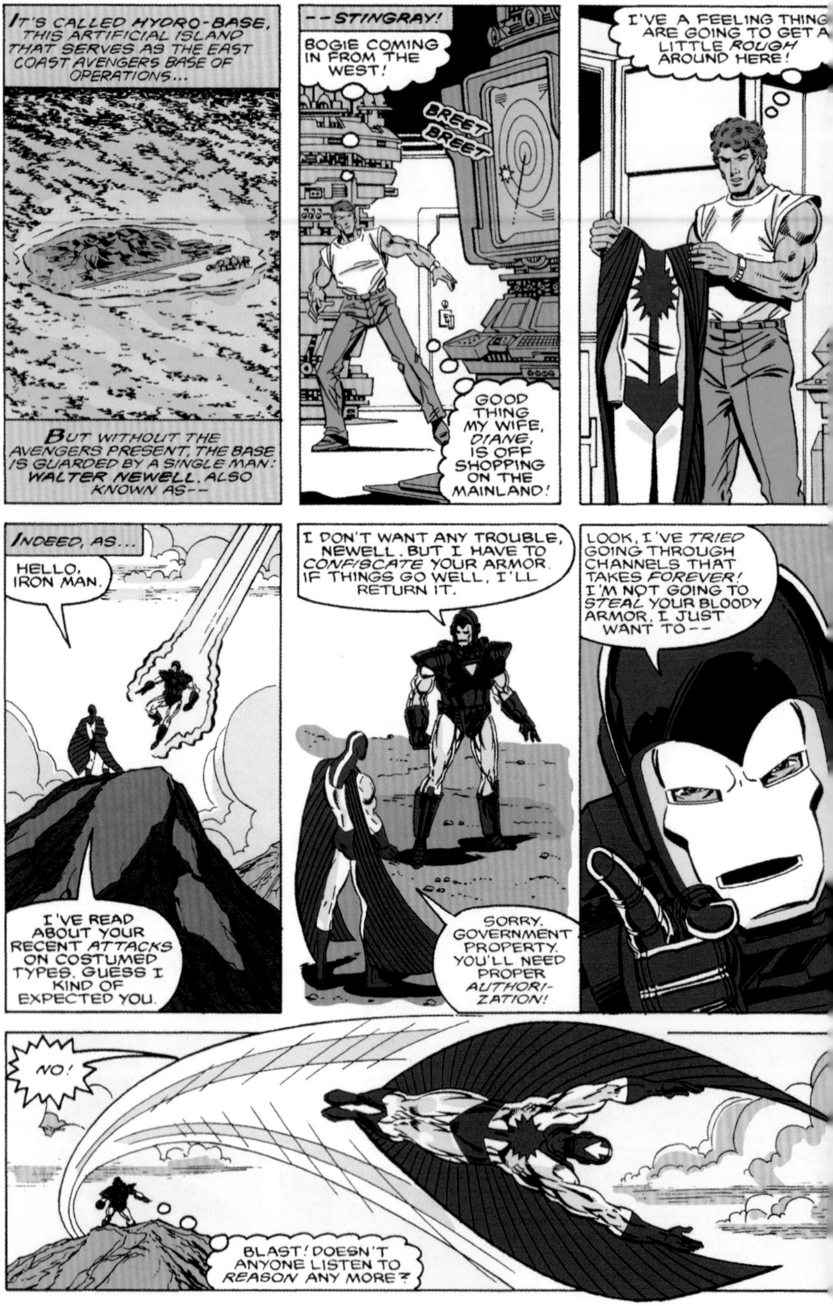
IT'S CALLED HYDRO-BASE, THIS ARTIFICIAL ISLAND THAT SERVES AS THE EAST COAST AVENGERS BASE OF OPERATIONS...
BUT WITHOUT THE AVENGERS PRESENT, THE BASE IS GUARDED BY A SINGLE MAN: WALTER NEWELL, ALSO KNOWN AS--
--STINGRAY!
BOGIE COMING IN FROM THE WEST!
BREET BREET
GOOD THING MY WIFE, DIANE, IS OFF SHOPPING ON THE MAINLAND!
I'VE A FEELING THINGS ARE GOING TO GET A LITTLE ROUGH AROUND HERE!
INDEED, AS...
HELLO, IRON MAN.
I'VE READ ABOUT YOUR RECENT ATTACKS ON COSTUMED TYPES. GUESS I KIND OF EXPECTED YOU.
I DON'T WANT ANY TROUBLE, NEWELL. BUT I HAVE TO CONFISCATE YOUR ARMOR. IF THINGS GO WELL, I'LL RETURN IT.
SORRY. GOVERNMENT PROPERTY. YOU'LL NEED PROPER AUTHORIZATION!
LOOK, I'VE TRIED GOING THROUGH CHANNELS THAT TAKES FOREVER! I'M NOT GOING TO STEAL YOUR BLOODY ARMOR. I JUST WANT TO--
NO!
BLAST! DOESN'T ANYONE LISTEN TO REASON ANY MORE?

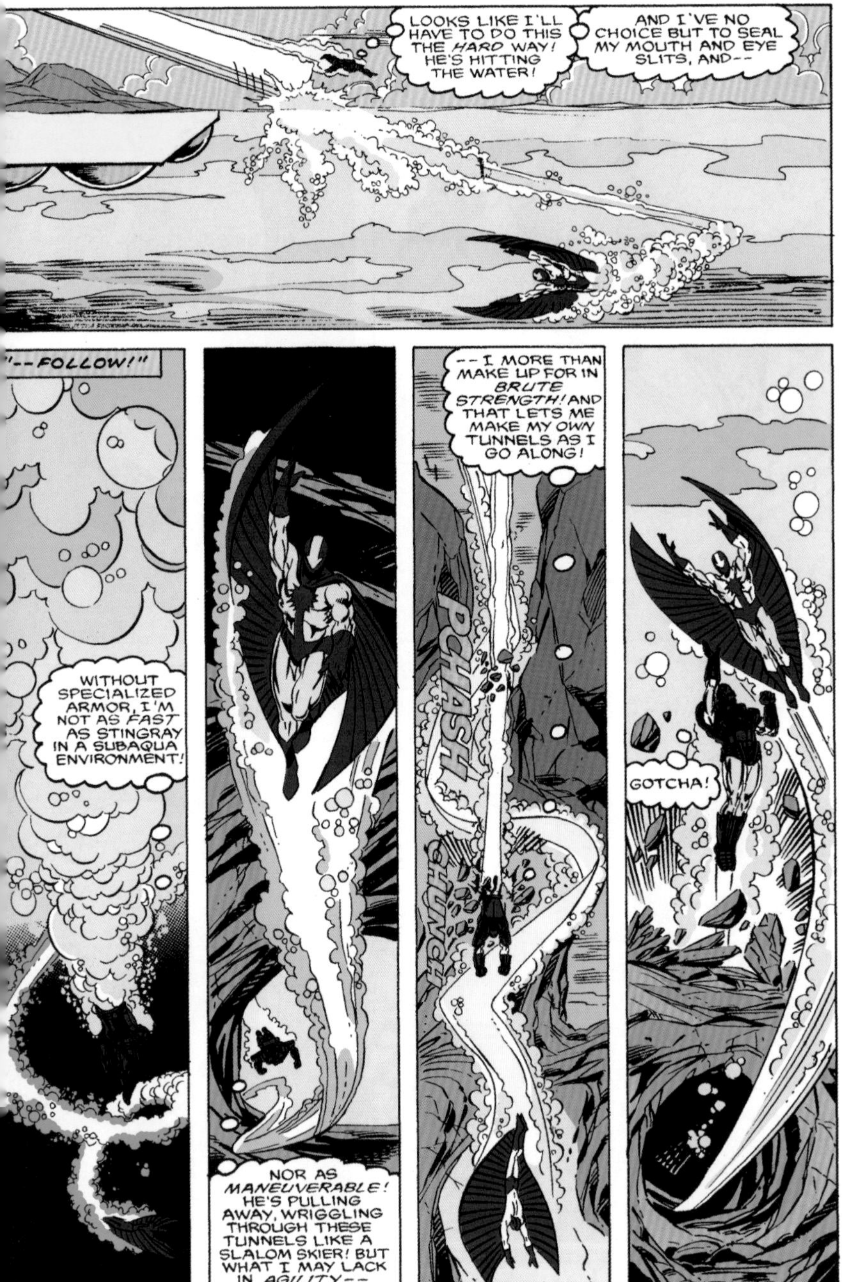

LOOKS LIKE I'LL HAVE TO DO THIS THE *HARD* WAY! HE'S HITTING THE WATER!
AND I'VE NO CHOICE BUT TO SEAL MY MOUTH AND EYE SLITS, AND--
"--FOLLOW!"
WITHOUT SPECIALIZED ARMOR, I'M NOT AS *FAST* AS STINGRAY IN A SUBAQUA ENVIRONMENT!
NOR AS *MANEUVERABLE!* HE'S PULLING AWAY, WRIGGLING THROUGH THESE TUNNELS LIKE A SLALOM SKIER! BUT WHAT I MAY LACK IN *AGILITY*--
--I MORE THAN MAKE UP FOR IN *BRUTE STRENGTH!* AND THAT LETS ME MAKE MY *OWN* TUNNELS AS I GO ALONG!
PCHASH!
CHUNCH
GOTCHA!

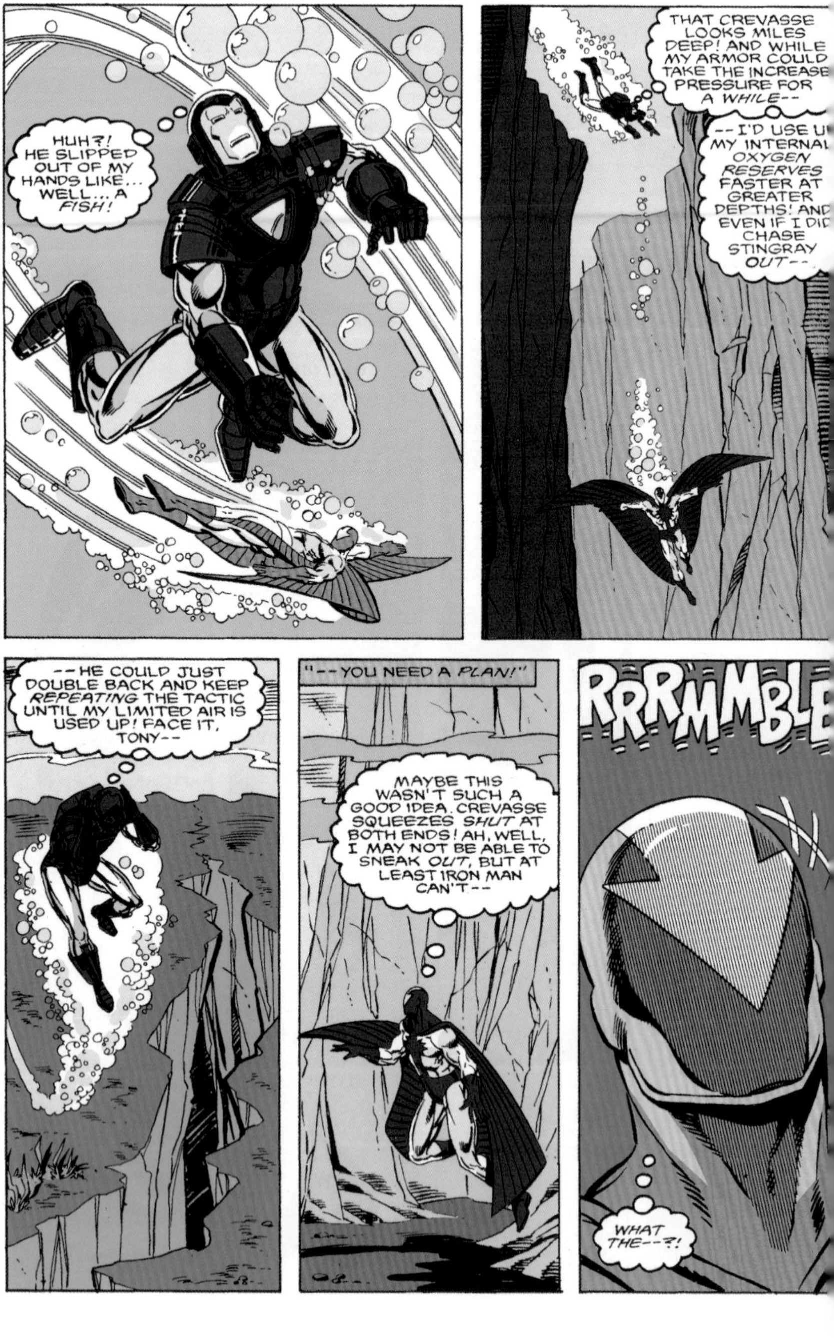

HUH?! HE SLIPPED OUT OF MY HANDS LIKE... WELL... A FISH!
THAT CREVASSE LOOKS MILES DEEP! AND WHILE MY ARMOR COULD TAKE THE INCREASE PRESSURE FOR A WHILE--
--I'D USE U MY INTERNAL OXYGEN RESERVES FASTER AT GREATER DEPTHS! AND EVEN IF I DID CHASE STINGRAY OUT--
--HE COULD JUST DOUBLE BACK AND KEEP REPEATING THE TACTIC UNTIL MY LIMITED AIR IS USED UP! FACE IT, TONY--
"--YOU NEED A PLAN!"
MAYBE THIS WASN'T SUCH A GOOD IDEA. CREVASSE SQUEEZES SHUT AT BOTH ENDS! AH, WELL, I MAY NOT BE ABLE TO SNEAK OUT, BUT AT LEAST IRON MAN CAN'T--
RRRMMBLE
WHAT THE--?!

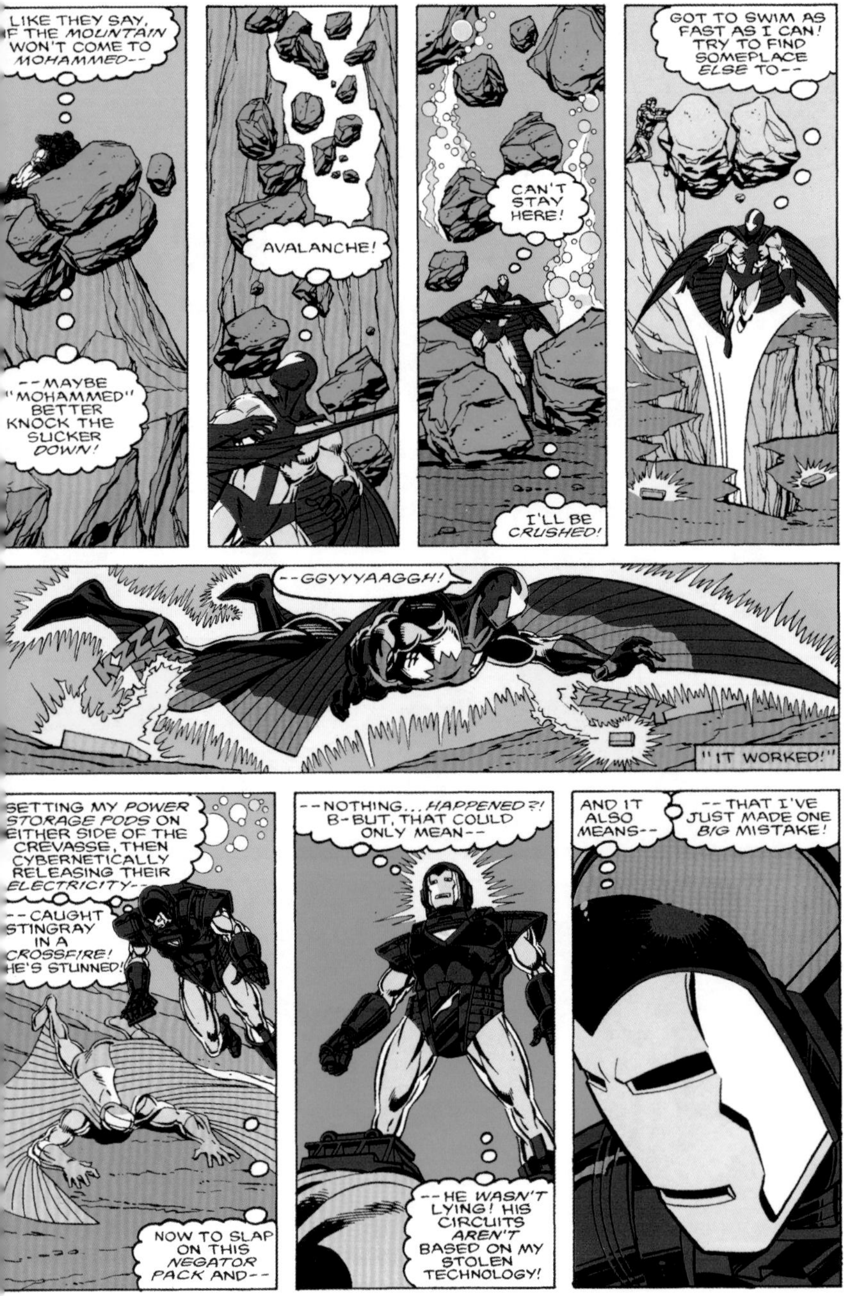
LIKE THEY SAY, IF THE MOUNTAIN WON'T COME TO MOHAMMED--
--MAYBE "MOHAMMED" BETTER KNOCK THE SUCKER DOWN!
AVALANCHE!
CAN'T STAY HERE!
I'LL BE CRUSHED!
GOT TO SWIM AS FAST AS I CAN! TRY TO FIND SOMEPLACE ELSE TO--
--GGYYYAAGGH!
KZZZ
ZZZK
"IT WORKED!"
SETTING MY POWER STORAGE PODS ON EITHER SIDE OF THE CREVASSE, THEN CYBERNETICALLY RELEASING THEIR ELECTRICITY--
--CAUGHT STINGRAY IN A CROSSFIRE! HE'S STUNNED!
NOW TO SLAP ON THIS NEGATOR PACK AND--
--NOTHING... HAPPENED?! B-BUT, THAT COULD ONLY MEAN--
--HE WASN'T LYING! HIS CIRCUITS AREN'T BASED ON MY STOLEN TECHNOLOGY!
AND IT ALSO MEANS--
--THAT I'VE JUST MADE ONE BIG MISTAKE!

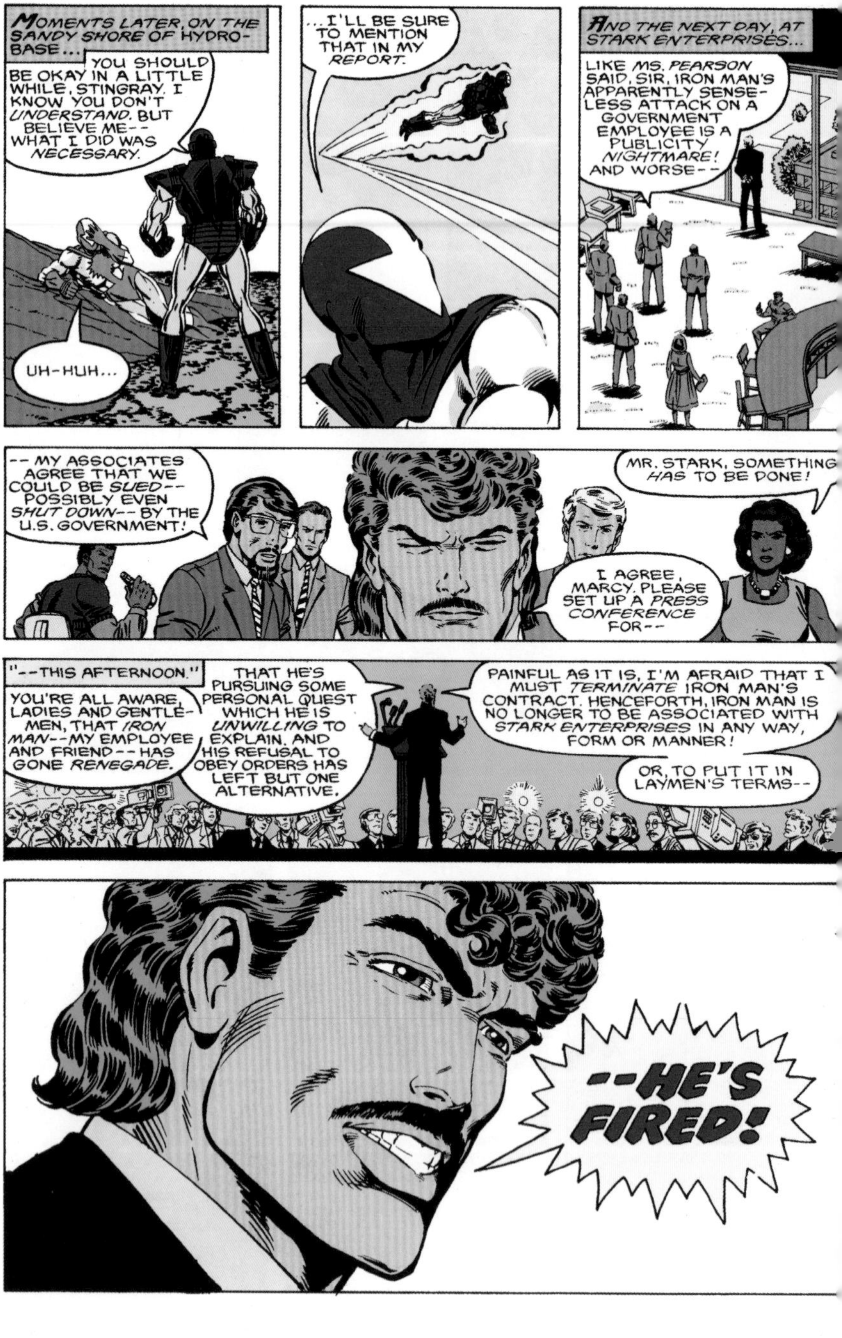
MOMENTS LATER, ON THE SANDY SHORE OF HYDRO-BASE...
YOU SHOULD BE OKAY IN A LITTLE WHILE, STINGRAY. I KNOW YOU DON'T UNDERSTAND, BUT BELIEVE ME-- WHAT I DID WAS NECESSARY.
UH-HUH...
...I'LL BE SURE TO MENTION THAT IN MY REPORT.
AND THE NEXT DAY, AT STARK ENTERPRISES...
LIKE MS. PEARSON SAID, SIR, IRON MAN'S APPARENTLY SENSELESS ATTACK ON A GOVERNMENT EMPLOYEE IS A PUBLICITY NIGHTMARE! AND WORSE--
-- MY ASSOCIATES AGREE THAT WE COULD BE SUED-- POSSIBLY EVEN SHUT DOWN-- BY THE U.S. GOVERNMENT!
MR. STARK, SOMETHING HAS TO BE DONE!
I AGREE, MARCY. PLEASE SET UP A PRESS CONFERENCE FOR--
"--THIS AFTERNOON."
YOU'RE ALL AWARE, LADIES AND GENTLEMEN, THAT IRON MAN--MY EMPLOYEE AND FRIEND--HAS GONE RENEGADE.
THAT HE'S PURSUING SOME PERSONAL QUEST WHICH HE IS UNWILLING TO EXPLAIN, AND HIS REFUSAL TO OBEY ORDERS HAS LEFT BUT ONE ALTERNATIVE.
PAINFUL AS IT IS, I'M AFRAID THAT I MUST TERMINATE IRON MAN'S CONTRACT. HENCEFORTH, IRON MAN IS NO LONGER TO BE ASSOCIATED WITH STARK ENTERPRISES IN ANY WAY, FORM OR MANNER!
OR, TO PUT IT IN LAYMEN'S TERMS--
--HE'S FIRED!

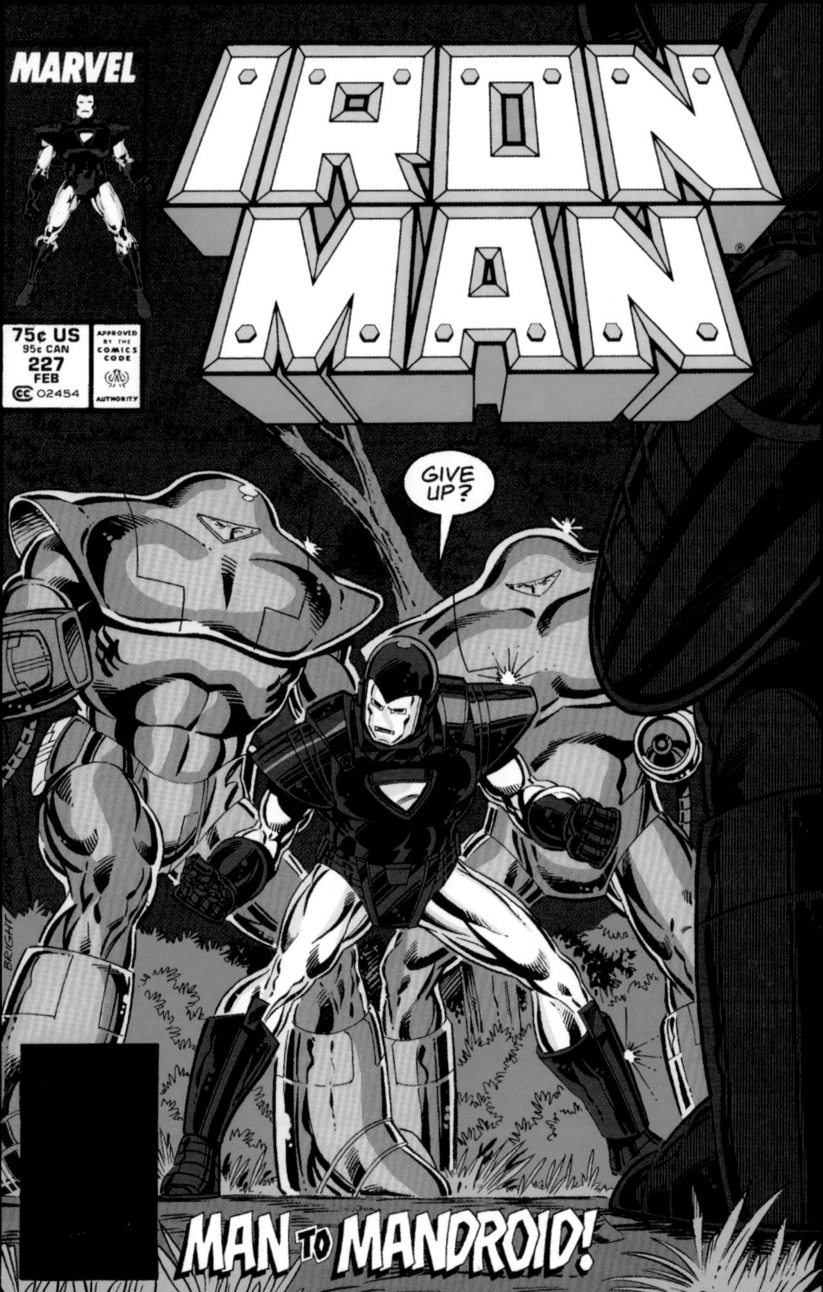
MARVEL
IRON MAN
75¢ US
95¢ CAN
227
FEB
02454
APPROVED BY THE COMICS CODE AUTHORITY
GIVE UP?
BRIGHT
MAN TO MANDROID!

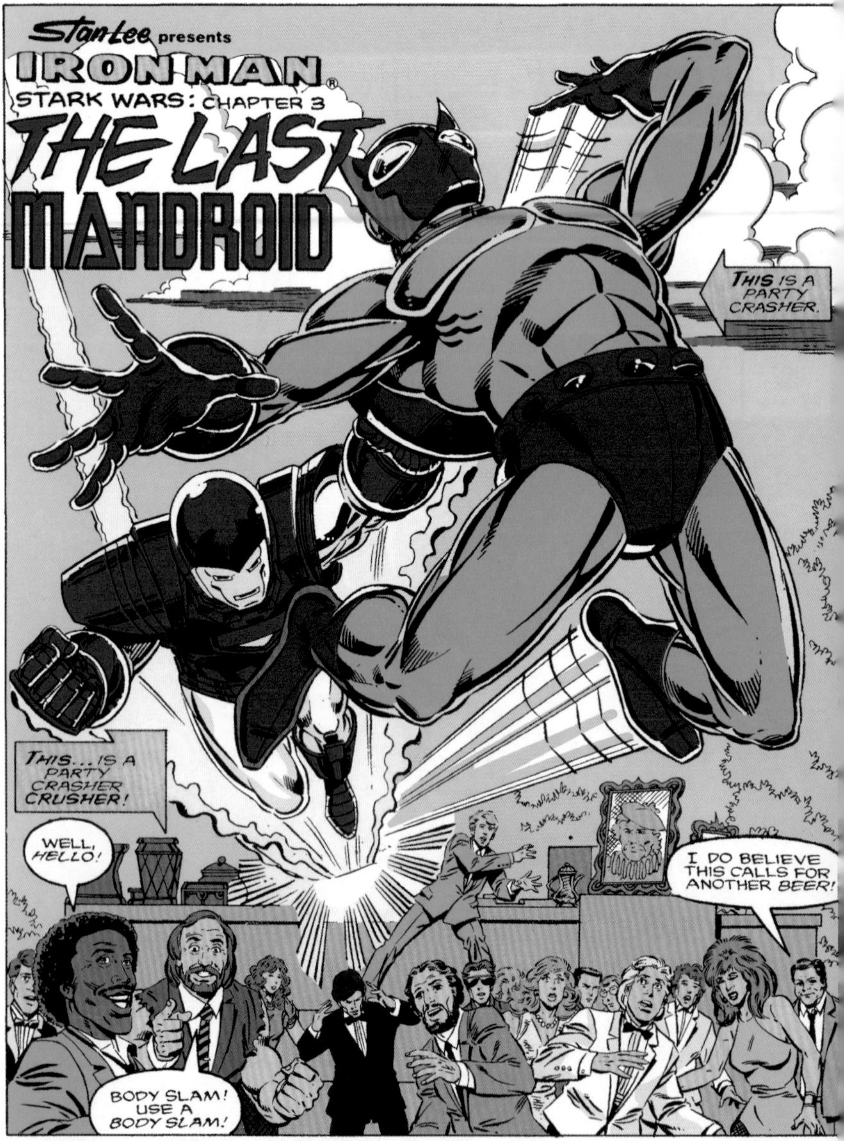
Stan Lee presents
IRON MAN®
STARK WARS: CHAPTER 3
THE LAST MANDROID
THIS IS A PARTY CRASHER.
THIS... IS A PARTY CRASHER CRUSHER!
WELL, HELLO!
I DO BELIEVE THIS CALLS FOR ANOTHER BEER!
BODY SLAM! USE A BODY SLAM!

DAVID MICHELINIE • PLOT/SCRIPT
MARK D. BRIGHT • BREAKDOWNS
BOB LAYTON • PLOT/ FINISHED ART
JANICE CHIANG • LETTERS
BOB SHAREN • COLORS
MARK GRUENWALD • EDITOR
TOM DeFALCO • EDITOR IN CHIEF

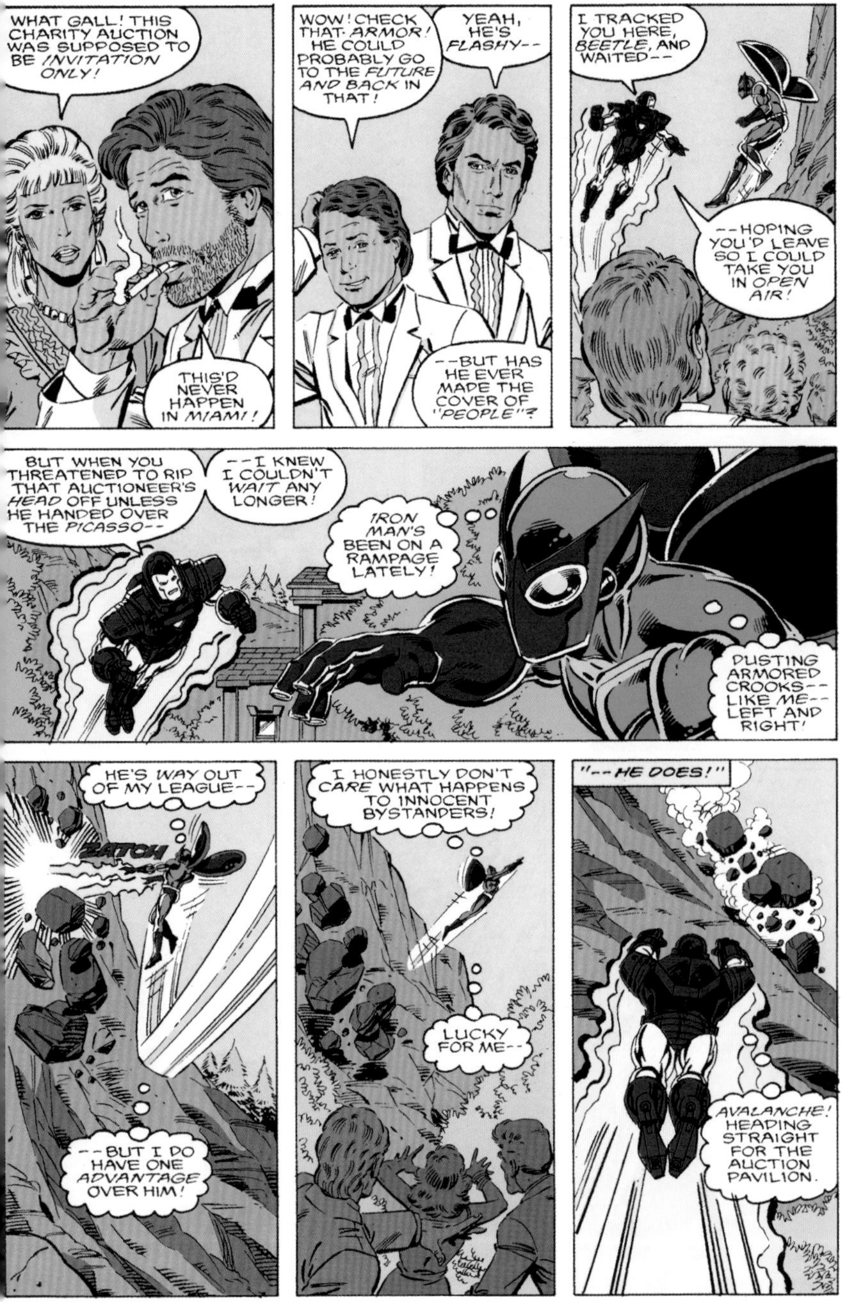
WHAT GALL! THIS CHARITY AUCTION WAS SUPPOSED TO BE *INVITATION ONLY!*
THIS'D NEVER HAPPEN IN *MIAMI!*
WOW! CHECK THAT *ARMOR!* HE COULD PROBABLY GO TO THE *FUTURE AND BACK* IN THAT!
YEAH, HE'S *FLASHY*--
--BUT HAS HE EVER MADE THE COVER OF "*PEOPLE*"?
I TRACKED YOU HERE, *BEETLE*, AND WAITED--
--HOPING YOU'D LEAVE SO I COULD TAKE YOU IN *OPEN AIR!*
BUT WHEN YOU THREATENED TO RIP THAT AUCTIONEER'S *HEAD* OFF UNLESS HE HANDED OVER THE *PICASSO*--
--I KNEW I COULDN'T *WAIT* ANY LONGER!
IRON MAN'S BEEN ON A RAMPAGE LATELY!
DUSTING ARMORED CROOKS--LIKE *ME*--LEFT AND RIGHT!
HE'S *WAY OUT* OF MY LEAGUE--
ZATCH
--BUT I DO HAVE ONE *ADVANTAGE* OVER HIM!
I HONESTLY DON'T *CARE* WHAT HAPPENS TO INNOCENT BYSTANDERS!
LUCKY FOR ME--
"--*HE DOES!*"
AVALANCHE! HEADING STRAIGHT FOR THE AUCTION PAVILION.

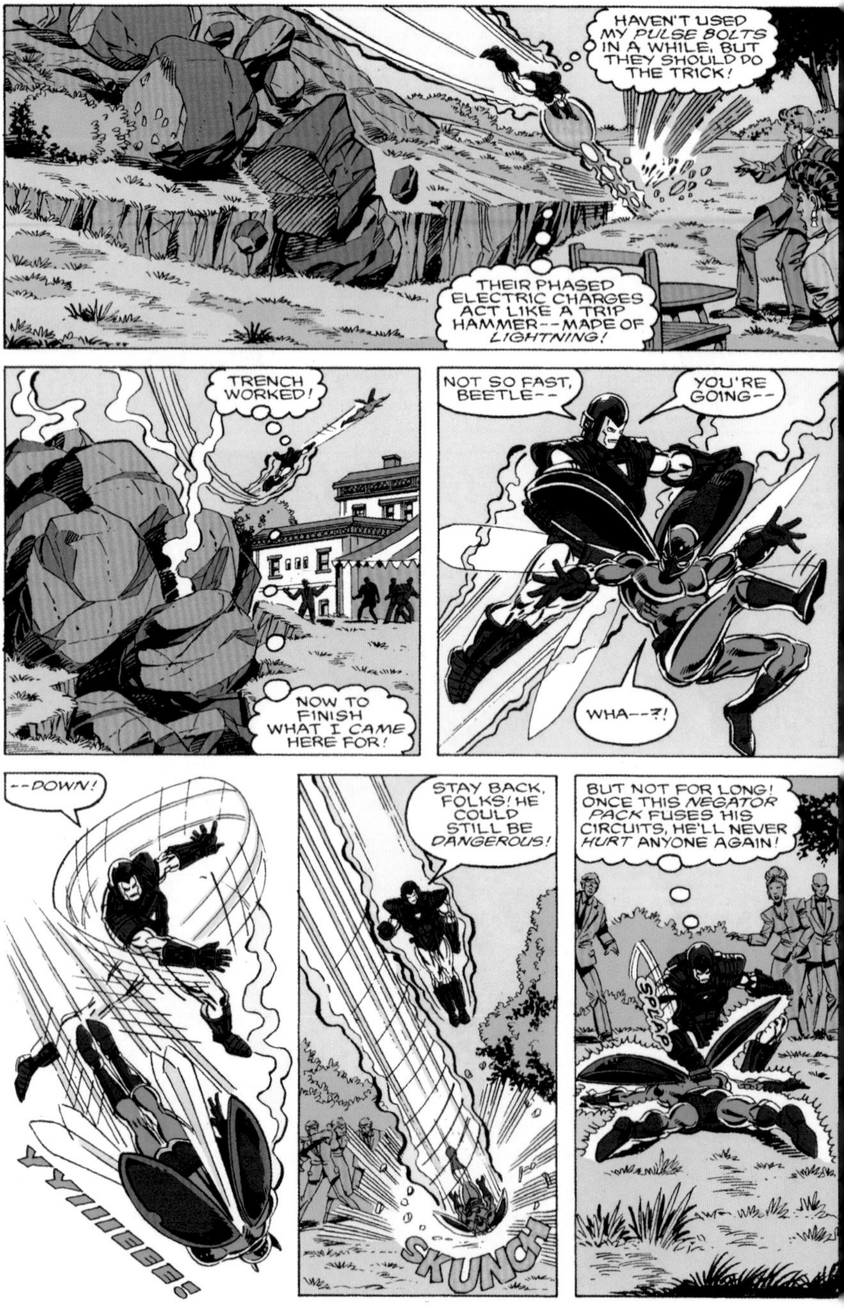

HAVEN'T USED MY PULSE BOLTS IN A WHILE, BUT THEY SHOULD DO THE TRICK!
THEIR PHASED ELECTRIC CHARGES ACT LIKE A TRIP HAMMER--MADE OF LIGHTNING!
TRENCH WORKED!
NOW TO FINISH WHAT I CAME HERE FOR!
NOT SO FAST, BEETLE--
YOU'RE GOING--
WHA--?!
--DOWN!
YYIIIIEEEE!
STAY BACK, FOLKS! HE COULD STILL BE DANGEROUS!
SKUNCH
BUT NOT FOR LONG! ONCE THIS NEGATOR PACK FUSES HIS CIRCUITS, HE'LL NEVER HURT ANYONE AGAIN!
SPLAP

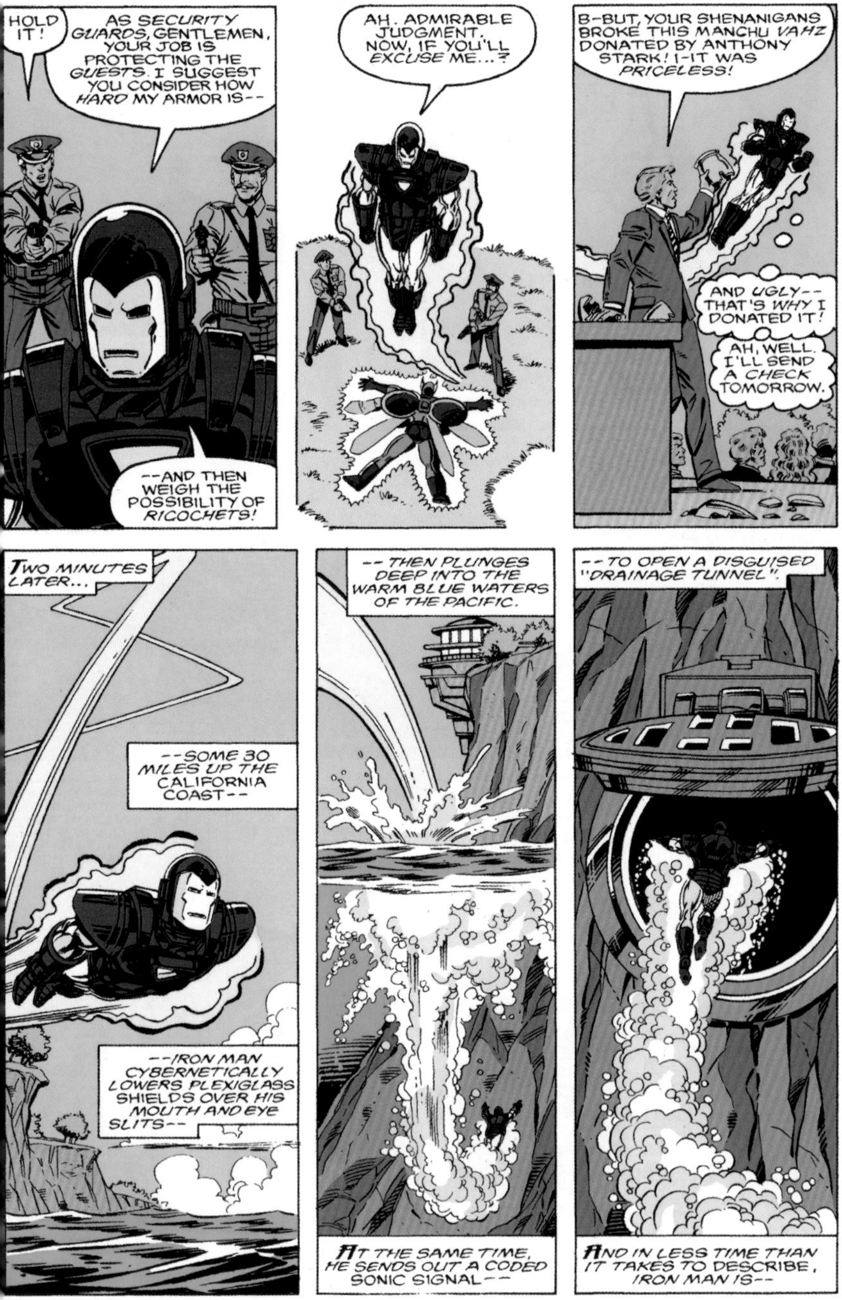

HOLD IT!
AS SECURITY GUARDS, GENTLEMEN, YOUR JOB IS PROTECTING THE GUESTS. I SUGGEST YOU CONSIDER HOW HARD MY ARMOR IS--
--AND THEN WEIGH THE POSSIBILITY OF RICOCHETS!
AH. ADMIRABLE JUDGMENT. NOW, IF YOU'LL EXCUSE ME...?
B-BUT, YOUR SHENANIGANS BROKE THIS MANCHU VAHZ DONATED BY ANTHONY STARK! I-IT WAS PRICELESS!
AND UGLY-- THAT'S WHY I DONATED IT!
AH, WELL. I'LL SEND A CHECK TOMORROW.
TWO MINUTES LATER...
--SOME 30 MILES UP THE CALIFORNIA COAST--
--IRON MAN CYBERNETICALLY LOWERS PLEXIGLASS SHIELDS OVER HIS MOUTH AND EYE SLITS--
--THEN PLUNGES DEEP INTO THE WARM BLUE WATERS OF THE PACIFIC.
AT THE SAME TIME, HE SENDS OUT A CODED SONIC SIGNAL--
--TO OPEN A DISGUISED "DRAINAGE TUNNEL".
AND IN LESS TIME THAN IT TAKES TO DESCRIBE, IRON MAN IS--

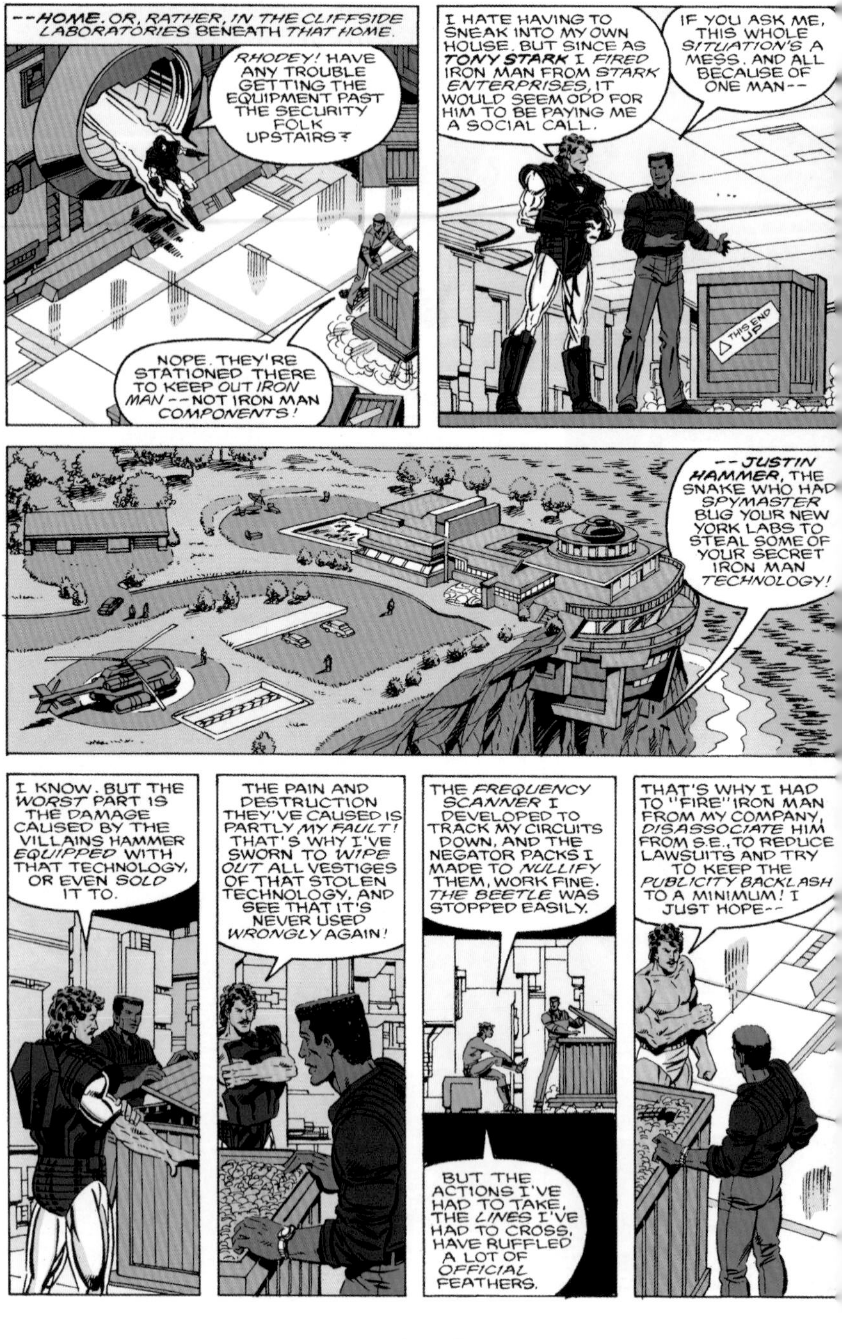
--HOME. OR, RATHER, IN THE CLIFFSIDE LABORATORIES BENEATH THAT HOME.
RHODEY! HAVE ANY TROUBLE GETTING THE EQUIPMENT PAST THE SECURITY FOLK UPSTAIRS?
NOPE. THEY'RE STATIONED THERE TO KEEP OUT IRON MAN --NOT IRON MAN COMPONENTS!
I HATE HAVING TO SNEAK INTO MY OWN HOUSE. BUT SINCE AS TONY STARK I FIRED IRON MAN FROM STARK ENTERPRISES, IT WOULD SEEM ODD FOR HIM TO BE PAYING ME A SOCIAL CALL.
IF YOU ASK ME, THIS WHOLE SITUATION'S A MESS. AND ALL BECAUSE OF ONE MAN--
...
THIS END UP
--JUSTIN HAMMER, THE SNAKE WHO HAD SPYMASTER BUG YOUR NEW YORK LABS TO STEAL SOME OF YOUR SECRET IRON MAN TECHNOLOGY!
I KNOW. BUT THE WORST PART IS THE DAMAGE CAUSED BY THE VILLAINS HAMMER EQUIPPED WITH THAT TECHNOLOGY, OR EVEN SOLD IT TO.
THE PAIN AND DESTRUCTION THEY'VE CAUSED IS PARTLY MY FAULT! THAT'S WHY I'VE SWORN TO WIPE OUT ALL VESTIGES OF THAT STOLEN TECHNOLOGY, AND SEE THAT IT'S NEVER USED WRONGLY AGAIN!
THE FREQUENCY SCANNER I DEVELOPED TO TRACK MY CIRCUITS DOWN, AND THE NEGATOR PACKS I MADE TO NULLIFY THEM, WORK FINE. THE BEETLE WAS STOPPED EASILY.
BUT THE ACTIONS I'VE HAD TO TAKE, THE LINES I'VE HAD TO CROSS, HAVE RUFFLED A LOT OF OFFICIAL FEATHERS.
THAT'S WHY I HAD TO "FIRE" IRON MAN FROM MY COMPANY, DISASSOCIATE HIM FROM S.E., TO REDUCE LAWSUITS AND TRY TO KEEP THE PUBLICITY BACKLASH TO A MINIMUM! I JUST HOPE--

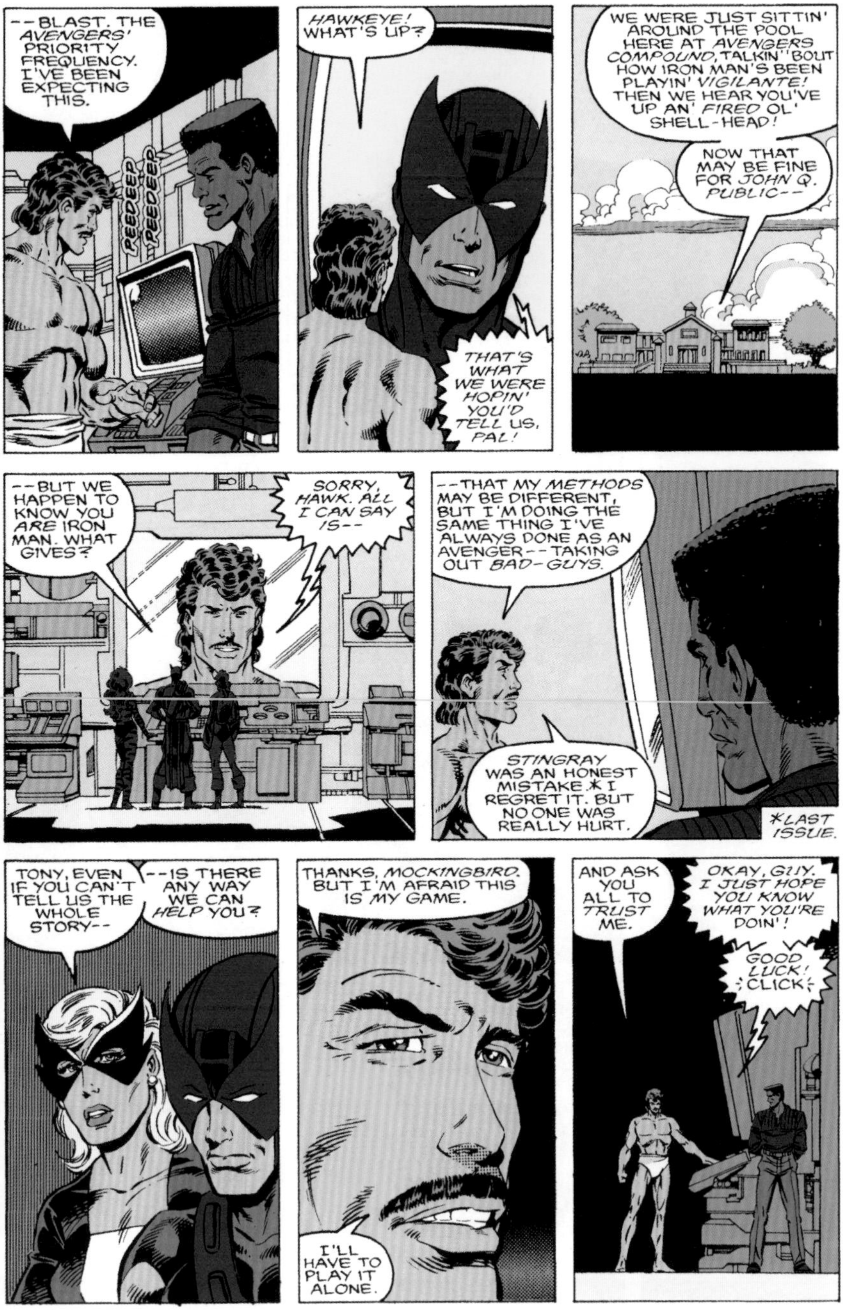
--BLAST. THE AVENGERS' PRIORITY FREQUENCY. I'VE BEEN EXPECTING THIS.
PEEDEEP PEEDEEP
HAWKEYE! WHAT'S UP?
THAT'S WHAT WE WERE HOPIN' YOU'D TELL US, PAL!
WE WERE JUST SITTIN' AROUND THE POOL HERE AT AVENGERS COMPOUND, TALKIN' 'BOUT HOW IRON MAN'S BEEN PLAYIN' VIGILANTE! THEN WE HEAR YOU'VE UP AN' FIRED OL' SHELL-HEAD!
NOW THAT MAY BE FINE FOR JOHN Q. PUBLIC--
--BUT WE HAPPEN TO KNOW YOU ARE IRON MAN. WHAT GIVES?
SORRY, HAWK. ALL I CAN SAY IS--
--THAT MY METHODS MAY BE DIFFERENT, BUT I'M DOING THE SAME THING I'VE ALWAYS DONE AS AN AVENGER--TAKING OUT BAD-GUYS.
STINGRAY WAS AN HONEST MISTAKE.* I REGRET IT. BUT NO ONE WAS REALLY HURT.
*LAST ISSUE.
TONY, EVEN IF YOU CAN'T TELL US THE WHOLE STORY--
--IS THERE ANY WAY WE CAN HELP YOU?
THANKS, MOCKINGBIRD. BUT I'M AFRAID THIS IS MY GAME.
I'LL HAVE TO PLAY IT ALONE.
AND ASK YOU ALL TO TRUST ME.
OKAY, GUY. I JUST HOPE YOU KNOW WHAT YOU'RE DOIN'!
GOOD LUCK! CLICK

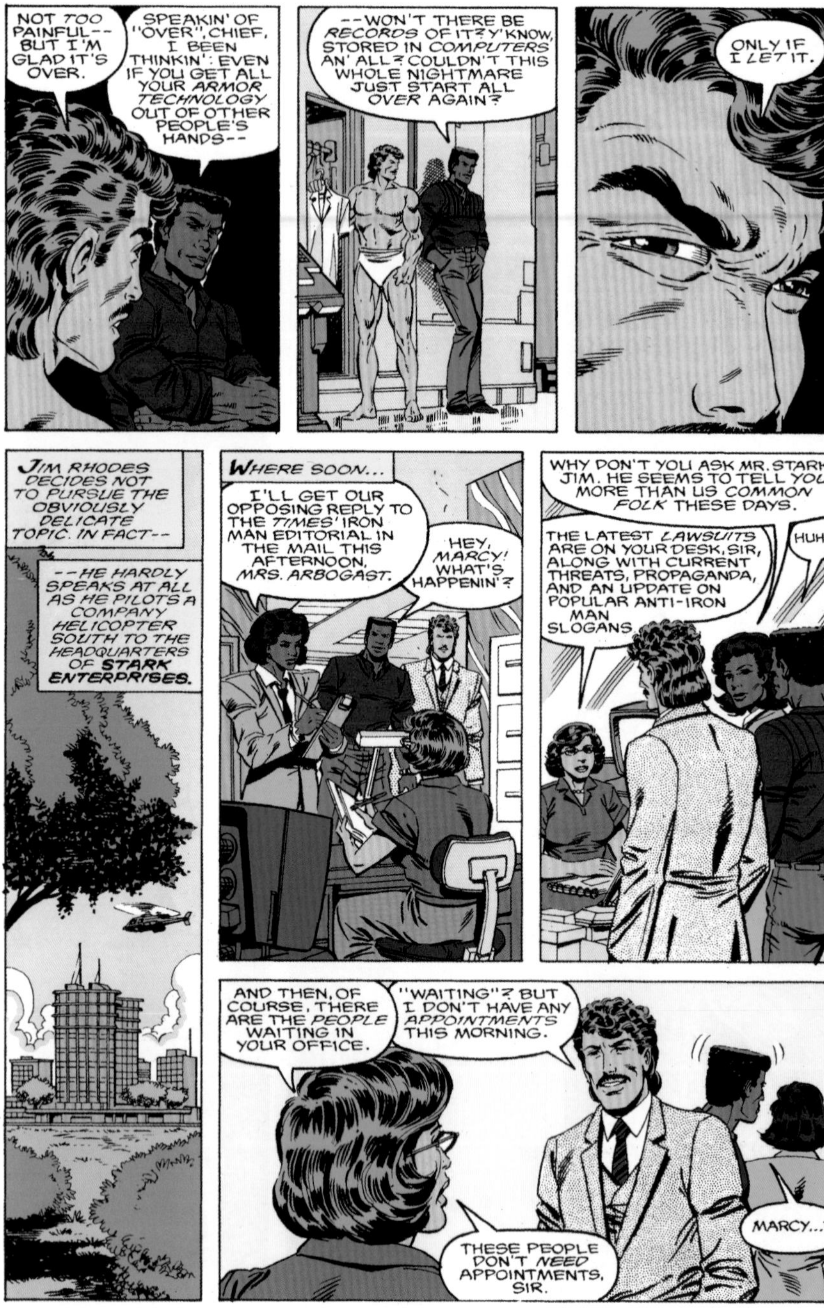
NOT TOO PAINFUL-- BUT I'M GLAD IT'S OVER.
SPEAKIN' OF "OVER", CHIEF, I BEEN THINKIN': EVEN IF YOU GET ALL YOUR ARMOR TECHNOLOGY OUT OF OTHER PEOPLE'S HANDS--
--WON'T THERE BE RECORDS OF IT? Y'KNOW, STORED IN COMPUTERS AN' ALL? COULDN'T THIS WHOLE NIGHTMARE JUST START ALL OVER AGAIN?
ONLY IF I LET IT.
JIM RHODES DECIDES NOT TO PURSUE THE OBVIOUSLY DELICATE TOPIC. IN FACT--
--HE HARDLY SPEAKS AT ALL AS HE PILOTS A COMPANY HELICOPTER SOUTH TO THE HEADQUARTERS OF STARK ENTERPRISES.
WHERE SOON...
I'LL GET OUR OPPOSING REPLY TO THE TIMES' IRON MAN EDITORIAL IN THE MAIL THIS AFTERNOON, MRS. ARBOGAST.
HEY, MARCY! WHAT'S HAPPENIN'?
WHY DON'T YOU ASK MR. STARK, JIM. HE SEEMS TO TELL YOU MORE THAN US COMMON FOLK THESE DAYS.
THE LATEST LAWSUITS ARE ON YOUR DESK, SIR, ALONG WITH CURRENT THREATS, PROPAGANDA, AND AN UPDATE ON POPULAR ANTI-IRON MAN SLOGANS.
HUH?
AND THEN, OF COURSE, THERE ARE THE PEOPLE WAITING IN YOUR OFFICE.
"WAITING"? BUT I DON'T HAVE ANY APPOINTMENTS THIS MORNING.
THESE PEOPLE DON'T NEED APPOINTMENTS, SIR.
MARCY...?

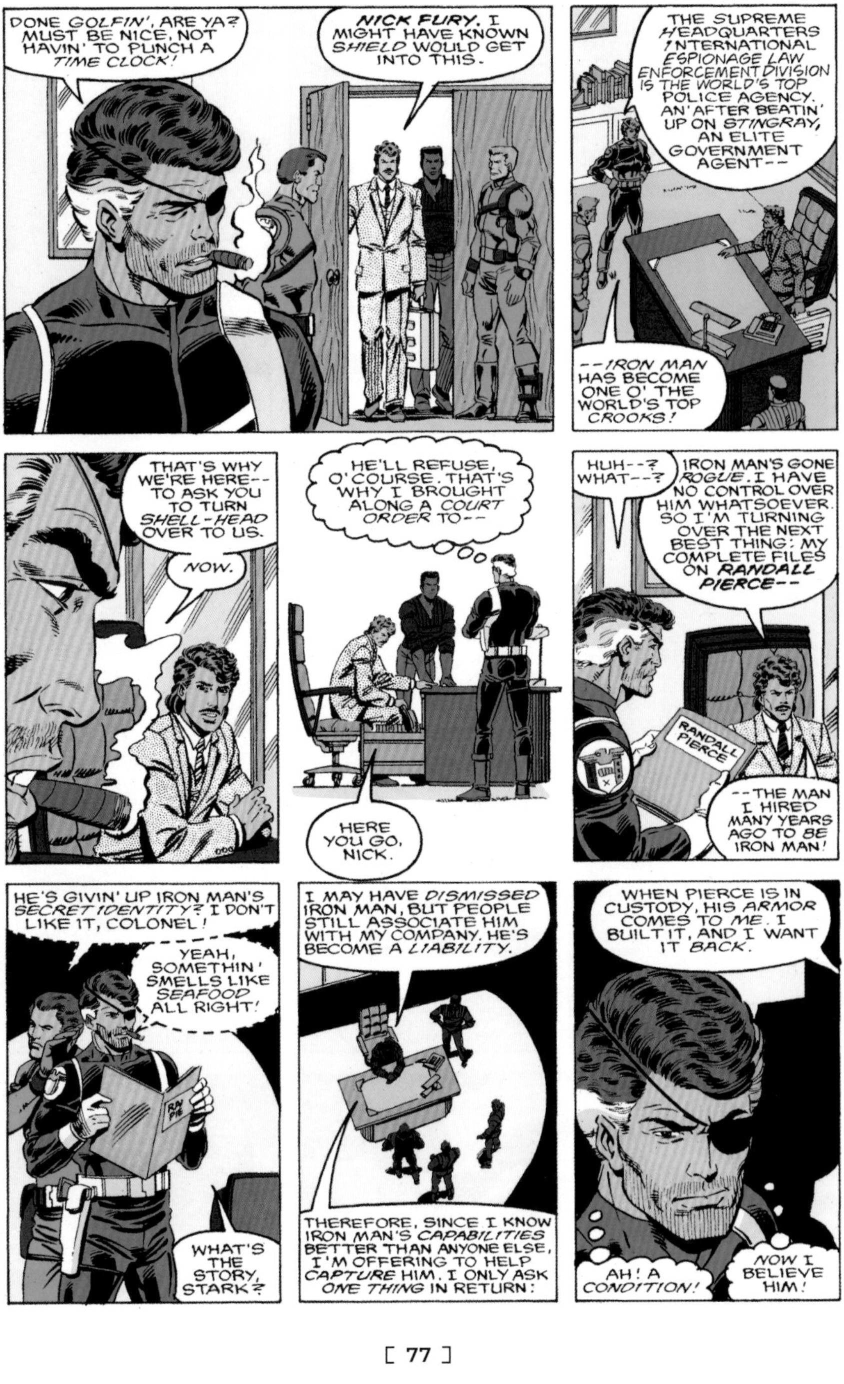
DONE GOLFIN', ARE YA? MUST BE NICE, NOT HAVIN' TO PUNCH A TIME CLOCK!
NICK FURY. I MIGHT HAVE KNOWN SHIELD WOULD GET INTO THIS.
THE SUPREME HEADQUARTERS INTERNATIONAL ESPIONAGE LAW ENFORCEMENT DIVISION IS THE WORLD'S TOP POLICE AGENCY. AN' AFTER BEATIN' UP ON STINGRAY, AN ELITE GOVERNMENT AGENT--
--IRON MAN HAS BECOME ONE O' THE WORLD'S TOP CROOKS!
THAT'S WHY WE'RE HERE-- TO ASK YOU TO TURN SHELL-HEAD OVER TO US.
NOW.
HE'LL REFUSE, O' COURSE. THAT'S WHY I BROUGHT ALONG A COURT ORDER TO--
HERE YOU GO, NICK.
HUH--? WHAT--?
IRON MAN'S GONE ROGUE. I HAVE NO CONTROL OVER HIM WHATSOEVER. SO I'M TURNING OVER THE NEXT BEST THING: MY COMPLETE FILES ON RANDALL PIERCE--
RANDALL PIERCE
--THE MAN I HIRED MANY YEARS AGO TO BE IRON MAN!
HE'S GIVIN' UP IRON MAN'S SECRET IDENTITY? I DON'T LIKE IT, COLONEL!
YEAH, SOMETHIN' SMELLS LIKE SEAFOOD ALL RIGHT!
WHAT'S THE STORY, STARK?
I MAY HAVE DISMISSED IRON MAN, BUT PEOPLE STILL ASSOCIATE HIM WITH MY COMPANY. HE'S BECOME A LIABILITY.
THEREFORE, SINCE I KNOW IRON MAN'S CAPABILITIES BETTER THAN ANYONE ELSE, I'M OFFERING TO HELP CAPTURE HIM. I ONLY ASK ONE THING IN RETURN:
WHEN PIERCE IS IN CUSTODY, HIS ARMOR COMES TO ME. I BUILT IT, AND I WANT IT BACK.
AH! A CONDITION!
NOW I BELIEVE HIM!

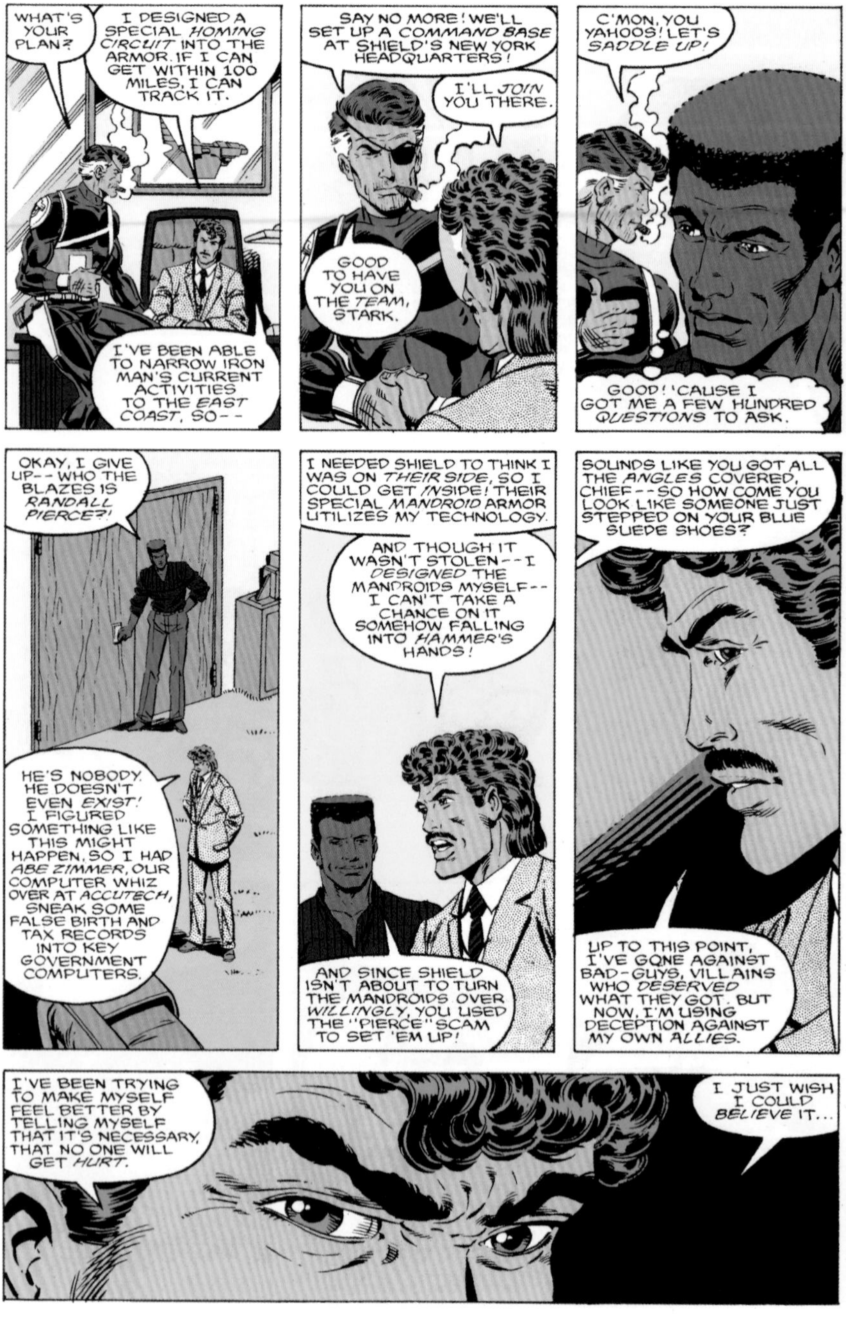
WHAT'S YOUR PLAN?
I DESIGNED A SPECIAL HOMING CIRCUIT INTO THE ARMOR. IF I CAN GET WITHIN 100 MILES, I CAN TRACK IT.
I'VE BEEN ABLE TO NARROW IRON MAN'S CURRENT ACTIVITIES TO THE EAST COAST, SO--
SAY NO MORE! WE'LL SET UP A COMMAND BASE AT SHIELD'S NEW YORK HEADQUARTERS!
I'LL JOIN YOU THERE.
GOOD TO HAVE YOU ON THE TEAM, STARK.
C'MON, YOU YAHOOS! LET'S SADDLE UP!
GOOD! 'CAUSE I GOT ME A FEW HUNDRED QUESTIONS TO ASK.
OKAY, I GIVE UP-- WHO THE BLAZES IS RANDALL PIERCE?!
HE'S NOBODY. HE DOESN'T EVEN EXIST! I FIGURED SOMETHING LIKE THIS MIGHT HAPPEN, SO I HAD ABE ZIMMER, OUR COMPUTER WHIZ OVER AT ACCUTECH, SNEAK SOME FALSE BIRTH AND TAX RECORDS INTO KEY GOVERNMENT COMPUTERS.
I NEEDED SHIELD TO THINK I WAS ON THEIR SIDE, SO I COULD GET INSIDE! THEIR SPECIAL MANDROID ARMOR UTILIZES MY TECHNOLOGY.
AND THOUGH IT WASN'T STOLEN--I DESIGNED THE MANDROIDS MYSELF-- I CAN'T TAKE A CHANCE ON IT SOMEHOW FALLING INTO HAMMER'S HANDS!
AND SINCE SHIELD ISN'T ABOUT TO TURN THE MANDROIDS OVER WILLINGLY, YOU USED THE "PIERCE" SCAM TO SET 'EM UP!
SOUNDS LIKE YOU GOT ALL THE ANGLES COVERED, CHIEF--SO HOW COME YOU LOOK LIKE SOMEONE JUST STEPPED ON YOUR BLUE SUEDE SHOES?
UP TO THIS POINT, I'VE GONE AGAINST BAD-GUYS, VILLAINS WHO DESERVED WHAT THEY GOT. BUT NOW, I'M USING DECEPTION AGAINST MY OWN ALLIES.
I'VE BEEN TRYING TO MAKE MYSELF FEEL BETTER BY TELLING MYSELF THAT IT'S NECESSARY, THAT NO ONE WILL GET HURT.
I JUST WISH I COULD BELIEVE IT...

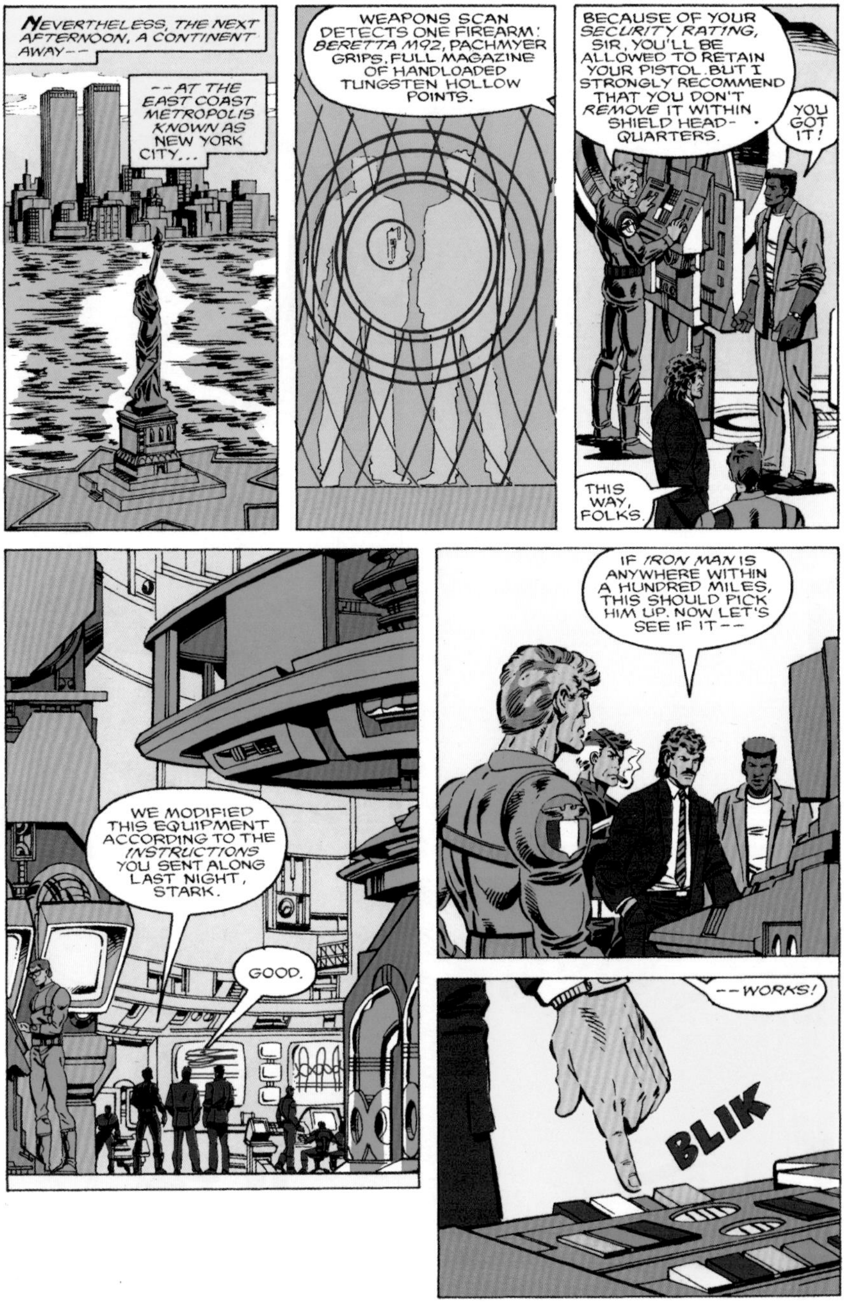
NEVERTHELESS, THE NEXT AFTERNOON, A CONTINENT AWAY--
--AT THE EAST COAST METROPOLIS KNOWN AS NEW YORK CITY...
WEAPONS SCAN DETECTS ONE FIREARM: BERETTA M92, PACHMYER GRIPS, FULL MAGAZINE OF HANDLOADED TUNGSTEN HOLLOW POINTS.
BECAUSE OF YOUR SECURITY RATING, SIR, YOU'LL BE ALLOWED TO RETAIN YOUR PISTOL. BUT I STRONGLY RECOMMEND THAT YOU DON'T REMOVE IT WITHIN SHIELD HEAD-QUARTERS.
YOU GOT IT!
THIS WAY, FOLKS.
WE MODIFIED THIS EQUIPMENT ACCORDING TO THE INSTRUCTIONS YOU SENT ALONG LAST NIGHT, STARK.
GOOD.
IF IRON MAN IS ANYWHERE WITHIN A HUNDRED MILES, THIS SHOULD PICK HIM UP. NOW LET'S SEE IF IT--
--WORKS!
BLIK

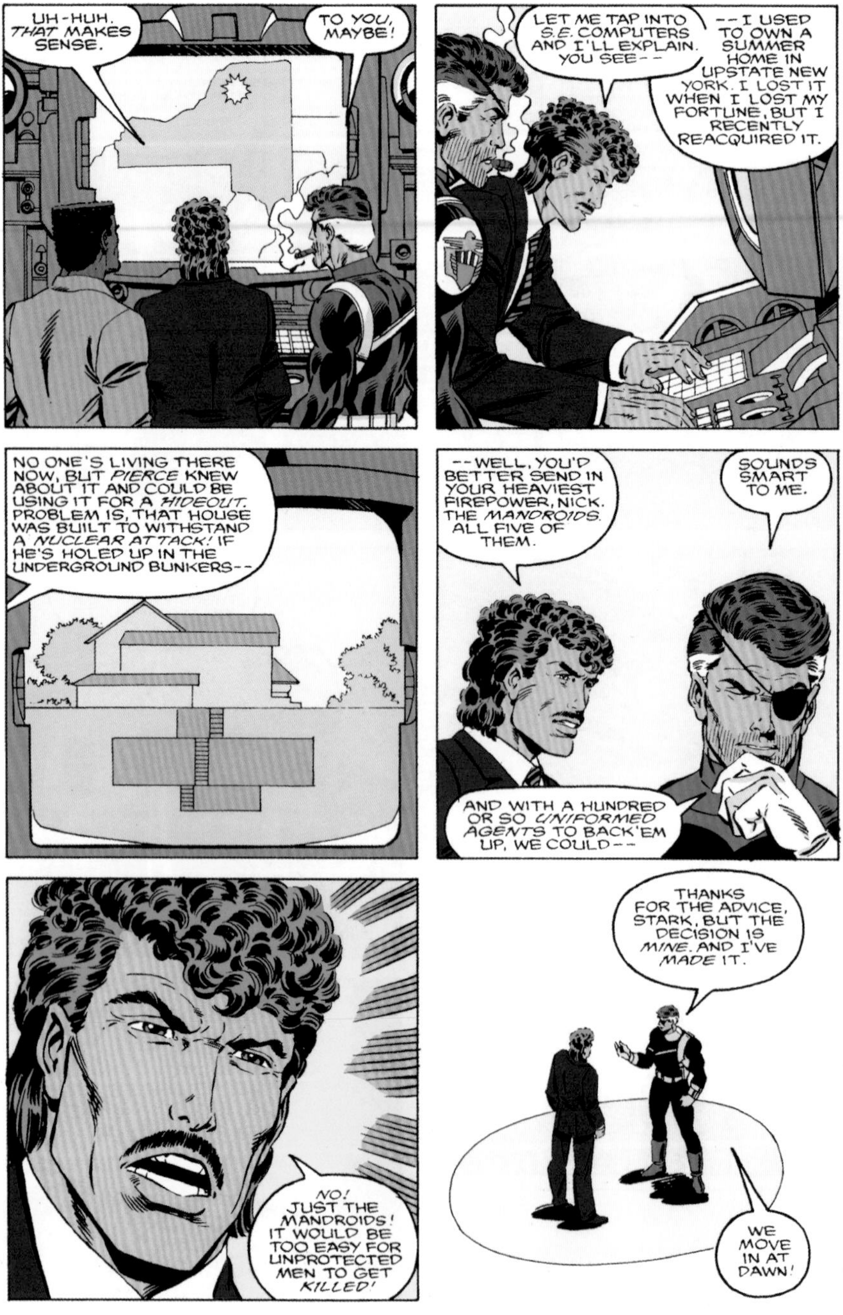
UH-HUH. THAT MAKES SENSE.
TO YOU, MAYBE!
LET ME TAP INTO S.E. COMPUTERS AND I'LL EXPLAIN. YOU SEE--
--I USED TO OWN A SUMMER HOME IN UPSTATE NEW YORK. I LOST IT WHEN I LOST MY FORTUNE, BUT I RECENTLY REACQUIRED IT.
NO ONE'S LIVING THERE NOW, BUT PIERCE KNEW ABOUT IT AND COULD BE USING IT FOR A HIDEOUT. PROBLEM IS, THAT HOUSE WAS BUILT TO WITHSTAND A NUCLEAR ATTACK! IF HE'S HOLED UP IN THE UNDERGROUND BUNKERS--
--WELL, YOU'D BETTER SEND IN YOUR HEAVIEST FIREPOWER, NICK. THE MANDROIDS. ALL FIVE OF THEM.
SOUNDS SMART TO ME.
AND WITH A HUNDRED OR SO UNIFORMED AGENTS TO BACK'EM UP, WE COULD--
NO! JUST THE MANDROIDS! IT WOULD BE TOO EASY FOR UNPROTECTED MEN TO GET KILLED!
THANKS FOR THE ADVICE, STARK, BUT THE DECISION IS MINE. AND I'VE MADE IT.
WE MOVE IN AT DAWN!

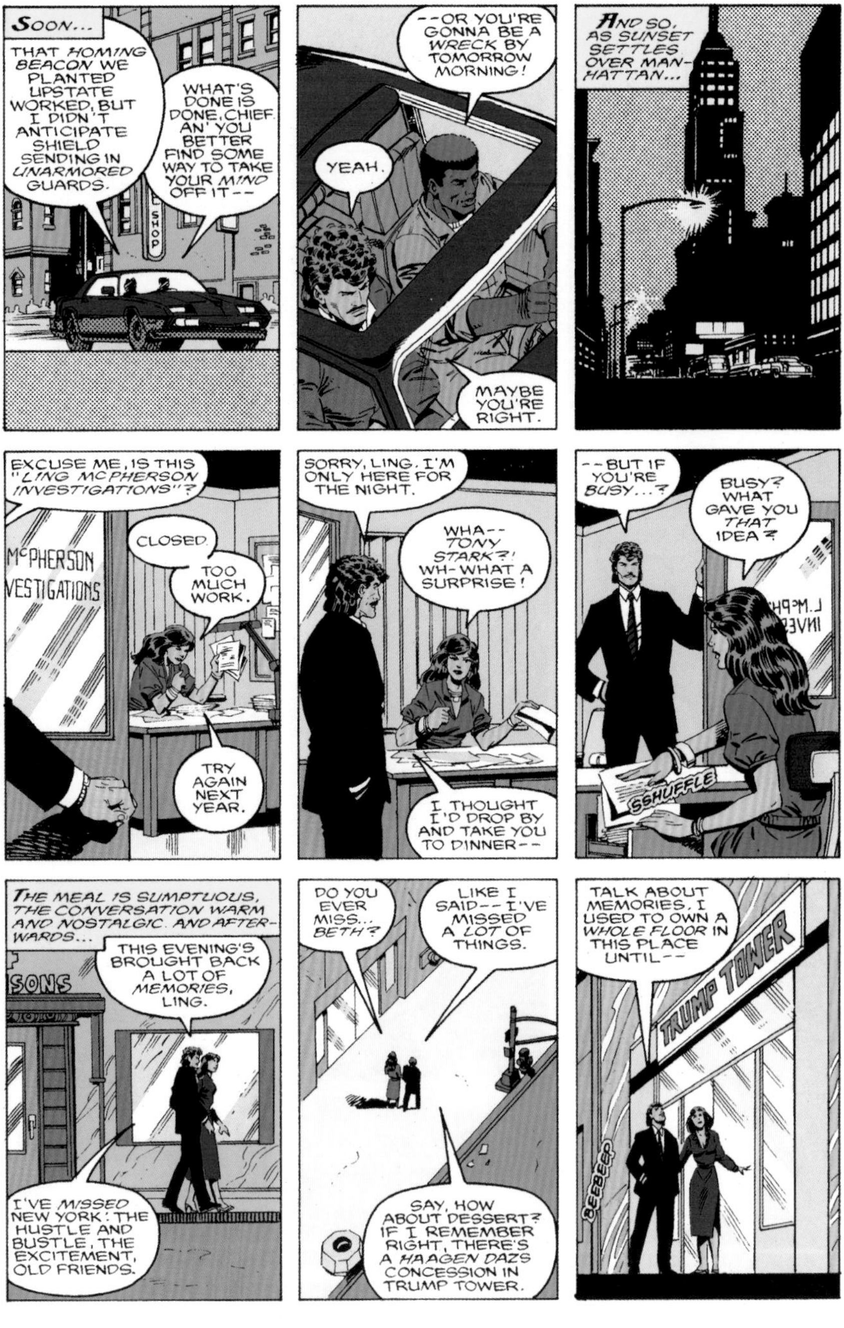
SOON...
THAT HOMING BEACON WE PLANTED UPSTATE WORKED, BUT I DIDN'T ANTICIPATE SHIELD SENDING IN UNARMORED GUARDS.
WHAT'S DONE IS DONE, CHIEF. AN' YOU BETTER FIND SOME WAY TO TAKE YOUR MIND OFF IT--
SHOP
--OR YOU'RE GONNA BE A WRECK BY TOMORROW MORNING!
YEAH.
MAYBE YOU'RE RIGHT.
AND SO, AS SUNSET SETTLES OVER MANHATTAN...
EXCUSE ME, IS THIS "LING MCPHERSON INVESTIGATIONS"?
MCPHERSON
VESTIGATIONS
CLOSED.
TOO MUCH WORK.
TRY AGAIN NEXT YEAR.
SORRY, LING. I'M ONLY HERE FOR THE NIGHT.
WHA-- TONY STARK?! WH-WHAT A SURPRISE!
I THOUGHT I'D DROP BY AND TAKE YOU TO DINNER--
--BUT IF YOU'RE BUSY...?
BUSY? WHAT GAVE YOU THAT IDEA?
SSHUFFLE
THE MEAL IS SUMPTUOUS, THE CONVERSATION WARM AND NOSTALGIC. AND AFTERWARDS...
THIS EVENING'S BROUGHT BACK A LOT OF MEMORIES, LING.
SONS
I'VE MISSED NEW YORK: THE HUSTLE AND BUSTLE, THE EXCITEMENT, OLD FRIENDS.
DO YOU EVER MISS... BETH?
LIKE I SAID-- I'VE MISSED A LOT OF THINGS.
SAY, HOW ABOUT DESSERT? IF I REMEMBER RIGHT, THERE'S A HAAGEN DAZS CONCESSION IN TRUMP TOWER.
TALK ABOUT MEMORIES. I USED TO OWN A WHOLE FLOOR IN THIS PLACE UNTIL--
TRUMP TOWER
BEEBEEP

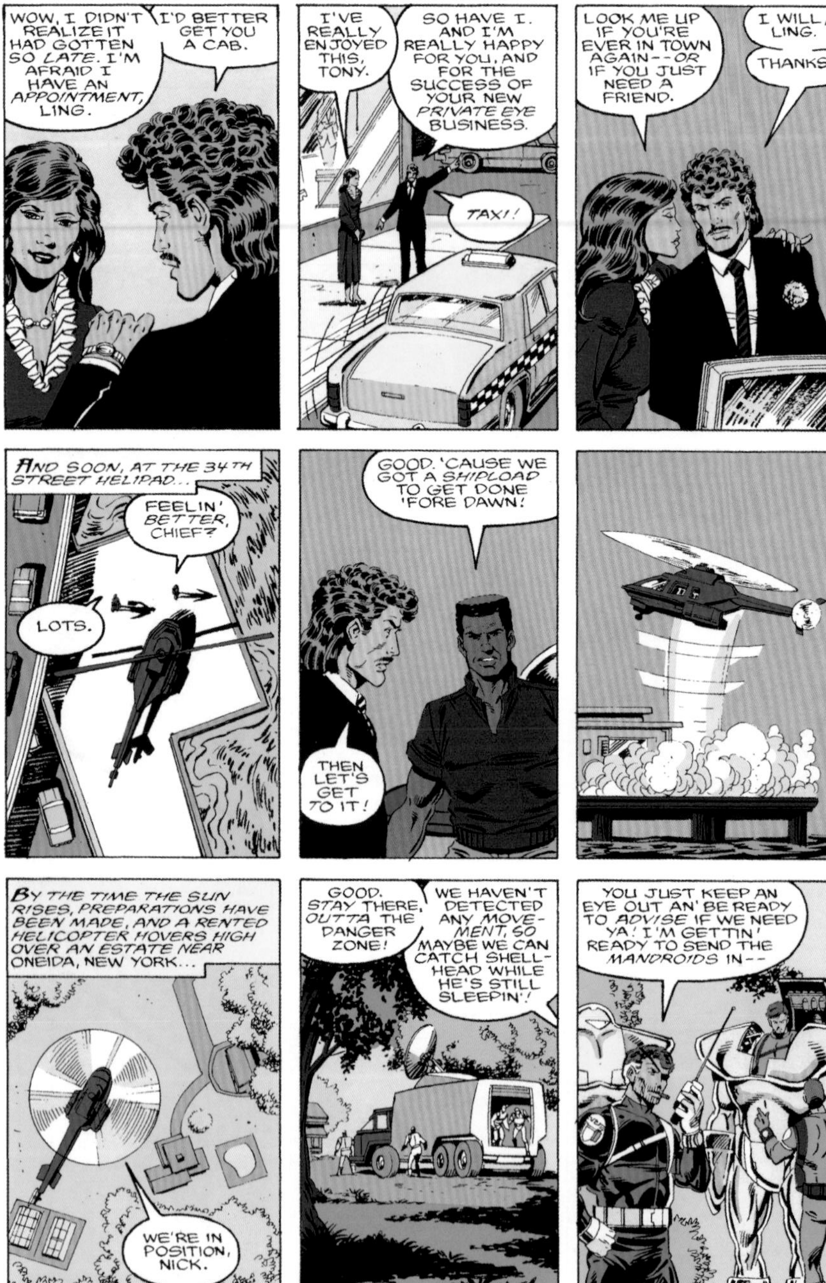
WOW, I DIDN'T REALIZE IT HAD GOTTEN SO LATE. I'M AFRAID I HAVE AN APPOINTMENT, LING.
I'D BETTER GET YOU A CAB.
I'VE REALLY ENJOYED THIS, TONY.
SO HAVE I. AND I'M REALLY HAPPY FOR YOU, AND FOR THE SUCCESS OF YOUR NEW PRIVATE EYE BUSINESS.
TAXI!
LOOK ME UP IF YOU'RE EVER IN TOWN AGAIN--OR IF YOU JUST NEED A FRIEND.
I WILL, LING.
THANKS.
AND SOON, AT THE 34TH STREET HELIPAD...
FEELIN' BETTER, CHIEF?
LOTS.
GOOD. 'CAUSE WE GOT A SHIPLOAD TO GET DONE 'FORE DAWN!
THEN LET'S GET TO IT!
BY THE TIME THE SUN RISES, PREPARATIONS HAVE BEEN MADE, AND A RENTED HELICOPTER HOVERS HIGH OVER AN ESTATE NEAR ONEIDA, NEW YORK...
WE'RE IN POSITION, NICK.
GOOD. STAY THERE, OUTTA THE DANGER ZONE!
WE HAVEN'T DETECTED ANY MOVE-MENT, SO MAYBE WE CAN CATCH SHELL-HEAD WHILE HE'S STILL SLEEPIN'!
YOU JUST KEEP AN EYE OUT AN' BE READY TO ADVISE IF WE NEED YA! I'M GETTIN' READY TO SEND THE MANDROIDS IN--

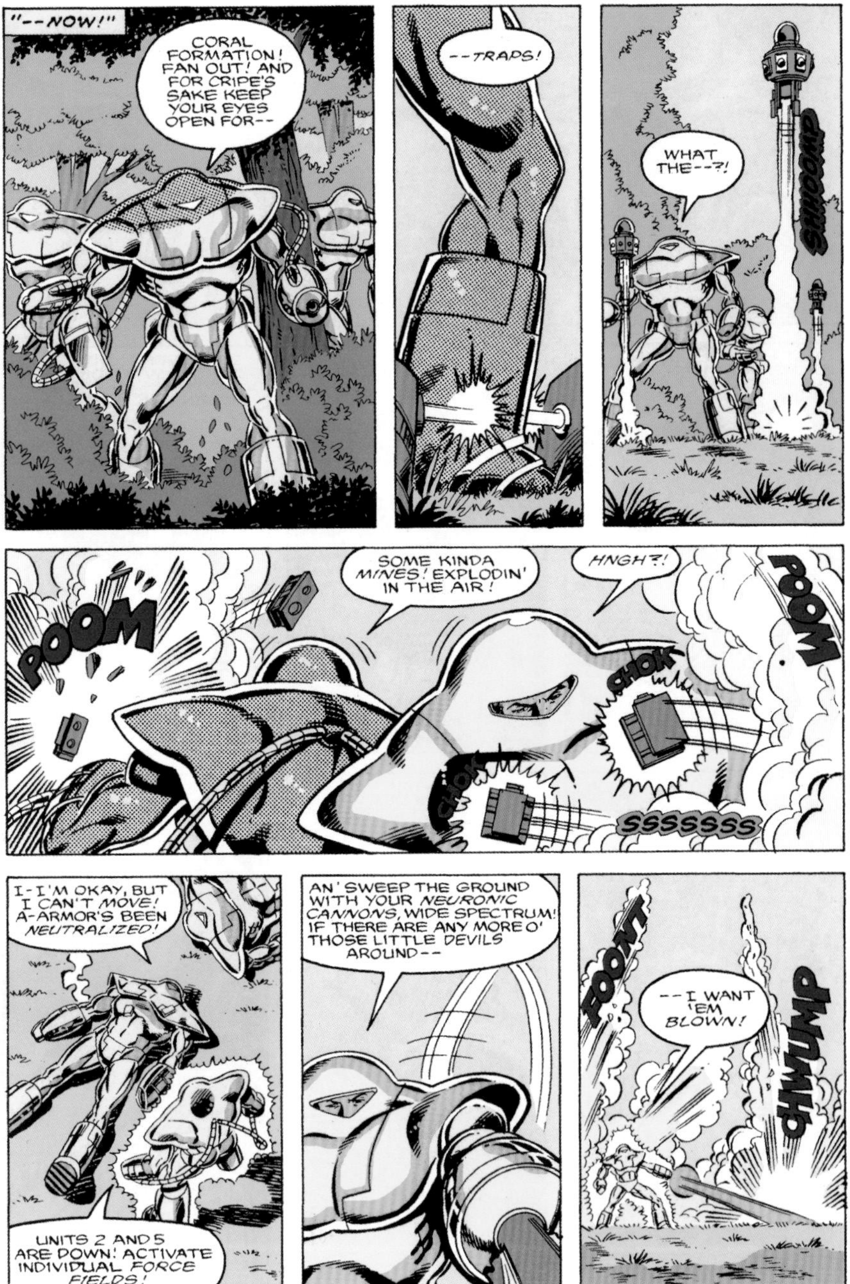
"--NOW!"
CORAL FORMATION! FAN OUT! AND FOR CRIPE'S SAKE KEEP YOUR EYES OPEN FOR--
--TRAPS!
WHAT THE--?!
SHWOOOO
SOME KINDA MINES! EXPLODIN' IN THE AIR!
HNGH?!
POOM
POOM
CHOK
CHOK
SSSSSSS
I-I'M OKAY, BUT I CAN'T MOVE! A-ARMOR'S BEEN NEUTRALIZED!
UNITS 2 AND 5 ARE DOWN! ACTIVATE INDIVIDUAL FORCE FIELDS!
AN' SWEEP THE GROUND WITH YOUR NEURONIC CANNONS, WIDE SPECTRUM! IF THERE ARE ANY MORE O' THOSE LITTLE DEVILS AROUND--
FOOM
--I WANT 'EM BLOWN!
CHWUMP

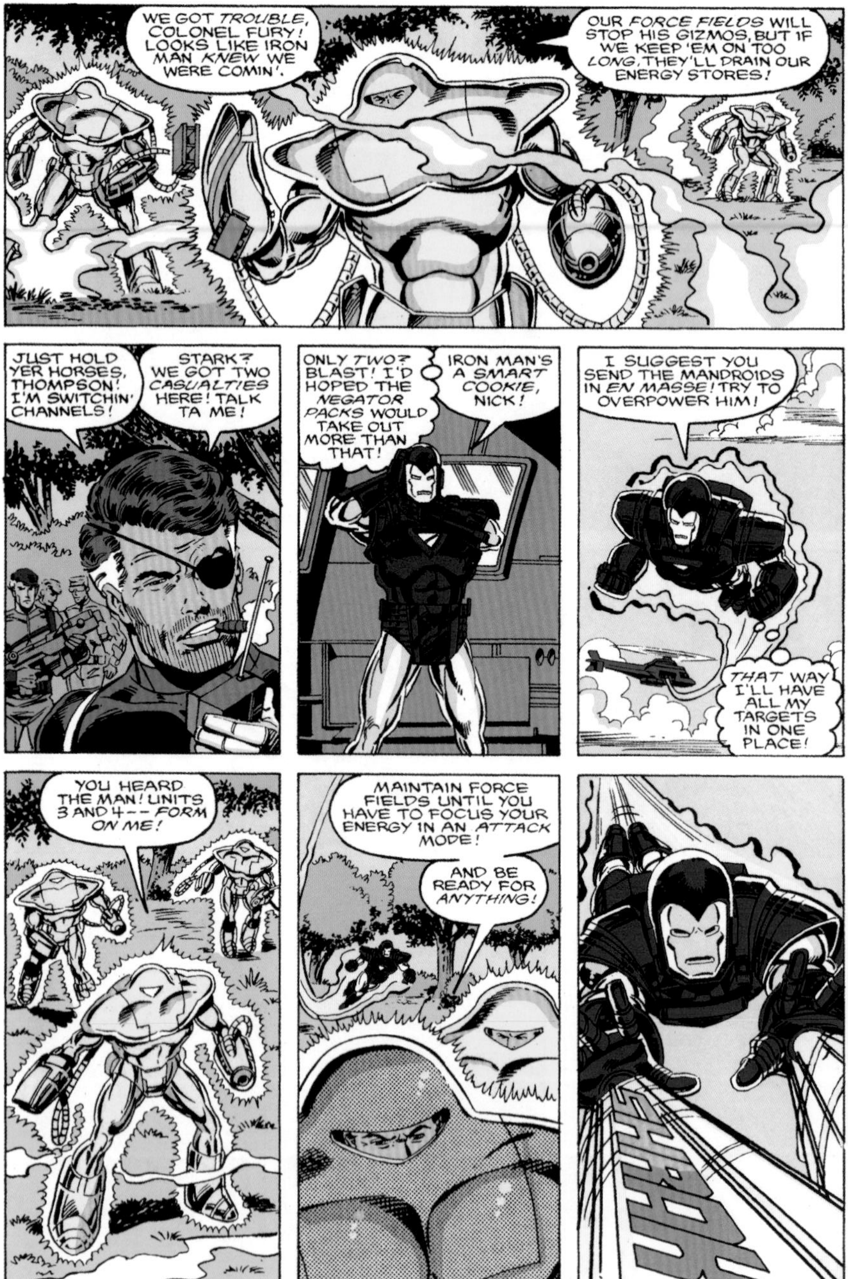
WE GOT TROUBLE, COLONEL FURY! LOOKS LIKE IRON MAN KNEW WE WERE COMIN'.
OUR FORCE FIELDS WILL STOP HIS GIZMOS, BUT IF WE KEEP 'EM ON TOO LONG, THEY'LL DRAIN OUR ENERGY STORES!
JUST HOLD YER HORSES, THOMPSON! I'M SWITCHIN' CHANNELS!
STARK? WE GOT TWO CASUALTIES HERE! TALK TA ME!
ONLY TWO? BLAST! I'D HOPED THE NEGATOR PACKS WOULD TAKE OUT MORE THAN THAT!
IRON MAN'S A SMART COOKIE, NICK!
I SUGGEST YOU SEND THE MANDROIDS IN EN MASSE! TRY TO OVERPOWER HIM!
THAT WAY I'LL HAVE ALL MY TARGETS IN ONE PLACE!
YOU HEARD THE MAN! UNITS 3 AND 4-- FORM ON ME!
MAINTAIN FORCE FIELDS UNTIL YOU HAVE TO FOCUS YOUR ENERGY IN AN ATTACK MODE!
AND BE READY FOR ANYTHING!
SHHH

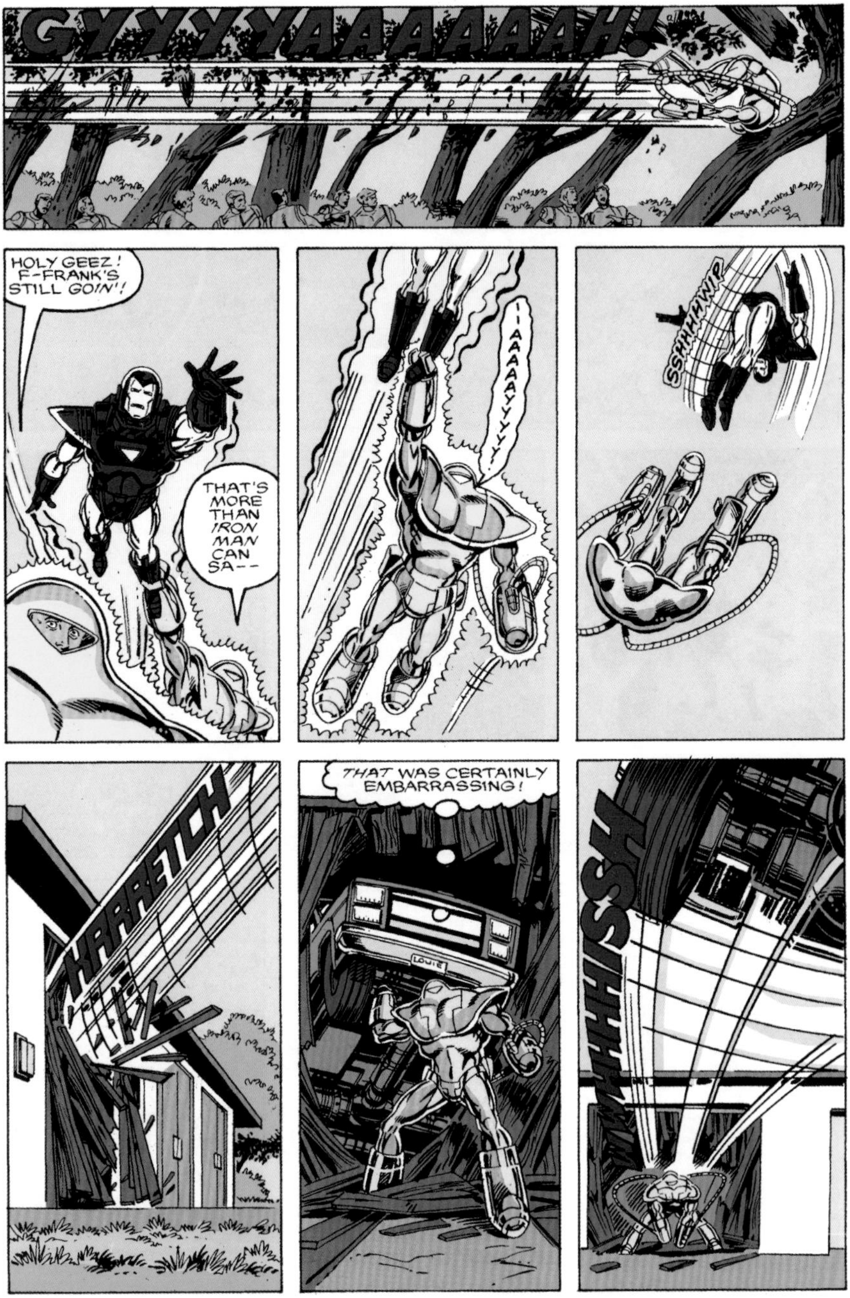
GYYYYAAAAAAAH!
HOLY GEEZ! F-FRANK'S STILL GOIN'!
THAT'S MORE THAN IRON MAN CAN SA--
AAAAAAYYYYY!
SSHHHWIP
KRRRETCH
THAT WAS CERTAINLY EMBARRASSING!
LOUIE
SSHHHHHH

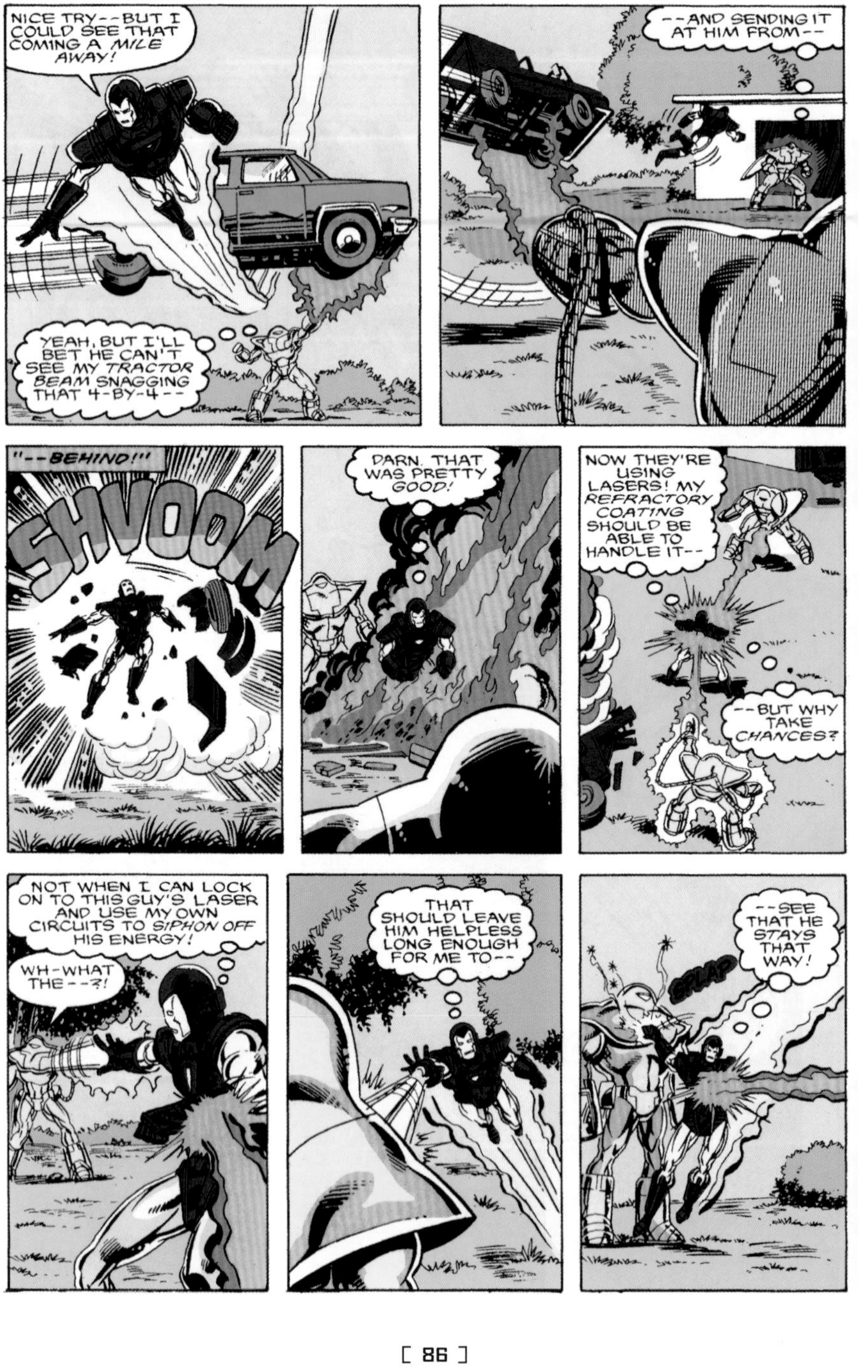
NICE TRY--BUT I COULD SEE THAT COMING A MILE AWAY!
YEAH, BUT I'LL BET HE CAN'T SEE MY TRACTOR BEAM SNAGGING THAT 4-BY-4--
--AND SENDING IT AT HIM FROM--
"--BEHIND!"
SHVOOM
DARN. THAT WAS PRETTY GOOD!
NOW THEY'RE USING LASERS! MY REFRACTORY COATING SHOULD BE ABLE TO HANDLE IT--
--BUT WHY TAKE CHANCES?
NOT WHEN I CAN LOCK ON TO THIS GUY'S LASER AND USE MY OWN CIRCUITS TO SIPHON OFF HIS ENERGY!
WH-WHAT THE--?!
THAT SHOULD LEAVE HIM HELPLESS LONG ENOUGH FOR ME TO--
SPLAP
--SEE THAT HE STAYS THAT WAY!

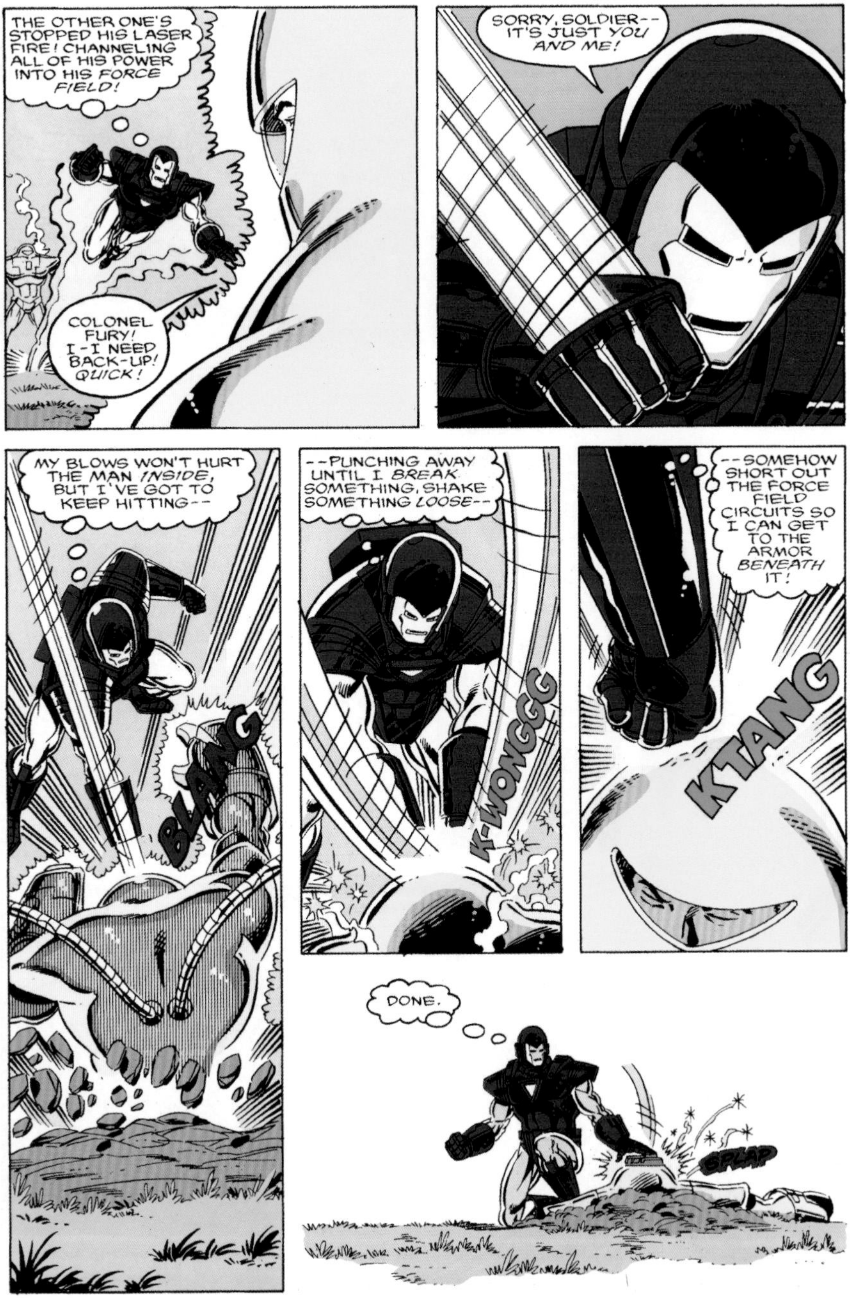
THE OTHER ONE'S STOPPED HIS LASER FIRE! CHANNELING ALL OF HIS POWER INTO HIS FORCE FIELD!
COLONEL FURY! I-I NEED BACK-UP! QUICK!
SORRY, SOLDIER-- IT'S JUST YOU AND ME!
MY BLOWS WON'T HURT THE MAN INSIDE, BUT I'VE GOT TO KEEP HITTING--
BLANG
--PUNCHING AWAY UNTIL I BREAK SOMETHING, SHAKE SOMETHING LOOSE--
K-WONGGG
--SOMEHOW SHORT OUT THE FORCE FIELD CIRCUITS SO I CAN GET TO THE ARMOR BENEATH IT!
KTANG
DONE.
SPLAP

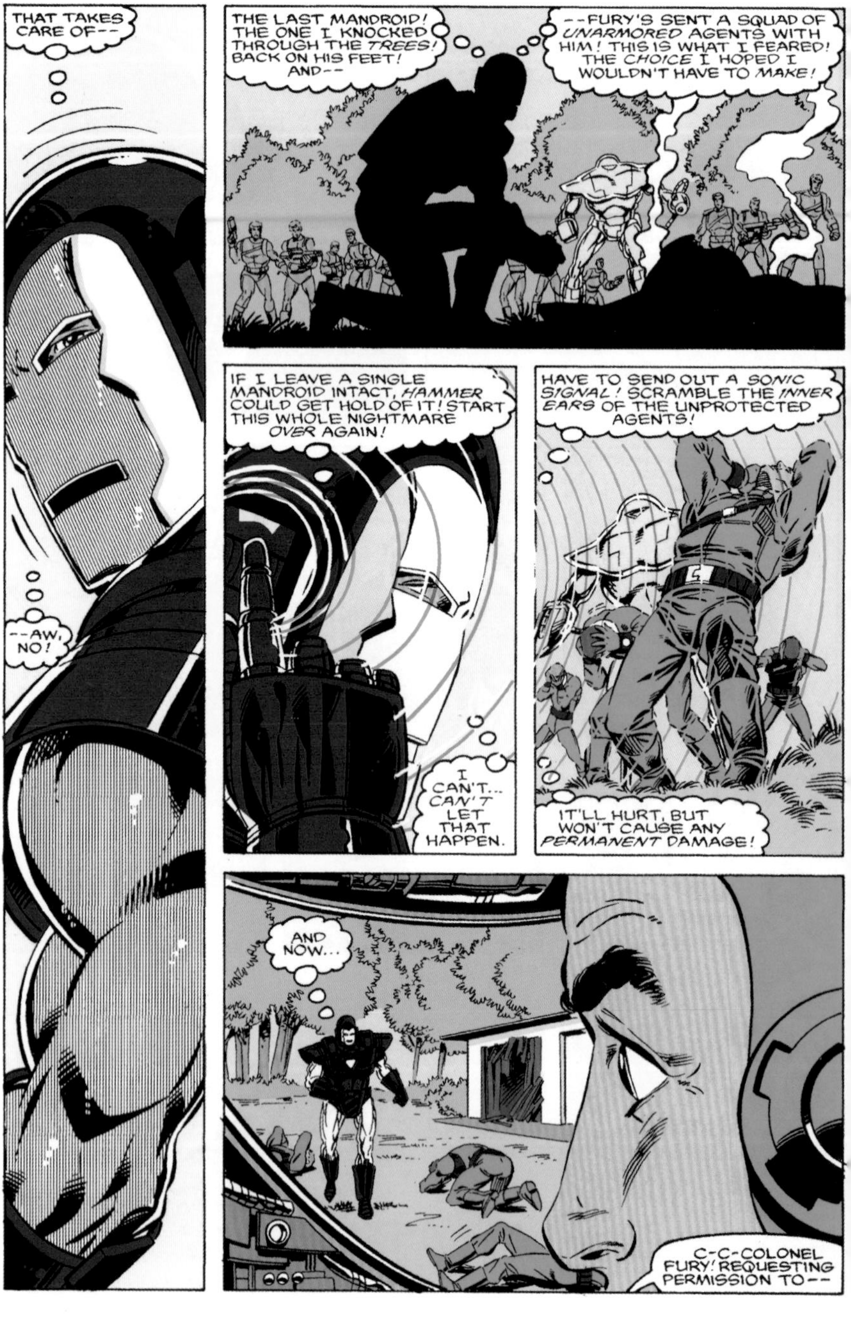
THAT TAKES CARE OF--
--AW, NO!
THE LAST MANDROID! THE ONE I KNOCKED THROUGH THE TREES! BACK ON HIS FEET! AND--
--FURY'S SENT A SQUAD OF UNARMORED AGENTS WITH HIM! THIS IS WHAT I FEARED! THE CHOICE I HOPED I WOULDN'T HAVE TO MAKE!
IF I LEAVE A SINGLE MANDROID INTACT, HAMMER COULD GET HOLD OF IT! START THIS WHOLE NIGHTMARE OVER AGAIN!
I CAN'T... CAN'T LET THAT HAPPEN.
HAVE TO SEND OUT A SONIC SIGNAL! SCRAMBLE THE INNER EARS OF THE UNPROTECTED AGENTS!
IT'LL HURT, BUT WON'T CAUSE ANY PERMANENT DAMAGE!
AND NOW...
C-C-COLONEL FURY! REQUESTING PERMISSION TO--

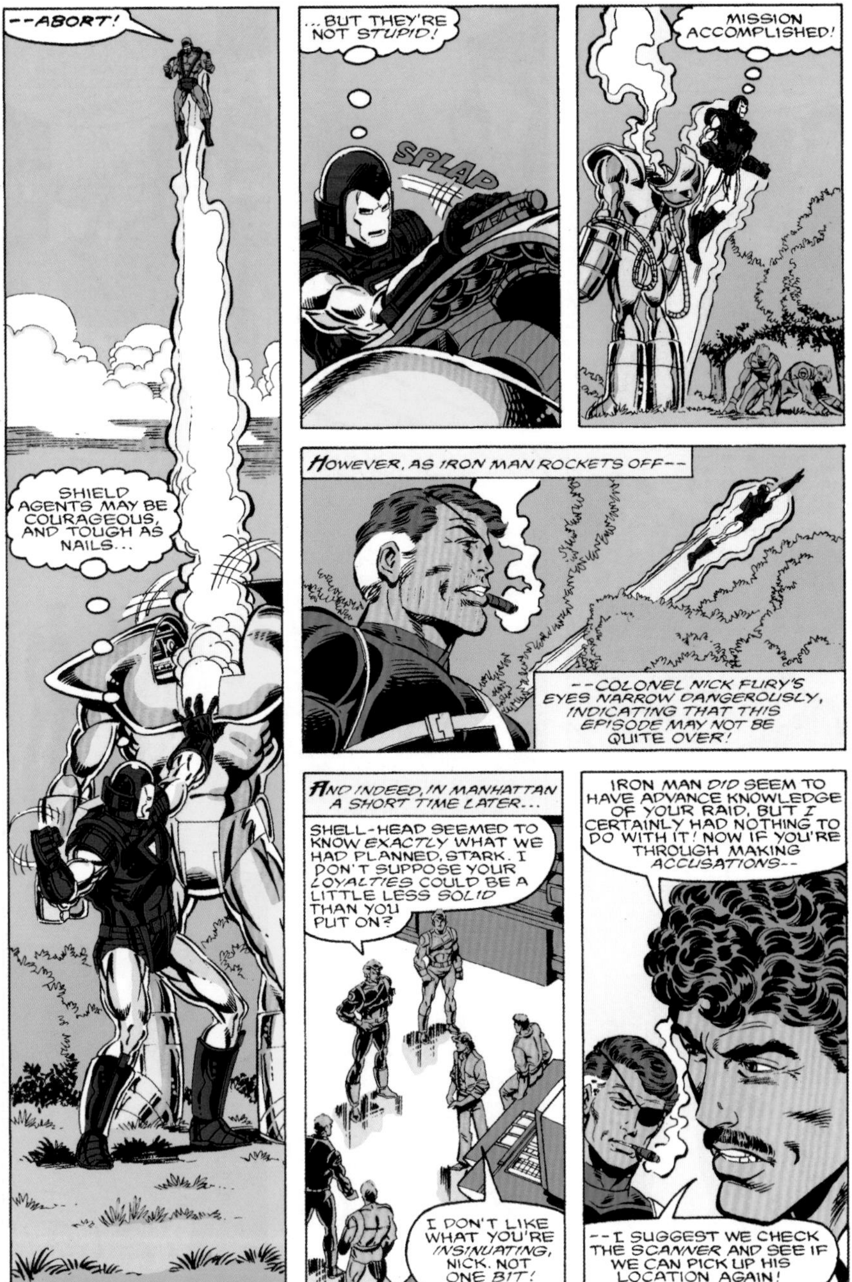
--ABORT!
SHIELD AGENTS MAY BE COURAGEOUS, AND TOUGH AS NAILS...
...BUT THEY'RE NOT STUPID!
SPLAP
MISSION ACCOMPLISHED!
HOWEVER, AS IRON MAN ROCKETS OFF--
--COLONEL NICK FURY'S EYES NARROW DANGEROUSLY, INDICATING THAT THIS EPISODE MAY NOT BE QUITE OVER!
AND INDEED, IN MANHATTAN A SHORT TIME LATER...
SHELL-HEAD SEEMED TO KNOW EXACTLY WHAT WE HAD PLANNED, STARK. I DON'T SUPPOSE YOUR LOYALTIES COULD BE A LITTLE LESS SOLID THAN YOU PUT ON?
I DON'T LIKE WHAT YOU'RE INSINUATING, NICK. NOT ONE BIT!
IRON MAN DID SEEM TO HAVE ADVANCE KNOWLEDGE OF YOUR RAID, BUT I CERTAINLY HAD NOTHING TO DO WITH IT! NOW IF YOU'RE THROUGH MAKING ACCUSATIONS--
--I SUGGEST WE CHECK THE SCANNER AND SEE IF WE CAN PICK UP HIS LOCATION AGAIN!

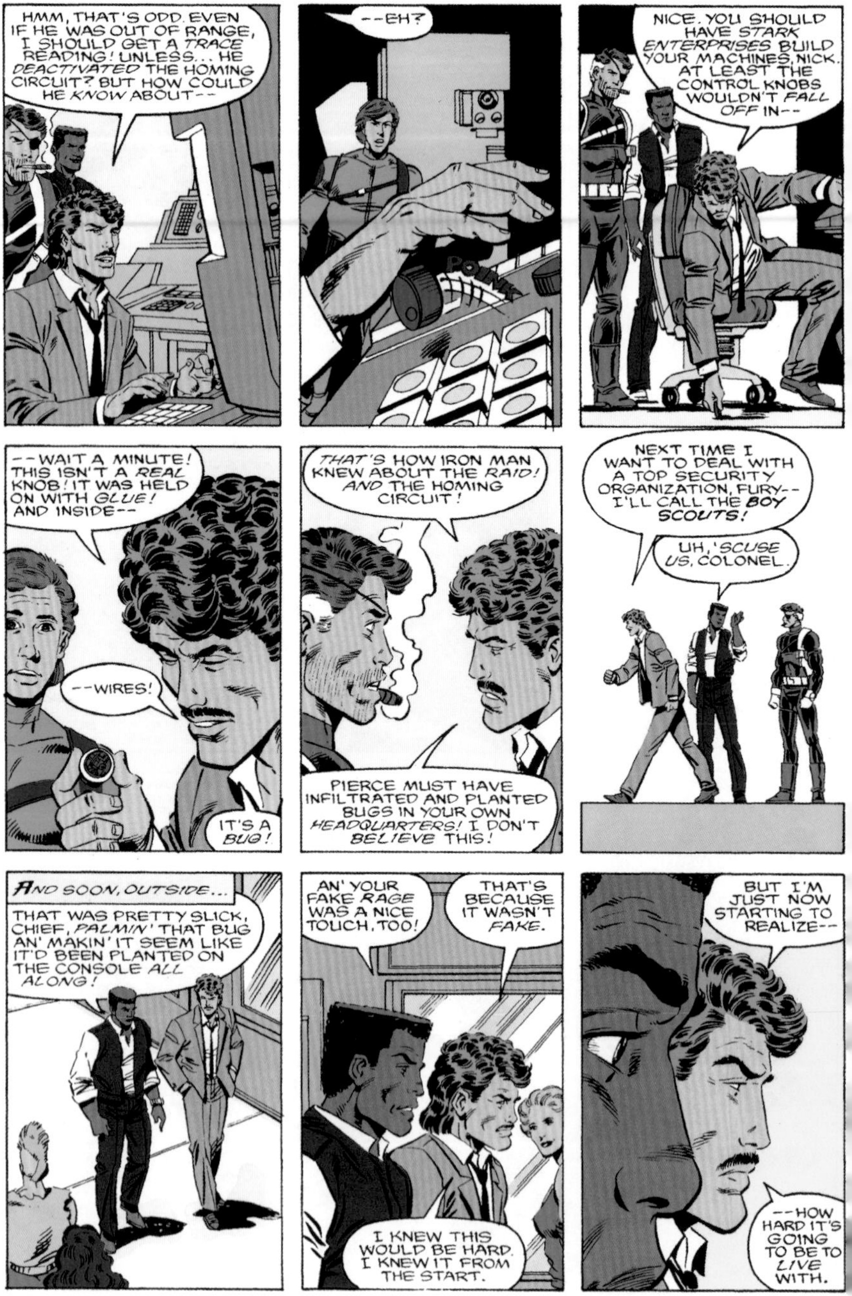
HMM, THAT'S ODD. EVEN IF HE WAS OUT OF RANGE, I SHOULD GET A *TRACE* READING! UNLESS... HE *DEACTIVATED* THE HOMING CIRCUIT? BUT HOW COULD HE *KNOW* ABOUT--
--EH?
POINK
NICE. YOU SHOULD HAVE *STARK ENTERPRISES* BUILD YOUR MACHINES, NICK. AT LEAST THE CONTROL KNOBS WOULDN'T *FALL OFF* IN--
--WAIT A MINUTE! THIS ISN'T A *REAL* KNOB! IT WAS HELD ON WITH *GLUE*! AND INSIDE--
--WIRES!
IT'S A *BUG*!
THAT'S HOW IRON MAN KNEW ABOUT THE *RAID*! *AND* THE HOMING CIRCUIT!
PIERCE MUST HAVE INFILTRATED AND PLANTED BUGS IN YOUR OWN *HEADQUARTERS*! I DON'T *BELIEVE* THIS!
NEXT TIME I WANT TO DEAL WITH A TOP SECURITY ORGANIZATION, FURY-- I'LL CALL THE *BOY SCOUTS*!
UH, 'SCUSE US, COLONEL.
AND SOON, OUTSIDE...
THAT WAS PRETTY SLICK, CHIEF, *PALMIN'* THAT BUG AN' MAKIN' IT SEEM LIKE IT'D BEEN PLANTED ON THE CONSOLE *ALL ALONG*!
AN' YOUR FAKE *RAGE* WAS A NICE TOUCH, TOO!
THAT'S BECAUSE IT WASN'T *FAKE*.
I KNEW THIS WOULD BE HARD. I KNEW IT FROM THE START.
BUT I'M JUST NOW STARTING TO REALIZE--
--HOW HARD IT'S GOING TO BE TO *LIVE* WITH.

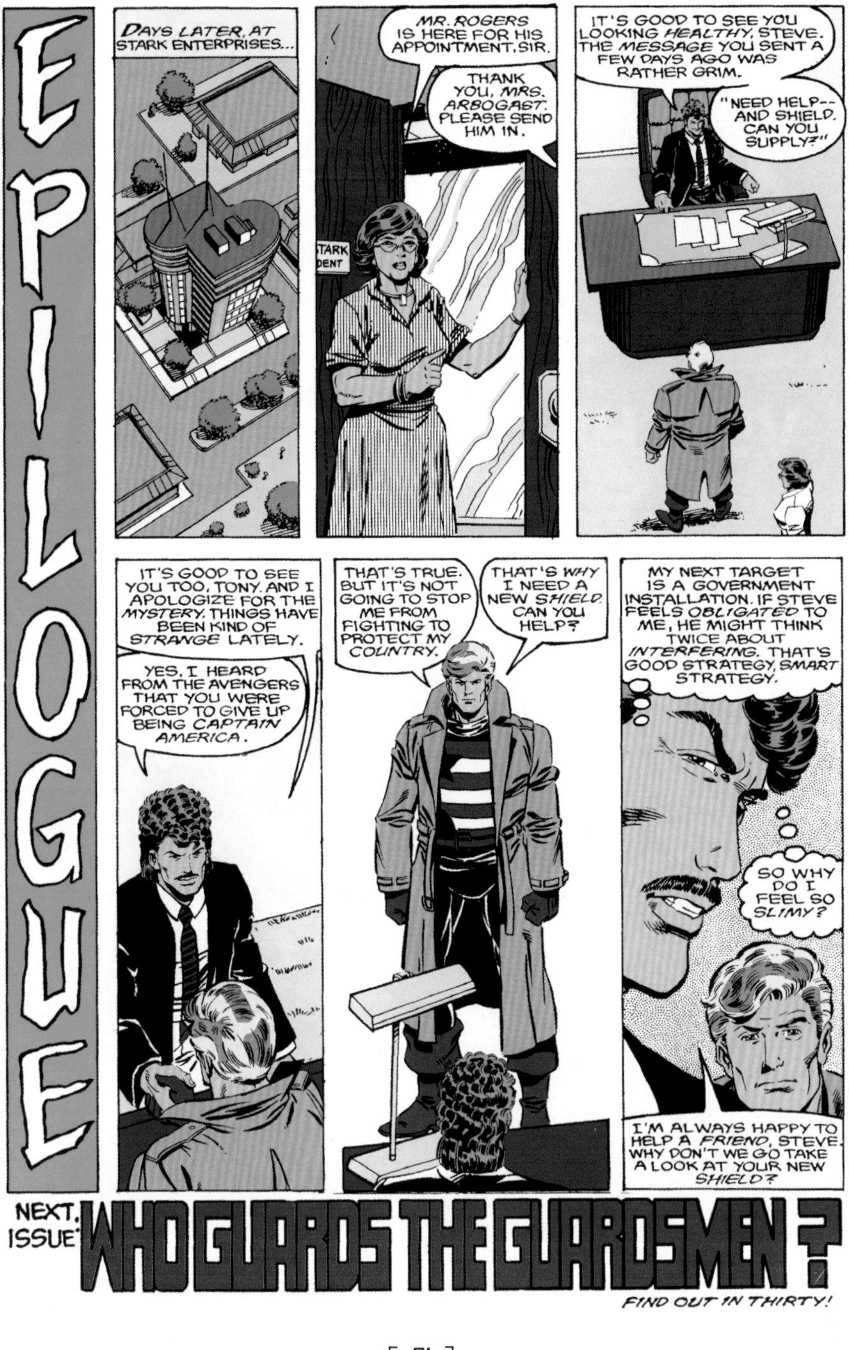
EPILOGUE
DAYS LATER, AT STARK ENTERPRISES...
MR. ROGERS IS HERE FOR HIS APPOINTMENT, SIR.
THANK YOU, MRS. ARBOGAST. PLEASE SEND HIM IN.
STARK
DENT
IT'S GOOD TO SEE YOU LOOKING HEALTHY, STEVE. THE MESSAGE YOU SENT A FEW DAYS AGO WAS RATHER GRIM.
"NEED HELP-- AND SHIELD. CAN YOU SUPPLY?"
IT'S GOOD TO SEE YOU TOO, TONY. AND I APOLOGIZE FOR THE MYSTERY. THINGS HAVE BEEN KIND OF STRANGE LATELY.
YES, I HEARD FROM THE AVENGERS THAT YOU WERE FORCED TO GIVE UP BEING CAPTAIN AMERICA.
THAT'S TRUE. BUT IT'S NOT GOING TO STOP ME FROM FIGHTING TO PROTECT MY COUNTRY.
THAT'S WHY I NEED A NEW SHIELD. CAN YOU HELP?
MY NEXT TARGET IS A GOVERNMENT INSTALLATION. IF STEVE FEELS OBLIGATED TO ME, HE MIGHT THINK TWICE ABOUT INTERFERING. THAT'S GOOD STRATEGY, SMART STRATEGY.
SO WHY DO I FEEL SO SLIMY?
I'M ALWAYS HAPPY TO HELP A FRIEND, STEVE. WHY DON'T WE GO TAKE A LOOK AT YOUR NEW SHIELD?
NEXT ISSUE: WHO GUARDS THE GUARDSMEN?
FIND OUT IN THIRTY!

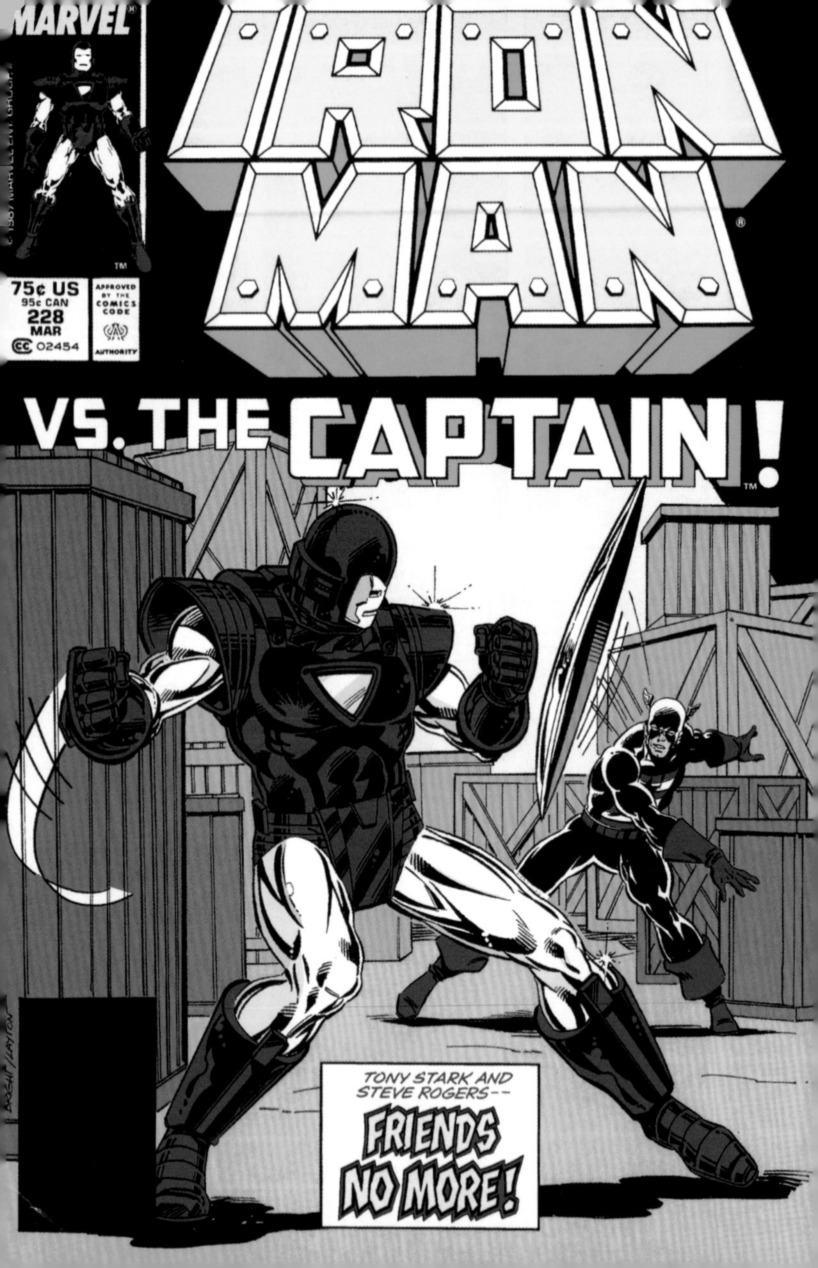
MARVEL
IRON MAN
75¢ US
95¢ CAN
228
MAR
02454
APPROVED BY THE COMICS CODE AUTHORITY
VS. THE CAPTAIN!
TONY STARK AND STEVE ROGERS--
FRIENDS NO MORE!

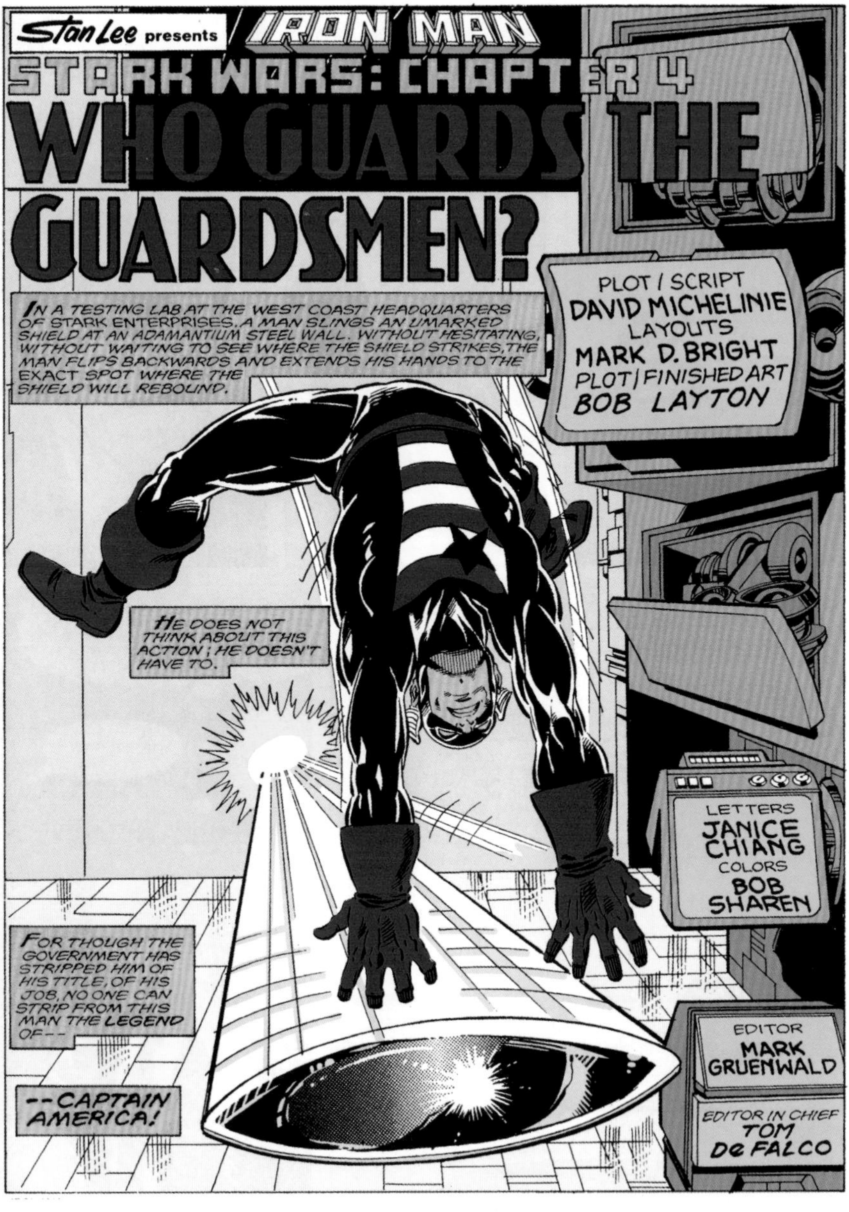
Stan Lee presents
IRON MAN
STARK WARS: CHAPTER 4
WHO GUARDS THE GUARDSMEN?
PLOT / SCRIPT DAVID MICHELINIE LAYOUTS MARK D. BRIGHT PLOT/FINISHED ART BOB LAYTON
IN A TESTING LAB AT THE WEST COAST HEADQUARTERS OF STARK ENTERPRISES, A MAN SLINGS AN UNMARKED SHIELD AT AN ADAMANTIUM STEEL WALL. WITHOUT HESITATING, WITHOUT WAITING TO SEE WHERE THE SHIELD STRIKES, THE MAN FLIPS BACKWARDS AND EXTENDS HIS HANDS TO THE EXACT SPOT WHERE THE SHIELD WILL REBOUND.
HE DOES NOT THINK ABOUT THIS ACTION; HE DOESN'T HAVE TO.
LETTERS JANICE CHIANG COLORS BOB SHAREN
FOR THOUGH THE GOVERNMENT HAS STRIPPED HIM OF HIS TITLE, OF HIS JOB, NO ONE CAN STRIP FROM THIS MAN THE LEGEND OF--
--CAPTAIN AMERICA!
EDITOR MARK GRUENWALD
EDITOR IN CHIEF TOM DeFALCO

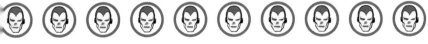

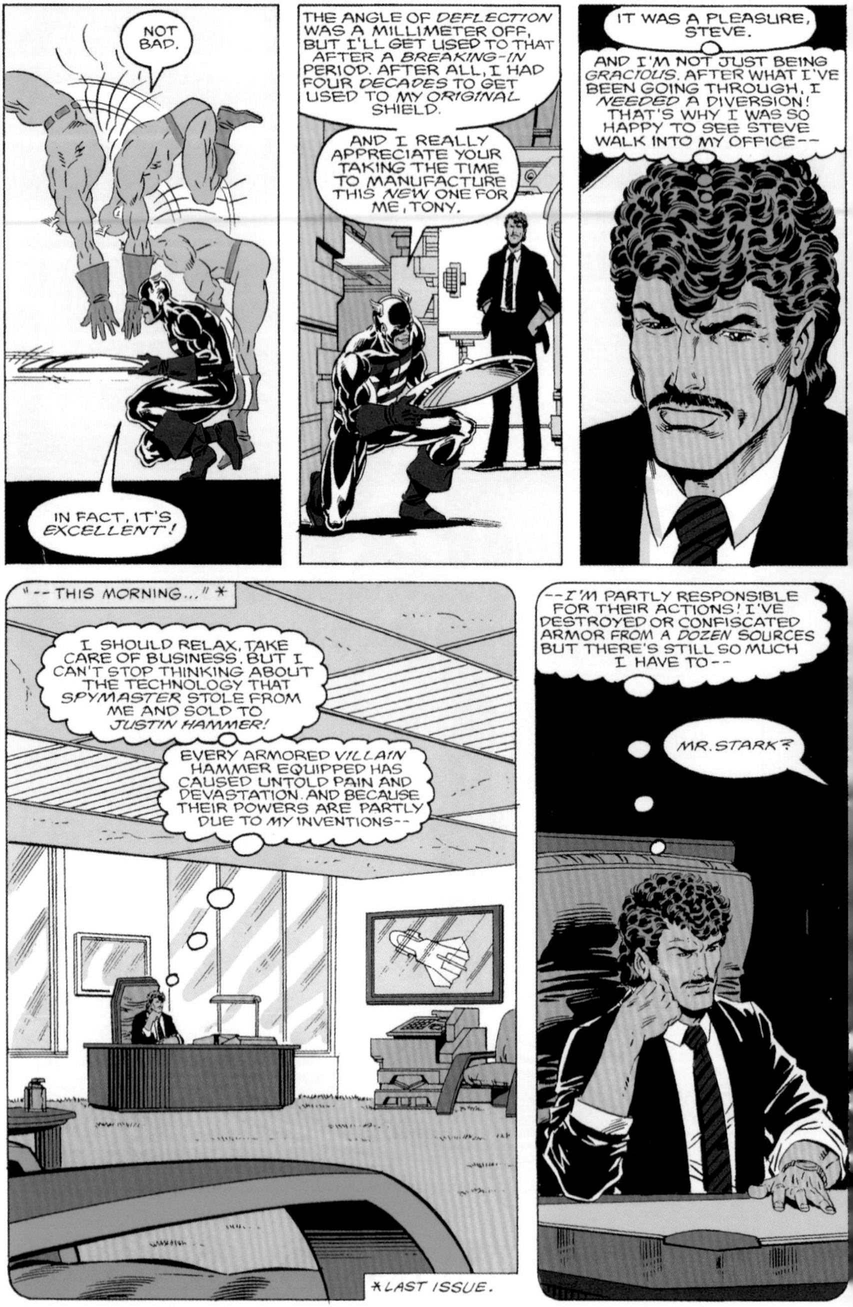

NOT BAD.
IN FACT, IT'S EXCELLENT!
THE ANGLE OF DEFLECTION WAS A MILLIMETER OFF, BUT I'LL GET USED TO THAT AFTER A BREAKING-IN PERIOD. AFTER ALL, I HAD FOUR DECADES TO GET USED TO MY ORIGINAL SHIELD.
AND I REALLY APPRECIATE YOUR TAKING THE TIME TO MANUFACTURE THIS NEW ONE FOR ME, TONY.
IT WAS A PLEASURE, STEVE.
AND I'M NOT JUST BEING GRACIOUS. AFTER WHAT I'VE BEEN GOING THROUGH, I NEEDED A DIVERSION! THAT'S WHY I WAS SO HAPPY TO SEE STEVE WALK INTO MY OFFICE--
"--THIS MORNING..." *
I SHOULD RELAX, TAKE CARE OF BUSINESS. BUT I CAN'T STOP THINKING ABOUT THE TECHNOLOGY THAT SPYMASTER STOLE FROM ME AND SOLD TO JUSTIN HAMMER!
EVERY ARMORED VILLAIN HAMMER EQUIPPED HAS CAUSED UNTOLD PAIN AND DEVASTATION. AND BECAUSE THEIR POWERS ARE PARTLY DUE TO MY INVENTIONS--
*LAST ISSUE.
--I'M PARTLY RESPONSIBLE FOR THEIR ACTIONS! I'VE DESTROYED OR CONFISCATED ARMOR FROM A DOZEN SOURCES BUT THERE'S STILL SO MUCH I HAVE TO--
MR. STARK?

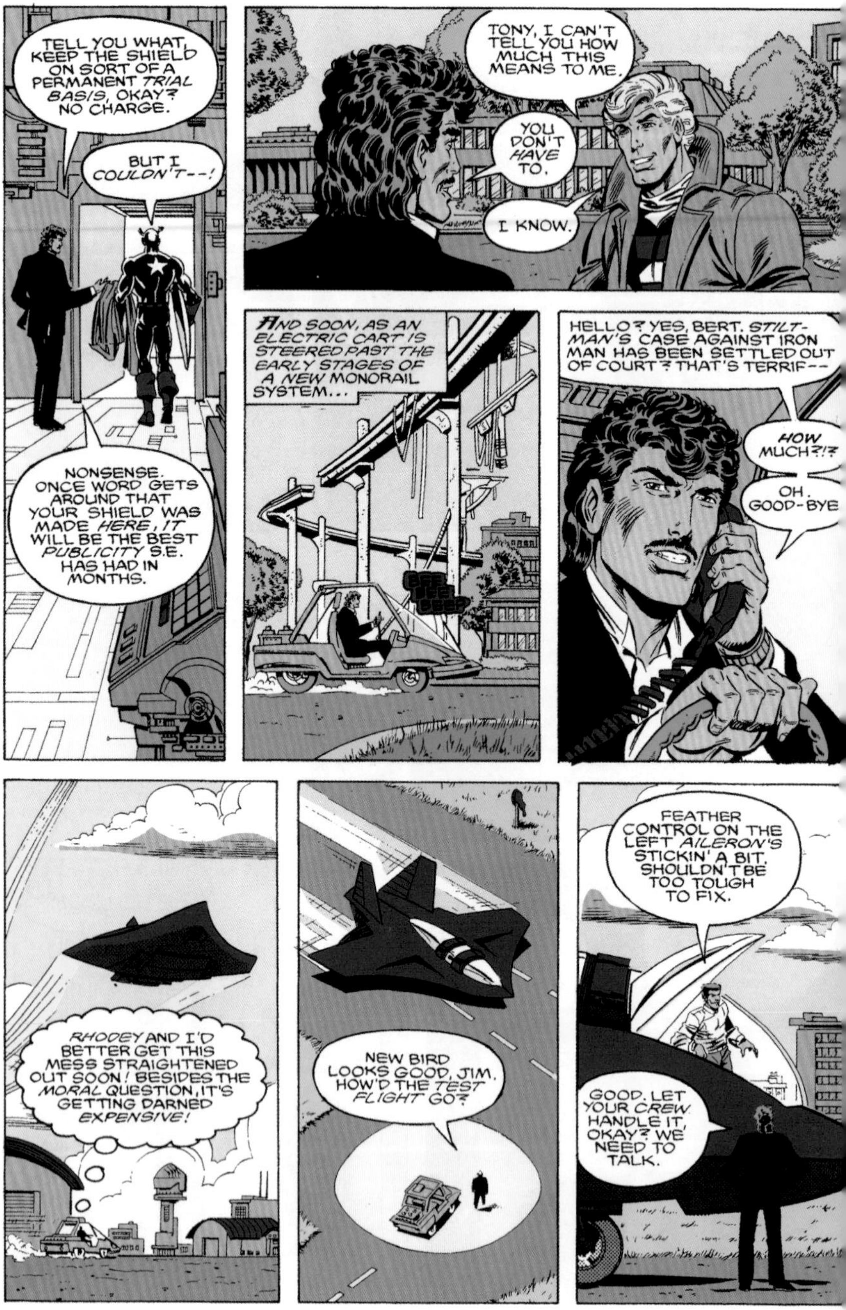
TELL YOU WHAT, KEEP THE SHIELD ON SORT OF A PERMANENT *TRIAL BASIS*, OKAY? NO CHARGE.
BUT I *COULDN'T*--!
NONSENSE. ONCE WORD GETS AROUND THAT YOUR SHIELD WAS MADE *HERE*, *IT* WILL BE THE BEST *PUBLICITY* S.E. HAS HAD IN MONTHS.
TONY, I CAN'T TELL YOU HOW MUCH THIS MEANS TO ME.
YOU DON'T *HAVE* TO.
I KNOW.
AND SOON, AS AN ELECTRIC CART IS STEERED PAST THE EARLY STAGES OF A *NEW* MONORAIL SYSTEM...
HELLO? YES, BERT. *STILT-MAN'S* CASE AGAINST IRON MAN HAS BEEN SETTLED OUT OF COURT? THAT'S TERRIF--
HOW MUCH?!?
OH. GOOD-BYE
RHODEY AND I'D BETTER GET THIS MESS STRAIGHTENED OUT SOON! BESIDES THE *MORAL* QUESTION, IT'S GETTING DARNED *EXPENSIVE*!
NEW BIRD LOOKS GOOD, JIM. HOW'D THE *TEST FLIGHT* GO?
FEATHER CONTROL ON THE LEFT *AILERON'S* STICKIN' A BIT. SHOULDN'T BE TOO TOUGH TO FIX.
GOOD. LET YOUR *CREW* HANDLE IT, OKAY? WE NEED TO TALK.

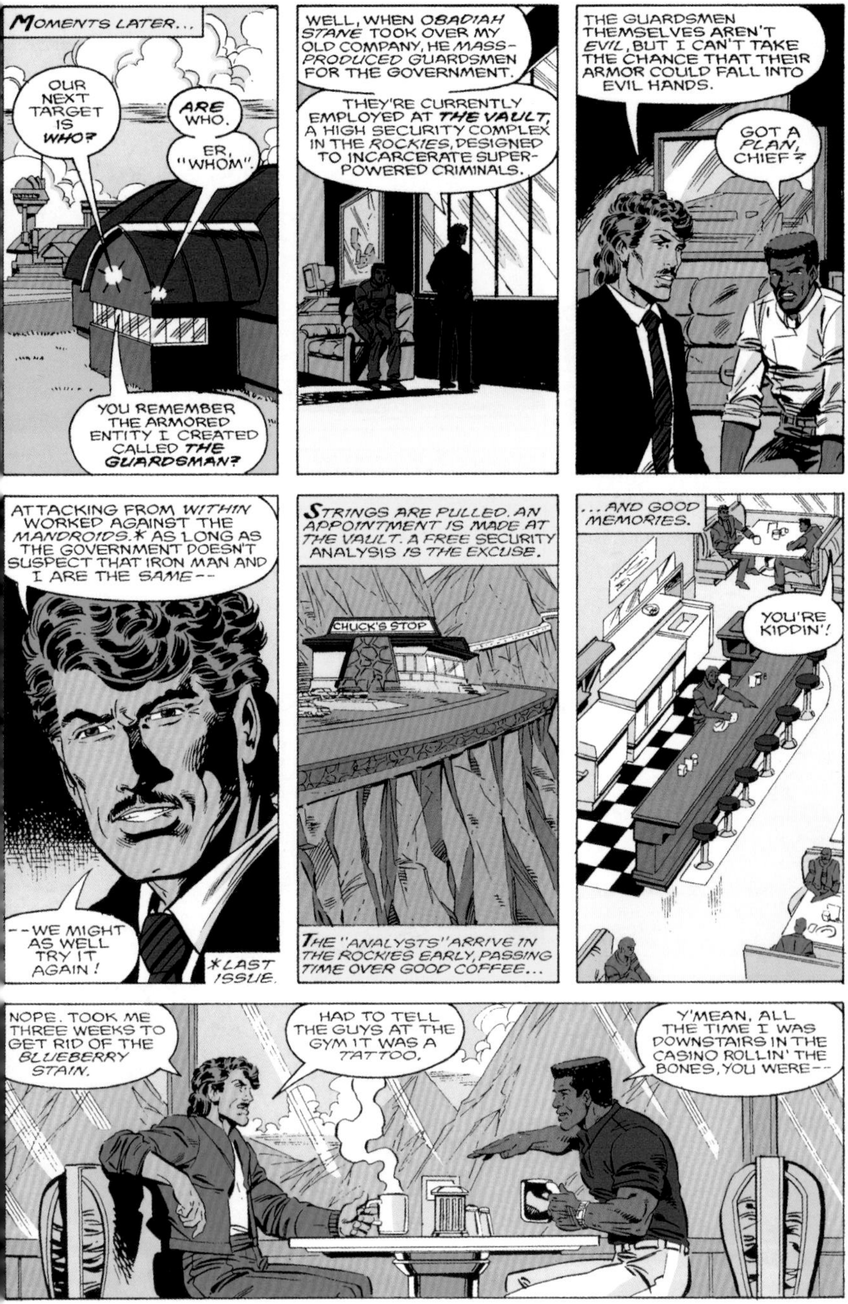
MOMENTS LATER...
OUR NEXT TARGET IS WHO?
ARE WHO.
ER, "WHOM".
YOU REMEMBER THE ARMORED ENTITY I CREATED CALLED THE GUARDSMAN?
WELL, WHEN OBADIAH STANE TOOK OVER MY OLD COMPANY, HE MASS-PRODUCED GUARDSMEN FOR THE GOVERNMENT.
THEY'RE CURRENTLY EMPLOYED AT THE VAULT, A HIGH SECURITY COMPLEX IN THE ROCKIES, DESIGNED TO INCARCERATE SUPER-POWERED CRIMINALS.
THE GUARDSMEN THEMSELVES AREN'T EVIL, BUT I CAN'T TAKE THE CHANCE THAT THEIR ARMOR COULD FALL INTO EVIL HANDS.
GOT A PLAN, CHIEF?
ATTACKING FROM WITHIN WORKED AGAINST THE MANDROIDS.* AS LONG AS THE GOVERNMENT DOESN'T SUSPECT THAT IRON MAN AND I ARE THE SAME--
--WE MIGHT AS WELL TRY IT AGAIN!
*LAST ISSUE.
STRINGS ARE PULLED. AN APPOINTMENT IS MADE AT THE VAULT. A FREE SECURITY ANALYSIS IS THE EXCUSE.
CHUCK'S STOP
THE "ANALYSTS" ARRIVE IN THE ROCKIES EARLY, PASSING TIME OVER GOOD COFFEE...
...AND GOOD MEMORIES.
YOU'RE KIDDIN'!
NOPE. TOOK ME THREE WEEKS TO GET RID OF THE BLUEBERRY STAIN.
HAD TO TELL THE GUYS AT THE GYM IT WAS A TATTOO.
Y'MEAN, ALL THE TIME I WAS DOWNSTAIRS IN THE CASINO ROLLIN' THE BONES, YOU WERE--

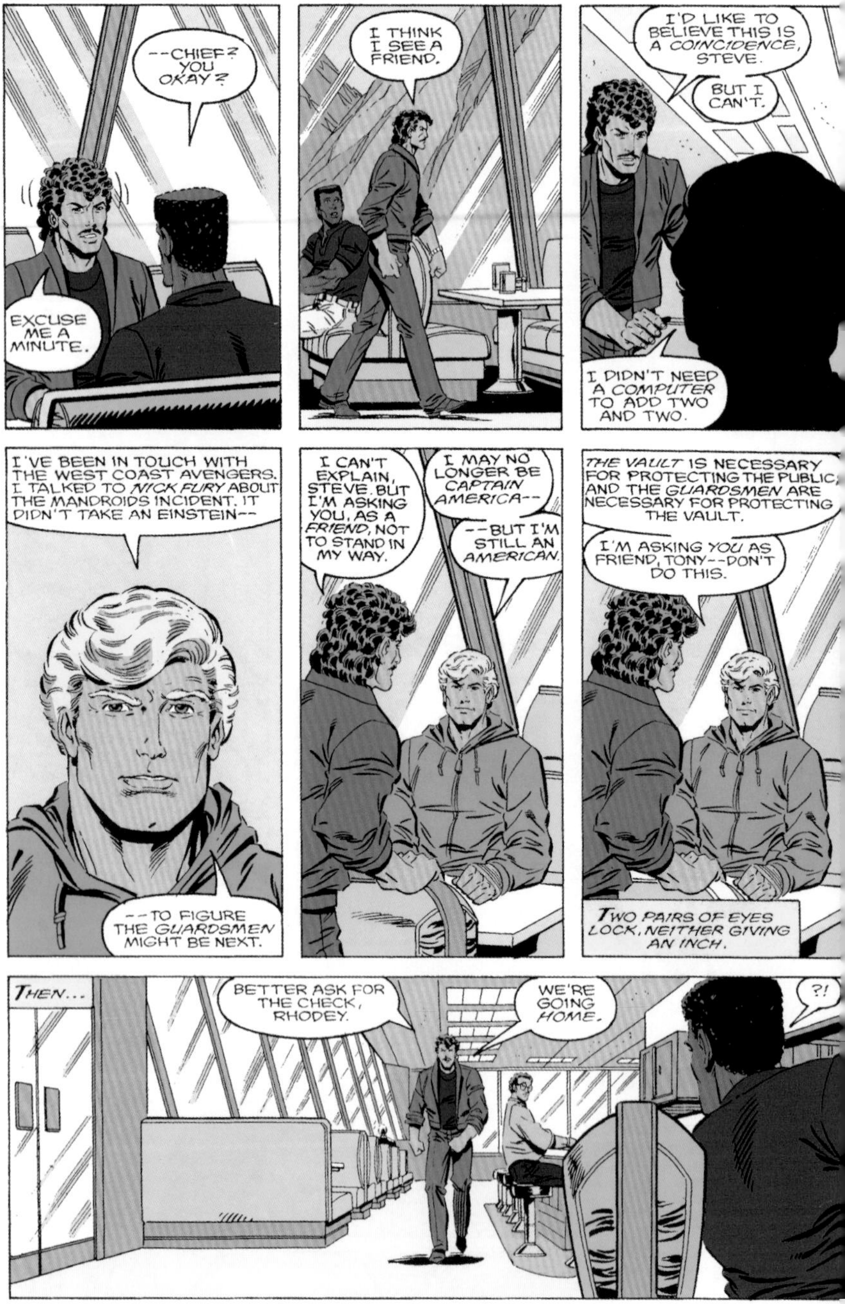
--CHIEF? YOU OKAY?
EXCUSE ME A MINUTE.
I THINK I SEE A FRIEND.
I'D LIKE TO BELIEVE THIS IS A COINCIDENCE, STEVE.
BUT I CAN'T.
I DIDN'T NEED A COMPUTER TO ADD TWO AND TWO.
I'VE BEEN IN TOUCH WITH THE WEST COAST AVENGERS. I TALKED TO NICK FURY ABOUT THE MANDROIDS INCIDENT. IT DIDN'T TAKE AN EINSTEIN--
--TO FIGURE THE GUARDSMEN MIGHT BE NEXT.
I CAN'T EXPLAIN, STEVE. BUT I'M ASKING YOU, AS A FRIEND, NOT TO STAND IN MY WAY.
I MAY NO LONGER BE CAPTAIN AMERICA--
--BUT I'M STILL AN AMERICAN.
THE VAULT IS NECESSARY FOR PROTECTING THE PUBLIC, AND THE GUARDSMEN ARE NECESSARY FOR PROTECTING THE VAULT.
I'M ASKING YOU AS FRIEND, TONY--DON'T DO THIS.
TWO PAIRS OF EYES LOCK, NEITHER GIVING AN INCH.
THEN...
BETTER ASK FOR THE CHECK, RHODEY.
WE'RE GOING HOME.
?!

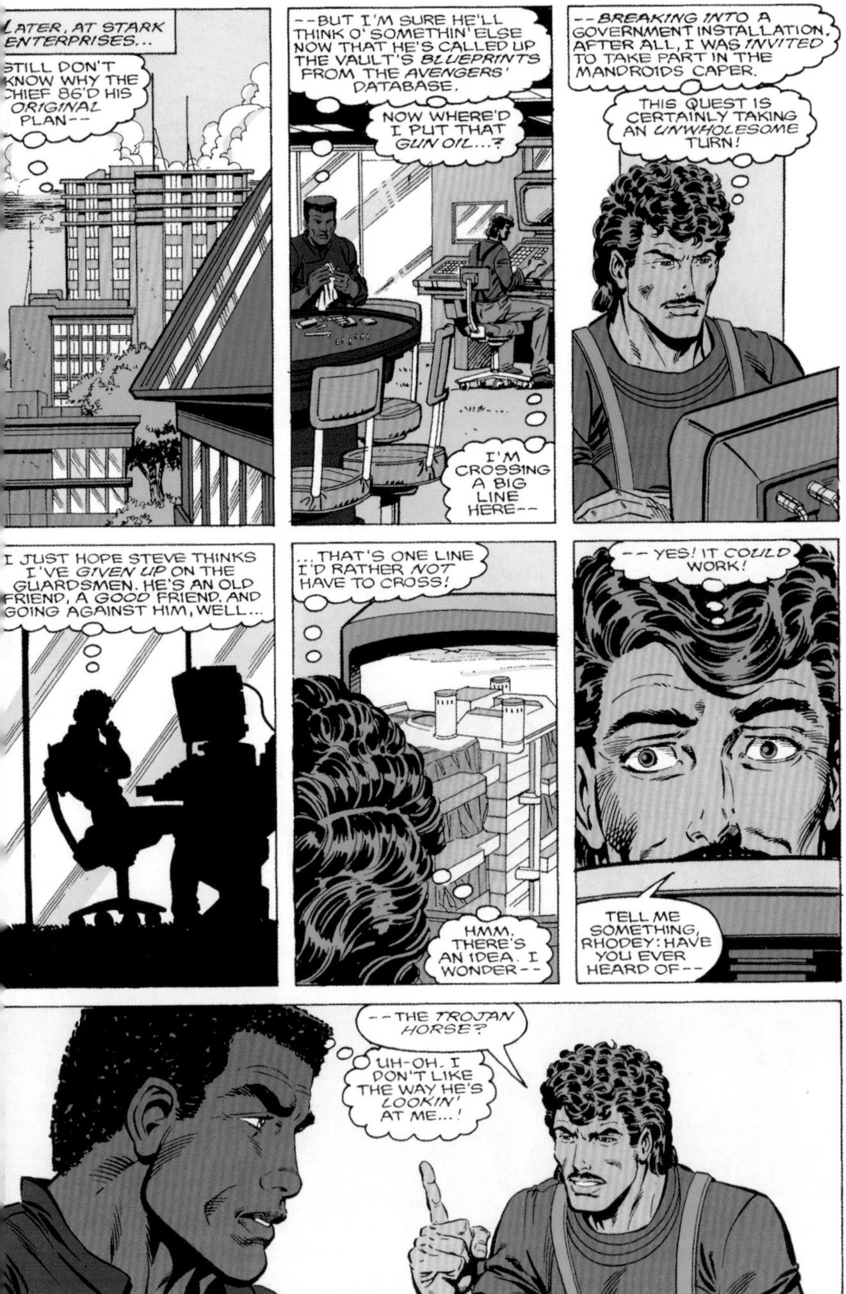
LATER, AT STARK ENTERPRISES...
STILL DON'T KNOW WHY THE CHIEF 86'D HIS ORIGINAL PLAN--
--BUT I'M SURE HE'LL THINK O' SOMETHIN' ELSE NOW THAT HE'S CALLED UP THE VAULT'S BLUEPRINTS FROM THE AVENGERS' DATABASE.
NOW WHERE'D I PUT THAT GUN OIL...?
I'M CROSSING A BIG LINE HERE--
--BREAKING INTO A GOVERNMENT INSTALLATION. AFTER ALL, I WAS INVITED TO TAKE PART IN THE MANDROIDS CAPER.
THIS QUEST IS CERTAINLY TAKING AN UNWHOLESOME TURN!
I JUST HOPE STEVE THINKS I'VE GIVEN UP ON THE GUARDSMEN. HE'S AN OLD FRIEND, A GOOD FRIEND, AND GOING AGAINST HIM, WELL...
...THAT'S ONE LINE I'D RATHER NOT HAVE TO CROSS!
HMM. THERE'S AN IDEA. I WONDER--
--YES! IT COULD WORK!
TELL ME SOMETHING, RHODEY: HAVE YOU EVER HEARD OF--
--THE TROJAN HORSE?
UH-OH. I DON'T LIKE THE WAY HE'S LOOKIN' AT ME...!

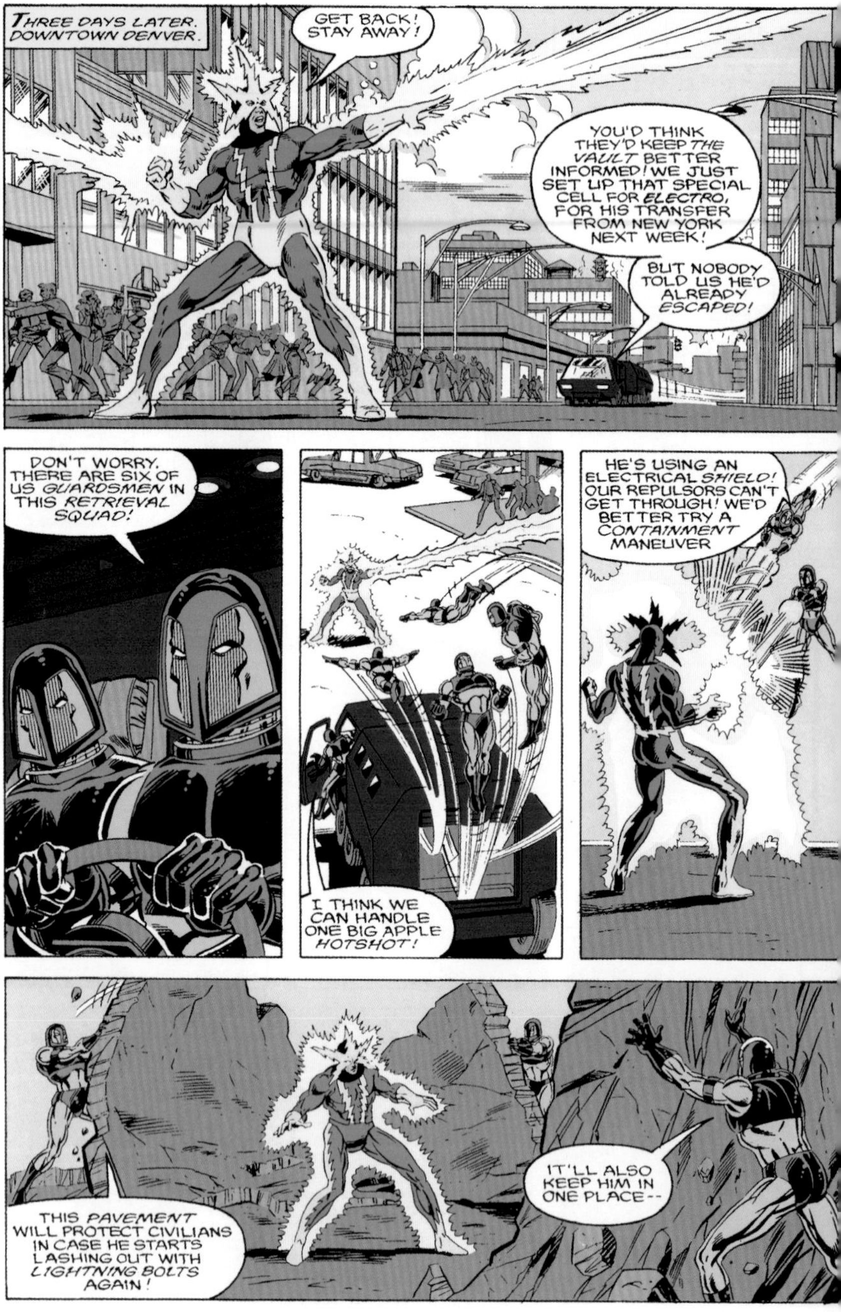

THREE DAYS LATER. DOWNTOWN DENVER.
GET BACK! STAY AWAY!
YOU'D THINK THEY'D KEEP THE VAULT BETTER INFORMED! WE JUST SET UP THAT SPECIAL CELL FOR ELECTRO, FOR HIS TRANSFER FROM NEW YORK NEXT WEEK!
BUT NOBODY TOLD US HE'D ALREADY ESCAPED!
DON'T WORRY. THERE ARE SIX OF US GUARDSMEN IN THIS RETRIEVAL SQUAD!
I THINK WE CAN HANDLE ONE BIG APPLE HOTSHOT!
HE'S USING AN ELECTRICAL SHIELD! OUR REPULSORS CAN'T GET THROUGH! WE'D BETTER TRY A CONTAINMENT MANEUVER
THIS PAVEMENT WILL PROTECT CIVILIANS IN CASE HE STARTS LASHING OUT WITH LIGHTNING BOLTS AGAIN!
IT'LL ALSO KEEP HIM IN ONE PLACE--

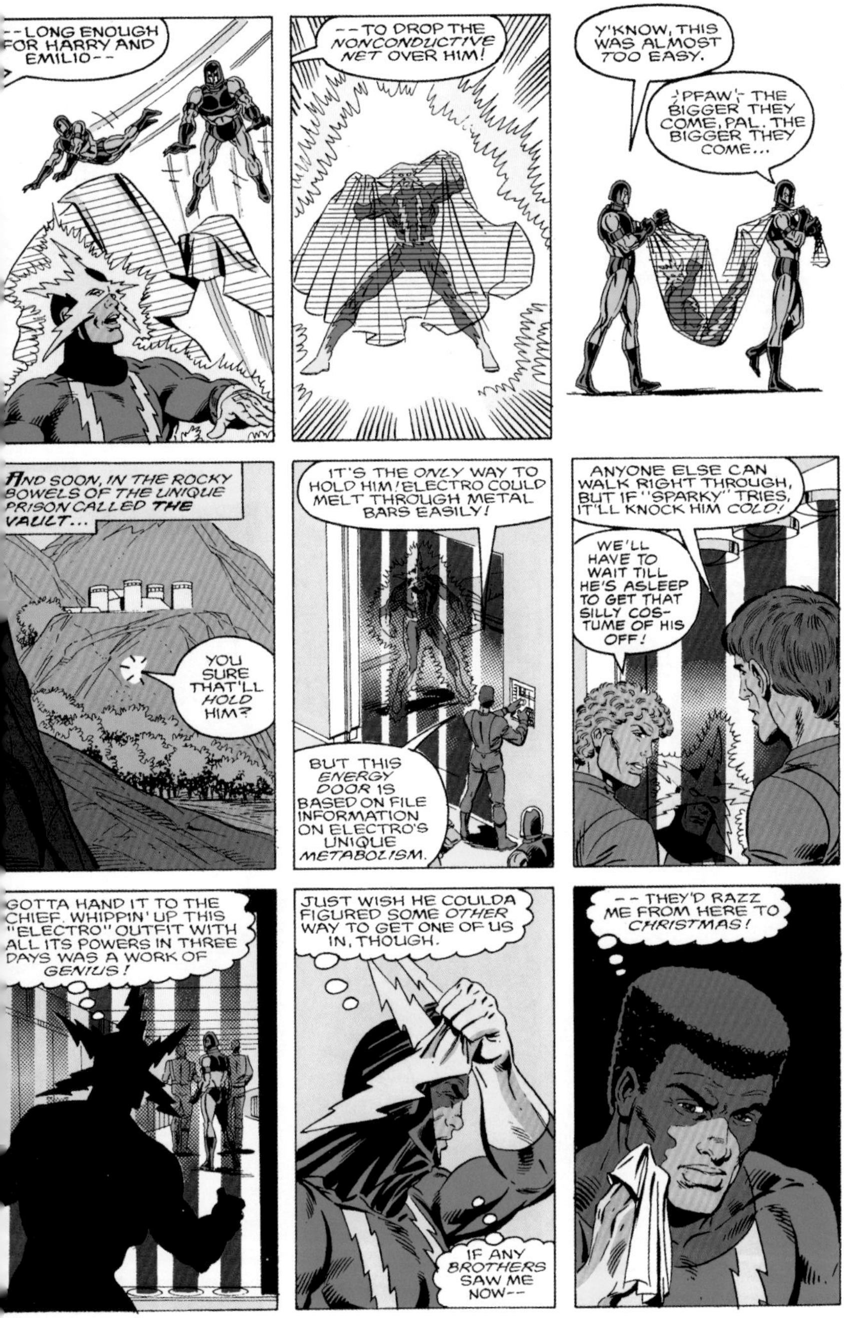

--LONG ENOUGH FOR HARRY AND EMILIO--
--TO DROP THE NONCONDUCTIVE NET OVER HIM!
Y'KNOW, THIS WAS ALMOST TOO EASY.
PFAW! THE BIGGER THEY COME, PAL. THE BIGGER THEY COME...
AND SOON, IN THE ROCKY BOWELS OF THE UNIQUE PRISON CALLED THE VAULT...
YOU SURE THAT'LL HOLD HIM?
IT'S THE ONLY WAY TO HOLD HIM! ELECTRO COULD MELT THROUGH METAL BARS EASILY!
BUT THIS ENERGY DOOR IS BASED ON FILE INFORMATION ON ELECTRO'S UNIQUE METABOLISM.
ANYONE ELSE CAN WALK RIGHT THROUGH, BUT IF "SPARKY" TRIES, IT'LL KNOCK HIM COLD!
WE'LL HAVE TO WAIT TILL HE'S ASLEEP TO GET THAT SILLY COSTUME OF HIS OFF!
GOTTA HAND IT TO THE CHIEF. WHIPPIN' UP THIS "ELECTRO" OUTFIT WITH ALL ITS POWERS IN THREE DAYS WAS A WORK OF GENIUS!
JUST WISH HE COULDA FIGURED SOME OTHER WAY TO GET ONE OF US IN, THOUGH.
IF ANY BROTHERS SAW ME NOW--
--THEY'D RAZZ ME FROM HERE TO CHRISTMAS!

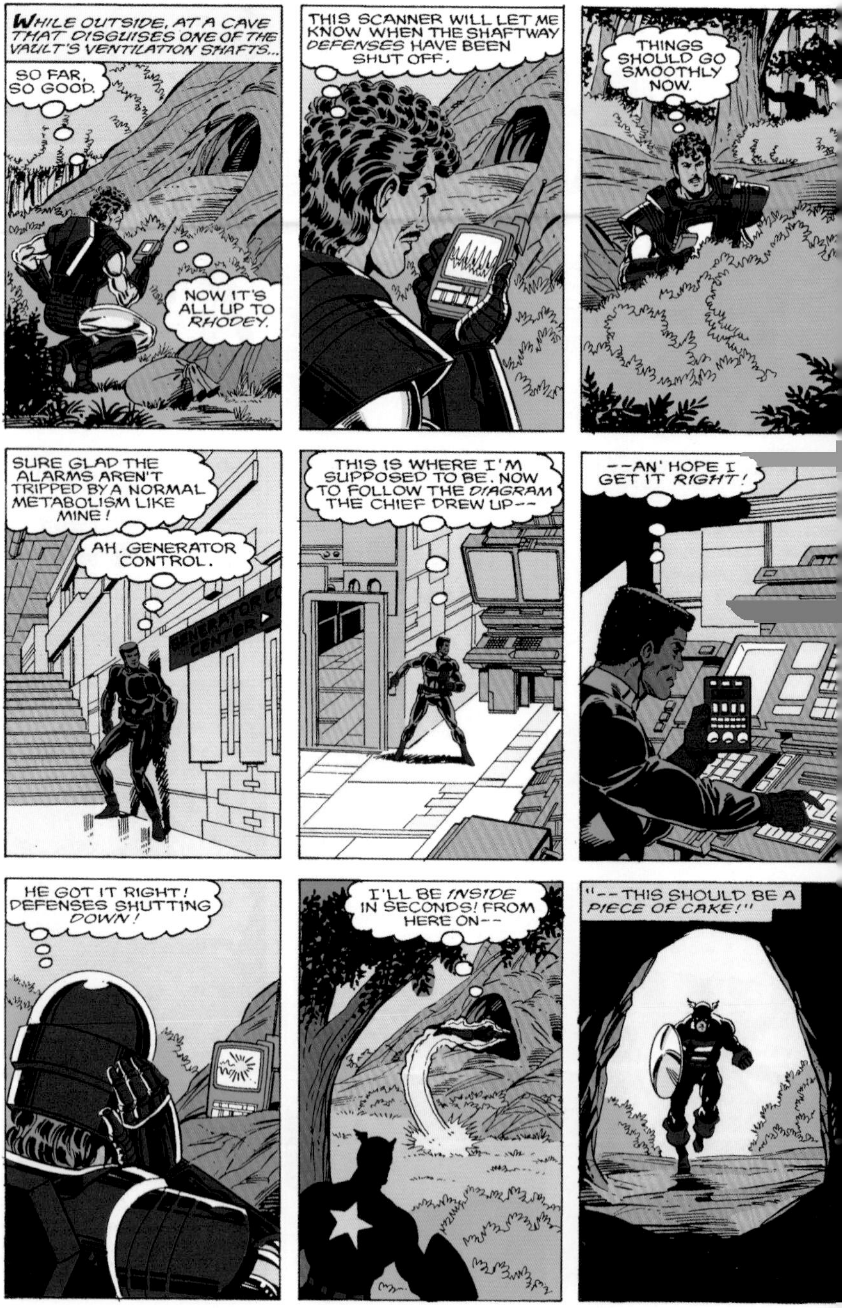
WHILE OUTSIDE, AT A CAVE THAT DISGUISES ONE OF THE VAULT'S VENTILATION SHAFTS...
SO FAR, SO GOOD.
NOW IT'S ALL UP TO RHODEY.
THIS SCANNER WILL LET ME KNOW WHEN THE SHAFTWAY DEFENSES HAVE BEEN SHUT OFF.
THINGS SHOULD GO SMOOTHLY NOW.
SURE GLAD THE ALARMS AREN'T TRIPPED BY A NORMAL METABOLISM LIKE MINE!
AH. GENERATOR CONTROL.
THIS IS WHERE I'M SUPPOSED TO BE. NOW TO FOLLOW THE DIAGRAM THE CHIEF DREW UP--
--AN' HOPE I GET IT RIGHT!
HE GOT IT RIGHT! DEFENSES SHUTTING DOWN!
I'LL BE INSIDE IN SECONDS! FROM HERE ON--
"--THIS SHOULD BE A PIECE OF CAKE!"

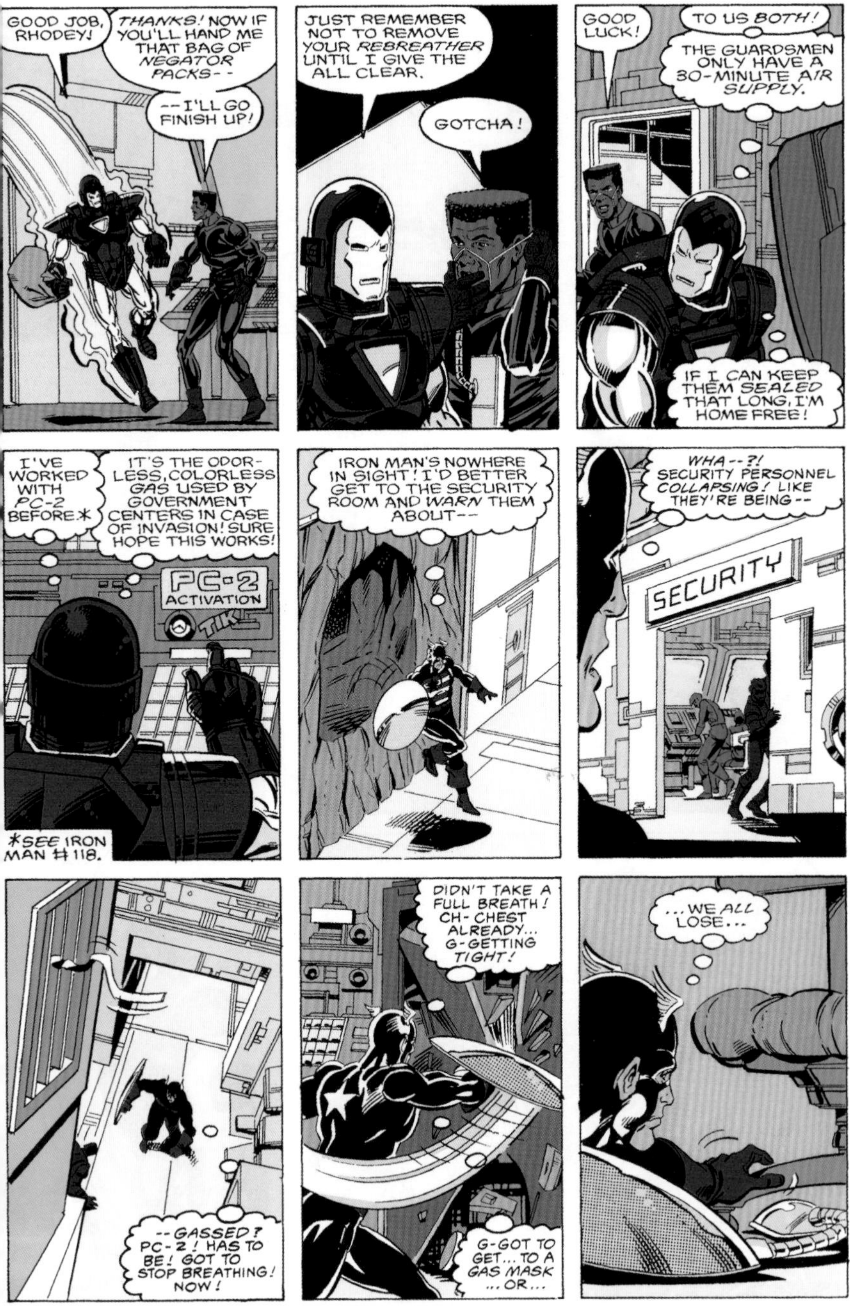
GOOD JOB, RHODEY!
THANKS! NOW IF YOU'LL HAND ME THAT BAG OF NEGATOR PACKS--
--I'LL GO FINISH UP!
JUST REMEMBER NOT TO REMOVE YOUR REBREATHER UNTIL I GIVE THE ALL CLEAR.
GOTCHA!
GOOD LUCK!
TO US BOTH!
THE GUARDSMEN ONLY HAVE A 30-MINUTE AIR SUPPLY.
IF I CAN KEEP THEM SEALED THAT LONG, I'M HOME FREE!
I'VE WORKED WITH PC-2 BEFORE.*
IT'S THE ODORLESS, COLORLESS GAS USED BY GOVERNMENT CENTERS IN CASE OF INVASION! SURE HOPE THIS WORKS!
PC-2 ACTIVATION
TIK
*SEE IRON MAN #118.
IRON MAN'S NOWHERE IN SIGHT! I'D BETTER GET TO THE SECURITY ROOM AND WARN THEM ABOUT--
WHA--?! SECURITY PERSONNEL COLLAPSING! LIKE THEY'RE BEING--
SECURITY
--GASSED? PC-2! HAS TO BE! GOT TO STOP BREATHING! NOW!
DIDN'T TAKE A FULL BREATH! CH-CHEST ALREADY... G-GETTING TIGHT!
G-GOT TO GET... TO A GAS MASK ...OR...
...WE ALL LOSE...

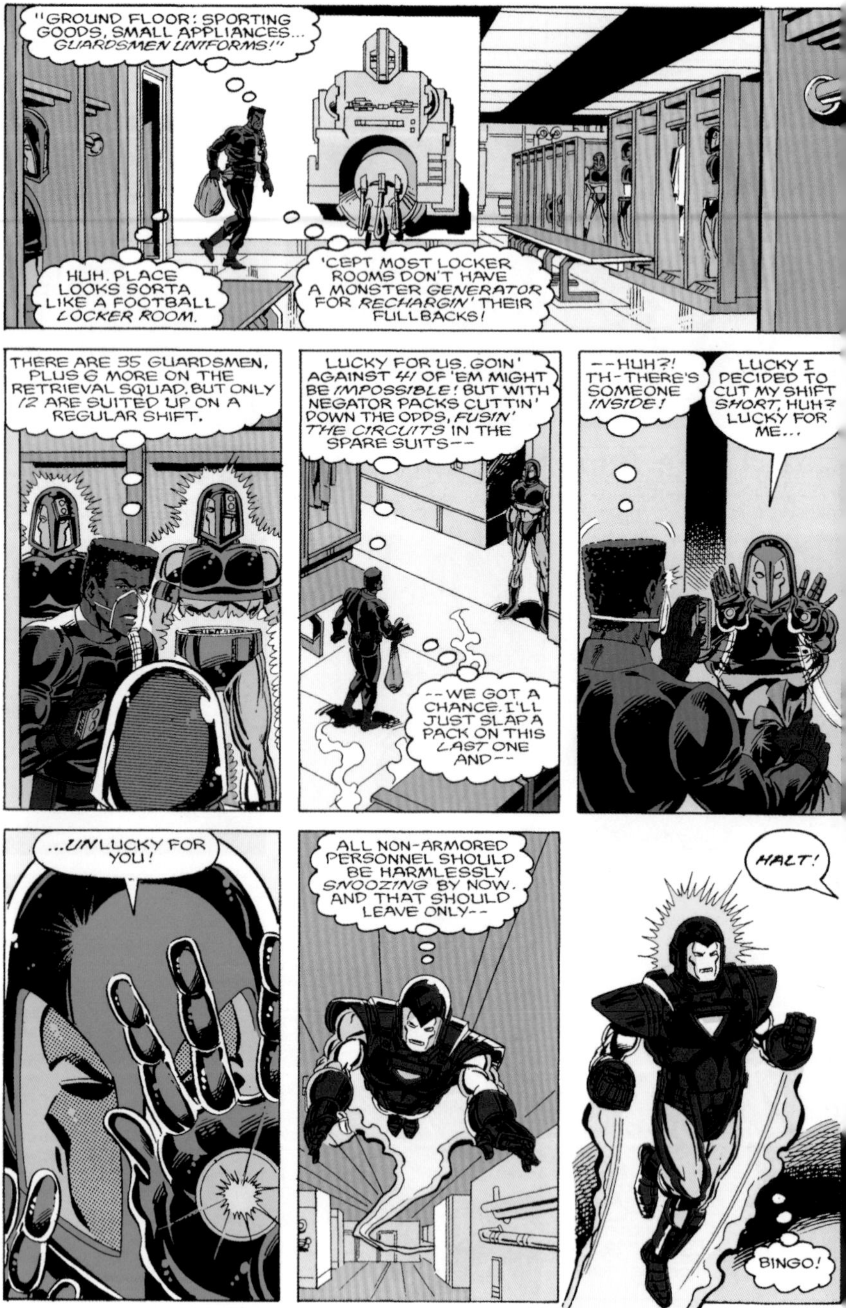
"GROUND FLOOR: SPORTING GOODS, SMALL APPLIANCES... GUARDSMEN UNIFORMS!"
HUH. PLACE LOOKS SORTA LIKE A FOOTBALL LOCKER ROOM.
'CEPT MOST LOCKER ROOMS DON'T HAVE A MONSTER GENERATOR FOR RECHARGIN' THEIR FULLBACKS!
THERE ARE 35 GUARDSMEN, PLUS 6 MORE ON THE RETRIEVAL SQUAD. BUT ONLY 12 ARE SUITED UP ON A REGULAR SHIFT.
LUCKY FOR US. GOIN' AGAINST 41 OF 'EM MIGHT BE IMPOSSIBLE! BUT WITH NEGATOR PACKS CUTTIN' DOWN THE ODDS, FUSIN' THE CIRCUITS IN THE SPARE SUITS--
--WE GOT A CHANCE. I'LL JUST SLAP A PACK ON THIS LAST ONE AND--
--HUH?! TH-THERE'S SOMEONE INSIDE!
LUCKY I DECIDED TO CUT MY SHIFT SHORT, HUH? LUCKY FOR ME...
...UNLUCKY FOR YOU!
ALL NON-ARMORED PERSONNEL SHOULD BE HARMLESSLY SNOOZING BY NOW. AND THAT SHOULD LEAVE ONLY--
HALT!
BINGO!

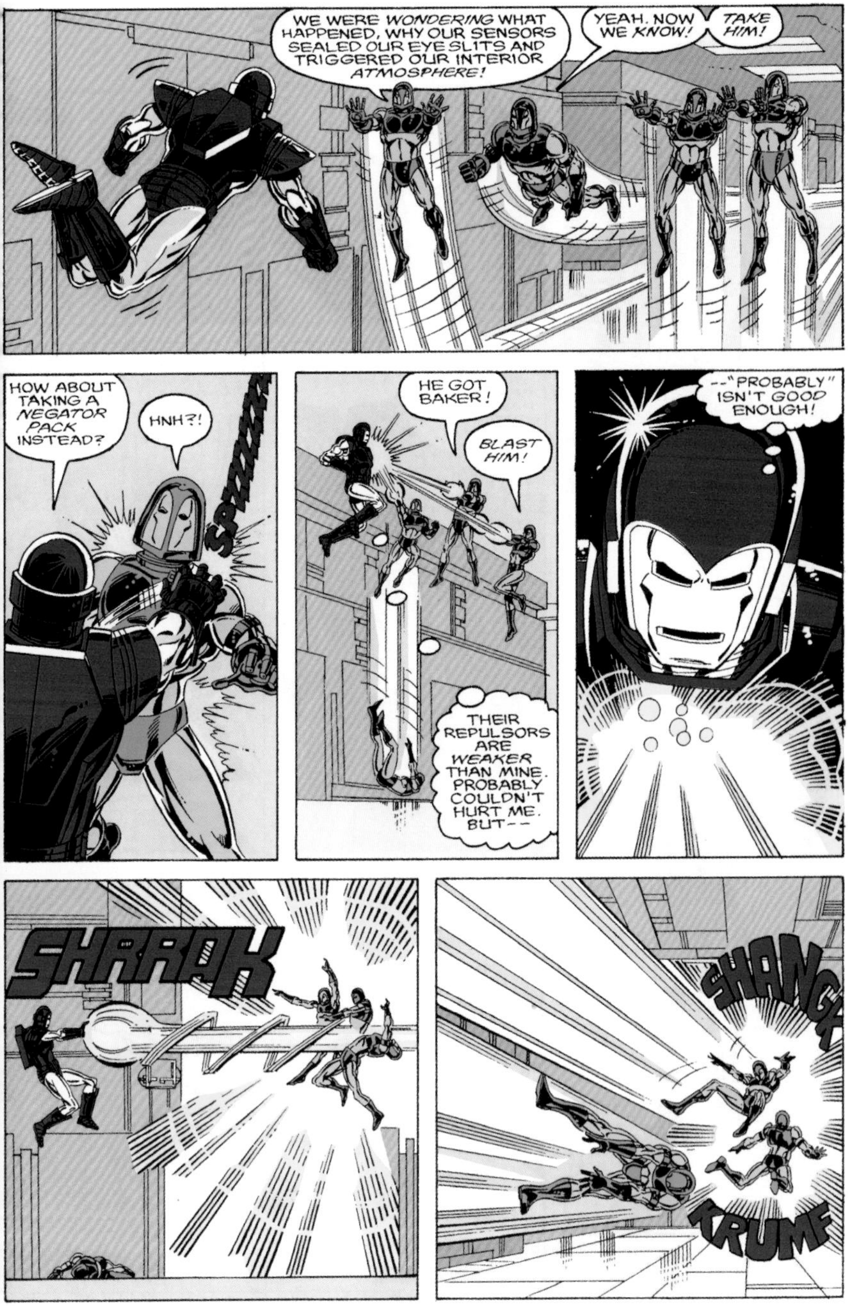
WE WERE WONDERING WHAT HAPPENED, WHY OUR SENSORS SEALED OUR EYE SLITS AND TRIGGERED OUR INTERIOR ATMOSPHERE!
YEAH. NOW WE KNOW!
TAKE HIM!
HOW ABOUT TAKING A NEGATOR PACK INSTEAD?
HNH?!
HE GOT BAKER!
BLAST HIM!
THEIR REPULSORS ARE WEAKER THAN MINE. PROBABLY COULDN'T HURT ME. BUT--
--"PROBABLY" ISN'T GOOD ENOUGH!
SHRAAK
SHANGK
KRUMF

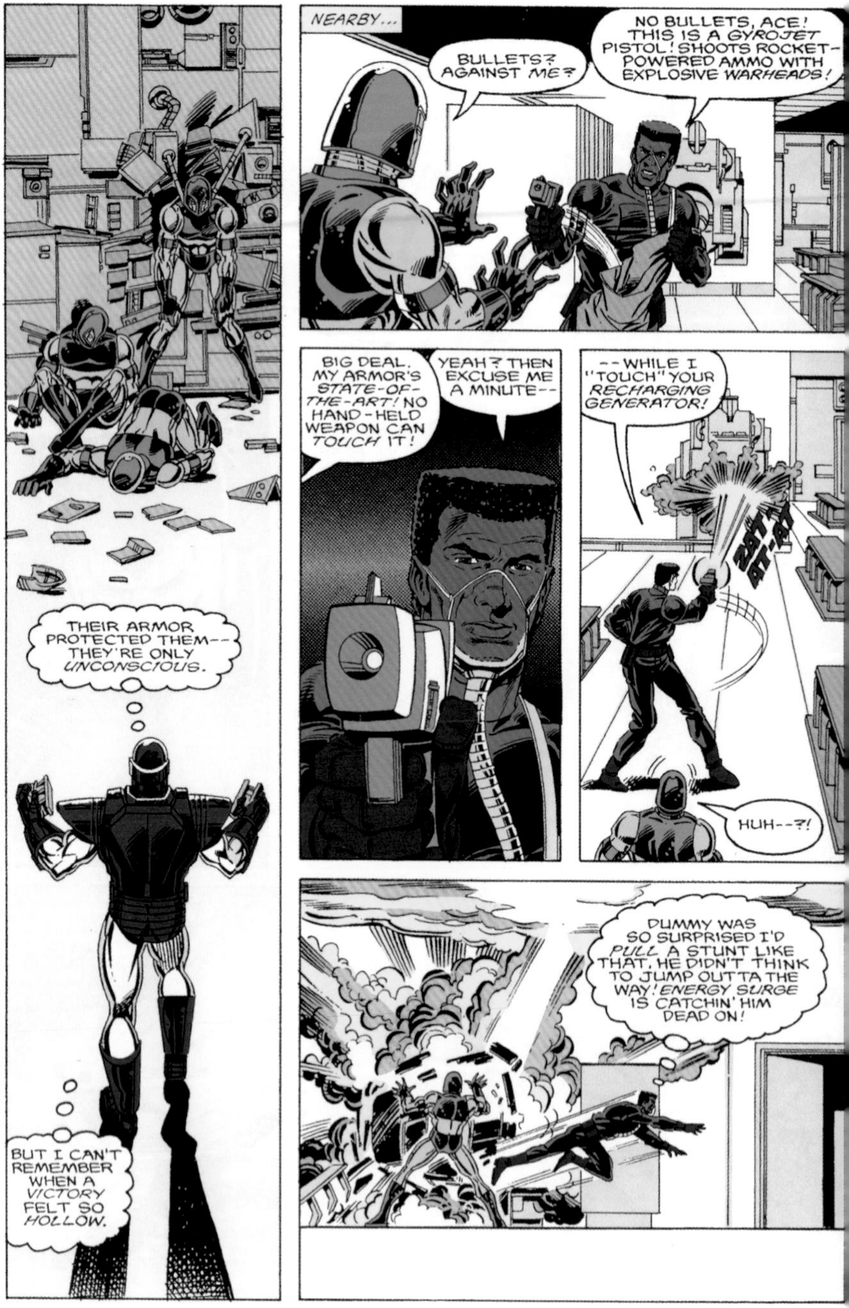
THEIR ARMOR PROTECTED THEM-- THEY'RE ONLY UNCONSCIOUS.
BUT I CAN'T REMEMBER WHEN A VICTORY FELT SO HOLLOW.
NEARBY...
BULLETS? AGAINST ME?
NO BULLETS, ACE! THIS IS A GYROJET PISTOL! SHOOTS ROCKET-POWERED AMMO WITH EXPLOSIVE WARHEADS!
BIG DEAL. MY ARMOR'S STATE-OF-THE-ART! NO HAND-HELD WEAPON CAN TOUCH IT!
YEAH? THEN EXCUSE ME A MINUTE--
--WHILE I "TOUCH" YOUR RECHARGING GENERATOR!
HUH--?!
DUMMY WAS SO SURPRISED I'D PULL A STUNT LIKE THAT, HE DIDN'T THINK TO JUMP OUTTA THE WAY! ENERGY SURGE IS CATCHIN' HIM DEAD ON!

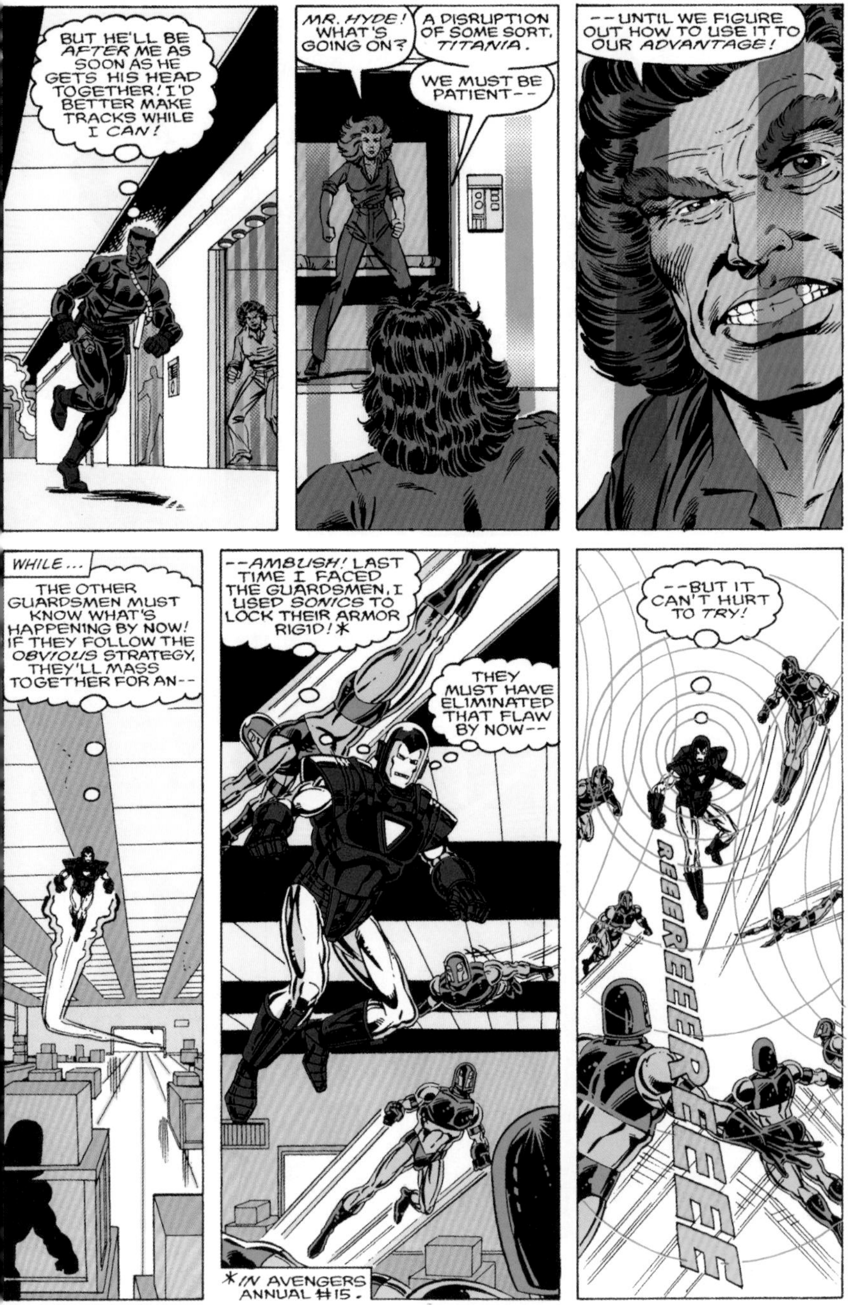
BUT HE'LL BE AFTER ME AS SOON AS HE GETS HIS HEAD TOGETHER! I'D BETTER MAKE TRACKS WHILE I CAN!
MR. HYDE! WHAT'S GOING ON?
A DISRUPTION OF SOME SORT, TITANIA.
WE MUST BE PATIENT--
--UNTIL WE FIGURE OUT HOW TO USE IT TO OUR ADVANTAGE!
WHILE...
THE OTHER GUARDSMEN MUST KNOW WHAT'S HAPPENING BY NOW! IF THEY FOLLOW THE OBVIOUS STRATEGY, THEY'LL MASS TOGETHER FOR AN--
--AMBUSH! LAST TIME I FACED THE GUARDSMEN, I USED SONICS TO LOCK THEIR ARMOR RIGID! *
THEY MUST HAVE ELIMINATED THAT FLAW BY NOW--
*IN AVENGERS ANNUAL #15.
--BUT IT CAN'T HURT TO TRY!
REEEREEEREEEEE

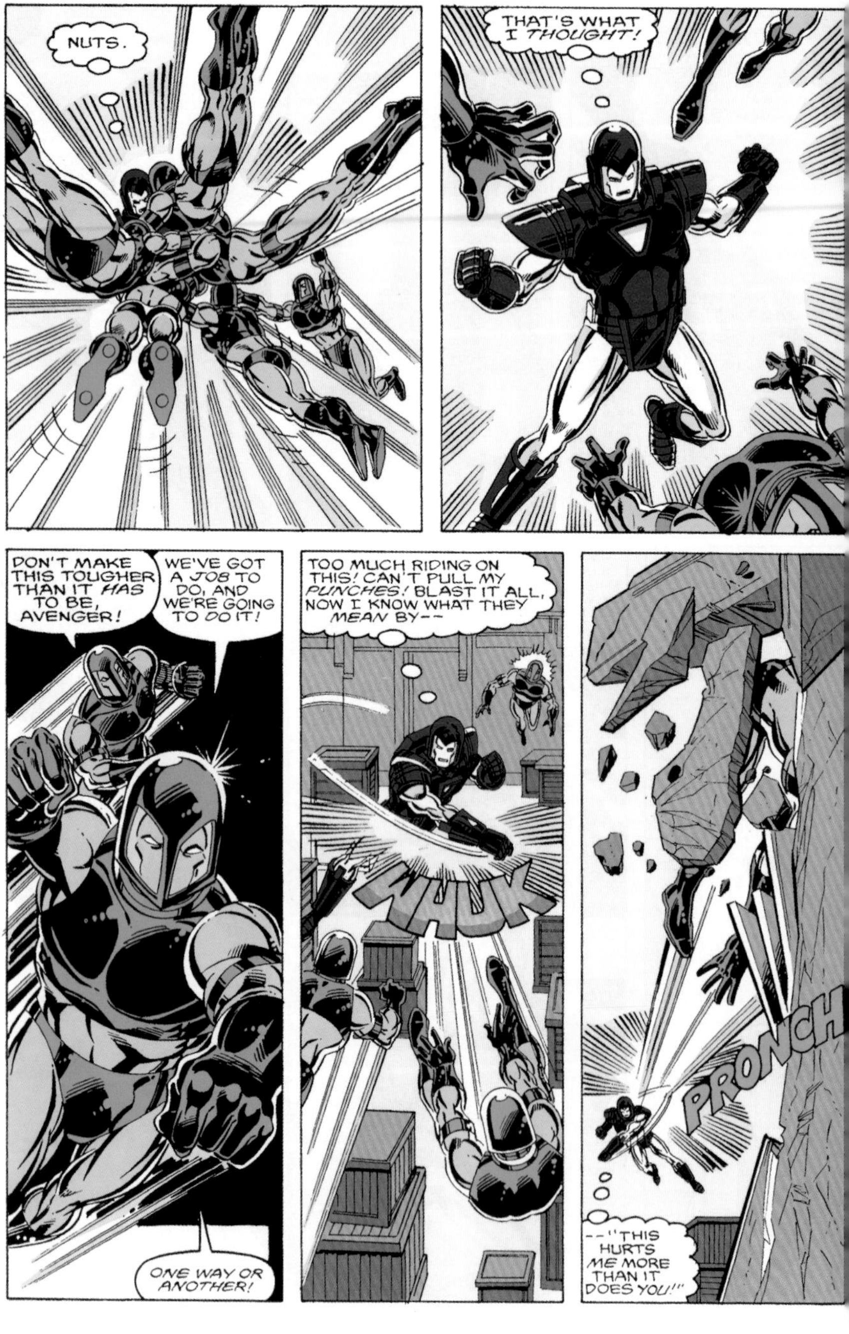
NUTS.
THAT'S WHAT I THOUGHT!
DON'T MAKE THIS TOUGHER THAN IT HAS TO BE, AVENGER!
WE'VE GOT A JOB TO DO, AND WE'RE GOING TO DO IT!
ONE WAY OR ANOTHER!
TOO MUCH RIDING ON THIS! CAN'T PULL MY PUNCHES! BLAST IT ALL, NOW I KNOW WHAT THEY MEAN BY--
WHUK
PRONCH
--"THIS HURTS ME MORE THAN IT DOES YOU!"

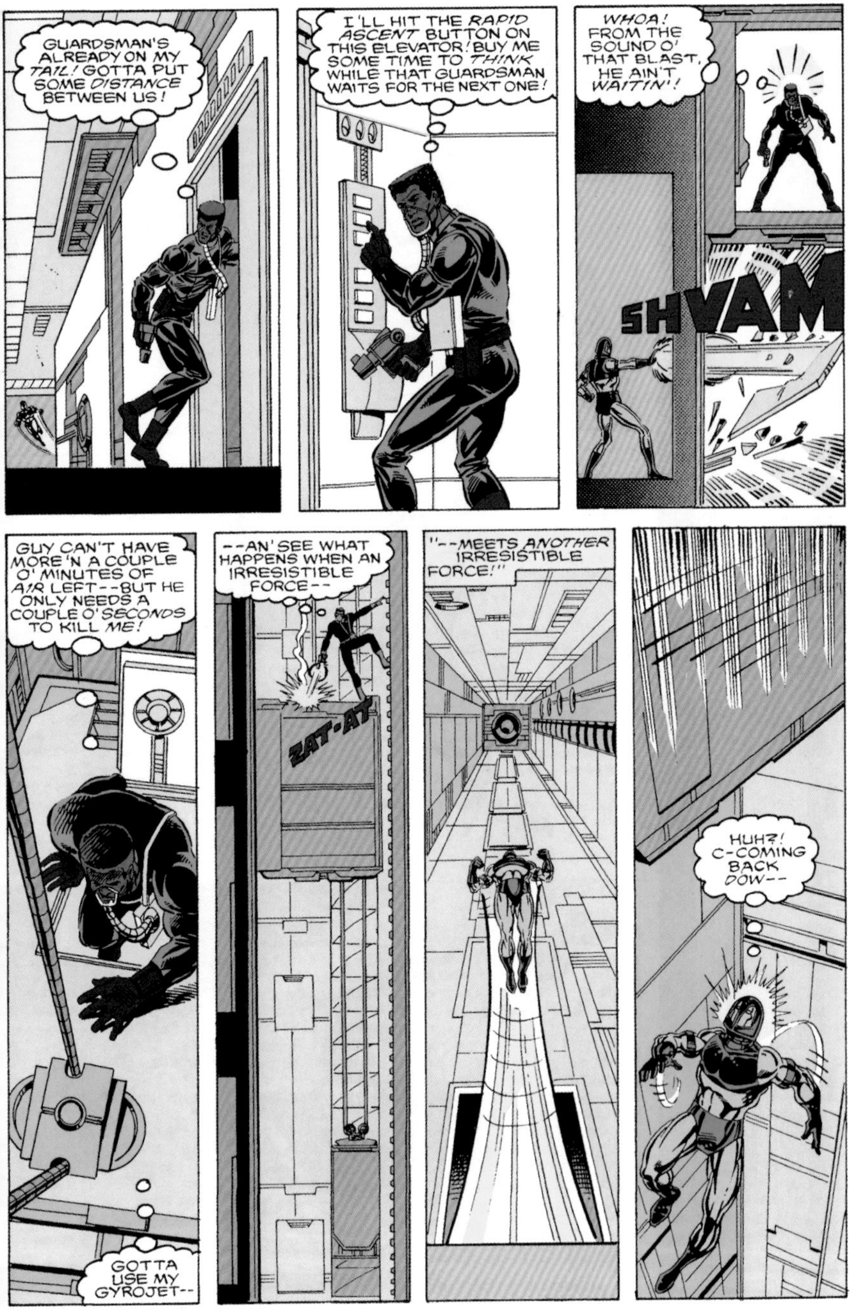
GUARDSMAN'S ALREADY ON MY TAIL! GOTTA PUT SOME DISTANCE BETWEEN US!
I'LL HIT THE RAPID ASCENT BUTTON ON THIS ELEVATOR! BUY ME SOME TIME TO THINK WHILE THAT GUARDSMAN WAITS FOR THE NEXT ONE!
WHOA! FROM THE SOUND O' THAT BLAST, HE AIN'T WAITIN'!
SHVAM
GUY CAN'T HAVE MORE 'N A COUPLE O' MINUTES OF AIR LEFT--BUT HE ONLY NEEDS A COUPLE O' SECONDS TO KILL ME!
GOTTA USE MY GYROJET--
--AN' SEE WHAT HAPPENS WHEN AN IRRESISTIBLE FORCE--
ZAT-AT
"--MEETS ANOTHER IRRESISTIBLE FORCE!"
HUH?! C-COMING BACK DOW--

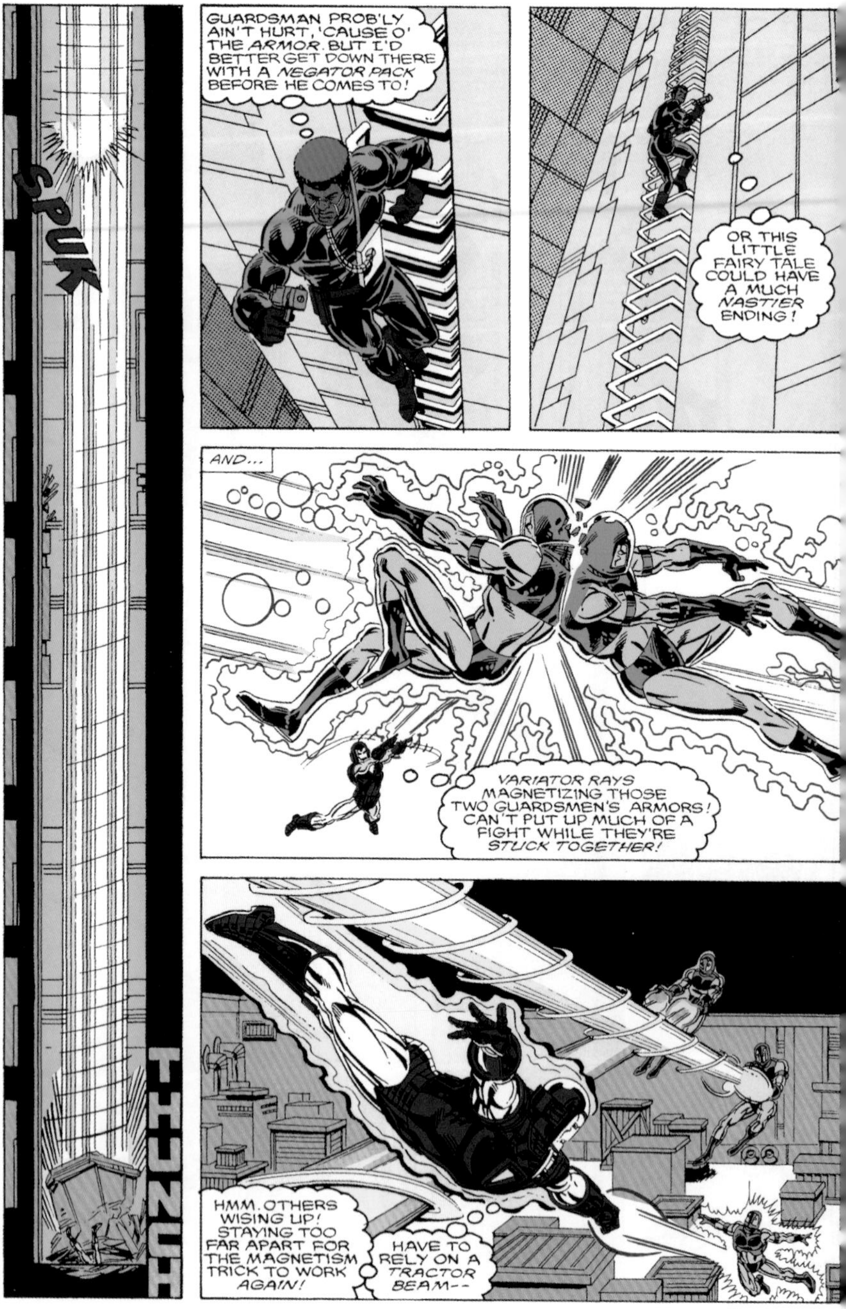
SPUK
THUNCH
GUARDSMAN PROB'LY AIN'T HURT, 'CAUSE O' THE ARMOR. BUT I'D BETTER GET DOWN THERE WITH A NEGATOR PACK BEFORE HE COMES TO!
OR THIS LITTLE FAIRY TALE COULD HAVE A MUCH NASTIER ENDING!
AND...
VARIATOR RAYS MAGNETIZING THOSE TWO GUARDSMEN'S ARMORS! CAN'T PUT UP MUCH OF A FIGHT WHILE THEY'RE STUCK TOGETHER!
HMM. OTHERS WISING UP! STAYING TOO FAR APART FOR THE MAGNETISM TRICK TO WORK AGAIN!
HAVE TO RELY ON A TRACTOR BEAM--

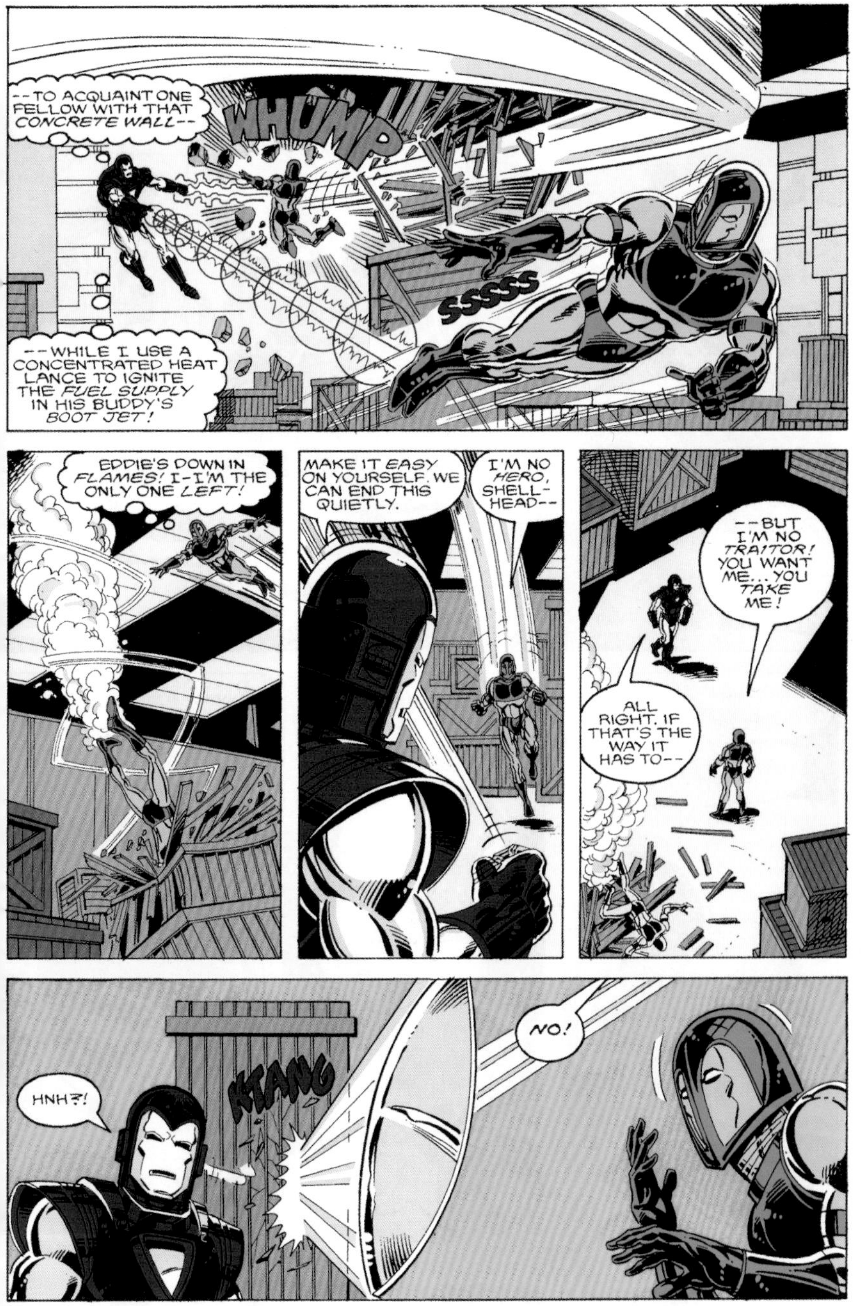
--TO ACQUAINT ONE FELLOW WITH THAT CONCRETE WALL--
WHUMP
--WHILE I USE A CONCENTRATED HEAT LANCE TO IGNITE THE FUEL SUPPLY IN HIS BUDDY'S BOOT JET!
SSSSS
EDDIE'S DOWN IN FLAMES! I-I'M THE ONLY ONE LEFT!
MAKE IT EASY ON YOURSELF. WE CAN END THIS QUIETLY.
I'M NO HERO, SHELL-HEAD--
--BUT I'M NO TRAITOR! YOU WANT ME... YOU TAKE ME!
ALL RIGHT. IF THAT'S THE WAY IT HAS TO--
NO!
HNH?!
KTANG

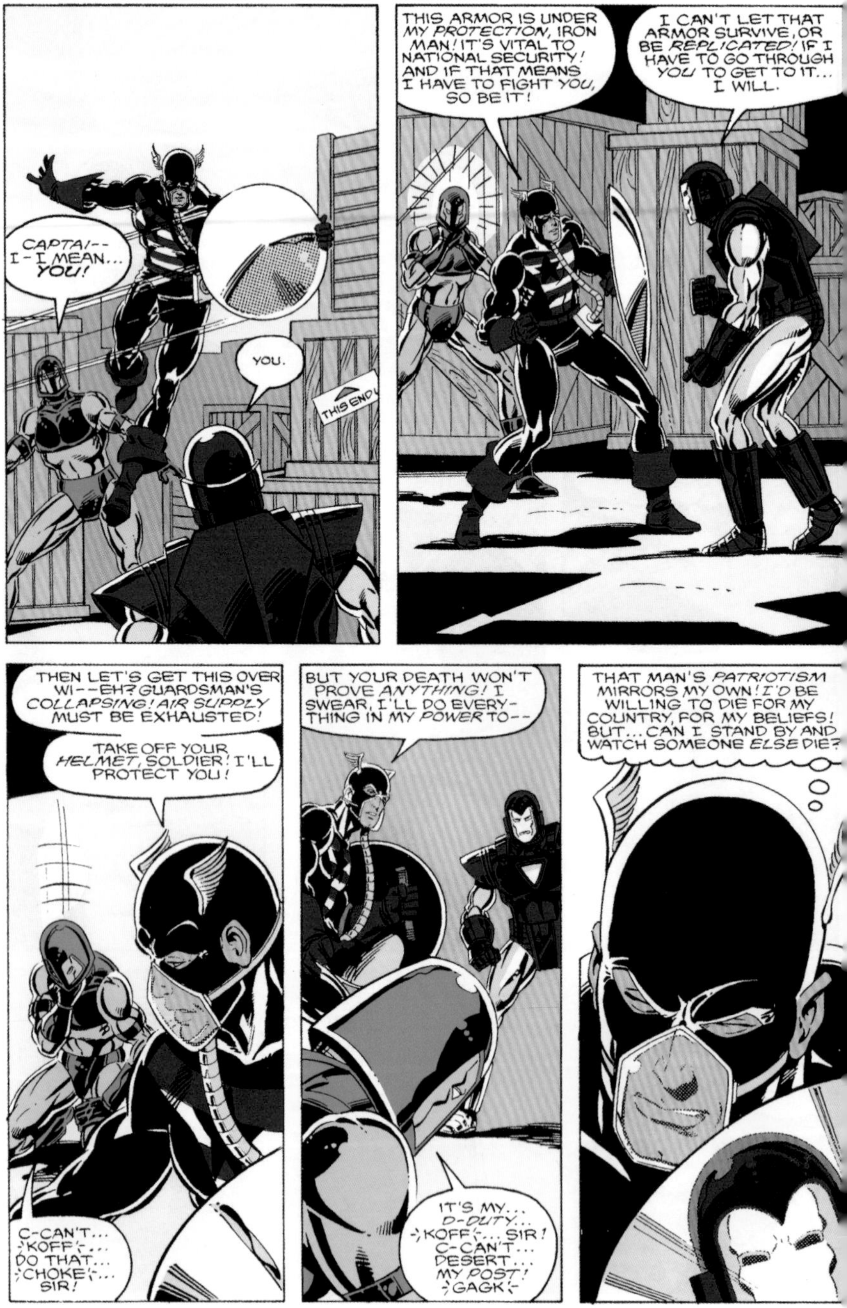

CAPTAI-- I-I MEAN... YOU!
YOU.
THIS END
THIS ARMOR IS UNDER MY PROTECTION, IRON MAN! IT'S VITAL TO NATIONAL SECURITY! AND IF THAT MEANS I HAVE TO FIGHT YOU, SO BE IT!
I CAN'T LET THAT ARMOR SURVIVE, OR BE REPLICATED! IF I HAVE TO GO THROUGH YOU TO GET TO IT... I WILL.
THEN LET'S GET THIS OVER WI--EH? GUARDSMAN'S COLLAPSING! AIR SUPPLY MUST BE EXHAUSTED!
TAKE OFF YOUR HELMET, SOLDIER! I'LL PROTECT YOU!
C-CAN'T... *KOFF*... DO THAT... *CHOKE*... SIR!
BUT YOUR DEATH WON'T PROVE ANYTHING! I SWEAR, I'LL DO EVERYTHING IN MY POWER TO--
IT'S MY... D-DUTY... *KOFF*... SIR! C-CAN'T... DESERT... MY POST! *GAGK*
THAT MAN'S PATRIOTISM MIRRORS MY OWN! I'D BE WILLING TO DIE FOR MY COUNTRY, FOR MY BELIEFS! BUT... CAN I STAND BY AND WATCH SOMEONE ELSE DIE?

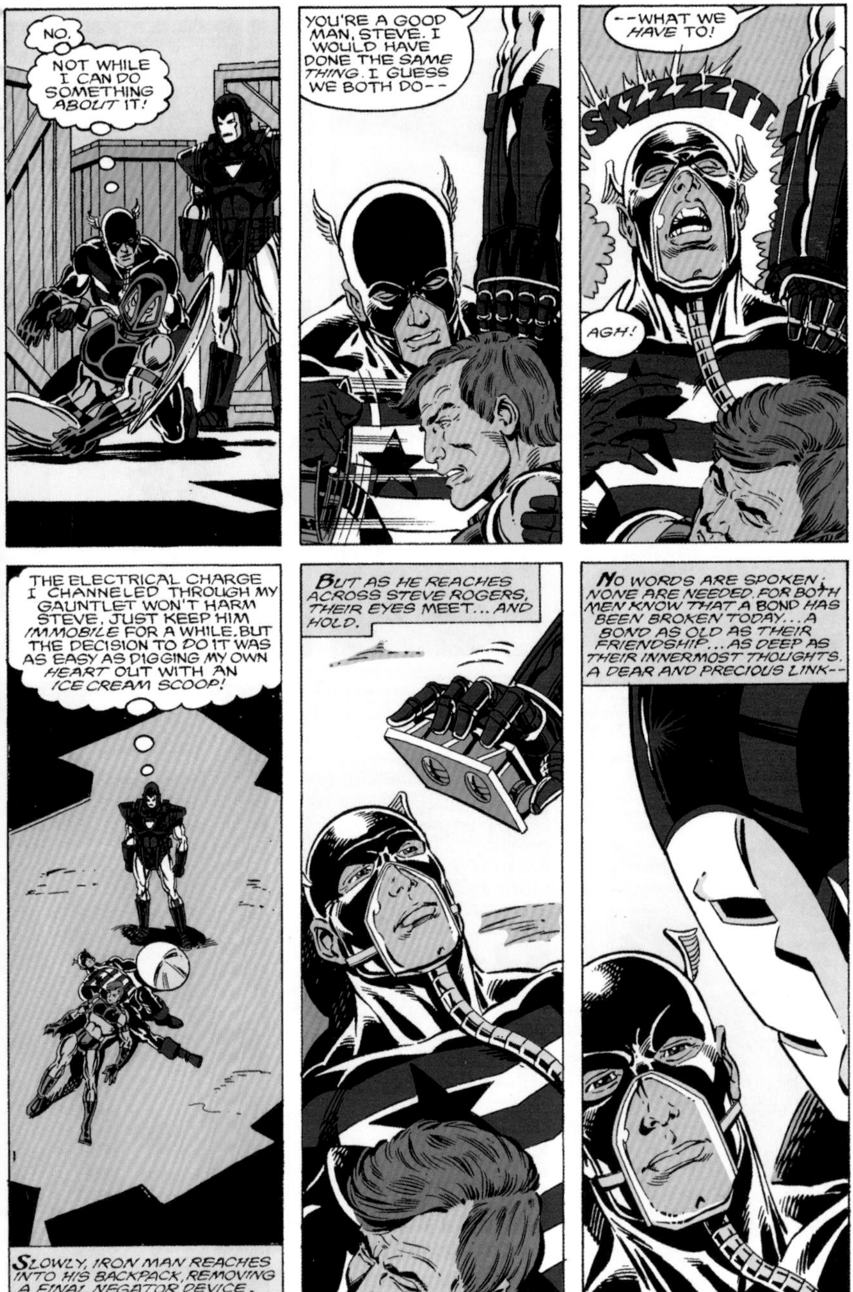

NO.
NOT WHILE I CAN DO SOMETHING ABOUT IT!
YOU'RE A GOOD MAN, STEVE. I WOULD HAVE DONE THE SAME THING. I GUESS WE BOTH DO--
--WHAT WE HAVE TO!
SKZZZZZTT
AGH!
THE ELECTRICAL CHARGE I CHANNELED THROUGH MY GAUNTLET WON'T HARM STEVE, JUST KEEP HIM IMMOBILE FOR A WHILE. BUT THE DECISION TO DO IT WAS AS EASY AS DIGGING MY OWN HEART OUT WITH AN ICE CREAM SCOOP!
SLOWLY, IRON MAN REACHES INTO HIS BACKPACK, REMOVING A FINAL NEGATOR DEVICE.
BUT AS HE REACHES ACROSS STEVE ROGERS, THEIR EYES MEET... AND HOLD.
NO WORDS ARE SPOKEN; NONE ARE NEEDED. FOR BOTH MEN KNOW THAT A BOND HAS BEEN BROKEN TODAY... A BOND AS OLD AS THEIR FRIENDSHIP... AS DEEP AS THEIR INNERMOST THOUGHTS. A DEAR AND PRECIOUS LINK--

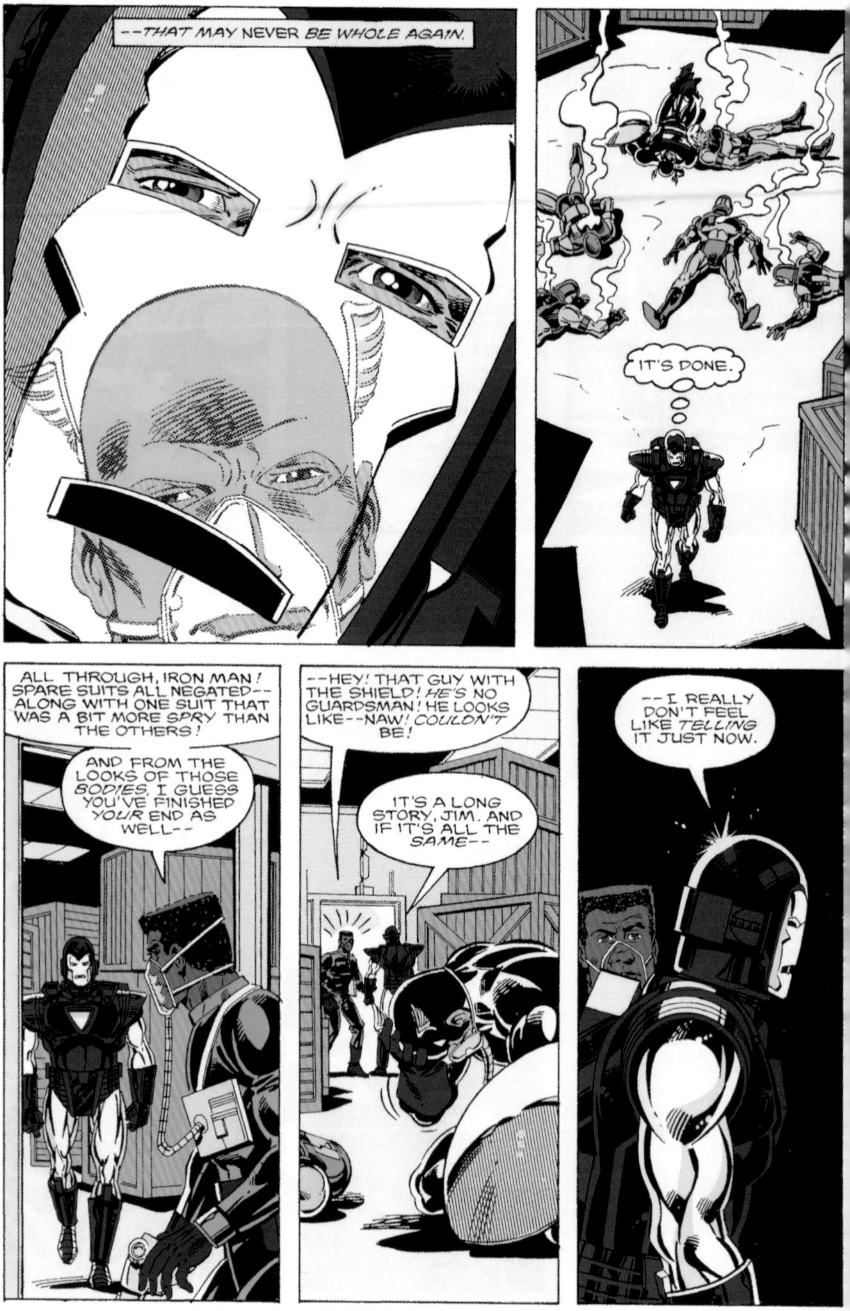
--THAT MAY NEVER BE WHOLE AGAIN.
IT'S DONE.
ALL THROUGH, IRON MAN! SPARE SUITS ALL NEGATED--ALONG WITH ONE SUIT THAT WAS A BIT MORE SPRY THAN THE OTHERS!
AND FROM THE LOOKS OF THOSE BODIES, I GUESS YOU'VE FINISHED YOUR END AS WELL--
--HEY! THAT GUY WITH THE SHIELD! HE'S NO GUARDSMAN! HE LOOKS LIKE--NAW! COULDN'T BE!
IT'S A LONG STORY, JIM. AND IF IT'S ALL THE SAME--
--I REALLY DON'T FEEL LIKE TELLING IT JUST NOW.

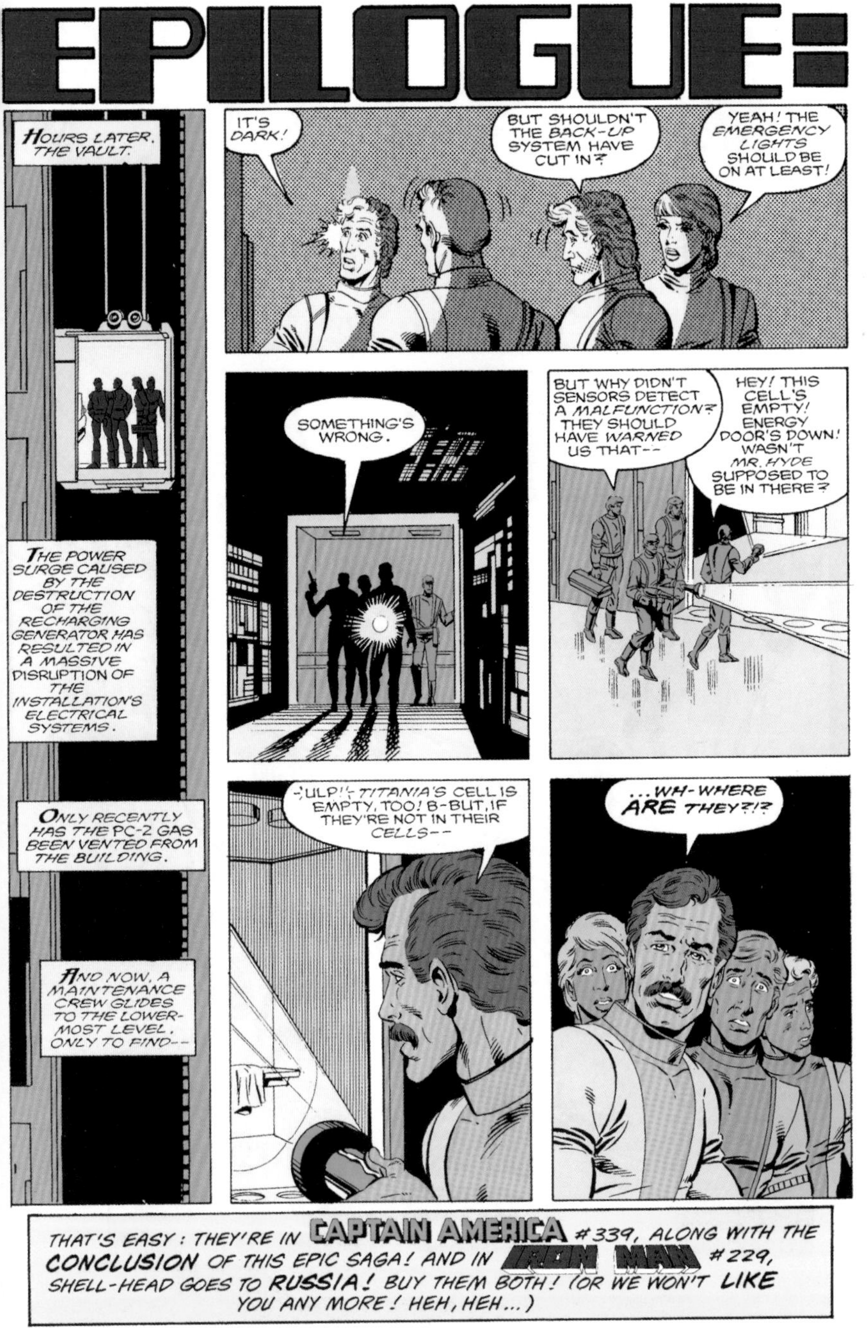
EPILOGUE:
HOURS LATER. THE VAULT.
THE POWER SURGE CAUSED BY THE DESTRUCTION OF THE RECHARGING GENERATOR HAS RESULTED IN A MASSIVE DISRUPTION OF THE INSTALLATION'S ELECTRICAL SYSTEMS.
ONLY RECENTLY HAS THE PC-2 GAS BEEN VENTED FROM THE BUILDING.
AND NOW, A MAINTENANCE CREW GLIDES TO THE LOWER-MOST LEVEL, ONLY TO FIND--
IT'S DARK!
BUT SHOULDN'T THE BACK-UP SYSTEM HAVE CUT IN?
YEAH! THE EMERGENCY LIGHTS SHOULD BE ON AT LEAST!
SOMETHING'S WRONG.
BUT WHY DIDN'T SENSORS DETECT A MALFUNCTION? THEY SHOULD HAVE WARNED US THAT--
HEY! THIS CELL'S EMPTY! ENERGY DOOR'S DOWN! WASN'T MR. HYDE SUPPOSED TO BE IN THERE?
-ULP!- TITANIA'S CELL IS EMPTY, TOO! B-BUT, IF THEY'RE NOT IN THEIR CELLS--
...WH-WHERE ARE THEY?!?
THAT'S EASY: THEY'RE IN CAPTAIN AMERICA #339, ALONG WITH THE CONCLUSION OF THIS EPIC SAGA! AND IN IRON MAN #229, SHELL-HEAD GOES TO RUSSIA! BUY THEM BOTH! (OR WE WON'T LIKE YOU ANY MORE! HEH, HEH...)

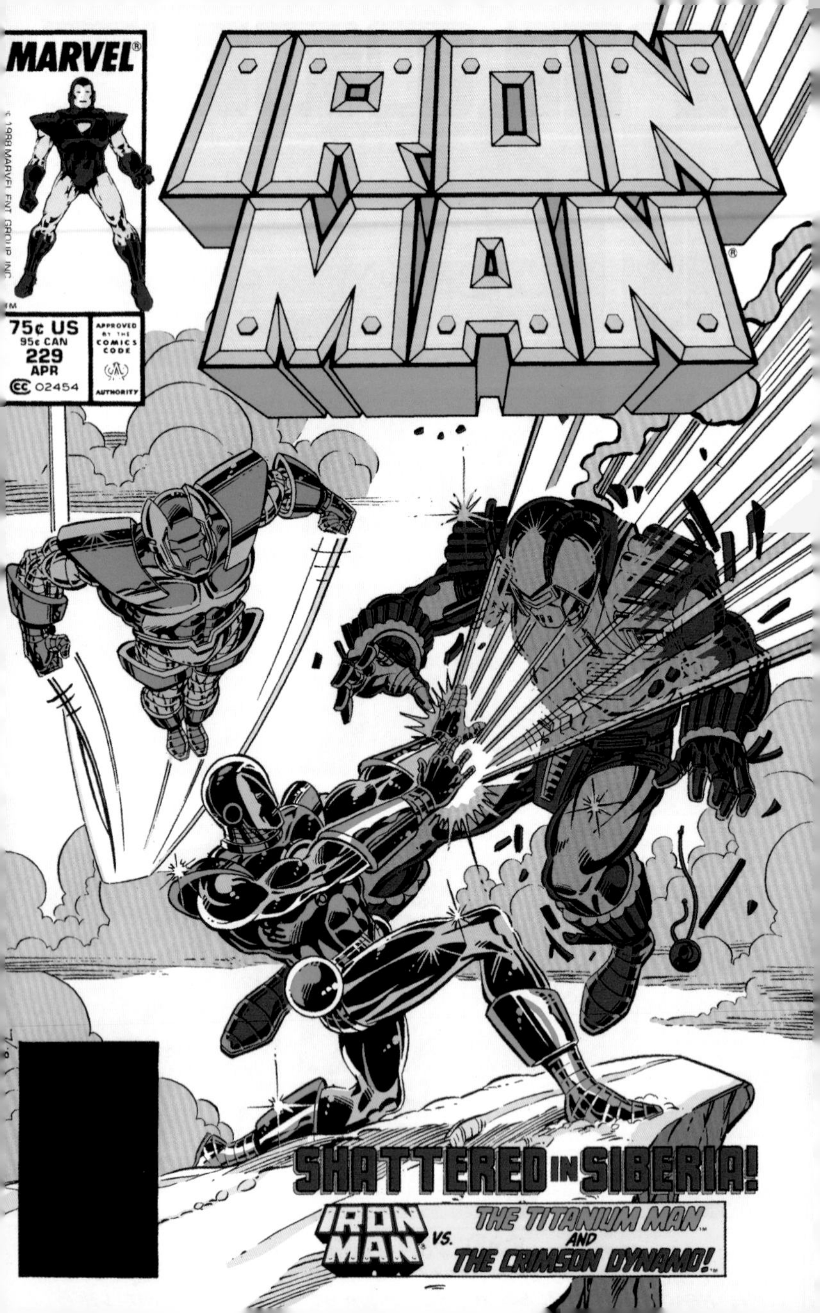
MARVEL®
© 1988 MARVEL ENT. GROUP, INC.
IRON MAN®
75¢ US
95¢ CAN
229
APR
02454
APPROVED BY THE COMICS CODE AUTHORITY
SHATTERED IN SIBERIA!
IRON MAN® VS. THE TITANIUM MAN™ AND THE CRIMSON DYNAMO!™

Stan Lee presents IRON MAN

DAVID MICHELINIE PLOT/SCRIPT • MARK D. BRIGHT BREAKDOWNS • BOB LAYTON PLOT/FINISHES • JANICE CHIANG LETTERS • BOB SHAREN COLORS • MARK GRUENWALD EDITOR • TOM DeFALCO EDITOR IN CHIEF

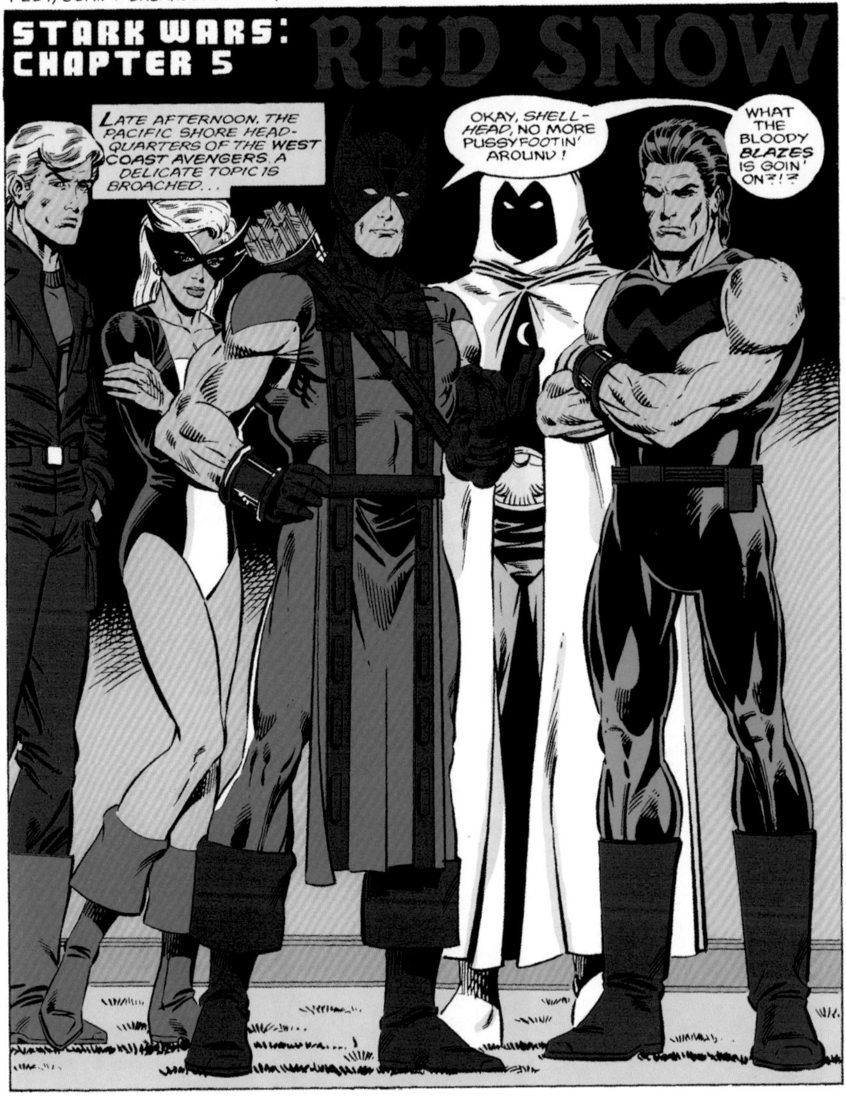
STARK WARS: CHAPTER 5
RED SNOW
LATE AFTERNOON. THE PACIFIC SHORE HEAD-QUARTERS OF THE WEST COAST AVENGERS. A DELICATE TOPIC IS BROACHED...
OKAY, SHELL-HEAD, NO MORE PUSSYFOOTIN' AROUND!
WHAT THE BLOODY BLAZES IS GOIN' ON?!?

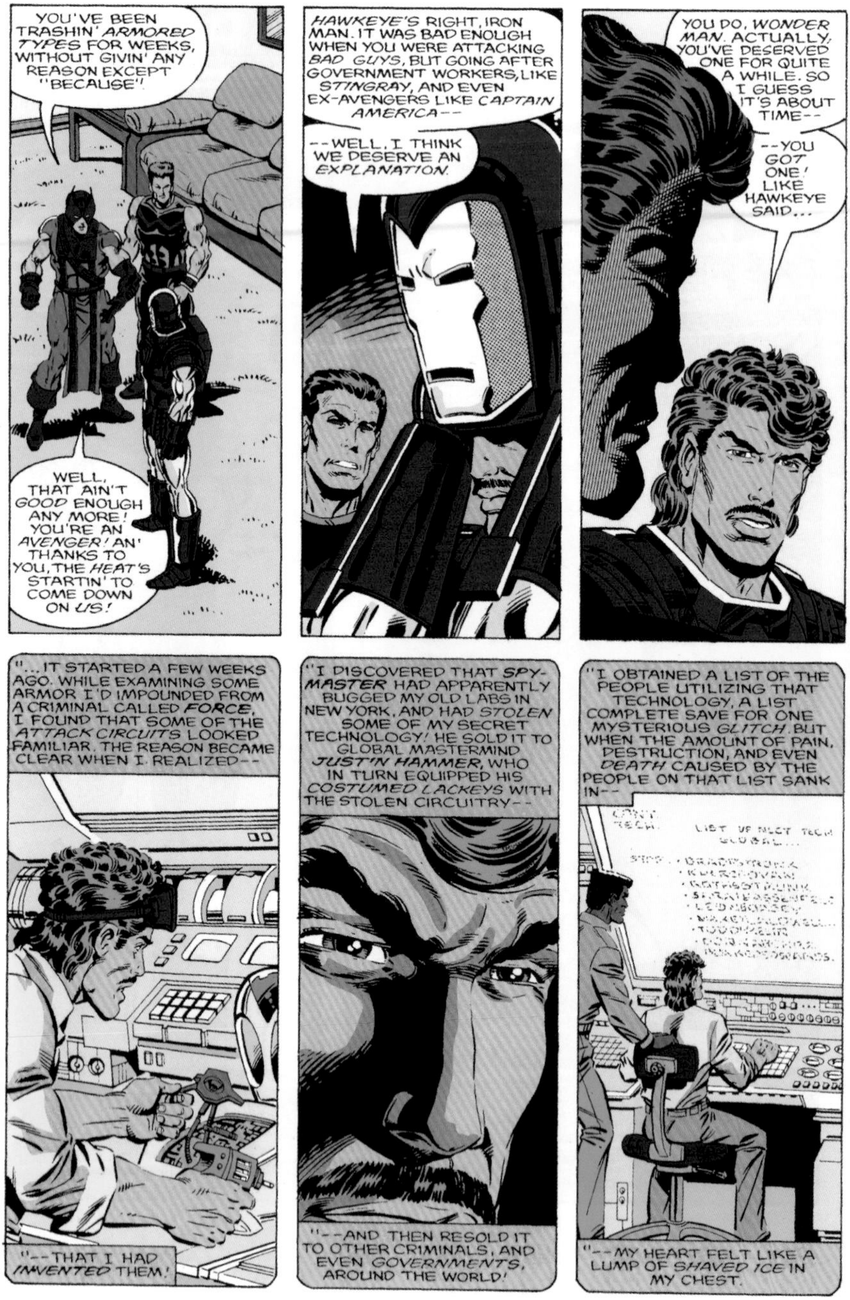
YOU'VE BEEN TRASHIN' ARMORED TYPES FOR WEEKS, WITHOUT GIVIN' ANY REASON EXCEPT "BECAUSE".
WELL, THAT AIN'T GOOD ENOUGH ANY MORE! YOU'RE AN AVENGER! AN' THANKS TO YOU, THE HEAT'S STARTIN' TO COME DOWN ON US!
HAWKEYE'S RIGHT, IRON MAN. IT WAS BAD ENOUGH WHEN YOU WERE ATTACKING BAD GUYS, BUT GOING AFTER GOVERNMENT WORKERS, LIKE STINGRAY, AND EVEN EX-AVENGERS LIKE CAPTAIN AMERICA--
--WELL, I THINK WE DESERVE AN EXPLANATION.
YOU DO, WONDER MAN. ACTUALLY, YOU'VE DESERVED ONE FOR QUITE A WHILE. SO I GUESS IT'S ABOUT TIME--
--YOU GOT ONE! LIKE HAWKEYE SAID...
"...IT STARTED A FEW WEEKS AGO. WHILE EXAMINING SOME ARMOR I'D IMPOUNDED FROM A CRIMINAL CALLED FORCE, I FOUND THAT SOME OF THE ATTACK CIRCUITS LOOKED FAMILIAR. THE REASON BECAME CLEAR WHEN I REALIZED--
"--THAT I HAD INVENTED THEM!
"I DISCOVERED THAT SPY-MASTER HAD APPARENTLY BUGGED MY OLD LABS IN NEW YORK, AND HAD STOLEN SOME OF MY SECRET TECHNOLOGY! HE SOLD IT TO GLOBAL MASTERMIND JUSTIN HAMMER, WHO IN TURN EQUIPPED HIS COSTUMED LACKEYS WITH THE STOLEN CIRCUITRY--
"--AND THEN RESOLD IT TO OTHER CRIMINALS, AND EVEN GOVERNMENTS, AROUND THE WORLD!
"I OBTAINED A LIST OF THE PEOPLE UTILIZING THAT TECHNOLOGY, A LIST COMPLETE SAVE FOR ONE MYSTERIOUS GLITCH. BUT WHEN THE AMOUNT OF PAIN, DESTRUCTION, AND EVEN DEATH CAUSED BY THE PEOPLE ON THAT LIST SANK IN--
"--MY HEART FELT LIKE A LUMP OF SHAVED ICE IN MY CHEST.

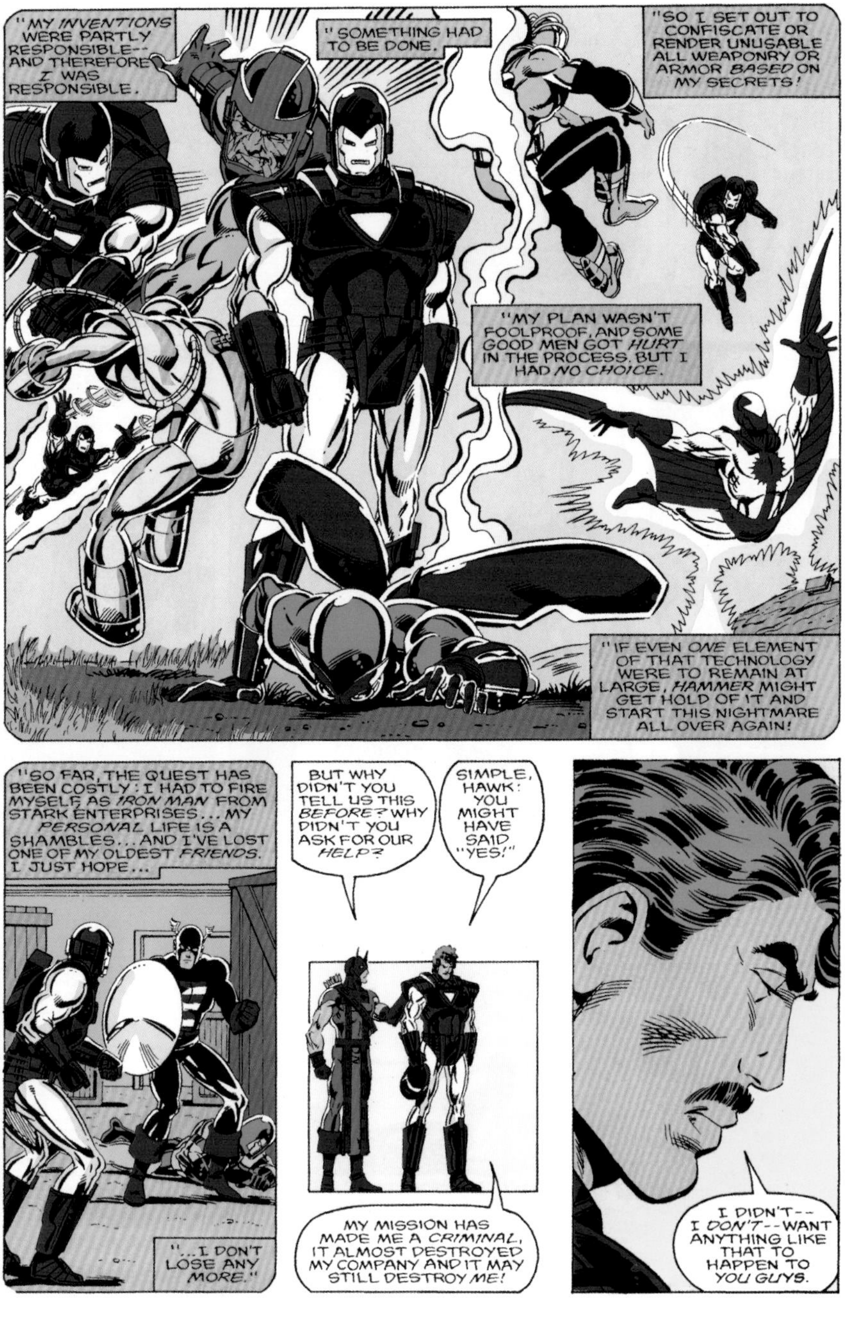
"MY INVENTIONS WERE PARTLY RESPONSIBLE-- AND THEREFORE I WAS RESPONSIBLE.
"SOMETHING HAD TO BE DONE.
"SO I SET OUT TO CONFISCATE OR RENDER UNUSABLE ALL WEAPONRY OR ARMOR BASED ON MY SECRETS!
"MY PLAN WASN'T FOOLPROOF, AND SOME GOOD MEN GOT HURT IN THE PROCESS. BUT I HAD NO CHOICE.
"IF EVEN ONE ELEMENT OF THAT TECHNOLOGY WERE TO REMAIN AT LARGE, HAMMER MIGHT GET HOLD OF IT AND START THIS NIGHTMARE ALL OVER AGAIN!
"SO FAR, THE QUEST HAS BEEN COSTLY: I HAD TO FIRE MYSELF AS IRON MAN FROM STARK ENTERPRISES... MY PERSONAL LIFE IS A SHAMBLES... AND I'VE LOST ONE OF MY OLDEST FRIENDS. I JUST HOPE...
"...I DON'T LOSE ANY MORE."
BUT WHY DIDN'T YOU TELL US THIS BEFORE? WHY DIDN'T YOU ASK FOR OUR HELP?
SIMPLE, HAWK: YOU MIGHT HAVE SAID "YES!"
MY MISSION HAS MADE ME A CRIMINAL, IT ALMOST DESTROYED MY COMPANY AND IT MAY STILL DESTROY ME!
I DIDN'T-- I DON'T--WANT ANYTHING LIKE THAT TO HAPPEN TO YOU GUYS.

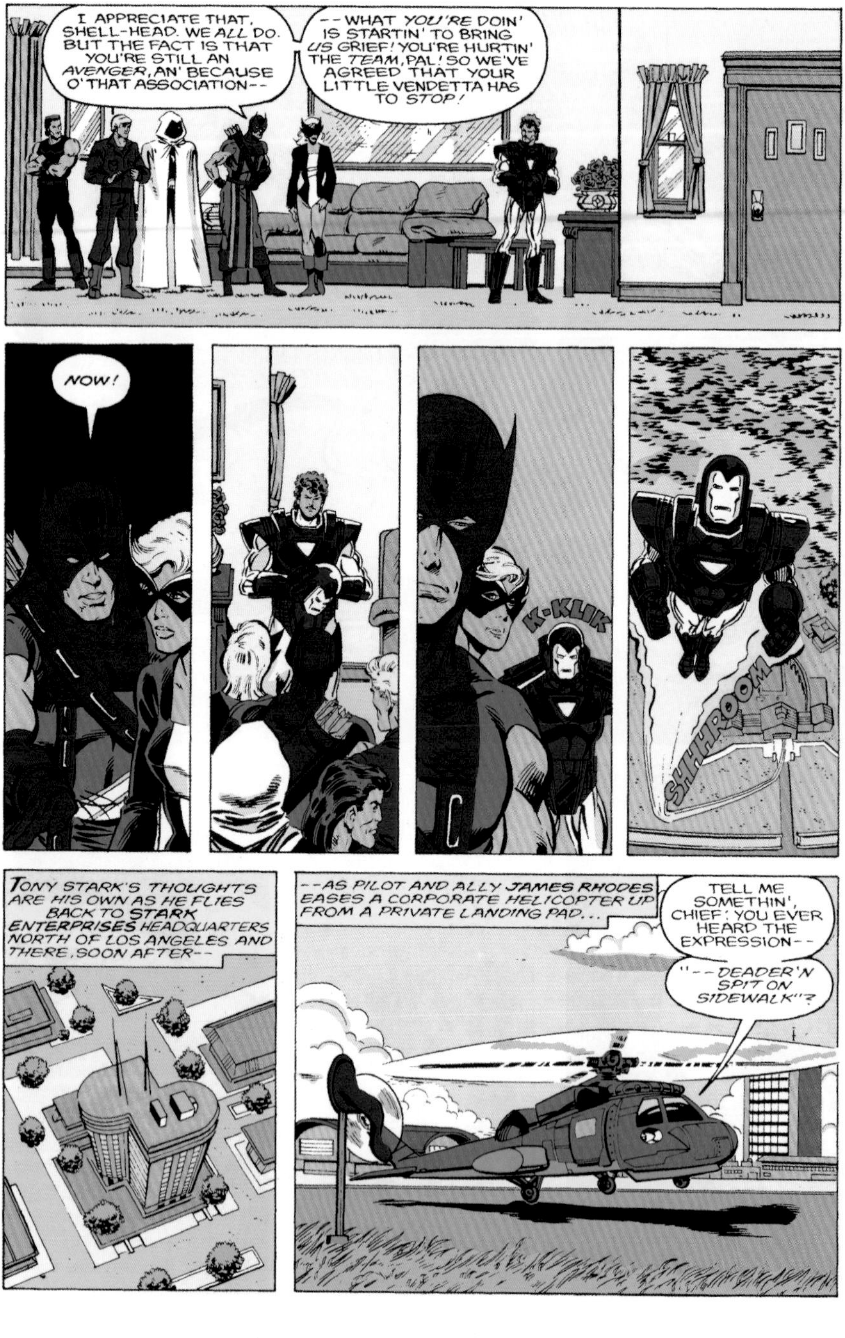
I APPRECIATE THAT, SHELL-HEAD. WE ALL DO. BUT THE FACT IS THAT YOU'RE STILL AN AVENGER, AN' BECAUSE O' THAT ASSOCIATION--
--WHAT YOU'RE DOIN' IS STARTIN' TO BRING US GRIEF! YOU'RE HURTIN' THE TEAM, PAL! SO WE'VE AGREED THAT YOUR LITTLE VENDETTA HAS TO STOP!
NOW!
K-KLIK
SHHHROOM
TONY STARK'S THOUGHTS ARE HIS OWN AS HE FLIES BACK TO STARK ENTERPRISES HEADQUARTERS NORTH OF LOS ANGELES AND THERE, SOON AFTER--
--AS PILOT AND ALLY JAMES RHODES EASES A CORPORATE HELICOPTER UP FROM A PRIVATE LANDING PAD...
TELL ME SOMETHIN', CHIEF: YOU EVER HEARD THE EXPRESSION--
"--DEADER'N SPIT ON SIDEWALK"?

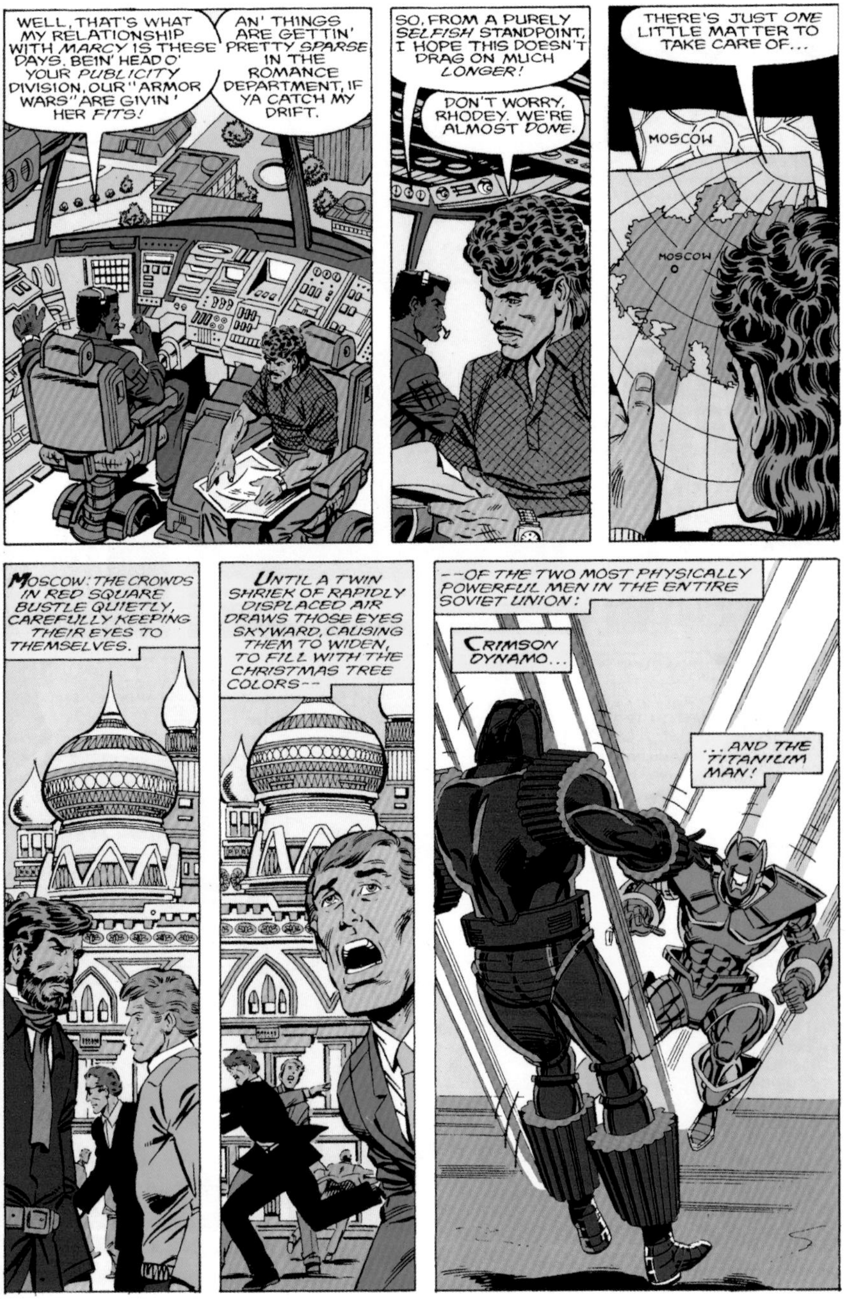
WELL, THAT'S WHAT MY RELATIONSHIP WITH MARCY IS THESE DAYS. BEIN' HEAD O' YOUR PUBLICITY DIVISION, OUR "ARMOR WARS" ARE GIVIN' HER FITS!
AN' THINGS ARE GETTIN' PRETTY SPARSE IN THE ROMANCE DEPARTMENT, IF YA CATCH MY DRIFT.
SO, FROM A PURELY SELFISH STANDPOINT, I HOPE THIS DOESN'T DRAG ON MUCH LONGER!
DON'T WORRY, RHODEY. WE'RE ALMOST DONE.
THERE'S JUST ONE LITTLE MATTER TO TAKE CARE OF...
MOSCOW
MOSCOW
MOSCOW: THE CROWDS IN RED SQUARE BUSTLE QUIETLY, CAREFULLY KEEPING THEIR EYES TO THEMSELVES.
UNTIL A TWIN SHRIEK OF RAPIDLY DISPLACED AIR DRAWS THOSE EYES SKYWARD, CAUSING THEM TO WIDEN, TO FILL WITH THE CHRISTMAS TREE COLORS--
--OF THE TWO MOST PHYSICALLY POWERFUL MEN IN THE ENTIRE SOVIET UNION:
CRIMSON DYNAMO...
...AND THE TITANIUM MAN!

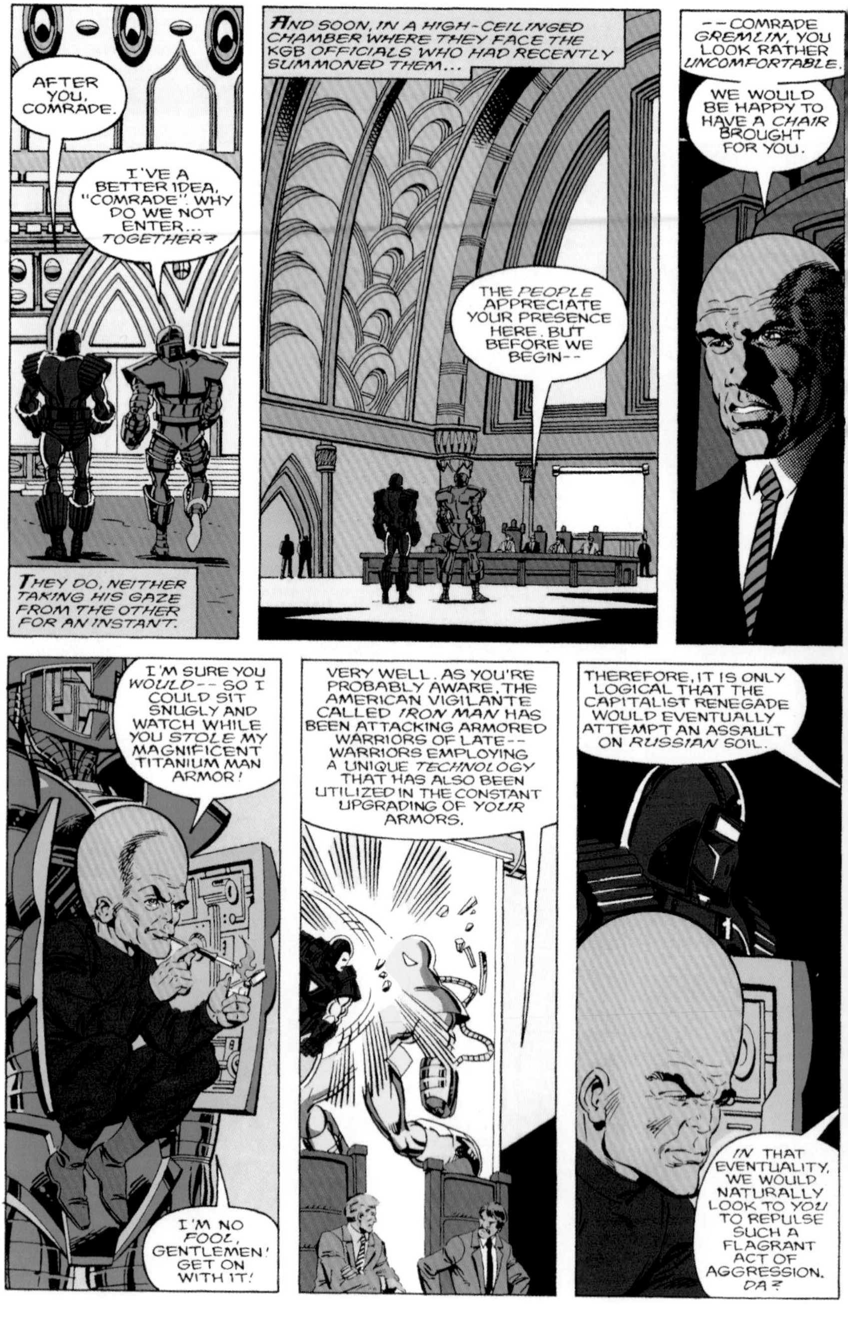
AFTER YOU, COMRADE.
I'VE A BETTER IDEA, "COMRADE". WHY DO WE NOT ENTER... TOGETHER?
THEY DO, NEITHER TAKING HIS GAZE FROM THE OTHER FOR AN INSTANT.
AND SOON, IN A HIGH-CEILINGED CHAMBER WHERE THEY FACE THE KGB OFFICIALS WHO HAD RECENTLY SUMMONED THEM...
THE PEOPLE APPRECIATE YOUR PRESENCE HERE. BUT BEFORE WE BEGIN--
--COMRADE GREMLIN, YOU LOOK RATHER UNCOMFORTABLE.
WE WOULD BE HAPPY TO HAVE A CHAIR BROUGHT FOR YOU.
I'M SURE YOU WOULD-- SO I COULD SIT SNUGLY AND WATCH WHILE YOU STOLE MY MAGNIFICENT TITANIUM MAN ARMOR!
I'M NO FOOL, GENTLEMEN! GET ON WITH IT!
VERY WELL. AS YOU'RE PROBABLY AWARE, THE AMERICAN VIGILANTE CALLED IRON MAN HAS BEEN ATTACKING ARMORED WARRIORS OF LATE-- WARRIORS EMPLOYING A UNIQUE TECHNOLOGY THAT HAS ALSO BEEN UTILIZED IN THE CONSTANT UPGRADING OF YOUR ARMORS.
THEREFORE, IT IS ONLY LOGICAL THAT THE CAPITALIST RENEGADE WOULD EVENTUALLY ATTEMPT AN ASSAULT ON RUSSIAN SOIL.
IN THAT EVENTUALITY, WE WOULD NATURALLY LOOK TO YOU TO REPULSE SUCH A FLAGRANT ACT OF AGGRESSION. DA?

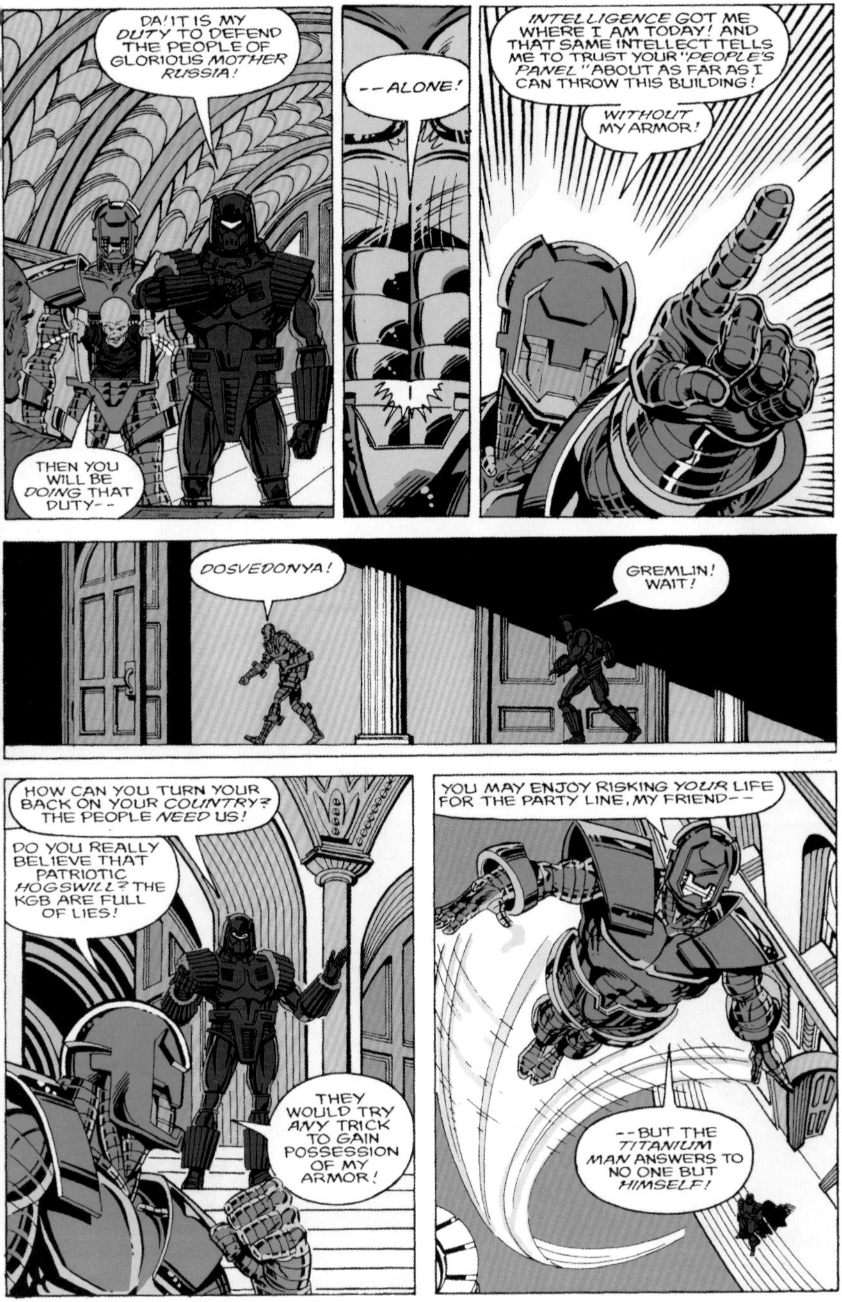
DA! IT IS MY DUTY TO DEFEND THE PEOPLE OF GLORIOUS MOTHER RUSSIA!
THEN YOU WILL BE DOING THAT DUTY--
--ALONE!
INTELLIGENCE GOT ME WHERE I AM TODAY! AND THAT SAME INTELLECT TELLS ME TO TRUST YOUR "PEOPLE'S PANEL" ABOUT AS FAR AS I CAN THROW THIS BUILDING!
WITHOUT MY ARMOR!
DOSVEDONYA!
GREMLIN! WAIT!
HOW CAN YOU TURN YOUR BACK ON YOUR COUNTRY? THE PEOPLE NEED US!
DO YOU REALLY BELIEVE THAT PATRIOTIC HOGSWILL? THE KGB ARE FULL OF LIES!
THEY WOULD TRY ANY TRICK TO GAIN POSSESSION OF MY ARMOR!
YOU MAY ENJOY RISKING YOUR LIFE FOR THE PARTY LINE, MY FRIEND--
--BUT THE TITANIUM MAN ANSWERS TO NO ONE BUT HIMSELF!

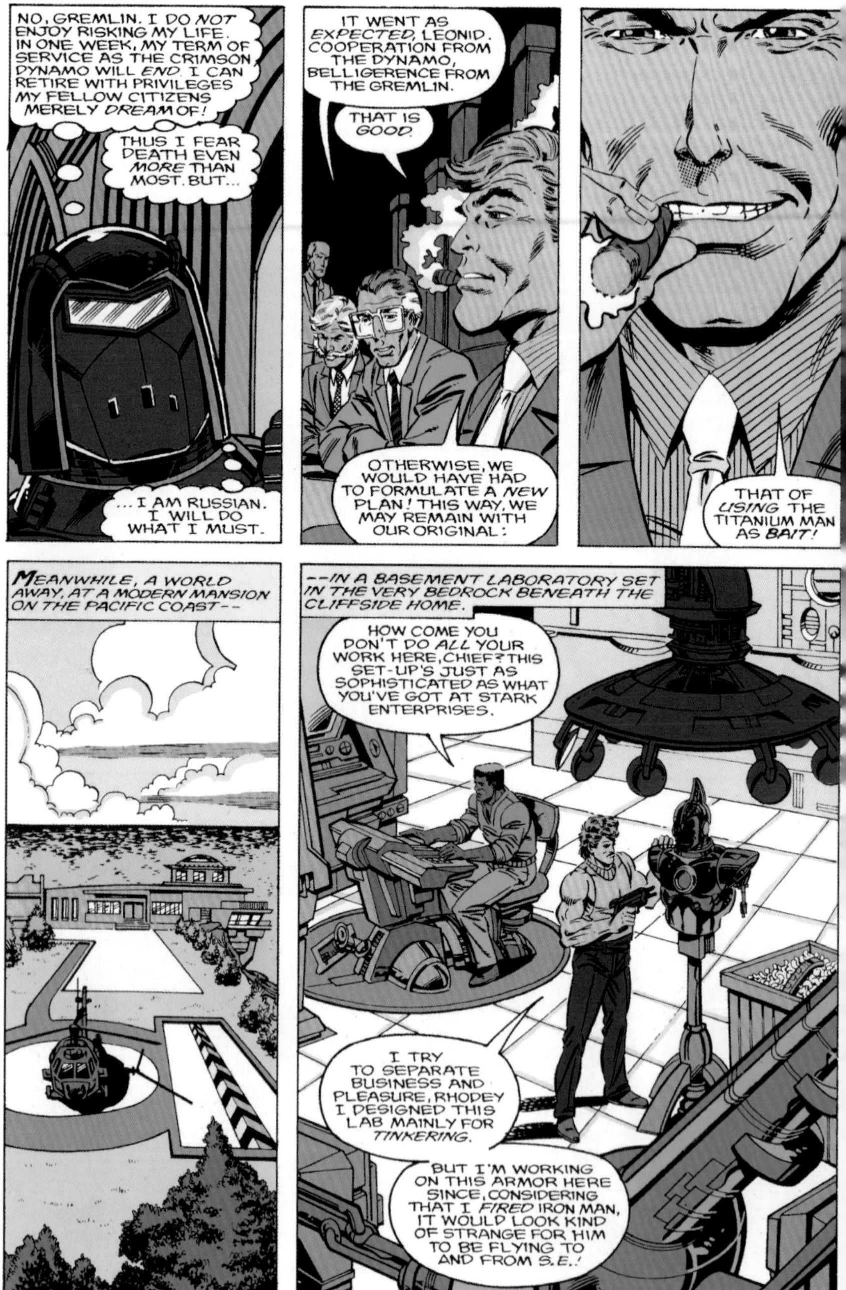
NO, GREMLIN. I DO NOT ENJOY RISKING MY LIFE. IN ONE WEEK, MY TERM OF SERVICE AS THE CRIMSON DYNAMO WILL END. I CAN RETIRE WITH PRIVILEGES MY FELLOW CITIZENS MERELY DREAM OF!
THUS I FEAR DEATH EVEN MORE THAN MOST. BUT...
... I AM RUSSIAN. I WILL DO WHAT I MUST.
IT WENT AS EXPECTED, LEONID. COOPERATION FROM THE DYNAMO, BELLIGERENCE FROM THE GREMLIN.
THAT IS GOOD.
OTHERWISE, WE WOULD HAVE HAD TO FORMULATE A NEW PLAN! THIS WAY, WE MAY REMAIN WITH OUR ORIGINAL:
THAT OF USING THE TITANIUM MAN AS BAIT!
MEANWHILE, A WORLD AWAY, AT A MODERN MANSION ON THE PACIFIC COAST--
--IN A BASEMENT LABORATORY SET IN THE VERY BEDROCK BENEATH THE CLIFFSIDE HOME.
HOW COME YOU DON'T DO ALL YOUR WORK HERE, CHIEF? THIS SET-UP'S JUST AS SOPHISTICATED AS WHAT YOU'VE GOT AT STARK ENTERPRISES.
I TRY TO SEPARATE BUSINESS AND PLEASURE, RHODEY. I DESIGNED THIS LAB MAINLY FOR TINKERING.
BUT I'M WORKING ON THIS ARMOR HERE SINCE, CONSIDERING THAT I FIRED IRON MAN, IT WOULD LOOK KIND OF STRANGE FOR HIM TO BE FLYING TO AND FROM S.E.!

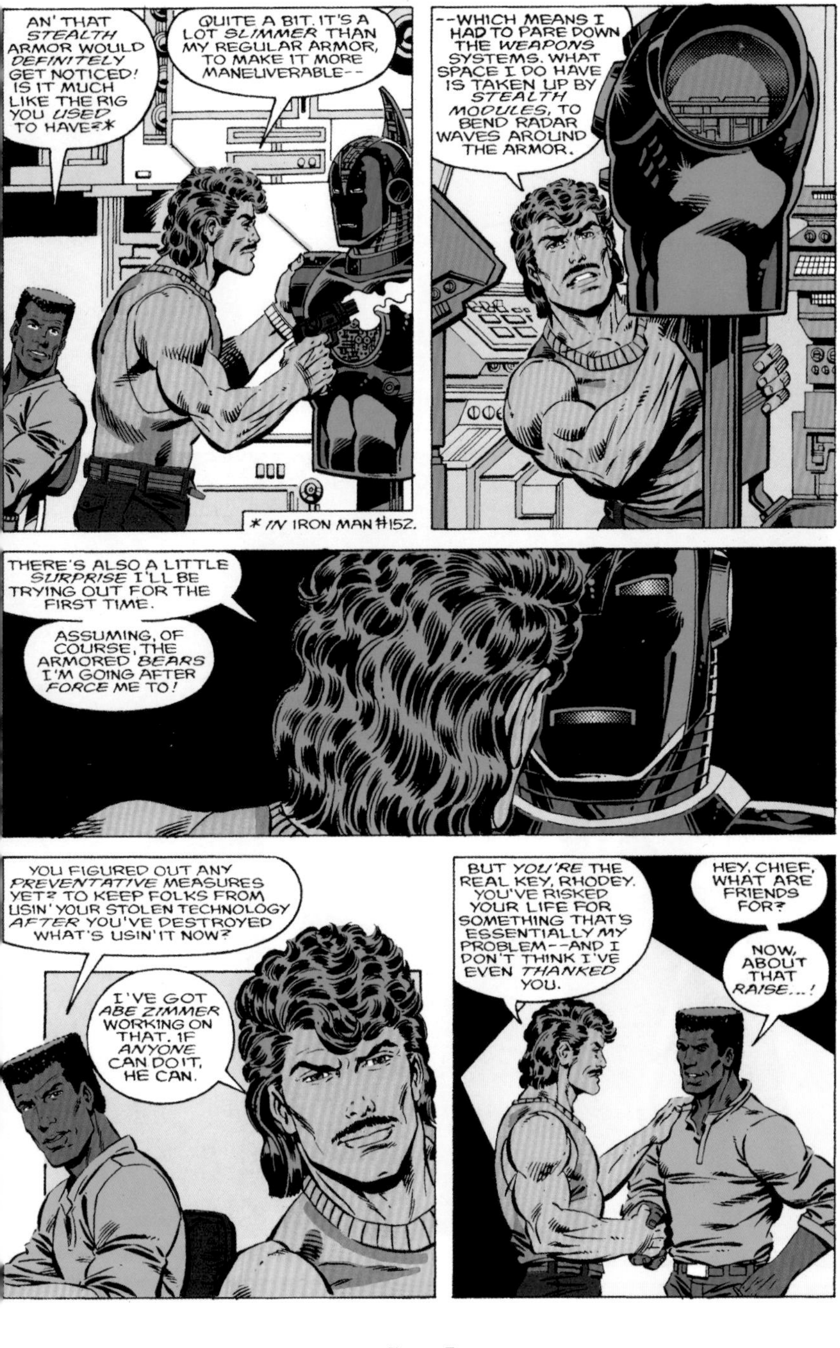

AN' THAT STEALTH ARMOR WOULD DEFINITELY GET NOTICED! IS IT MUCH LIKE THE RIG YOU USED TO HAVE?*
QUITE A BIT. IT'S A LOT SLIMMER THAN MY REGULAR ARMOR, TO MAKE IT MORE MANEUVERABLE--
* IN IRON MAN #152.
--WHICH MEANS I HAD TO PARE DOWN THE WEAPONS SYSTEMS. WHAT SPACE I DO HAVE IS TAKEN UP BY STEALTH MODULES, TO BEND RADAR WAVES AROUND THE ARMOR.
THERE'S ALSO A LITTLE SURPRISE I'LL BE TRYING OUT FOR THE FIRST TIME.
ASSUMING, OF COURSE, THE ARMORED BEARS I'M GOING AFTER FORCE ME TO!
YOU FIGURED OUT ANY PREVENTATIVE MEASURES YET? TO KEEP FOLKS FROM USIN' YOUR STOLEN TECHNOLOGY AFTER YOU'VE DESTROYED WHAT'S USIN' IT NOW?
I'VE GOT ABE ZIMMER WORKING ON THAT. IF ANYONE CAN DO IT, HE CAN.
BUT YOU'RE THE REAL KEY, RHODEY. YOU'VE RISKED YOUR LIFE FOR SOMETHING THAT'S ESSENTIALLY MY PROBLEM--AND I DON'T THINK I'VE EVEN THANKED YOU.
HEY, CHIEF, WHAT ARE FRIENDS FOR?
NOW, ABOUT THAT RAISE...!

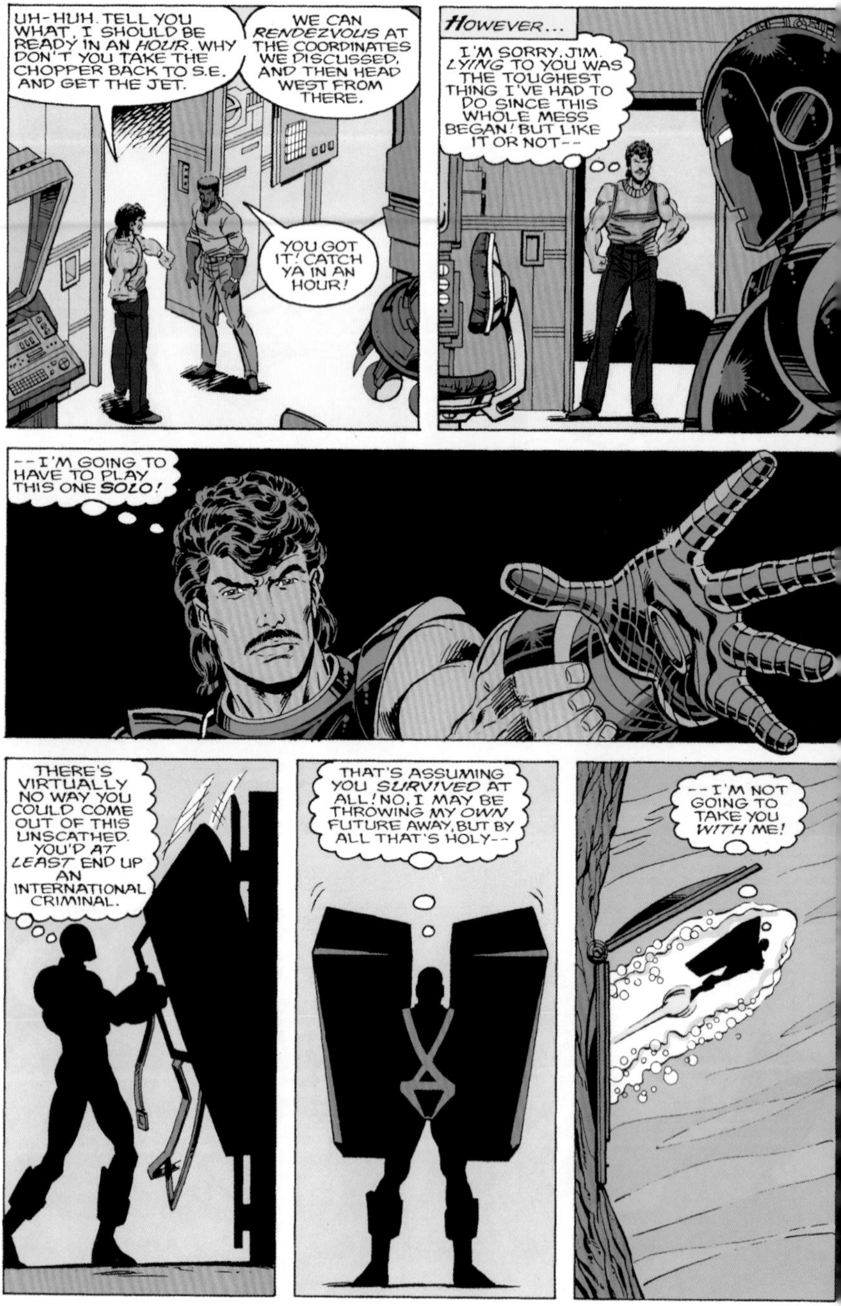

UH-HUH. TELL YOU WHAT, I SHOULD BE READY IN AN *HOUR*. WHY DON'T YOU TAKE THE CHOPPER BACK TO S.E. AND GET THE JET.
WE CAN *RENDEZVOUS* AT THE COORDINATES WE DISCUSSED, AND THEN HEAD WEST FROM THERE.
YOU GOT IT! CATCH YA IN AN HOUR!
HOWEVER...
I'M SORRY, JIM. *LYING* TO YOU WAS THE TOUGHEST THING I'VE HAD TO DO SINCE THIS WHOLE MESS BEGAN! BUT LIKE IT OR NOT--
--I'M GOING TO HAVE TO PLAY THIS ONE *SOLO*!
THERE'S VIRTUALLY NO WAY YOU COULD COME OUT OF THIS UNSCATHED. YOU'D *AT LEAST* END UP AN INTERNATIONAL CRIMINAL.
THAT'S ASSUMING YOU *SURVIVED* AT ALL! NO, I MAY BE THROWING *MY OWN* FUTURE AWAY, BUT BY ALL THAT'S HOLY--
--I'M NOT GOING TO TAKE YOU *WITH ME*!

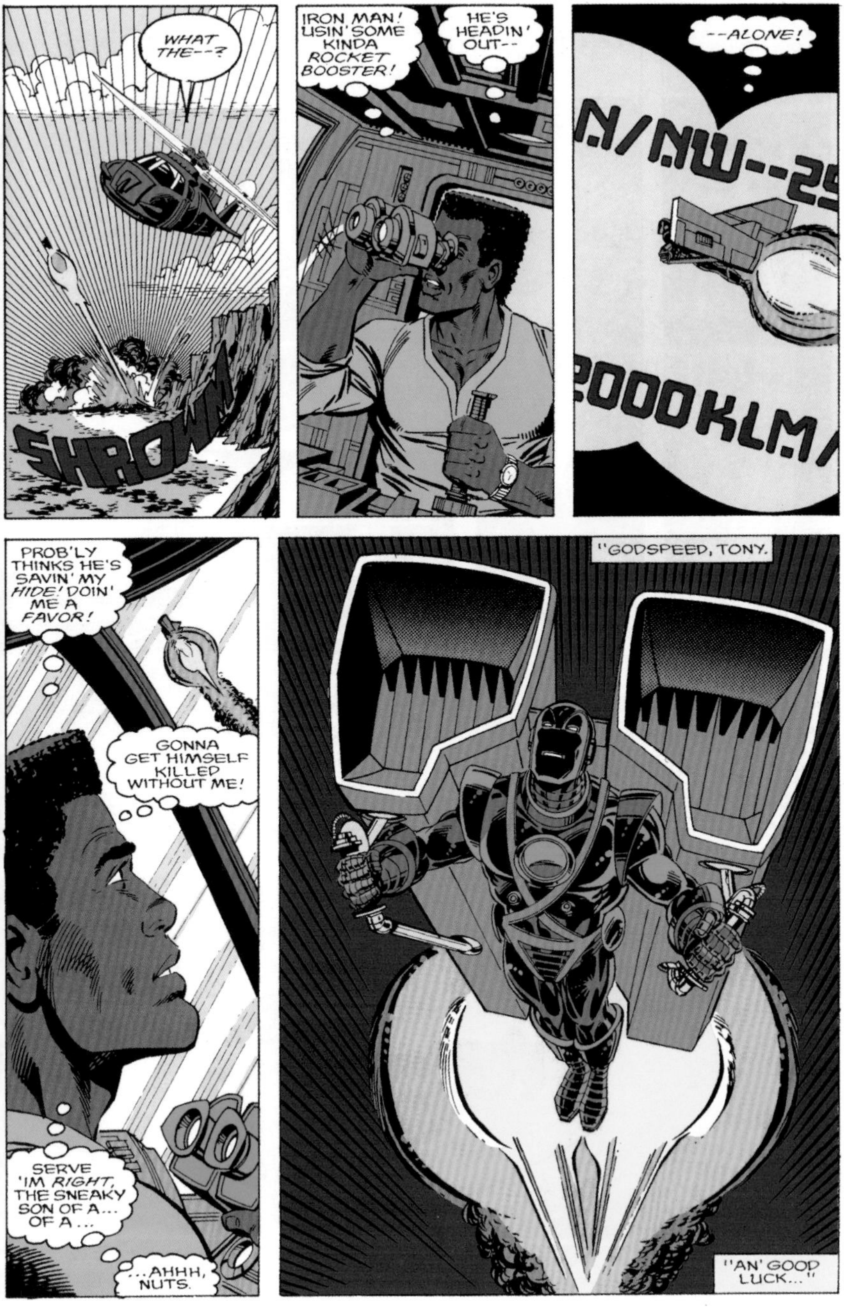
WHAT THE--?
SHROWM
IRON MAN! USIN' SOME KINDA ROCKET BOOSTER!
HE'S HEADIN' OUT--
--ALONE!
N/NW--25
2000 KLM
PROB'LY THINKS HE'S SAVIN' MY HIDE! DOIN' ME A FAVOR!
GONNA GET HIMSELF KILLED WITHOUT ME!
SERVE 'IM RIGHT, THE SNEAKY SON OF A... OF A...
...AHHH, NUTS.
"GODSPEED, TONY.
"AN' GOOD LUCK..."

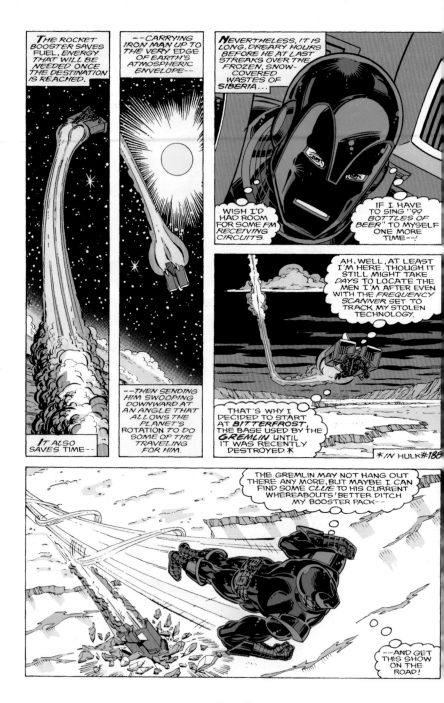

THE ROCKET BOOSTER SAVES FUEL, ENERGY THAT WILL BE NEEDED ONCE THE DESTINATION IS REACHED.

IT ALSO SAVES TIME--

--CARRYING IRON MAN UP TO THE VERY EDGE OF EARTH'S ATMOSPHERIC ENVELOPE--

--THEN SENDING HIM SWOOPING DOWNWARD AT AN ANGLE THAT ALLOWS THE PLANET'S ROTATION TO DO SOME OF THE TRAVELING FOR HIM.

NEVERTHELESS, IT IS LONG, DREARY HOURS BEFORE HE AT LAST STREAKS OVER THE FROZEN, SNOW-COVERED WASTES OF SIBERIA...

WISH I'D HAD ROOM FOR SOME FM RECEIVING CIRCUITS.

IF I HAVE TO SING "99 BOTTLES OF BEER" TO MYSELF ONE MORE TIME--!

AH, WELL, AT LEAST I'M HERE. THOUGH IT STILL MIGHT TAKE DAYS TO LOCATE THE MEN I'M AFTER EVEN WITH THE FREQUENCY SCANNER SET TO TRACK MY STOLEN TECHNOLOGY.

THAT'S WHY I DECIDED TO START AT BITTERFROST, THE BASE USED BY THE GREMLIN UNTIL IT WAS RECENTLY DESTROYED *

*IN HULK #188

THE GREMLIN MAY NOT HANG OUT THERE ANY MORE, BUT MAYBE I CAN FIND SOME CLUE TO HIS CURRENT WHEREABOUTS! BETTER DITCH MY BOOSTER PACK--

--AND GET THIS SHOW ON THE ROAD!

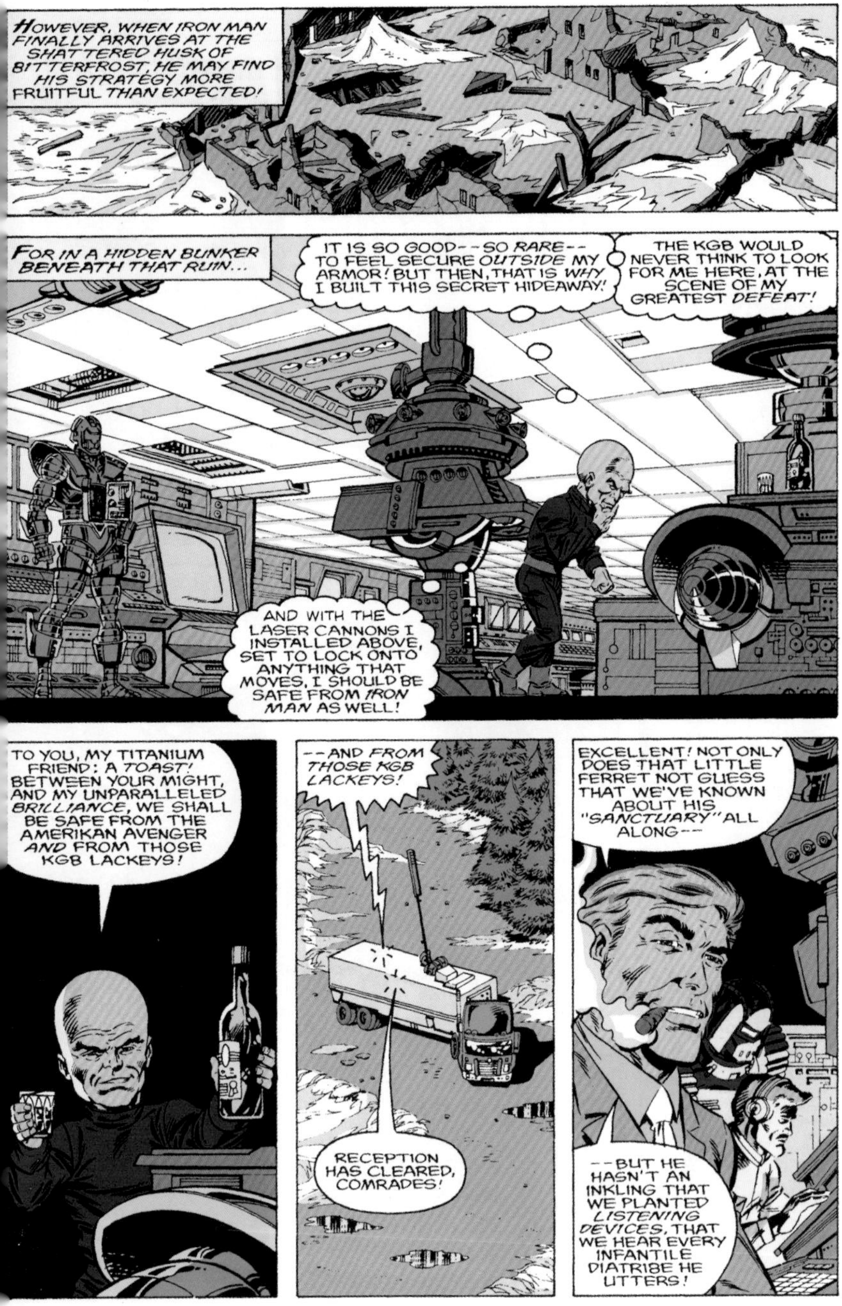
HOWEVER, WHEN IRON MAN FINALLY ARRIVES AT THE SHATTERED HUSK OF BITTERFROST, HE MAY FIND HIS STRATEGY MORE FRUITFUL THAN EXPECTED!
FOR IN A HIDDEN BUNKER BENEATH THAT RUIN...
IT IS SO GOOD--SO RARE--TO FEEL SECURE OUTSIDE MY ARMOR! BUT THEN, THAT IS WHY I BUILT THIS SECRET HIDEAWAY!
THE KGB WOULD NEVER THINK TO LOOK FOR ME HERE, AT THE SCENE OF MY GREATEST DEFEAT!
AND WITH THE LASER CANNONS I INSTALLED ABOVE, SET TO LOCK ONTO ANYTHING THAT MOVES, I SHOULD BE SAFE FROM IRON MAN AS WELL!
TO YOU, MY TITANIUM FRIEND: A TOAST! BETWEEN YOUR MIGHT, AND MY UNPARALLELED BRILLIANCE, WE SHALL BE SAFE FROM THE AMERIKAN AVENGER AND FROM THOSE KGB LACKEYS!
--AND FROM THOSE KGB LACKEYS!
RECEPTION HAS CLEARED, COMRADES!
EXCELLENT! NOT ONLY DOES THAT LITTLE FERRET NOT GUESS THAT WE'VE KNOWN ABOUT HIS "SANCTUARY" ALL ALONG--
--BUT HE HASN'T AN INKLING THAT WE PLANTED LISTENING DEVICES, THAT WE HEAR EVERY INFANTILE DIATRIBE HE UTTERS!

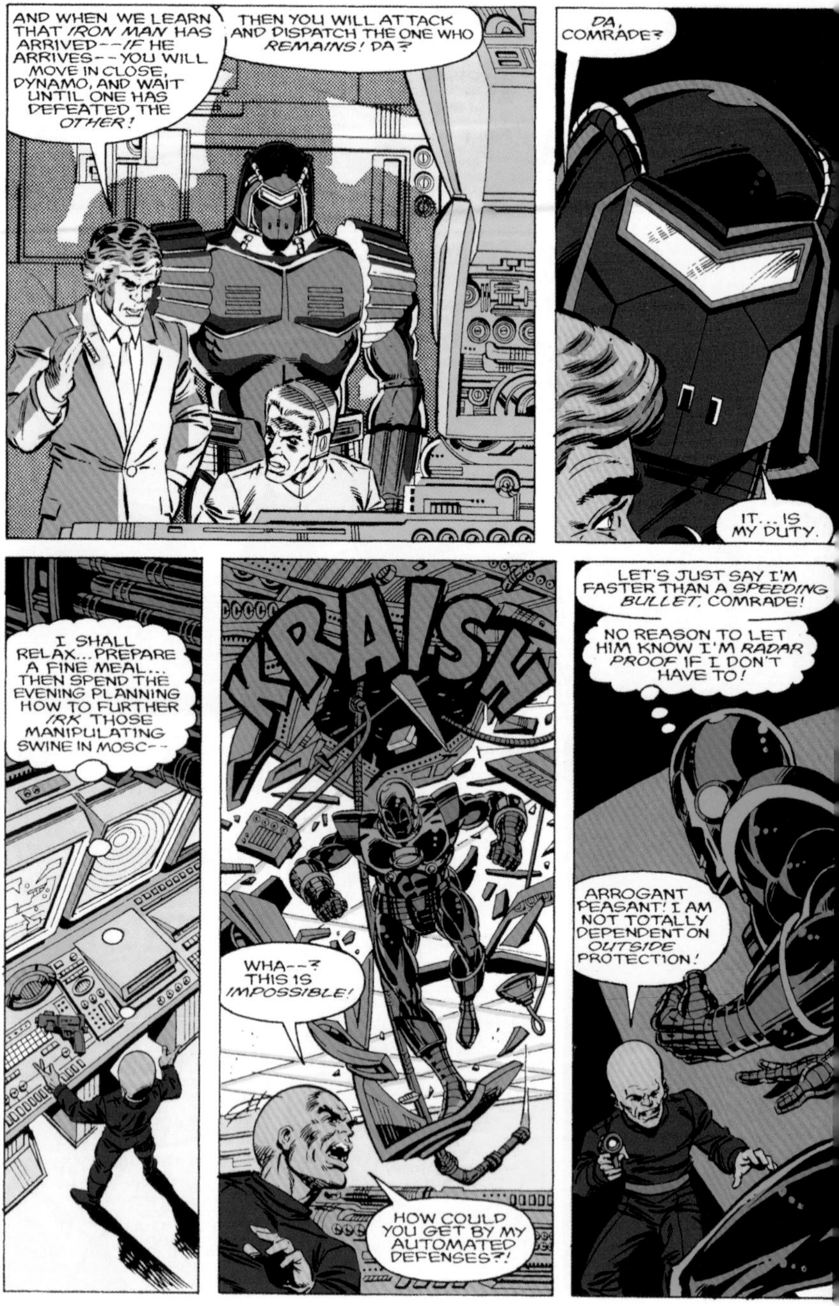

AND WHEN WE LEARN THAT *IRON MAN* HAS ARRIVED--*IF* HE ARRIVES--YOU WILL MOVE IN CLOSE, DYNAMO, AND WAIT UNTIL ONE HAS DEFEATED THE *OTHER*!
THEN YOU WILL ATTACK AND DISPATCH THE ONE WHO *REMAINS*! *DA*?
DA, COMRADE?
IT... IS MY DUTY.
I SHALL RELAX... PREPARE A FINE MEAL... THEN SPEND THE EVENING PLANNING HOW TO FURTHER *IRK* THOSE MANIPULATING SWINE IN *MOSC*--
KRAISH
WHA--? THIS IS *IMPOSSIBLE*!
HOW COULD YOU GET BY MY AUTOMATED DEFENSES?!
LET'S JUST SAY I'M FASTER THAN A *SPEEDING BULLET*, COMRADE!
NO REASON TO LET HIM KNOW I'M *RADAR PROOF* IF I DON'T HAVE TO!
ARROGANT PEASANT! I AM NOT TOTALLY DEPENDENT ON *OUTSIDE* PROTECTION!

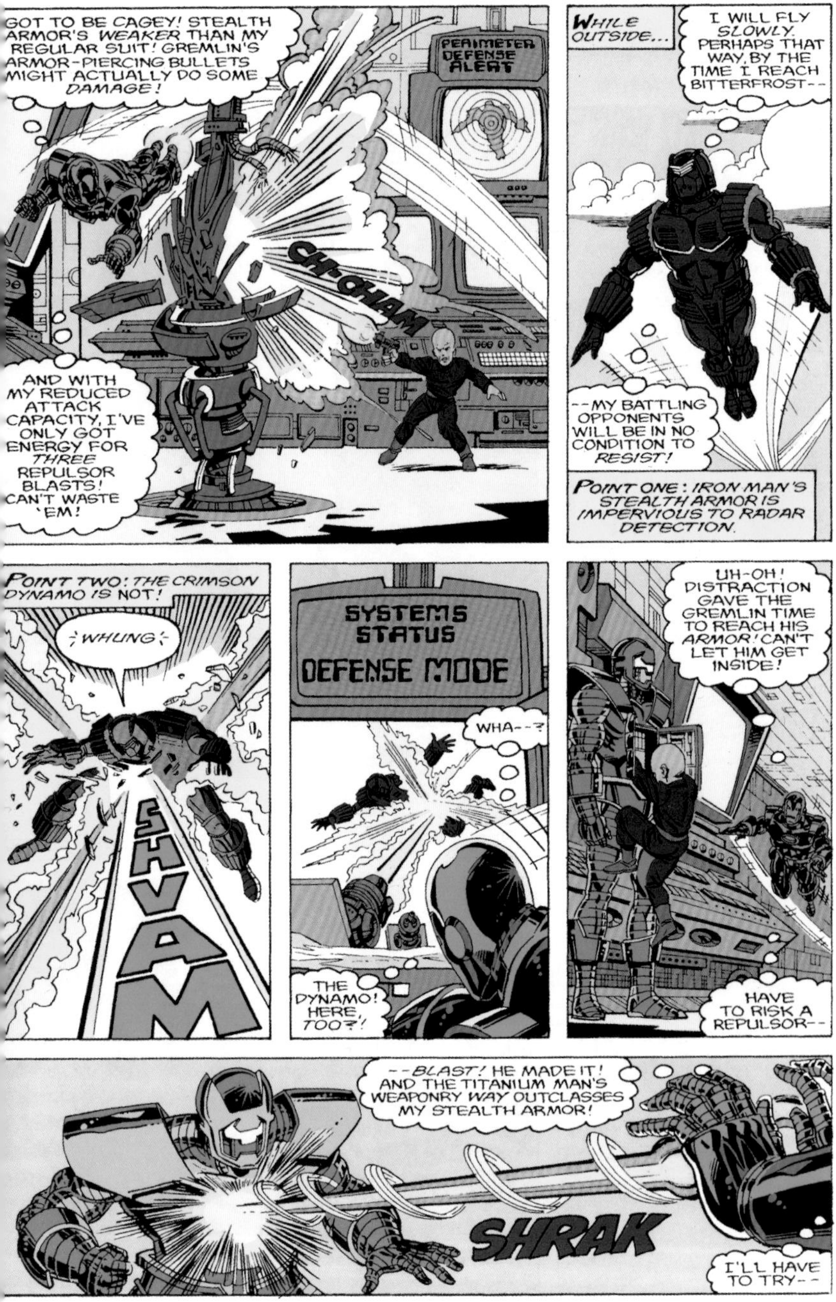
GOT TO BE CAGEY! STEALTH ARMOR'S WEAKER THAN MY REGULAR SUIT! GREMLIN'S ARMOR-PIERCING BULLETS MIGHT ACTUALLY DO SOME DAMAGE!
PERIMETER DEFENSE ALERT
CH-CHAM
AND WITH MY REDUCED ATTACK CAPACITY, I'VE ONLY GOT ENERGY FOR THREE REPULSOR BLASTS! CAN'T WASTE 'EM!
WHILE OUTSIDE...
I WILL FLY SLOWLY. PERHAPS THAT WAY, BY THE TIME I REACH BITTERFROST--
--MY BATTLING OPPONENTS WILL BE IN NO CONDITION TO RESIST!
POINT ONE: IRON MAN'S STEALTH ARMOR IS IMPERVIOUS TO RADAR DETECTION.
POINT TWO: THE CRIMSON DYNAMO IS NOT!
WHUNG
SHVAM
SYSTEMS STATUS
DEFENSE MODE
WHA--?
THE DYNAMO! HERE, TOO?!
UH-OH! DISTRACTION GAVE THE GREMLIN TIME TO REACH HIS ARMOR! CAN'T LET HIM GET INSIDE!
HAVE TO RISK A REPULSOR--
--BLAST! HE MADE IT! AND THE TITANIUM MAN'S WEAPONRY WAY OUTCLASSES MY STEALTH ARMOR!
SHRAK
I'LL HAVE TO TRY--

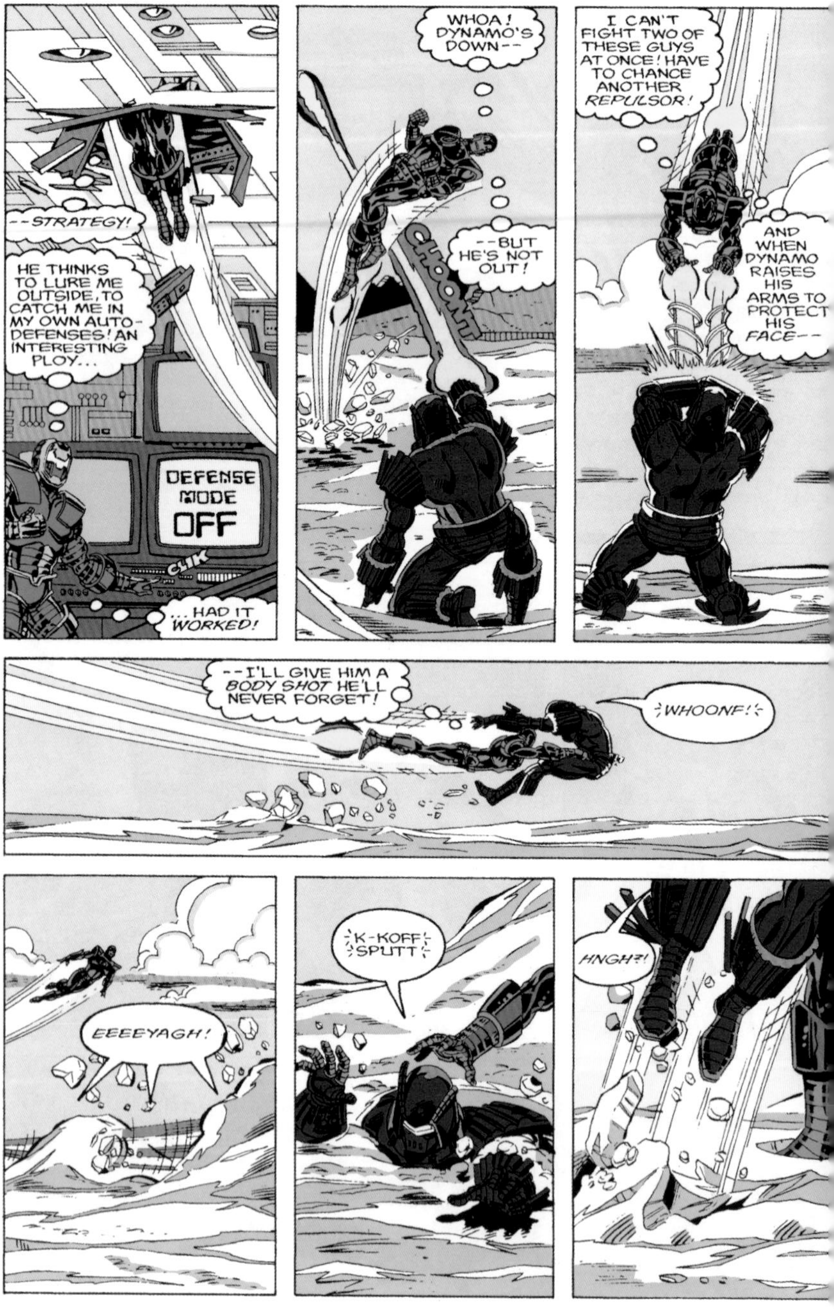
--STRATEGY!
HE THINKS TO LURE ME OUTSIDE, TO CATCH ME IN MY OWN AUTO-DEFENSES! AN INTERESTING PLOY...
DEFENSE MODE OFF
CLIK
...HAD IT WORKED!
WHOA! DYNAMO'S DOWN--
--BUT HE'S NOT OUT!
CHOOM
I CAN'T FIGHT TWO OF THESE GUYS AT ONCE! HAVE TO CHANCE ANOTHER REPULSOR!
AND WHEN DYNAMO RAISES HIS ARMS TO PROTECT HIS FACE--
--I'LL GIVE HIM A BODY SHOT HE'LL NEVER FORGET!
WHOONF!
EEEEYAGH!
K-KOFF SPUTT
HNGH?!

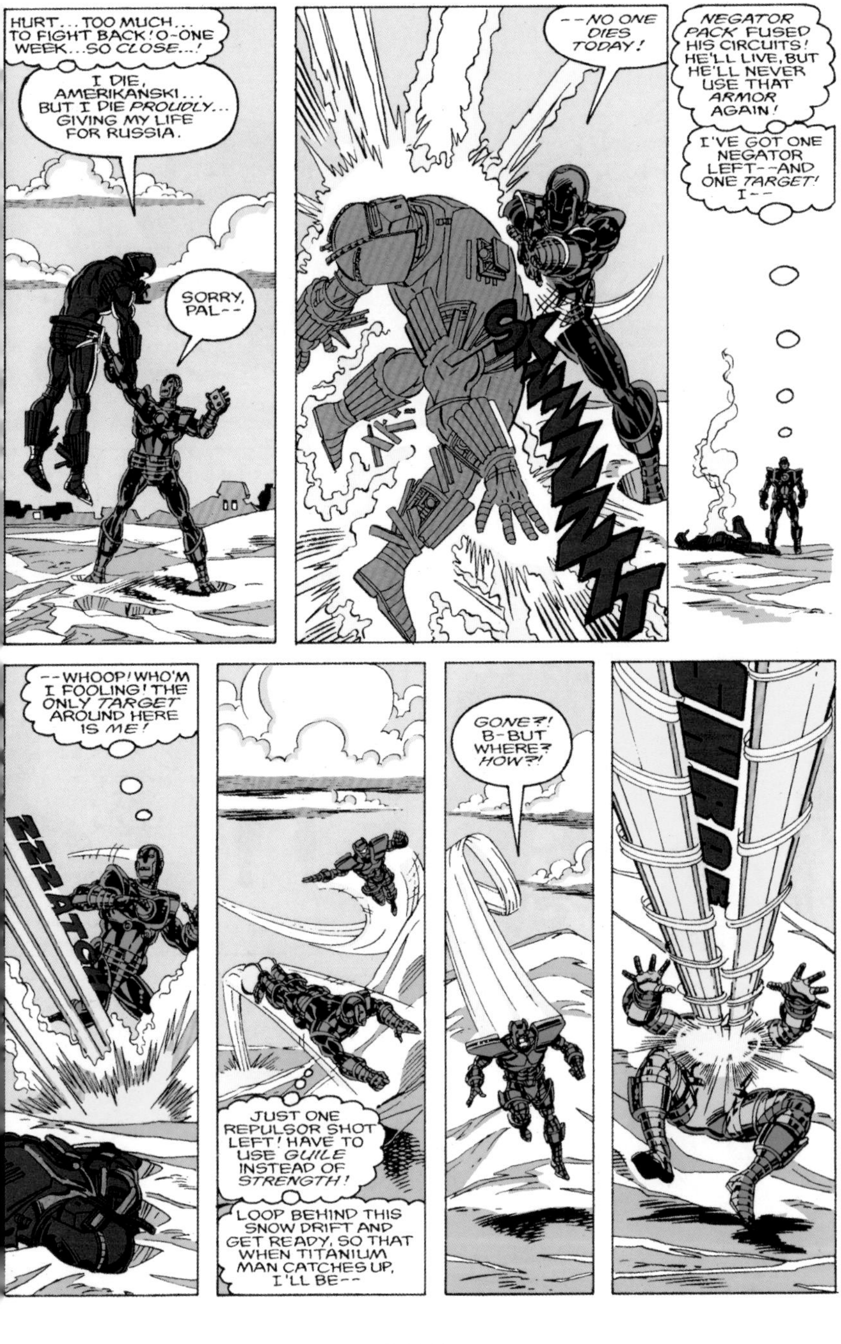
HURT... TOO MUCH... TO FIGHT BACK! O-ONE WEEK...SO CLOSE...!
I DIE, AMERIKANSKI... BUT I DIE PROUDLY... GIVING MY LIFE FOR RUSSIA.
SORRY, PAL--
--NO ONE DIES TODAY!
NEGATOR PACK FUSED HIS CIRCUITS! HE'LL LIVE, BUT HE'LL NEVER USE THAT ARMOR AGAIN!
I'VE GOT ONE NEGATOR LEFT--AND ONE TARGET! I--
--WHOOP! WHO'M I FOOLING! THE ONLY TARGET AROUND HERE IS ME!
JUST ONE REPULSOR SHOT LEFT! HAVE TO USE GUILE INSTEAD OF STRENGTH!
LOOP BEHIND THIS SNOW DRIFT AND GET READY, SO THAT WHEN TITANIUM MAN CATCHES UP, I'LL BE--
GONE?! B-BUT WHERE? HOW?!

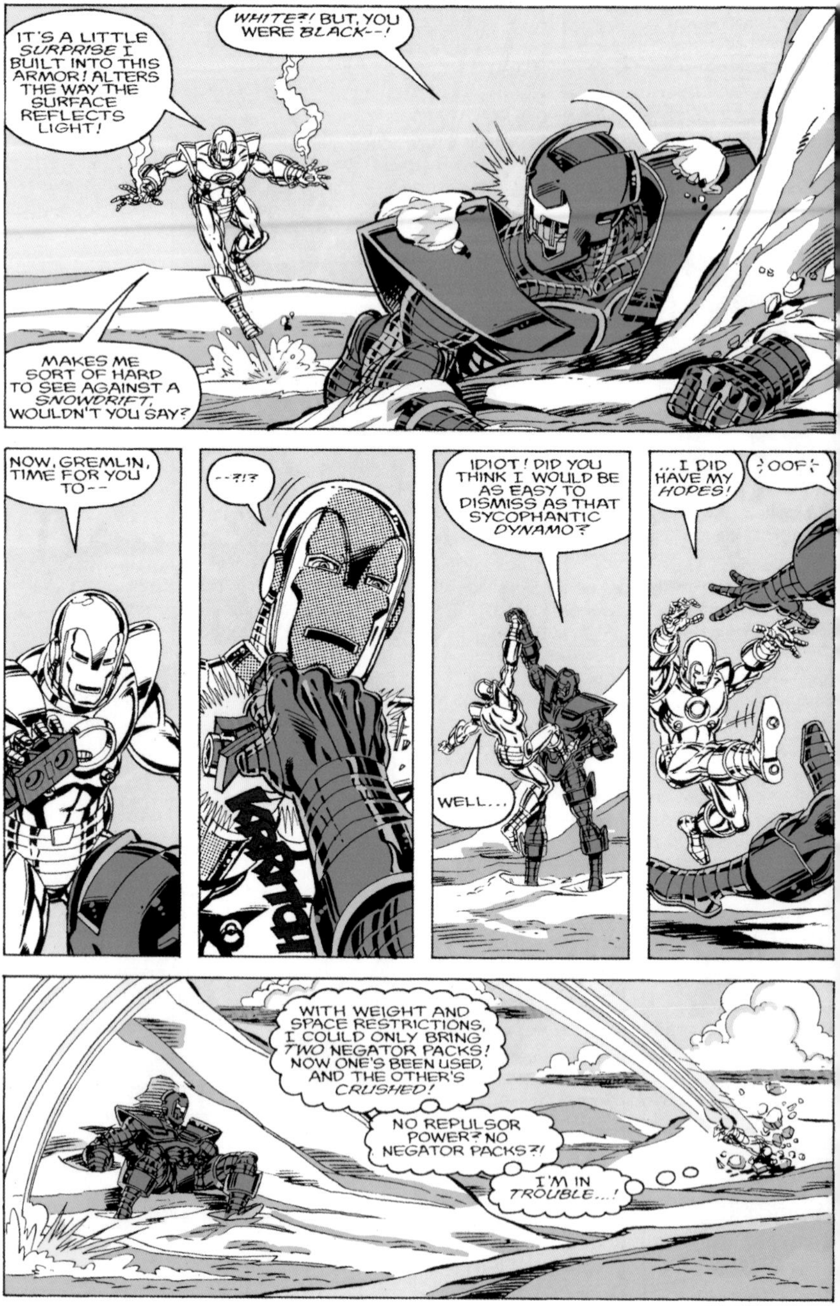
IT'S A LITTLE SURPRISE I BUILT INTO THIS ARMOR! ALTERS THE WAY THE SURFACE REFLECTS LIGHT!
WHITE?! BUT, YOU WERE BLACK--!
MAKES ME SORT OF HARD TO SEE AGAINST A SNOWDRIFT, WOULDN'T YOU SAY?
NOW, GREMLIN, TIME FOR YOU TO--
--?!?
IDIOT! DID YOU THINK I WOULD BE AS EASY TO DISMISS AS THAT SYCOPHANTIC DYNAMO?
WELL...
...I DID HAVE MY HOPES!
OOF
WITH WEIGHT AND SPACE RESTRICTIONS, I COULD ONLY BRING TWO NEGATOR PACKS! NOW ONE'S BEEN USED, AND THE OTHER'S CRUSHED!
NO REPULSOR POWER? NO NEGATOR PACKS?!
I'M IN TROUBLE...!

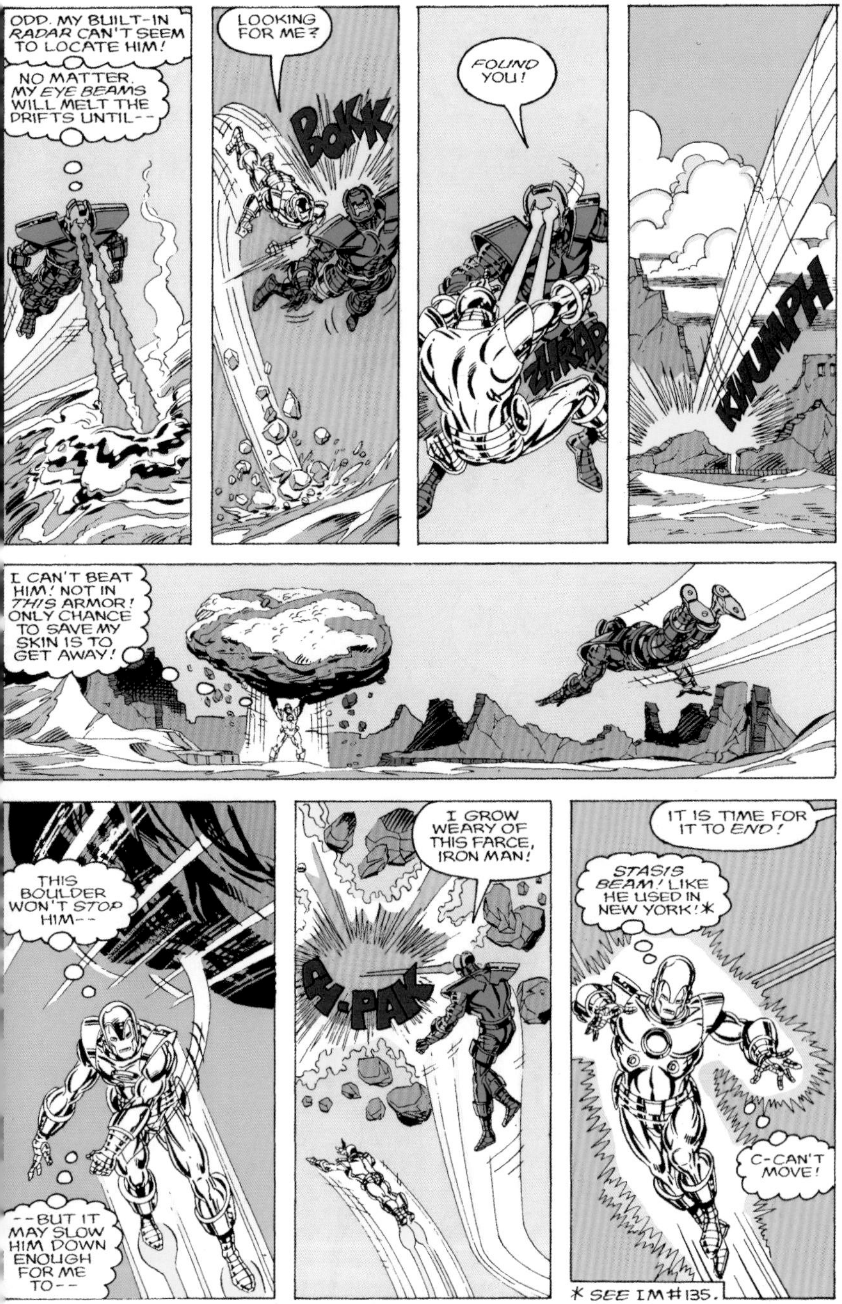
ODD. MY BUILT-IN RADAR CAN'T SEEM TO LOCATE HIM!
NO MATTER. MY EYE BEAMS WILL MELT THE DRIFTS UNTIL--
LOOKING FOR ME?
BOKK
FOUND YOU!
ZHRAP
KWUMPH
I CAN'T BEAT HIM! NOT IN THIS ARMOR! ONLY CHANCE TO SAVE MY SKIN IS TO GET AWAY!
THIS BOULDER WON'T STOP HIM--
--BUT IT MAY SLOW HIM DOWN ENOUGH FOR ME TO--
I GROW WEARY OF THIS FARCE, IRON MAN!
CH-PAK
IT IS TIME FOR IT TO END!
STASIS BEAM! LIKE HE USED IN NEW YORK!*
C-CAN'T MOVE!
* SEE IM #135.

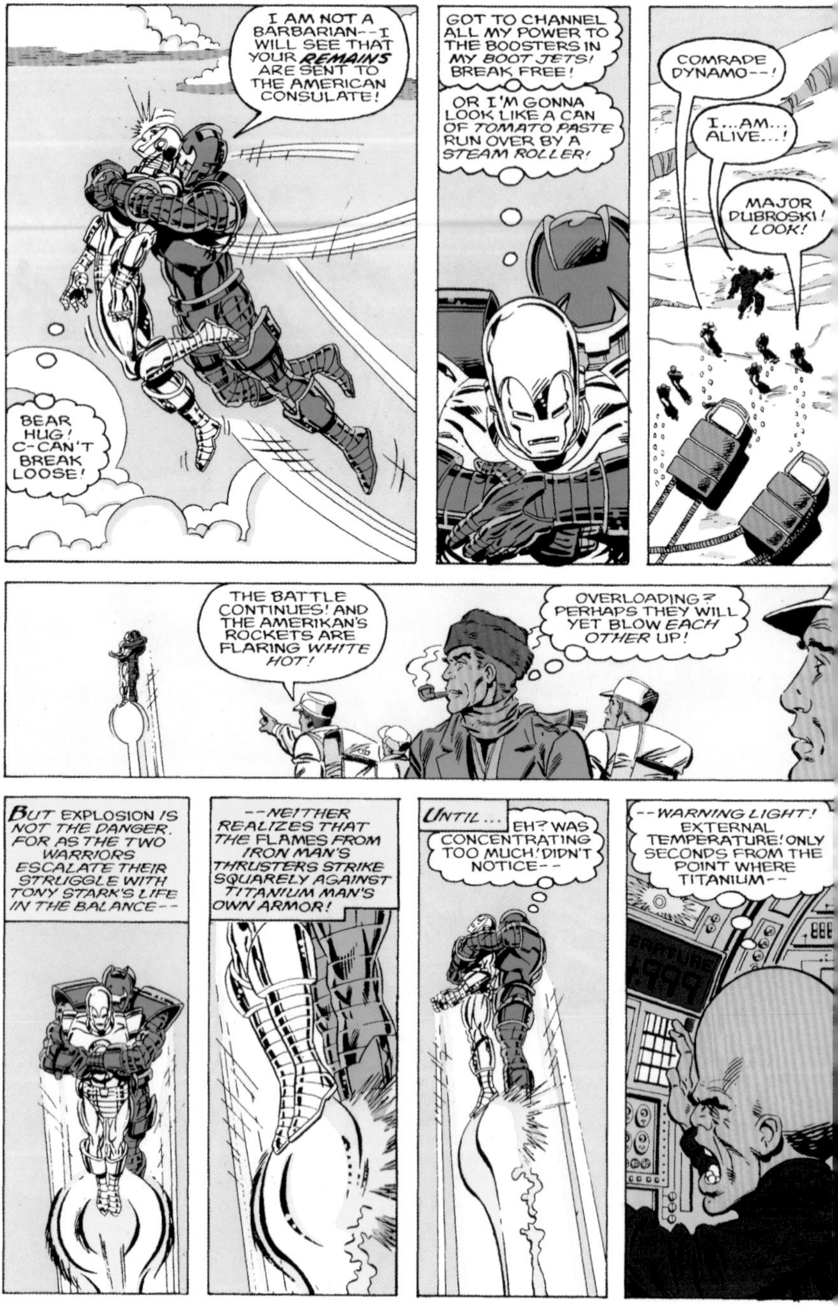
BEAR HUG! C-CAN'T BREAK LOOSE!
I AM NOT A BARBARIAN--I WILL SEE THAT YOUR REMAINS ARE SENT TO THE AMERICAN CONSULATE!
GOT TO CHANNEL ALL MY POWER TO THE BOOSTERS IN MY BOOT JETS! BREAK FREE!
OR I'M GONNA LOOK LIKE A CAN OF TOMATO PASTE RUN OVER BY A STEAM ROLLER!
COMRADE DYNAMO--!
I...AM... ALIVE...!
MAJOR DUBROSKI! LOOK!
THE BATTLE CONTINUES! AND THE AMERIKAN'S ROCKETS ARE FLARING WHITE HOT!
OVERLOADING? PERHAPS THEY WILL YET BLOW EACH OTHER UP!
BUT EXPLOSION IS NOT THE DANGER. FOR AS THE TWO WARRIORS ESCALATE THEIR STRUGGLE WITH TONY STARK'S LIFE IN THE BALANCE--
--NEITHER REALIZES THAT THE FLAMES FROM IRON MAN'S THRUSTERS STRIKE SQUARELY AGAINST TITANIUM MAN'S OWN ARMOR!
UNTIL...
EH? WAS CONCENTRATING TOO MUCH! DIDN'T NOTICE--
--WARNING LIGHT! EXTERNAL TEMPERATURE! ONLY SECONDS FROM THE POINT WHERE TITANIUM--

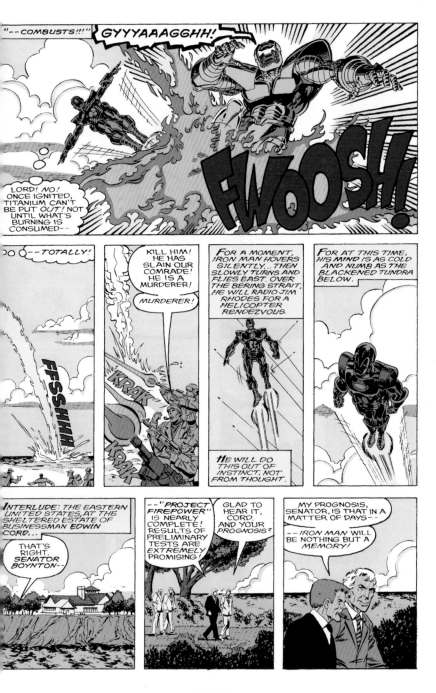

"--COMBUSTS!!!" GYYYAAAGGHH!

LORD! *NO!* ONCE IGNITED, TITANIUM CAN'T BE PUT OUT! NOT UNTIL WHAT'S BURNING IS CONSUMED--

FWOOSH!

00 --*TOTALLY!*

KILL HIM! HE HAS *SLAIN* OUR COMRADE! HE IS A *MURDERER!*

MURDERER!

FFSSHHH

KRAK

KRAK

FOR A MOMENT, IRON MAN HOVERS SILENTLY...THEN SLOWLY TURNS AND FLIES EAST, OVER THE BERING STRAIT; HE WILL RADIO JIM RHODES FOR A HELICOPTER RENDEZVOUS.

HE WILL DO THIS OUT OF INSTINCT, NOT FROM THOUGHT.

FOR AT THIS TIME, HIS MIND IS AS COLD AND NUMB AS THE BLACKENED TUNDRA BELOW.

INTERLUDE: THE EASTERN UNITED STATES, AT THE SHELTERED ESTATE OF BUSINESSMAN EDWIN CORD...

THAT'S RIGHT, *SENATOR BOYNTON*--

--"*PROJECT FIREPOWER*" IS NEARLY *COMPLETE!* RESULTS OF PRELIMINARY TESTS ARE *EXTREMELY PROMISING!*

GLAD TO HEAR IT, CORD. AND YOUR *PROGNOSIS?*

MY PROGNOSIS, SENATOR, IS THAT IN A MATTER OF *DAYS*--

--*IRON MAN* WILL BE NOTHING BUT A *MEMORY!*

[137]

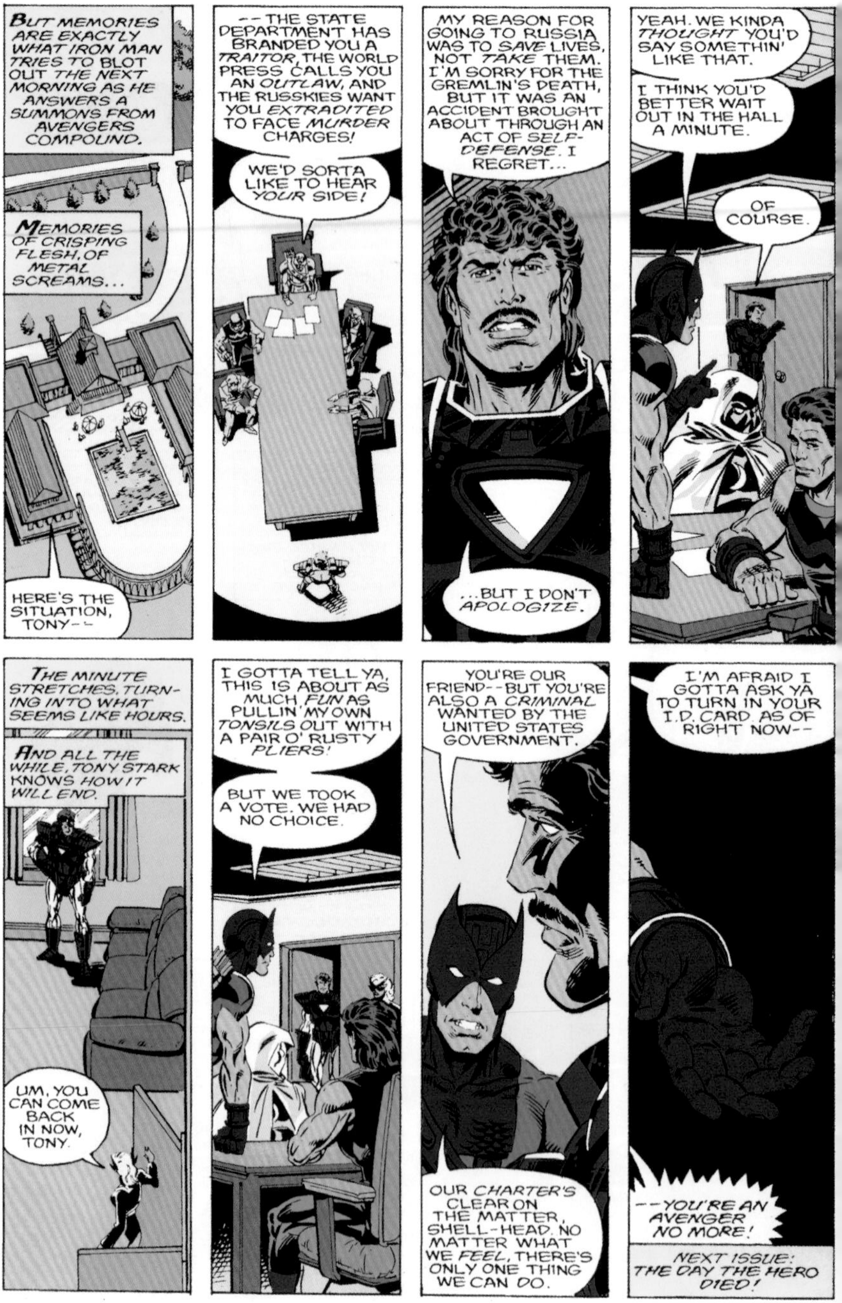
BUT MEMORIES ARE EXACTLY WHAT IRON MAN TRIES TO BLOT OUT THE NEXT MORNING AS HE ANSWERS A SUMMONS FROM AVENGERS COMPOUND.
MEMORIES OF CRISPING FLESH, OF METAL SCREAMS...
HERE'S THE SITUATION, TONY--
--THE STATE DEPARTMENT HAS BRANDED YOU A TRAITOR, THE WORLD PRESS CALLS YOU AN OUTLAW, AND THE RUSSKIES WANT YOU EXTRADITED TO FACE MURDER CHARGES!
WE'D SORTA LIKE TO HEAR YOUR SIDE!
MY REASON FOR GOING TO RUSSIA WAS TO SAVE LIVES, NOT TAKE THEM. I'M SORRY FOR THE GREMLIN'S DEATH, BUT IT WAS AN ACCIDENT BROUGHT ABOUT THROUGH AN ACT OF SELF-DEFENSE. I REGRET...
...BUT I DON'T APOLOGIZE.
YEAH. WE KINDA THOUGHT YOU'D SAY SOMETHIN' LIKE THAT.
I THINK YOU'D BETTER WAIT OUT IN THE HALL A MINUTE.
OF COURSE.
THE MINUTE STRETCHES, TURNING INTO WHAT SEEMS LIKE HOURS.
AND ALL THE WHILE, TONY STARK KNOWS HOW IT WILL END.
UM, YOU CAN COME BACK IN NOW, TONY.
I GOTTA TELL YA, THIS IS ABOUT AS MUCH FUN AS PULLIN' MY OWN TONSILS OUT WITH A PAIR O' RUSTY PLIERS!
BUT WE TOOK A VOTE. WE HAD NO CHOICE.
YOU'RE OUR FRIEND--BUT YOU'RE ALSO A CRIMINAL WANTED BY THE UNITED STATES GOVERNMENT.
OUR CHARTER'S CLEAR ON THE MATTER, SHELL-HEAD. NO MATTER WHAT WE FEEL, THERE'S ONLY ONE THING WE CAN DO.
I'M AFRAID I GOTTA ASK YA TO TURN IN YOUR I.D. CARD AS OF RIGHT NOW--
--YOU'RE AN AVENGER NO MORE!
NEXT ISSUE: THE DAY THE HERO DIED!

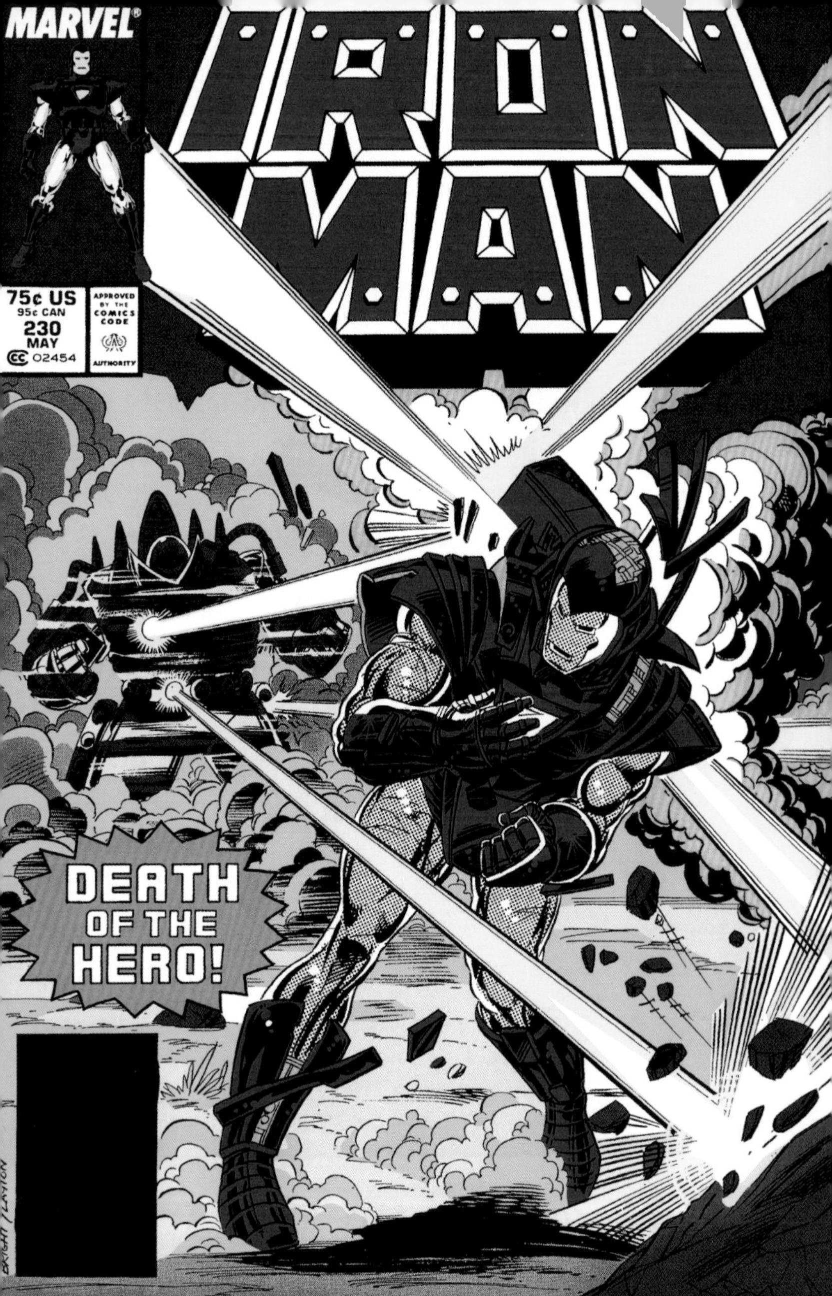
MARVEL®
IRON MAN
75¢ US
95¢ CAN
230
MAY
CC 02454
APPROVED BY THE COMICS CODE AUTHORITY
DEATH OF THE HERO!

STAN LEE PRESENTS:

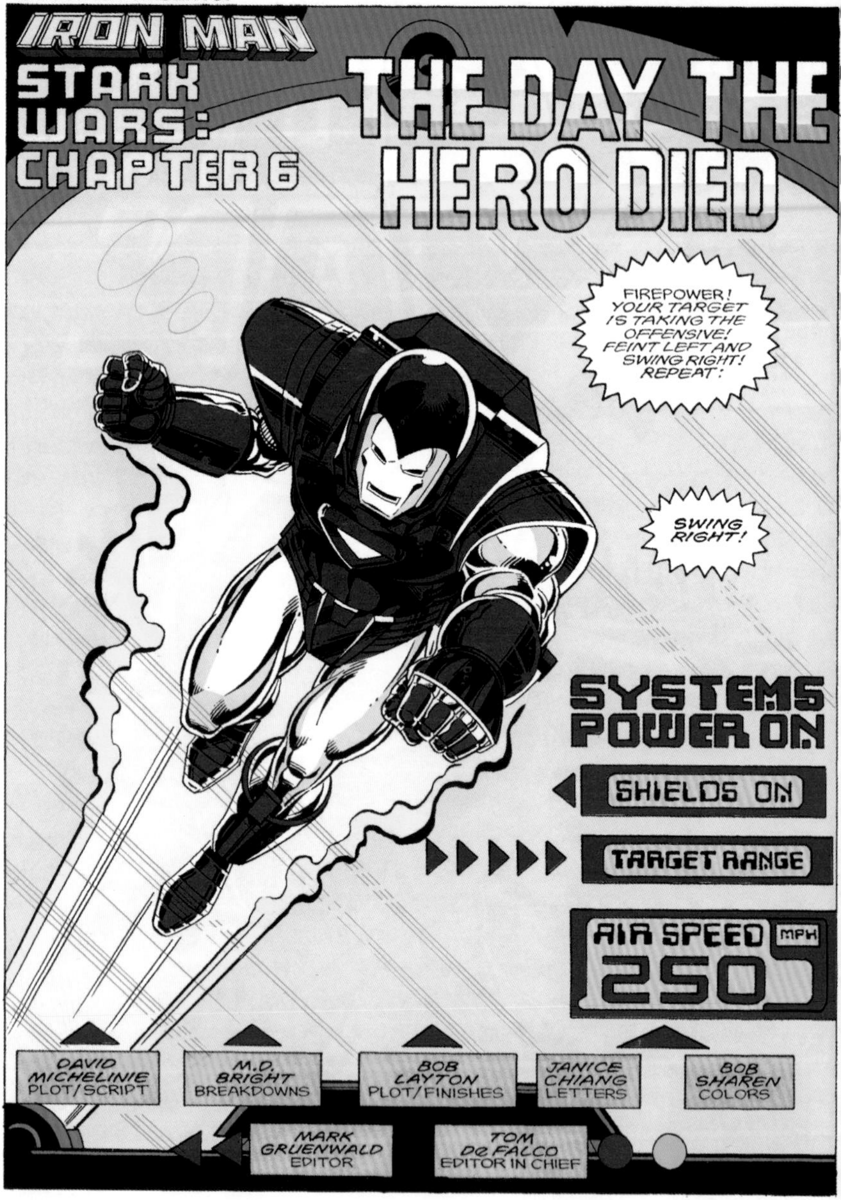

IRON MAN
STARK WARS: CHAPTER 6
THE DAY THE HERO DIED
FIREPOWER! YOUR TARGET IS TAKING THE OFFENSIVE! FEINT LEFT AND SWING RIGHT! REPEAT:
SWING RIGHT!
SYSTEMS POWER ON
SHIELDS ON
TARGET RANGE
AIR SPEED MPH
250
DAVID MICHELINIE PLOT/SCRIPT
M.D. BRIGHT BREAKDOWNS
BOB LAYTON PLOT/FINISHES
JANICE CHIANG LETTERS
BOB SHAREN COLORS
MARK GRUENWALD EDITOR
TOM DeFALCO EDITOR IN CHIEF

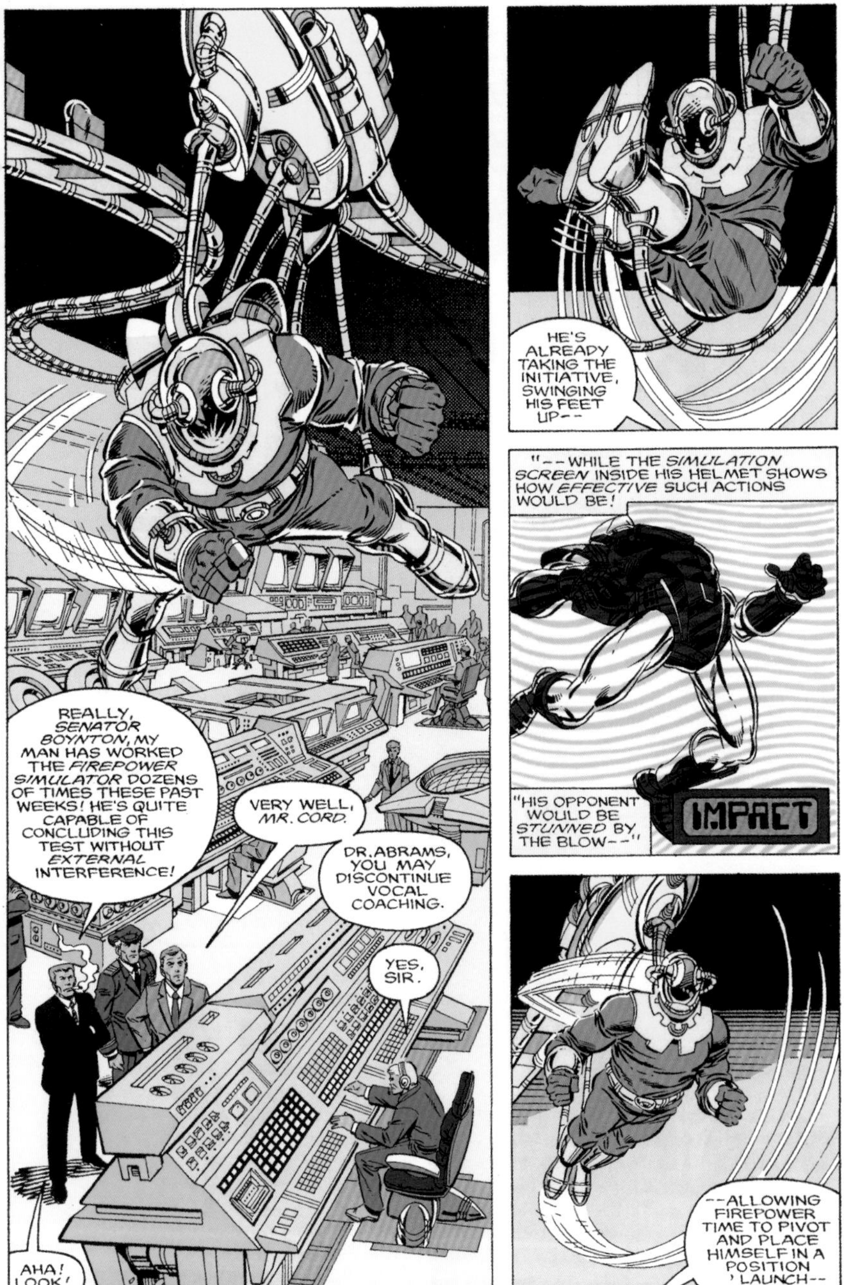
REALLY, SENATOR BOYNTON, MY MAN HAS WORKED THE FIREPOWER SIMULATOR DOZENS OF TIMES THESE PAST WEEKS! HE'S QUITE CAPABLE OF CONCLUDING THIS TEST WITHOUT EXTERNAL INTERFERENCE!
VERY WELL, MR. CORD.
DR. ABRAMS, YOU MAY DISCONTINUE VOCAL COACHING.
YES, SIR.
AHA! LOOK!
HE'S ALREADY TAKING THE INITIATIVE, SWINGING HIS FEET UP--
"--WHILE THE SIMULATION SCREEN INSIDE HIS HELMET SHOWS HOW EFFECTIVE SUCH ACTIONS WOULD BE!
IMPACT
"HIS OPPONENT WOULD BE STUNNED BY THE BLOW--"
--ALLOWING FIREPOWER TIME TO PIVOT AND PLACE HIMSELF IN A POSITION 'LAUNCH--

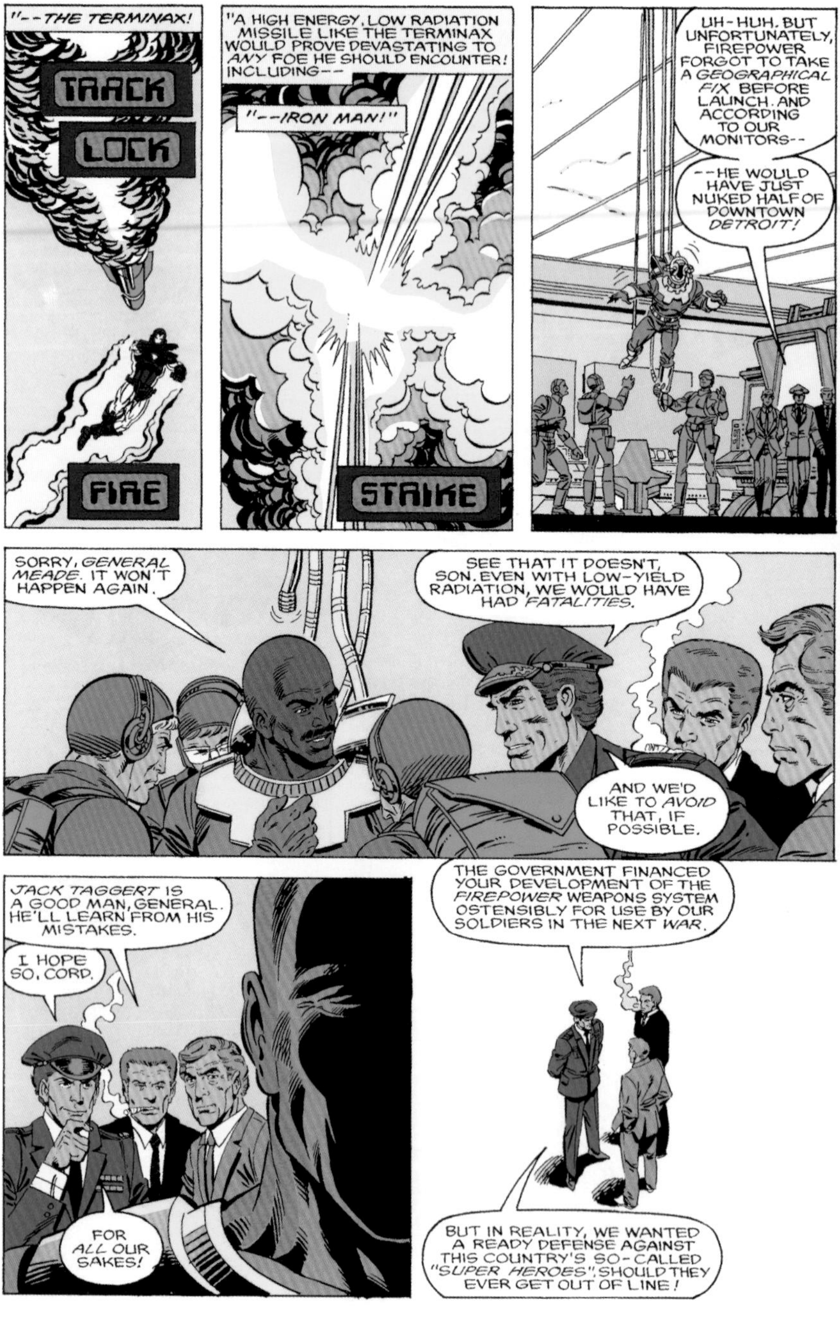
"--THE TERMINAX!
TRACK
LOCK
FIRE
"A HIGH ENERGY, LOW RADIATION MISSILE LIKE THE TERMINAX WOULD PROVE DEVASTATING TO ANY FOE HE SHOULD ENCOUNTER! INCLUDING--
"--IRON MAN!"
STRIKE
UH-HUH. BUT UNFORTUNATELY, FIREPOWER FORGOT TO TAKE A GEOGRAPHICAL FIX BEFORE LAUNCH. AND ACCORDING TO OUR MONITORS--
--HE WOULD HAVE JUST NUKED HALF OF DOWNTOWN DETROIT!
SORRY, GENERAL MEADE. IT WON'T HAPPEN AGAIN.
SEE THAT IT DOESN'T, SON. EVEN WITH LOW-YIELD RADIATION, WE WOULD HAVE HAD FATALITIES.
AND WE'D LIKE TO AVOID THAT, IF POSSIBLE.
JACK TAGGERT IS A GOOD MAN, GENERAL. HE'LL LEARN FROM HIS MISTAKES.
I HOPE SO, CORD.
FOR ALL OUR SAKES!
THE GOVERNMENT FINANCED YOUR DEVELOPMENT OF THE FIREPOWER WEAPONS SYSTEM OSTENSIBLY FOR USE BY OUR SOLDIERS IN THE NEXT WAR.
BUT IN REALITY, WE WANTED A READY DEFENSE AGAINST THIS COUNTRY'S SO-CALLED "SUPER HEROES", SHOULD THEY EVER GET OUT OF LINE!

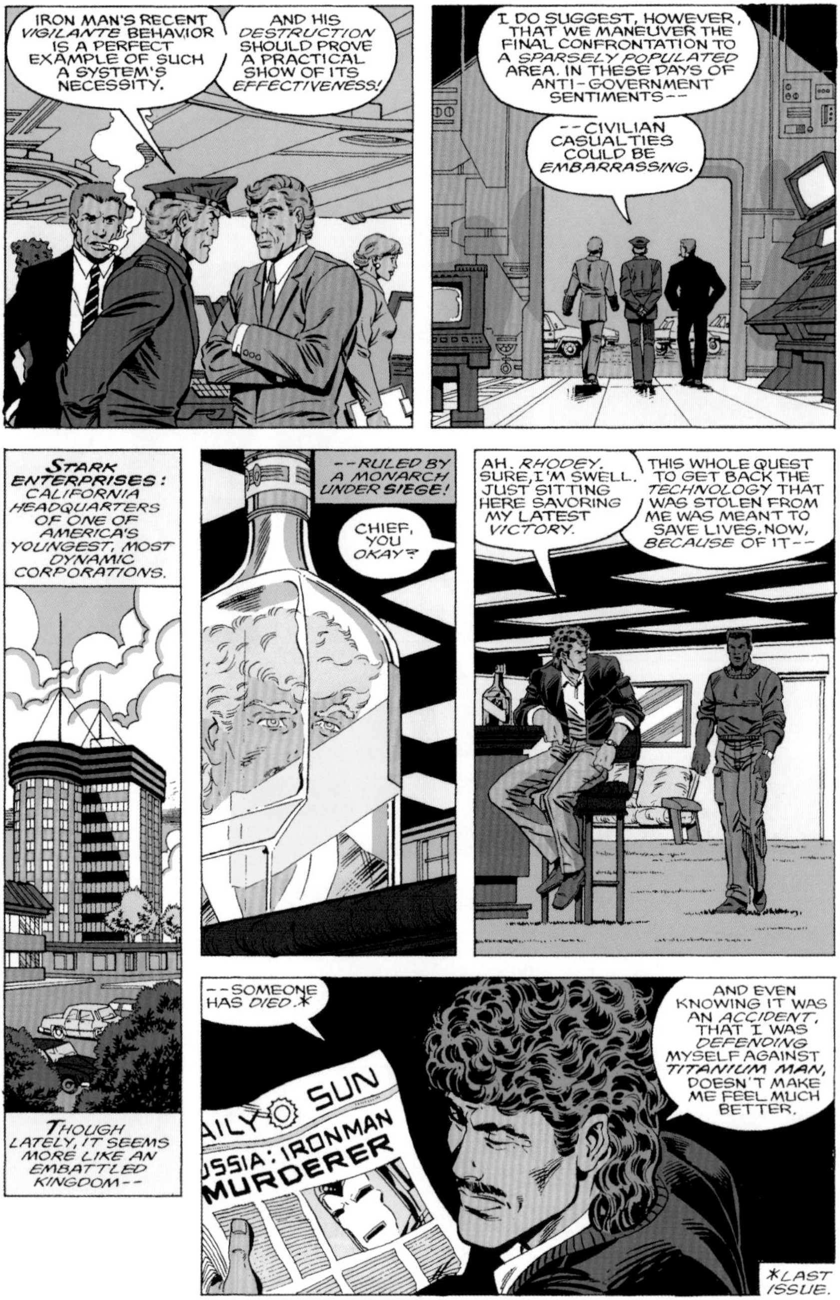
IRON MAN'S RECENT VIGILANTE BEHAVIOR IS A PERFECT EXAMPLE OF SUCH A SYSTEM'S NECESSITY.
AND HIS DESTRUCTION SHOULD PROVE A PRACTICAL SHOW OF ITS EFFECTIVENESS!
I DO SUGGEST, HOWEVER, THAT WE MANEUVER THE FINAL CONFRONTATION TO A SPARSELY POPULATED AREA. IN THESE DAYS OF ANTI-GOVERNMENT SENTIMENTS--
--CIVILIAN CASUALTIES COULD BE EMBARRASSING.
STARK ENTERPRISES: CALIFORNIA HEADQUARTERS OF ONE OF AMERICA'S YOUNGEST, MOST DYNAMIC CORPORATIONS.
THOUGH LATELY, IT SEEMS MORE LIKE AN EMBATTLED KINGDOM--
--RULED BY A MONARCH UNDER SIEGE!
CHIEF, YOU OKAY?
AH. RHODEY. SURE, I'M SWELL. JUST SITTING HERE SAVORING MY LATEST VICTORY.
THIS WHOLE QUEST TO GET BACK THE TECHNOLOGY THAT WAS STOLEN FROM ME WAS MEANT TO SAVE LIVES. NOW, BECAUSE OF IT--
--SOMEONE HAS DIED.*
AILY SUN
USSIA: IRONMAN MURDERER
AND EVEN KNOWING IT WAS AN ACCIDENT, THAT I WAS DEFENDING MYSELF AGAINST TITANIUM MAN, DOESN'T MAKE ME FEEL MUCH BETTER.
*LAST ISSUE.

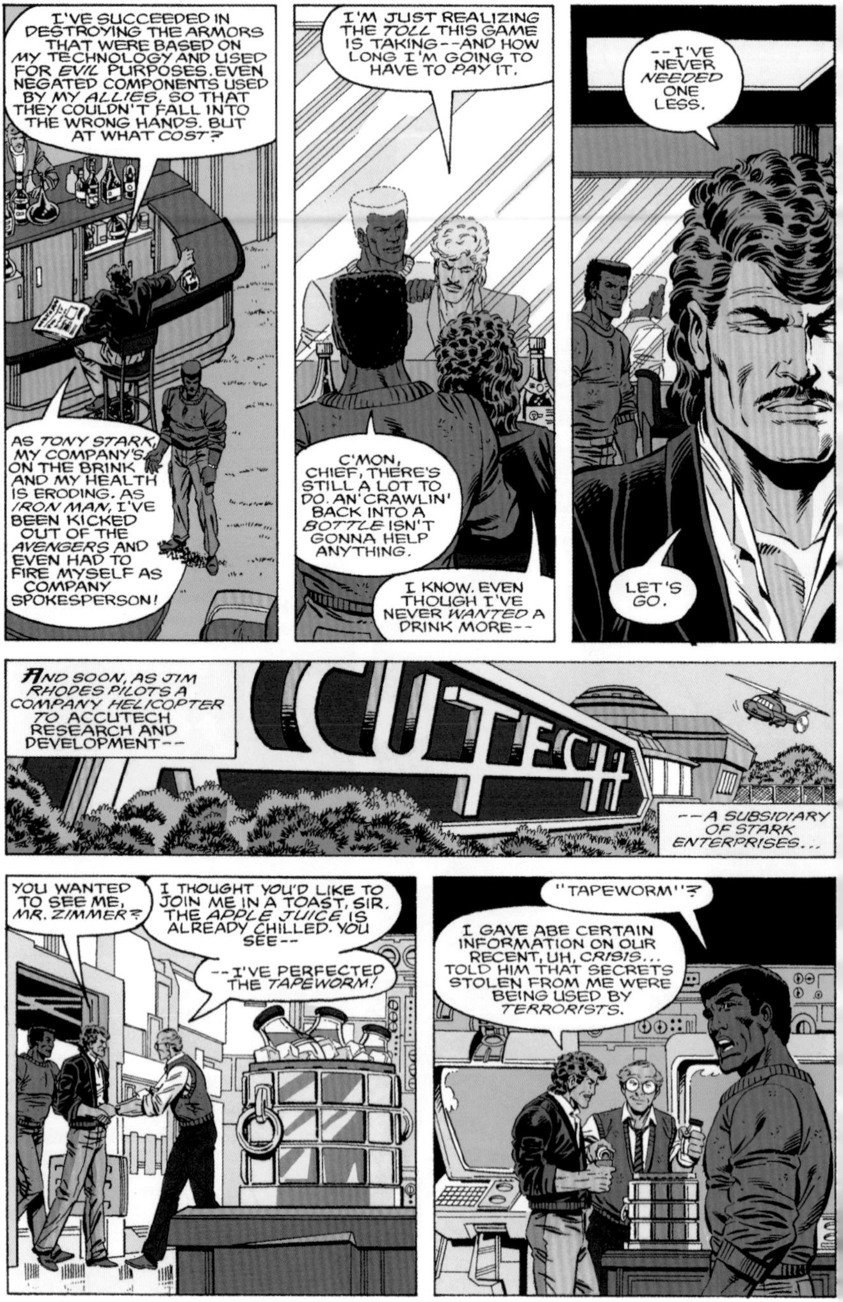

I'VE SUCCEEDED IN DESTROYING THE ARMORS THAT WERE BASED ON MY TECHNOLOGY AND USED FOR EVIL PURPOSES. EVEN NEGATED COMPONENTS USED BY MY ALLIES, SO THAT THEY COULDN'T FALL INTO THE WRONG HANDS. BUT AT WHAT COST?
AS TONY STARK, MY COMPANY'S ON THE BRINK AND MY HEALTH IS ERODING. AS IRON MAN, I'VE BEEN KICKED OUT OF THE AVENGERS AND EVEN HAD TO FIRE MYSELF AS COMPANY SPOKESPERSON!
I'M JUST REALIZING THE TOLL THIS GAME IS TAKING--AND HOW LONG I'M GOING TO HAVE TO PAY IT.
C'MON, CHIEF, THERE'S STILL A LOT TO DO. AN' CRAWLIN' BACK INTO A BOTTLE ISN'T GONNA HELP ANYTHING.
I KNOW. EVEN THOUGH I'VE NEVER WANTED A DRINK MORE--
--I'VE NEVER NEEDED ONE LESS.
LET'S GO.
AND SOON, AS JIM RHODES PILOTS A COMPANY HELICOPTER TO ACCUTECH RESEARCH AND DEVELOPMENT--
CUTECH
--A SUBSIDIARY OF STARK ENTERPRISES...
YOU WANTED TO SEE ME, MR. ZIMMER?
I THOUGHT YOU'D LIKE TO JOIN ME IN A TOAST, SIR. THE APPLE JUICE IS ALREADY CHILLED. YOU SEE--
--I'VE PERFECTED THE TAPEWORM!
"TAPEWORM"?
I GAVE ABE CERTAIN INFORMATION ON OUR RECENT, UH, CRISIS... TOLD HIM THAT SECRETS STOLEN FROM ME WERE BEING USED BY TERRORISTS.

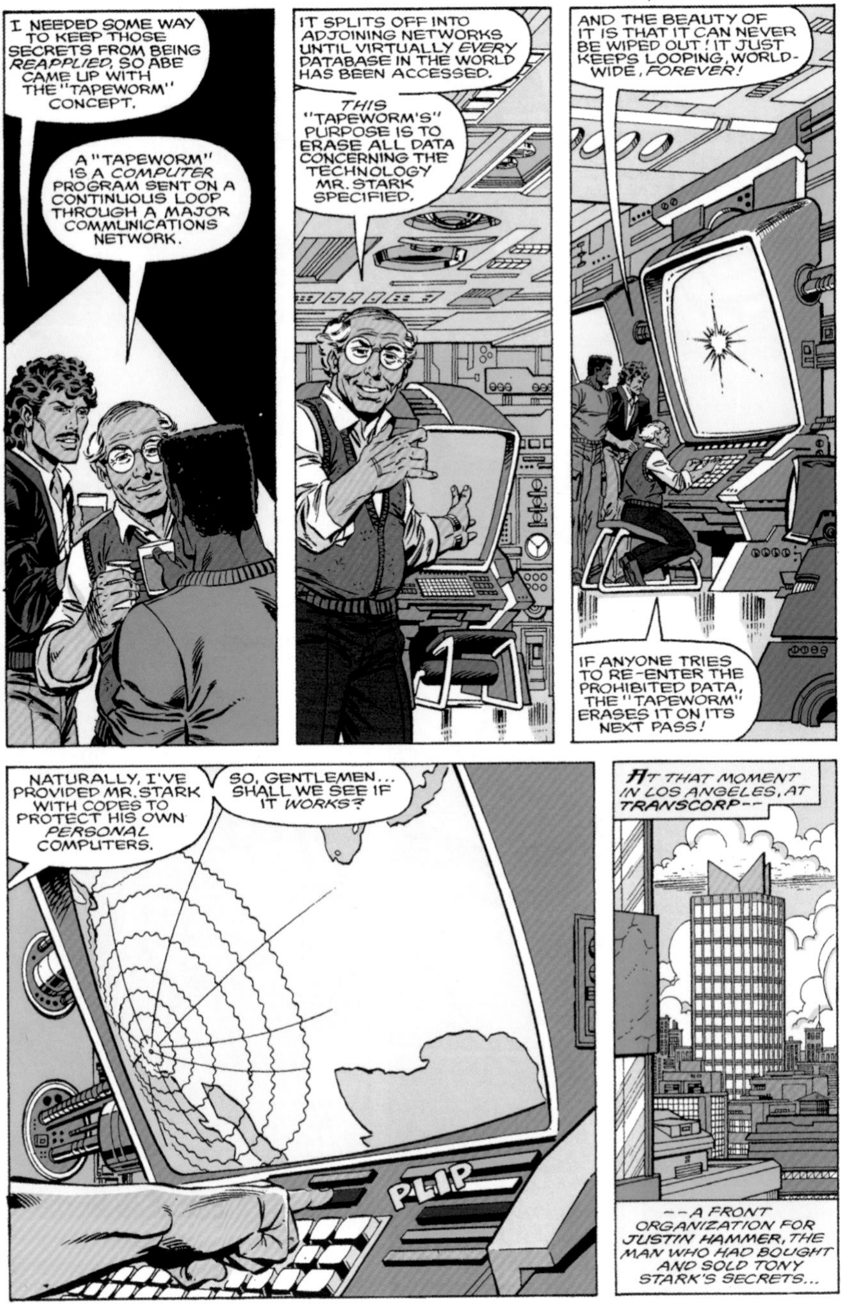
I NEEDED SOME WAY TO KEEP THOSE SECRETS FROM BEING *REAPPLIED*, SO ABE CAME UP WITH THE "TAPEWORM" CONCEPT.
A "TAPEWORM" IS A *COMPUTER* PROGRAM SENT ON A CONTINUOUS LOOP THROUGH A MAJOR COMMUNICATIONS NETWORK.
IT SPLITS OFF INTO ADJOINING NETWORKS UNTIL VIRTUALLY *EVERY* DATABASE IN THE WORLD HAS BEEN ACCESSED.
THIS "TAPEWORM'S" PURPOSE IS TO ERASE ALL DATA CONCERNING THE TECHNOLOGY MR. STARK SPECIFIED.
AND THE BEAUTY OF IT IS THAT IT CAN NEVER BE WIPED OUT! IT JUST KEEPS LOOPING, WORLD-WIDE, *FOREVER!*
IF ANYONE TRIES TO RE-ENTER THE PROHIBITED DATA, THE "TAPEWORM" ERASES IT ON ITS NEXT PASS!
NATURALLY, I'VE PROVIDED MR. STARK WITH CODES TO PROTECT HIS OWN *PERSONAL* COMPUTERS.
SO, GENTLEMEN... SHALL WE SEE IF IT *WORKS?*
PLIP
AT THAT MOMENT IN LOS ANGELES, AT TRANSCORP--
--A FRONT ORGANIZATION FOR JUSTIN HAMMER, THE MAN WHO HAD BOUGHT AND SOLD TONY STARK'S SECRETS...

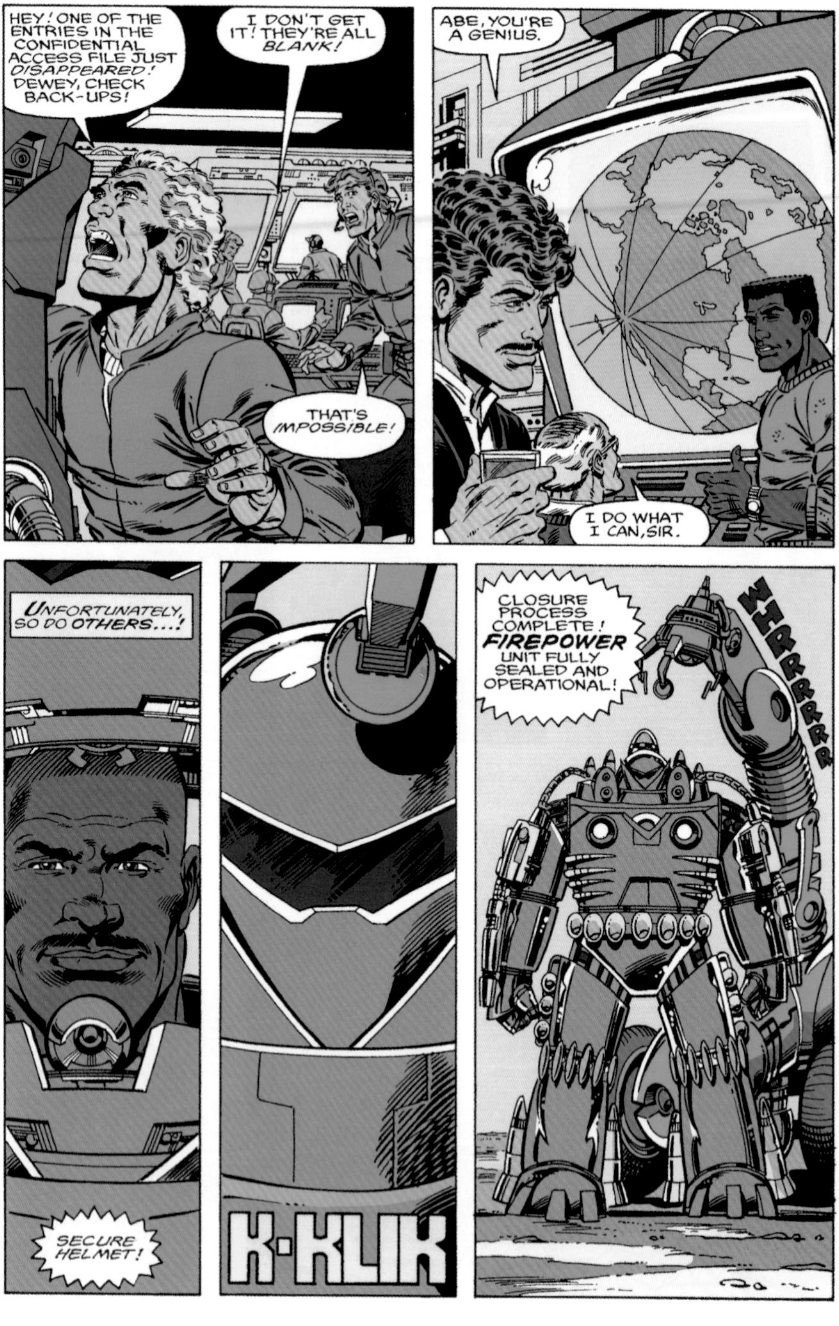
HEY! ONE OF THE ENTRIES IN THE CONFIDENTIAL ACCESS FILE JUST DISAPPEARED! DEWEY, CHECK BACK-UPS!
I DON'T GET IT! THEY'RE ALL BLANK!
THAT'S IMPOSSIBLE!
ABE, YOU'RE A GENIUS.
I DO WHAT I CAN, SIR.
UNFORTUNATELY, SO DO OTHERS...!
SECURE HELMET!
K-KLIK
CLOSURE PROCESS COMPLETE! FIREPOWER UNIT FULLY SEALED AND OPERATIONAL!
WHRRRRRRR

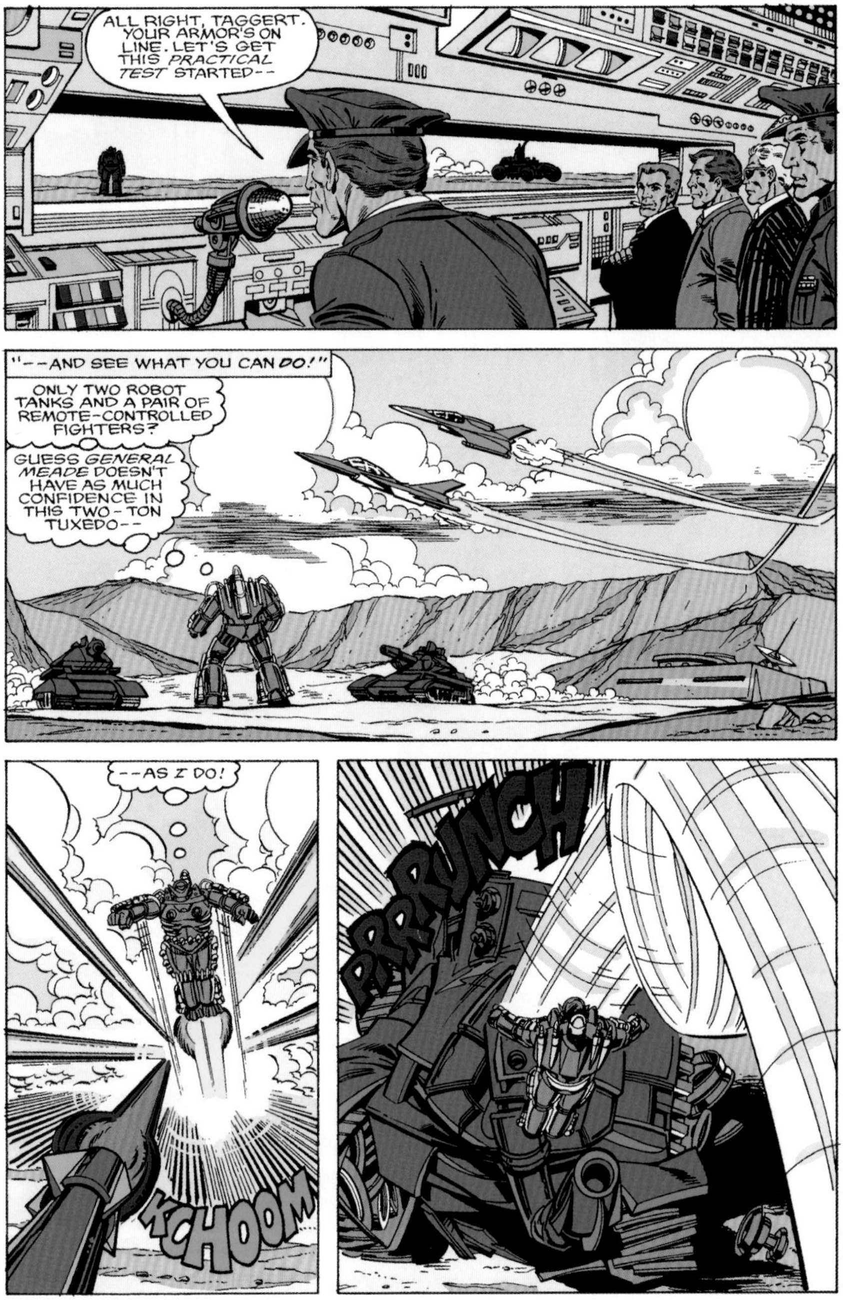
ALL RIGHT, TAGGERT. YOUR ARMOR'S ON LINE. LET'S GET THIS PRACTICAL TEST STARTED--
"--AND SEE WHAT YOU CAN DO!"
ONLY TWO ROBOT TANKS AND A PAIR OF REMOTE-CONTROLLED FIGHTERS?
GUESS GENERAL MEADE DOESN'T HAVE AS MUCH CONFIDENCE IN THIS TWO-TON TUXEDO--
--AS I DO!
KCHOOM
PRRRUNCH

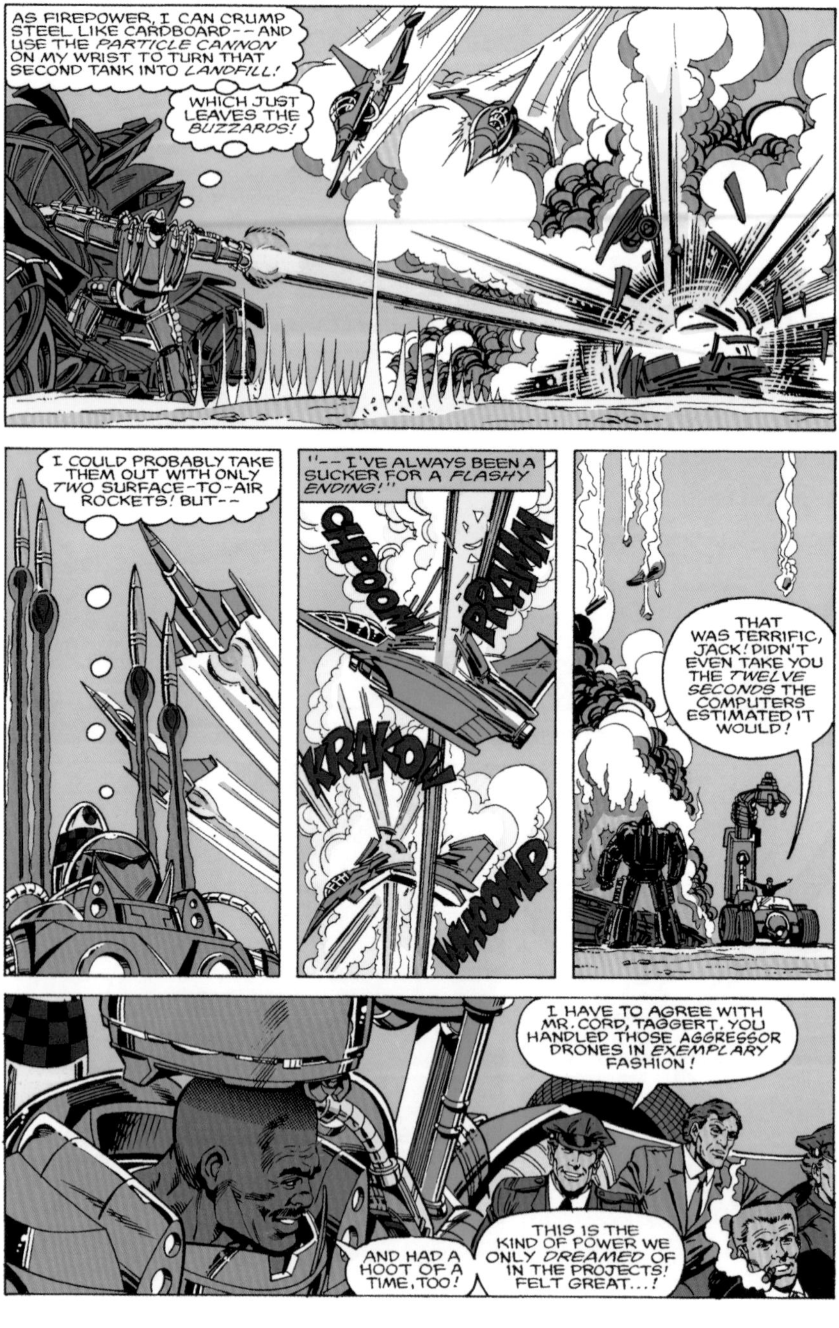
AS FIREPOWER, I CAN CRUMP STEEL LIKE CARDBOARD-- AND USE THE PARTICLE CANNON ON MY WRIST TO TURN THAT SECOND TANK INTO LANDFILL!
WHICH JUST LEAVES THE BUZZARDS!
I COULD PROBABLY TAKE THEM OUT WITH ONLY TWO SURFACE-TO-AIR ROCKETS! BUT--
"-- I'VE ALWAYS BEEN A SUCKER FOR A FLASHY ENDING!"
CHPOOOM
PRAMM
KRAKOW
WHOOMP
THAT WAS TERRIFIC, JACK! DIDN'T EVEN TAKE YOU THE TWELVE SECONDS THE COMPUTERS ESTIMATED IT WOULD!
I HAVE TO AGREE WITH MR. CORD, TAGGERT. YOU HANDLED THOSE AGGRESSOR DRONES IN EXEMPLARY FASHION!
AND HAD A HOOT OF A TIME, TOO!
THIS IS THE KIND OF POWER WE ONLY DREAMED OF IN THE PROJECTS! FELT GREAT...!

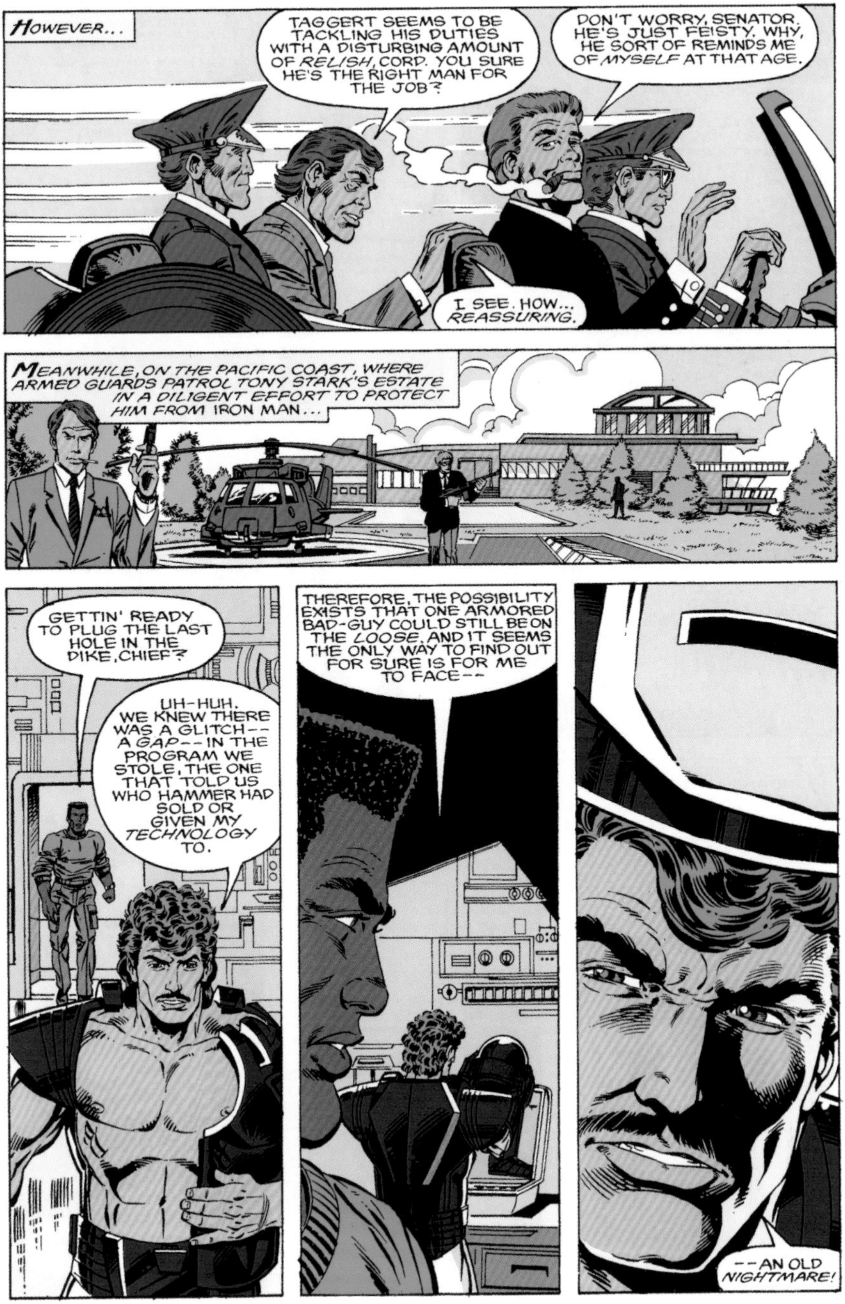
HOWEVER...
TAGGERT SEEMS TO BE TACKLING HIS DUTIES WITH A DISTURBING AMOUNT OF RELISH, CORD. YOU SURE HE'S THE RIGHT MAN FOR THE JOB?
DON'T WORRY, SENATOR. HE'S JUST FEISTY. WHY, HE SORT OF REMINDS ME OF MYSELF AT THAT AGE.
I SEE. HOW... REASSURING.
MEANWHILE, ON THE PACIFIC COAST, WHERE ARMED GUARDS PATROL TONY STARK'S ESTATE IN A DILIGENT EFFORT TO PROTECT HIM FROM IRON MAN...
GETTIN' READY TO PLUG THE LAST HOLE IN THE DIKE, CHIEF?
UH-HUH. WE KNEW THERE WAS A GLITCH-- A GAP-- IN THE PROGRAM WE STOLE, THE ONE THAT TOLD US WHO HAMMER HAD SOLD OR GIVEN MY TECHNOLOGY TO.
THEREFORE, THE POSSIBILITY EXISTS THAT ONE ARMORED BAD-GUY COULD STILL BE ON THE LOOSE. AND IT SEEMS THE ONLY WAY TO FIND OUT FOR SURE IS FOR ME TO FACE--
--AN OLD NIGHTMARE!

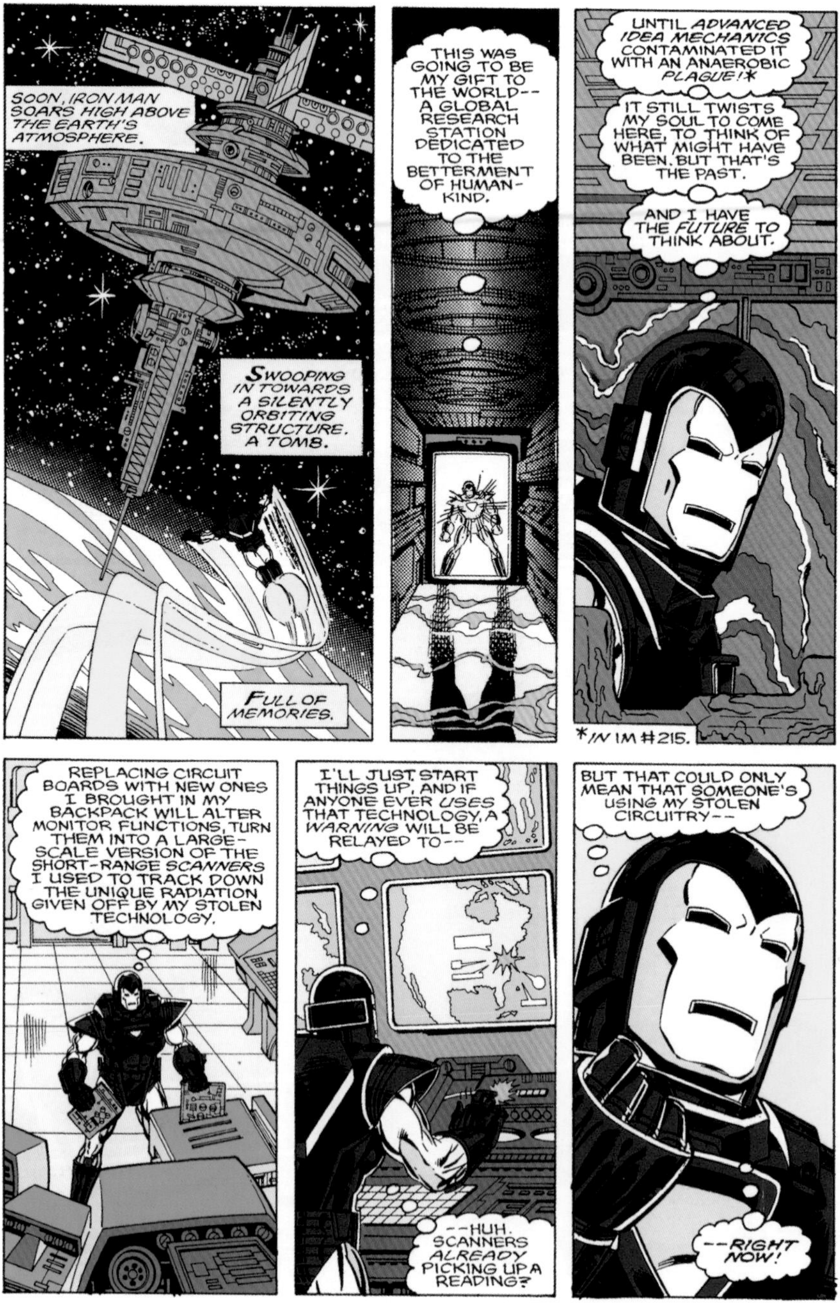
SOON, IRON MAN SOARS HIGH ABOVE THE EARTH'S ATMOSPHERE.
SWOOPING IN TOWARDS A SILENTLY ORBITING STRUCTURE. A TOMB.
FULL OF MEMORIES.
THIS WAS GOING TO BE MY GIFT TO THE WORLD-- A GLOBAL RESEARCH STATION DEDICATED TO THE BETTERMENT OF HUMAN-KIND.
UNTIL ADVANCED IDEA MECHANICS CONTAMINATED IT WITH AN ANAEROBIC PLAGUE!*
IT STILL TWISTS MY SOUL TO COME HERE, TO THINK OF WHAT MIGHT HAVE BEEN. BUT THAT'S THE PAST.
AND I HAVE THE FUTURE TO THINK ABOUT.
*IN IM #215.
REPLACING CIRCUIT BOARDS WITH NEW ONES I BROUGHT IN MY BACKPACK WILL ALTER MONITOR FUNCTIONS, TURN THEM INTO A LARGE-SCALE VERSION OF THE SHORT-RANGE SCANNERS I USED TO TRACK DOWN THE UNIQUE RADIATION GIVEN OFF BY MY STOLEN TECHNOLOGY.
I'LL JUST START THINGS UP, AND IF ANYONE EVER USES THAT TECHNOLOGY, A WARNING WILL BE RELAYED TO--
--HUH. SCANNERS ALREADY PICKING UP A READING?
BUT THAT COULD ONLY MEAN THAT SOMEONE'S USING MY STOLEN CIRCUITRY--
--RIGHT NOW!

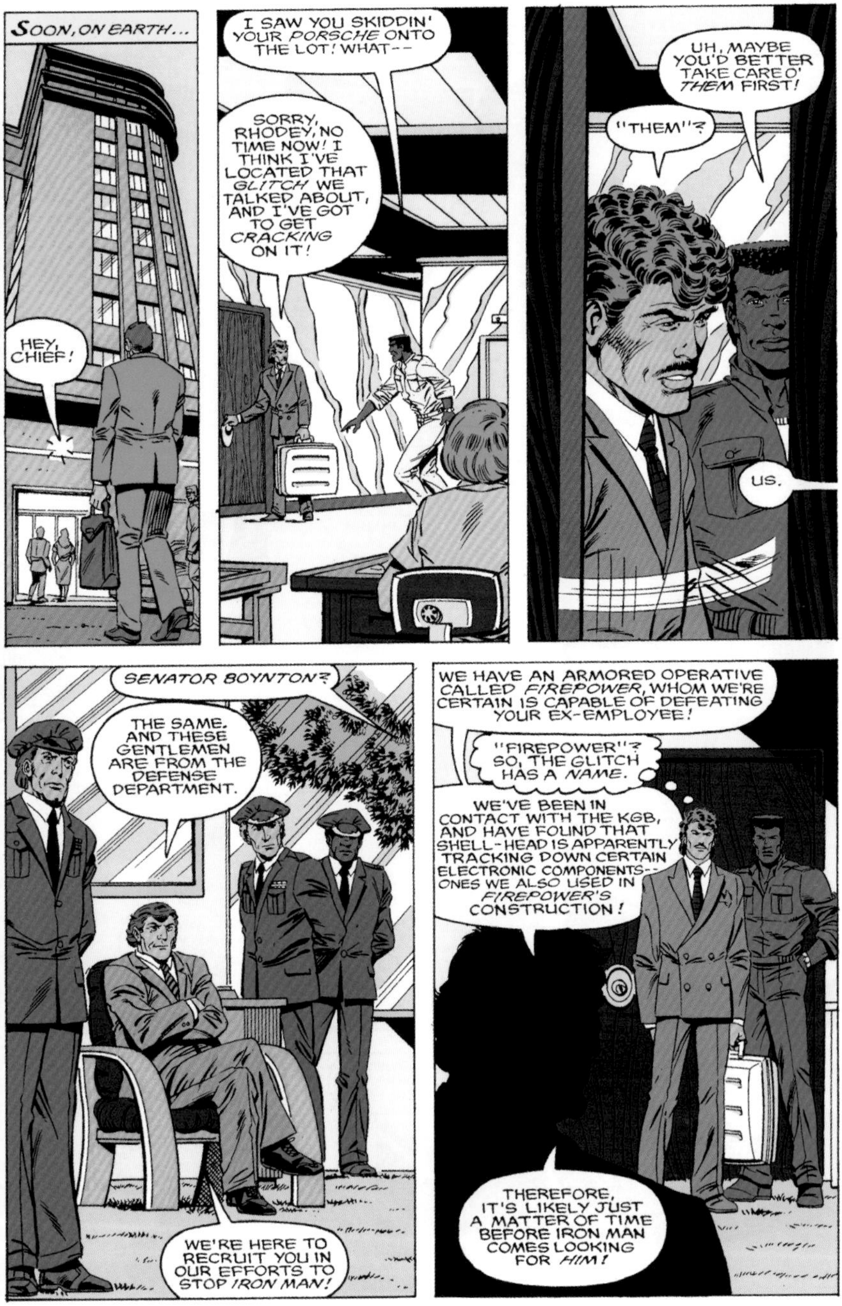
SOON, ON EARTH...
HEY, CHIEF!
I SAW YOU SKIDDIN' YOUR PORSCHE ONTO THE LOT! WHAT--
SORRY, RHODEY, NO TIME NOW! I THINK I'VE LOCATED THAT GLITCH WE TALKED ABOUT, AND I'VE GOT TO GET CRACKING ON IT!
UH, MAYBE YOU'D BETTER TAKE CARE O' THEM FIRST!
"THEM"?
US.
SENATOR BOYNTON?
THE SAME. AND THESE GENTLEMEN ARE FROM THE DEFENSE DEPARTMENT.
WE'RE HERE TO RECRUIT YOU IN OUR EFFORTS TO STOP IRON MAN!
WE HAVE AN ARMORED OPERATIVE CALLED FIREPOWER, WHOM WE'RE CERTAIN IS CAPABLE OF DEFEATING YOUR EX-EMPLOYEE!
"FIREPOWER"? SO, THE GLITCH HAS A NAME.
WE'VE BEEN IN CONTACT WITH THE KGB, AND HAVE FOUND THAT SHELL-HEAD IS APPARENTLY TRACKING DOWN CERTAIN ELECTRONIC COMPONENTS--ONES WE ALSO USED IN FIREPOWER'S CONSTRUCTION!
THEREFORE, IT'S LIKELY JUST A MATTER OF TIME BEFORE IRON MAN COMES LOOKING FOR HIM!

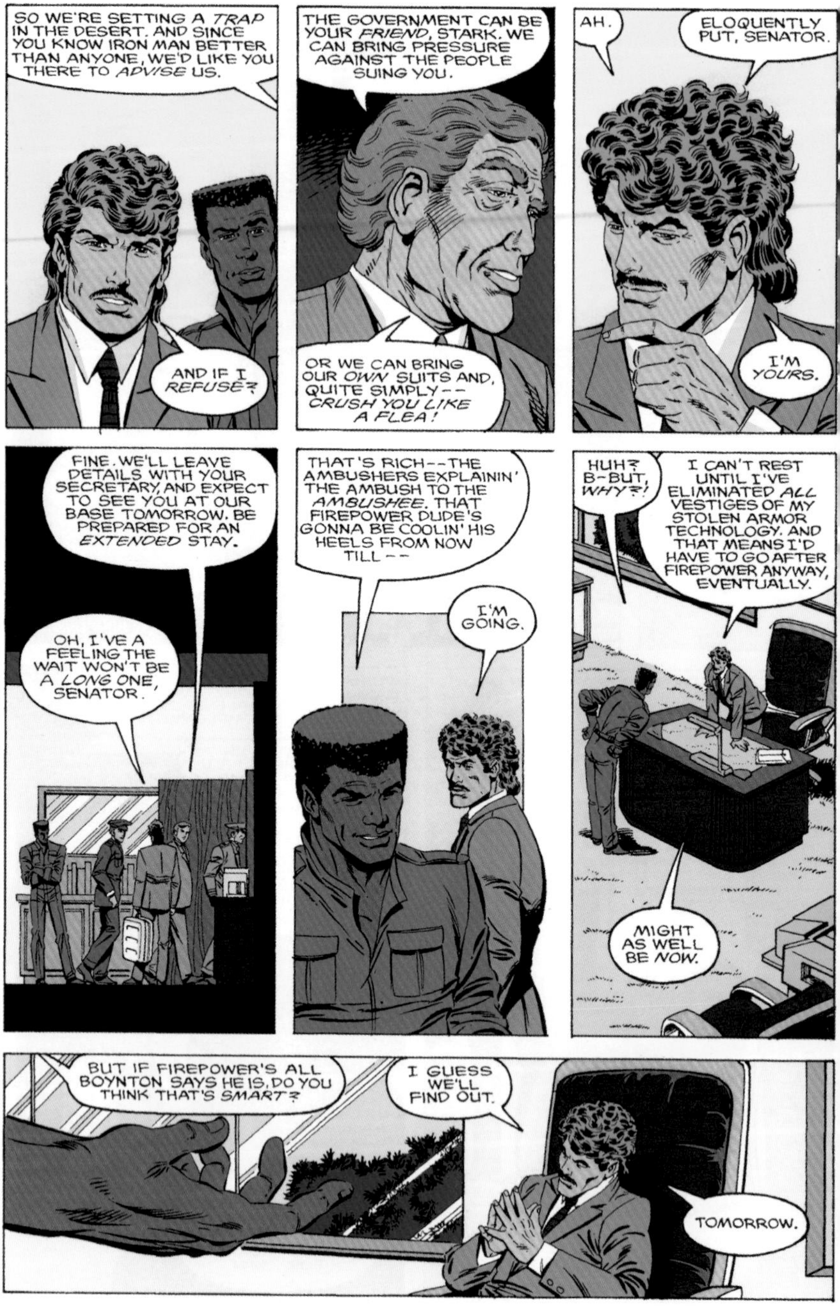
SO WE'RE SETTING A TRAP IN THE DESERT. AND SINCE YOU KNOW IRON MAN BETTER THAN ANYONE, WE'D LIKE YOU THERE TO ADVISE US.
AND IF I REFUSE?
THE GOVERNMENT CAN BE YOUR FRIEND, STARK. WE CAN BRING PRESSURE AGAINST THE PEOPLE SUING YOU.
OR WE CAN BRING OUR OWN SUITS AND, QUITE SIMPLY-- CRUSH YOU LIKE A FLEA!
AH.
ELOQUENTLY PUT, SENATOR.
I'M YOURS.
FINE. WE'LL LEAVE DETAILS WITH YOUR SECRETARY, AND EXPECT TO SEE YOU AT OUR BASE TOMORROW. BE PREPARED FOR AN EXTENDED STAY.
OH, I'VE A FEELING THE WAIT WON'T BE A LONG ONE, SENATOR.
THAT'S RICH--THE AMBUSHERS EXPLAININ' THE AMBUSH TO THE AMBUSHEE. THAT FIREPOWER DUDE'S GONNA BE COOLIN' HIS HEELS FROM NOW TILL--
I'M GOING.
HUH? B-BUT, WHY?!
I CAN'T REST UNTIL I'VE ELIMINATED ALL VESTIGES OF MY STOLEN ARMOR TECHNOLOGY. AND THAT MEANS I'D HAVE TO GO AFTER FIREPOWER ANYWAY, EVENTUALLY.
MIGHT AS WELL BE NOW.
BUT IF FIREPOWER'S ALL BOYNTON SAYS HE IS, DO YOU THINK THAT'S SMART?
I GUESS WE'LL FIND OUT.
TOMORROW.

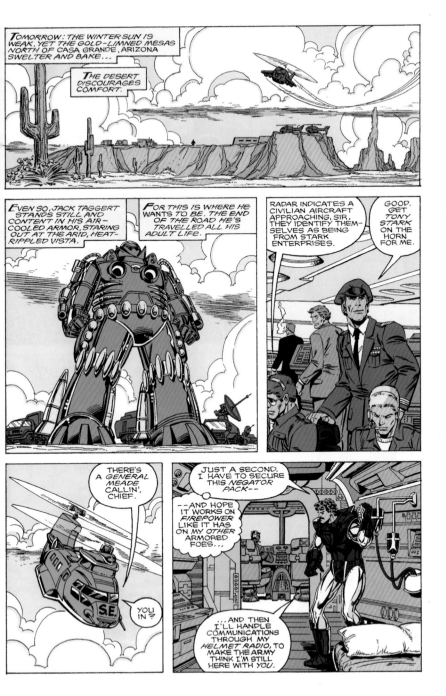

TOMORROW: THE WINTER SUN IS WEAK, YET THE GOLD-LIMNED MESAS NORTH OF CASA GRANDE, ARIZONA SWELTER AND BAKE...

THE DESERT DISCOURAGES COMFORT.

EVEN SO, JACK TAGGERT STANDS STILL AND CONTENT IN HIS AIR-COOLED ARMOR, STARING OUT AT THE ARID, HEAT-RIPPLED VISTA.

FOR THIS IS WHERE HE WANTS TO BE. THE END OF THE ROAD HE'S TRAVELLED ALL HIS ADULT LIFE.

RADAR INDICATES A CIVILIAN AIRCRAFT APPROACHING, SIR. THEY IDENTIFY THEM-SELVES AS BEING FROM STARK ENTERPRISES.

GOOD. GET TONY STARK ON THE HORN FOR ME.

THERE'S A GENERAL MEADE CALLIN', CHIEF.

YOU IN?

JUST A SECOND. I HAVE TO SECURE THIS NEGATOR PACK--

--AND HOPE IT WORKS ON FIREPOWER LIKE IT HAS ON MY OTHER ARMORED FOES...

...AND THEN I'LL HANDLE COMMUNICATIONS THROUGH MY HELMET RADIO, TO MAKE THE ARMY THINK I'M STILL HERE WITH YOU.

S.E.

[153]

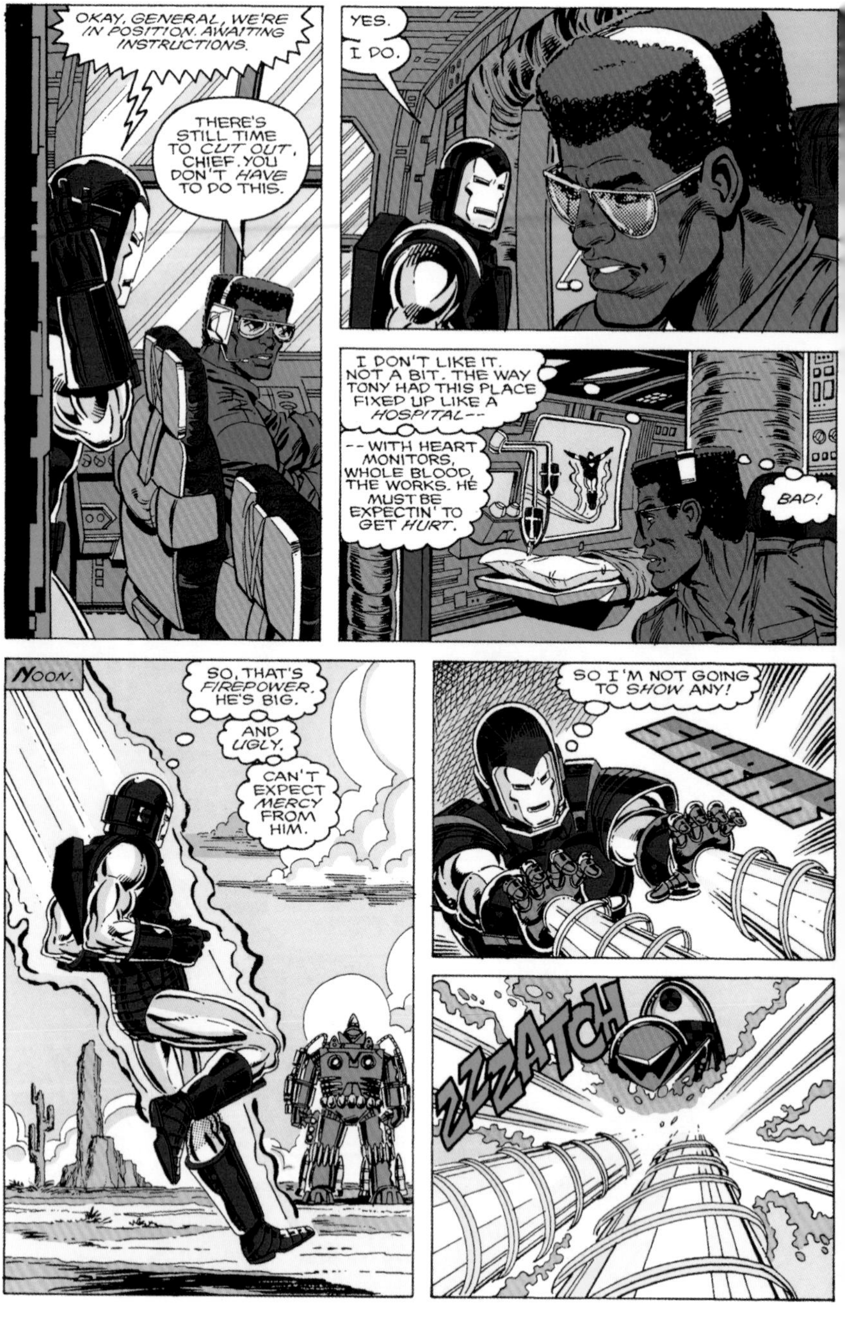
OKAY, GENERAL, WE'RE IN POSITION. AWAITING INSTRUCTIONS.
THERE'S STILL TIME TO CUT OUT, CHIEF. YOU DON'T HAVE TO DO THIS.
YES.
I DO.
I DON'T LIKE IT. NOT A BIT. THE WAY TONY HAD THIS PLACE FIXED UP LIKE A HOSPITAL--
--WITH HEART MONITORS, WHOLE BLOOD, THE WORKS. HE MUST BE EXPECTIN' TO GET HURT.
BAD!
NOON.
SO, THAT'S FIREPOWER. HE'S BIG.
AND UGLY.
CAN'T EXPECT MERCY FROM HIM.
SO I'M NOT GOING TO SHOW ANY!
ZZZATCH

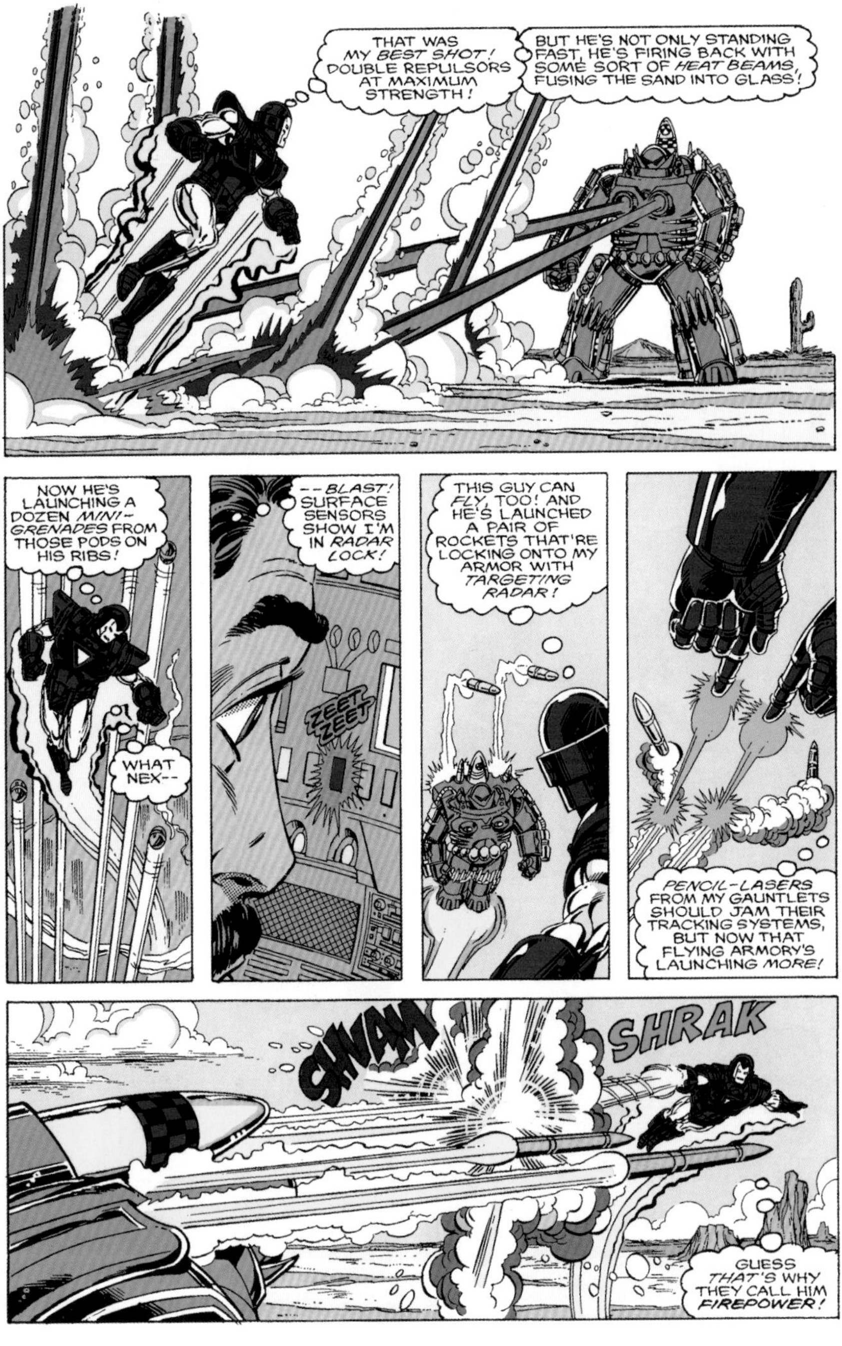
THAT WAS MY BEST SHOT! DOUBLE REPULSORS AT MAXIMUM STRENGTH!
BUT HE'S NOT ONLY STANDING FAST, HE'S FIRING BACK WITH SOME SORT OF HEAT BEAMS, FUSING THE SAND INTO GLASS!
NOW HE'S LAUNCHING A DOZEN MINI-GRENADES FROM THOSE PODS ON HIS RIBS!
WHAT NEX--
--BLAST! SURFACE SENSORS SHOW I'M IN RADAR LOCK!
ZEET ZEET
THIS GUY CAN FLY, TOO! AND HE'S LAUNCHED A PAIR OF ROCKETS THAT'RE LOCKING ONTO MY ARMOR WITH TARGETING RADAR!
PENCIL-LASERS FROM MY GAUNTLETS SHOULD JAM THEIR TRACKING SYSTEMS, BUT NOW THAT FLYING ARMORY'S LAUNCHING MORE!
SHWAM
SHRAK
GUESS THAT'S WHY THEY CALL HIM FIREPOWER!

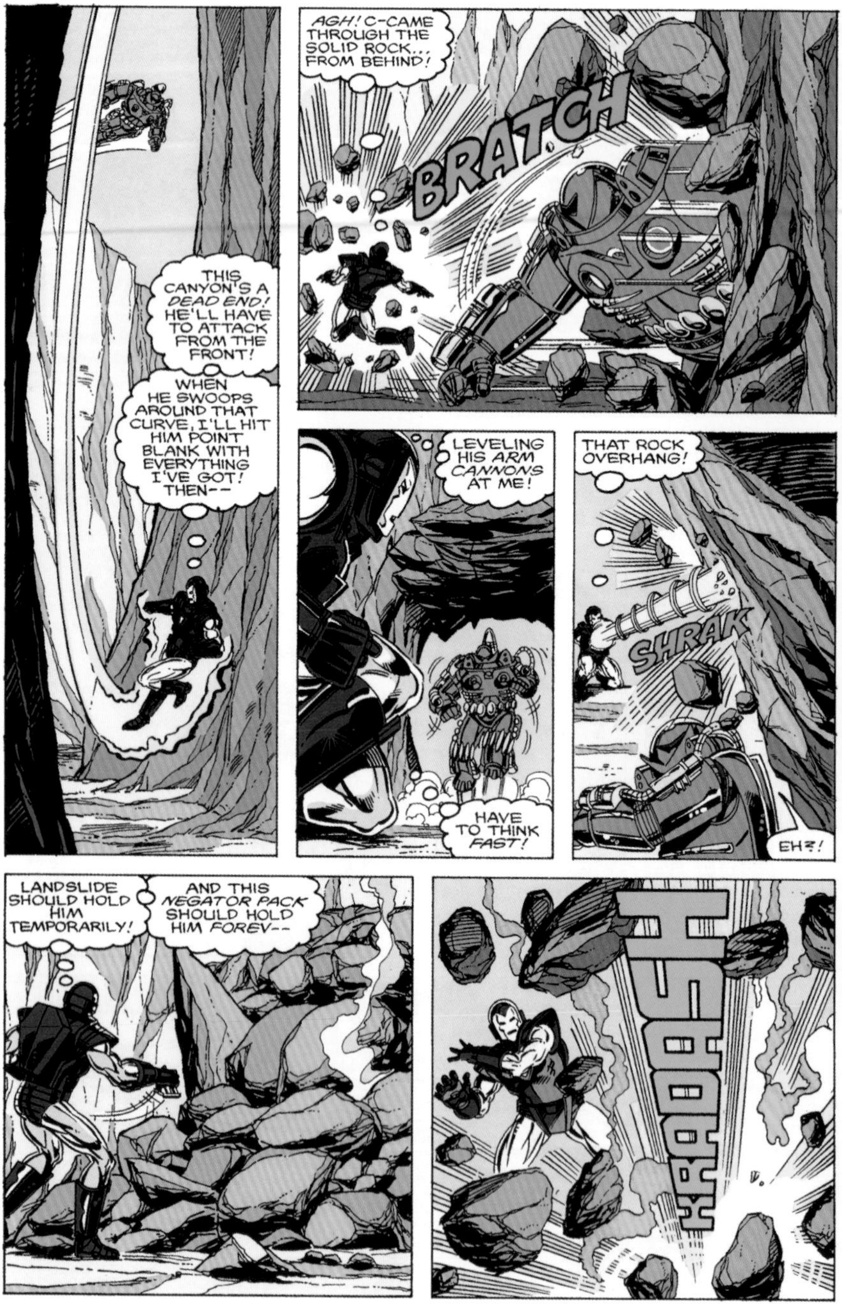
THIS CANYON'S A DEAD END! HE'LL HAVE TO ATTACK FROM THE FRONT!
WHEN HE SWOOPS AROUND THAT CURVE, I'LL HIT HIM POINT BLANK WITH EVERYTHING I'VE GOT! THEN--
AGH! C-CAME THROUGH THE SOLID ROCK... FROM BEHIND!
BRATCH
LEVELING HIS ARM CANNONS AT ME!
HAVE TO THINK FAST!
THAT ROCK OVERHANG!
SHRAK
EH?!
LANDSLIDE SHOULD HOLD HIM TEMPORARILY!
AND THIS NEGATOR PACK SHOULD HOLD HIM FOREV--
KRADASH

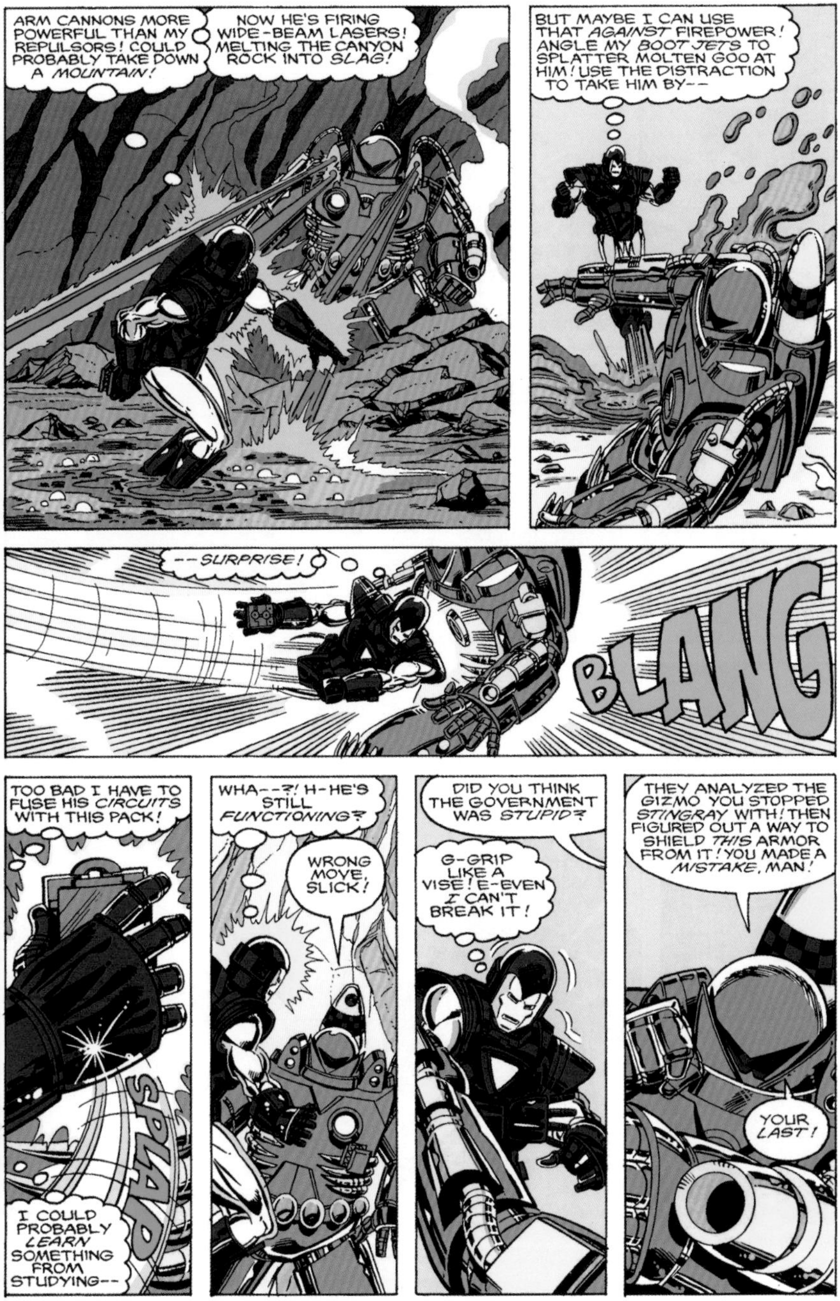
ARM CANNONS MORE POWERFUL THAN MY REPULSORS! COULD PROBABLY TAKE DOWN A *MOUNTAIN*!
NOW HE'S FIRING WIDE-BEAM LASERS! MELTING THE CANYON ROCK INTO *SLAG*!
BUT MAYBE I CAN USE THAT *AGAINST* FIREPOWER! ANGLE MY *BOOT JETS* TO SPLATTER MOLTEN GOO AT HIM! USE THE DISTRACTION TO TAKE HIM BY--
--*SURPRISE*!
BLANG
TOO BAD I HAVE TO FUSE HIS *CIRCUITS* WITH THIS PACK!
SPLAP
I COULD PROBABLY *LEARN* SOMETHING FROM STUDYING--
WHA--?! H-HE'S STILL *FUNCTIONING*?
WRONG MOVE, SLICK!
DID YOU THINK THE GOVERNMENT WAS *STUPID*?
G-GRIP LIKE A VISE! E-EVEN *I* CAN'T BREAK IT!
THEY ANALYZED THE GIZMO YOU STOPPED *STINGRAY* WITH! THEN FIGURED OUT A WAY TO SHIELD *THIS* ARMOR FROM IT! YOU MADE A *MISTAKE*, MAN!
YOUR *LAST*!

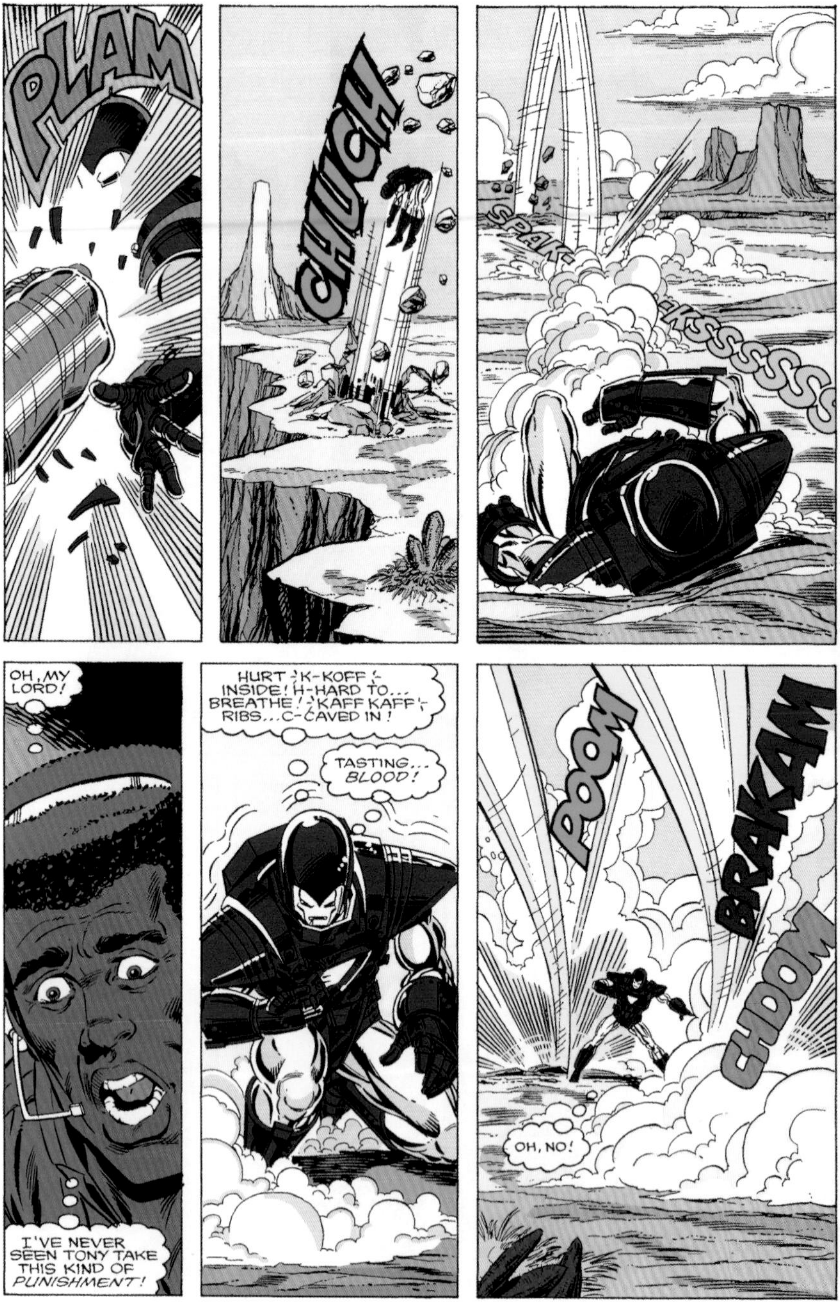

PLAM
CHUCH
SPAK
KSSSSSS
OH, MY LORD!
I'VE NEVER SEEN TONY TAKE THIS KIND OF *PUNISHMENT!*
HURT -K-KOFF- INSIDE! H-HARD TO... BREATHE! -KAFF KAFF- RIBS... C-CAVED IN!
TASTING... *BLOOD!*
POOM
BRAKAM
CHOOM
OH, NO!

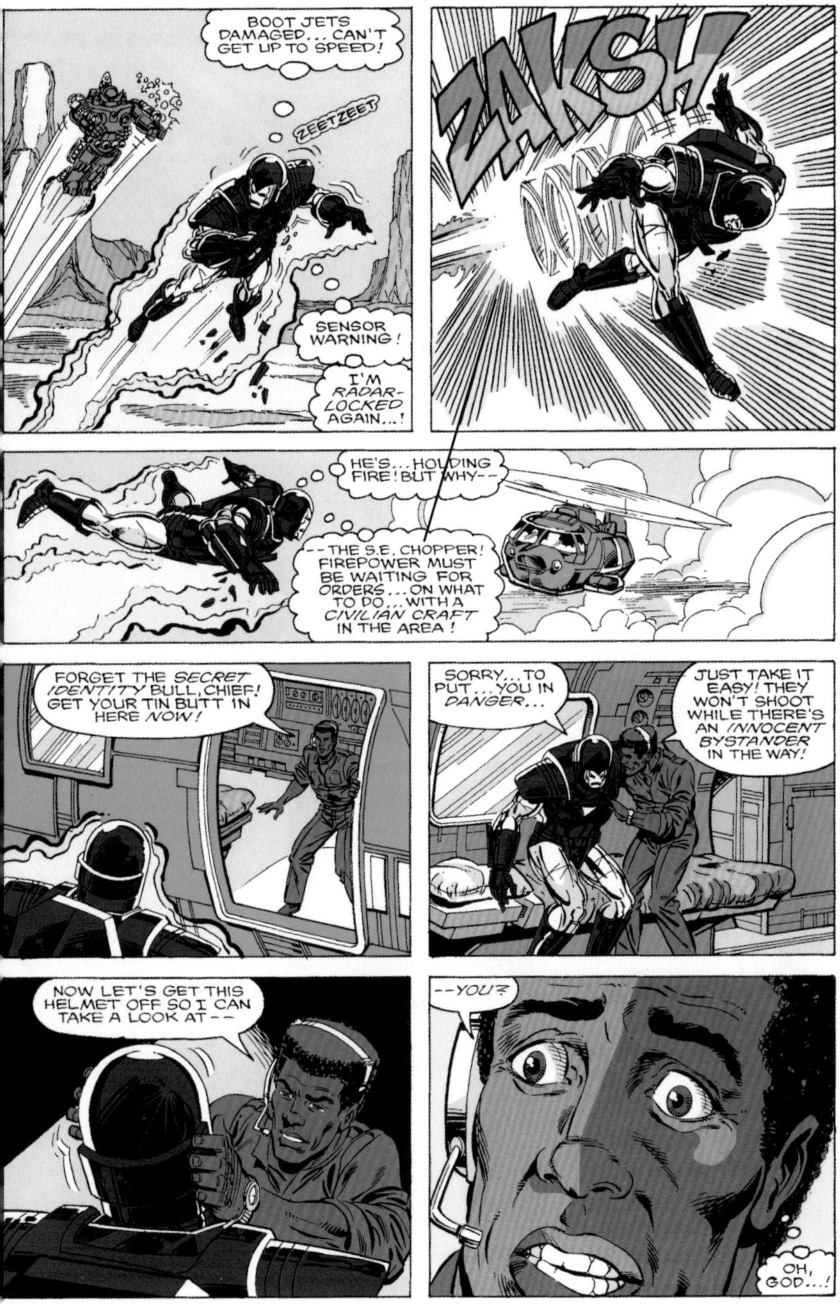
BOOT JETS DAMAGED... CAN'T GET UP TO SPEED!
ZEETZEET
SENSOR WARNING!
I'M RADAR-LOCKED AGAIN...!
ZAKSH
HE'S... HOLDING FIRE! BUT WHY--
--THE S.E. CHOPPER! FIREPOWER MUST BE WAITING FOR ORDERS... ON WHAT TO DO... WITH A CIVILIAN CRAFT IN THE AREA!
FORGET THE SECRET IDENTITY BULL, CHIEF! GET YOUR TIN BUTT IN HERE NOW!
SORRY... TO PUT... YOU IN DANGER...
JUST TAKE IT EASY! THEY WON'T SHOOT WHILE THERE'S AN INNOCENT BYSTANDER IN THE WAY!
NOW LET'S GET THIS HELMET OFF SO I CAN TAKE A LOOK AT --
--YOU?
OH, GOD...!

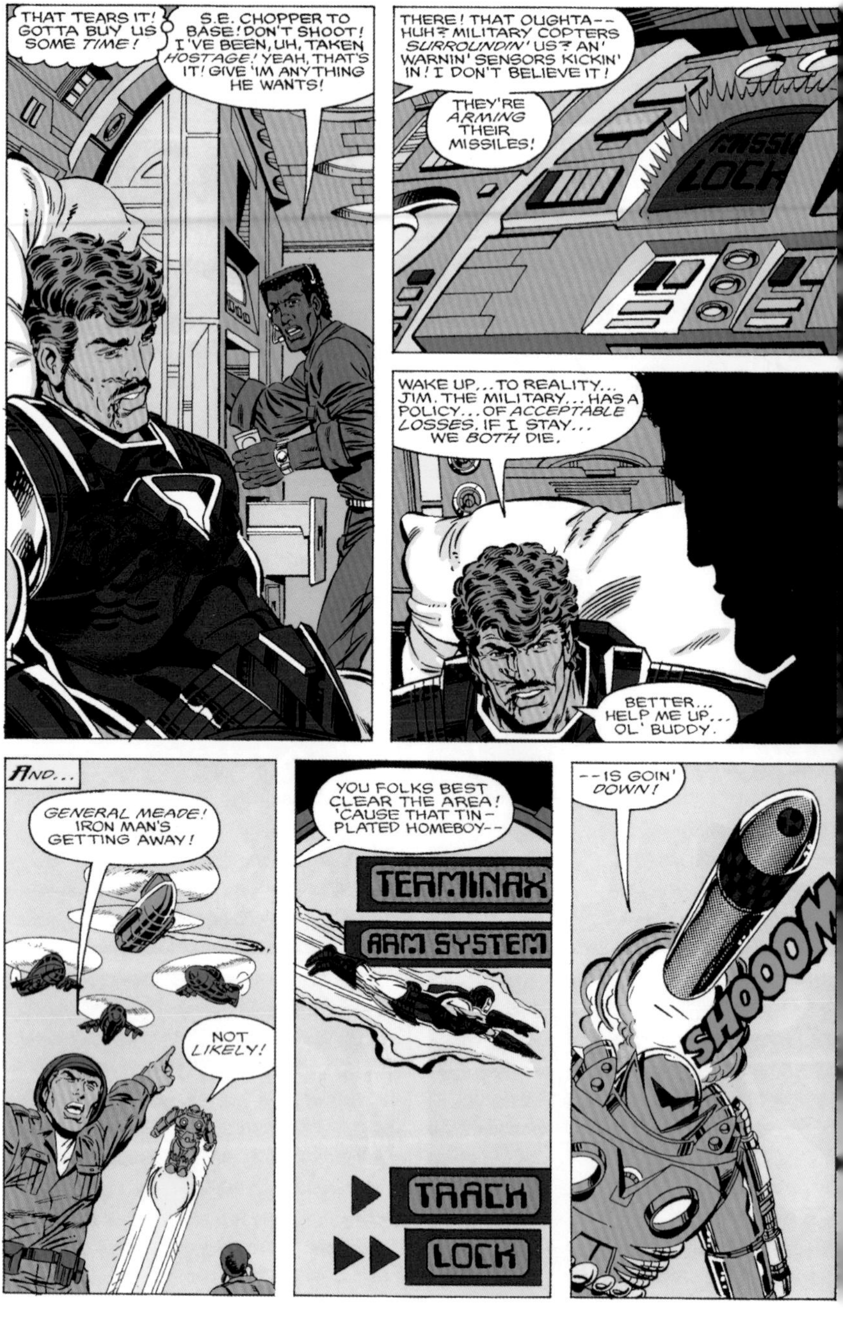
THAT TEARS IT! GOTTA BUY US SOME TIME!
S.E. CHOPPER TO BASE! DON'T SHOOT! I'VE BEEN, UH, TAKEN HOSTAGE! YEAH, THAT'S IT! GIVE 'IM ANYTHING HE WANTS!
THERE! THAT OUGHTA-- HUH? MILITARY COPTERS SURROUNDIN' US? AN' WARNIN' SENSORS KICKIN' IN! I DON'T BELIEVE IT!
THEY'RE ARMING THEIR MISSILES!
LOCK
WAKE UP,...TO REALITY... JIM. THE MILITARY... HAS A POLICY... OF ACCEPTABLE LOSSES. IF I STAY... WE BOTH DIE.
BETTER... HELP ME UP... OL' BUDDY.
AND...
GENERAL MEADE! IRON MAN'S GETTING AWAY!
NOT LIKELY!
YOU FOLKS BEST CLEAR THE AREA! 'CAUSE THAT TIN-PLATED HOMEBOY--
TERMINAX
ARM SYSTEM
TRACK
LOCK
--IS GOIN' DOWN!
SHOOOM

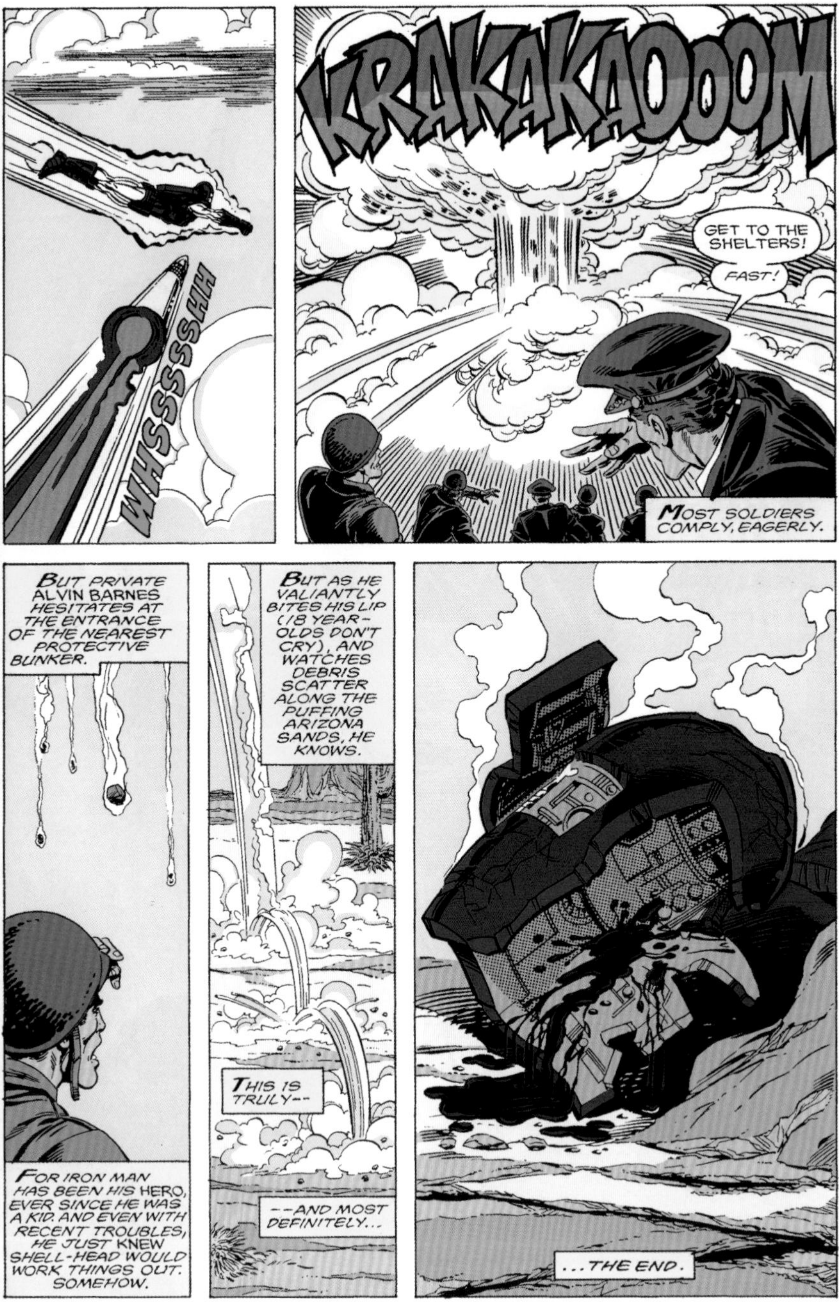
WHSSSSSSHH
KRAKAKAOOOM
GET TO THE SHELTERS!
FAST!
MOST SOLDIERS COMPLY, EAGERLY.
BUT PRIVATE ALVIN BARNES HESITATES AT THE ENTRANCE OF THE NEAREST PROTECTIVE BUNKER.
FOR IRON MAN HAS BEEN HIS HERO, EVER SINCE HE WAS A KID. AND EVEN WITH RECENT TROUBLES, HE JUST KNEW SHELL-HEAD WOULD WORK THINGS OUT. SOMEHOW.
BUT AS HE VALIANTLY BITES HIS LIP (18 YEAR-OLDS DON'T CRY), AND WATCHES DEBRIS SCATTER ALONG THE PUFFING ARIZONA SANDS, HE KNOWS.
THIS IS TRULY--
--AND MOST DEFINITELY...
...THE END.

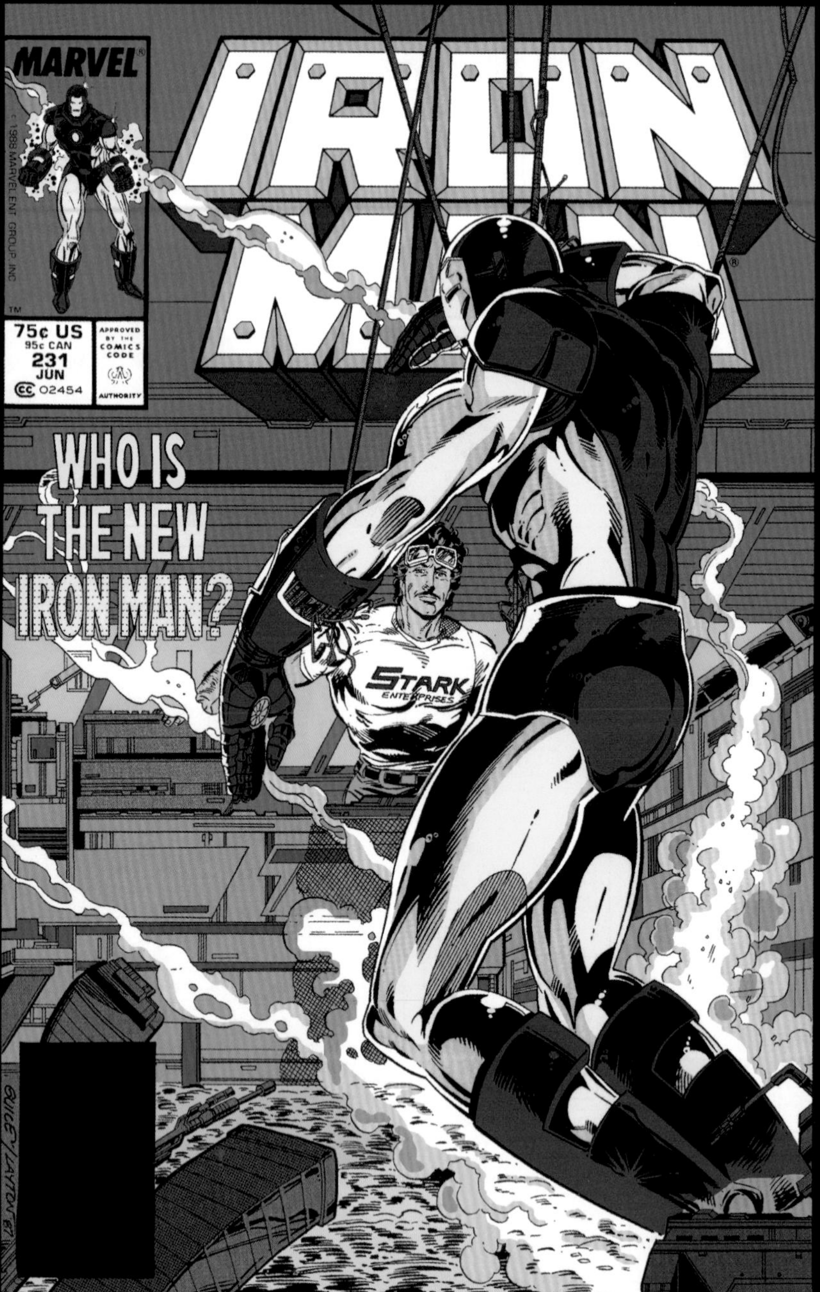
MARVEL®
© 1988 MARVEL ENT. GROUP, INC.
TM
IRON MAN®
75¢ US
95¢ CAN
231
JUN
CC 02454
APPROVED BY THE COMICS CODE AUTHORITY
WHO IS THE NEW IRON MAN?
STARK ENTERPRISES
QUICE/LAYTON '87

STAN LEE PRESENTS:

STARK WARS: CHAPTER 7

REBORN AGAIN

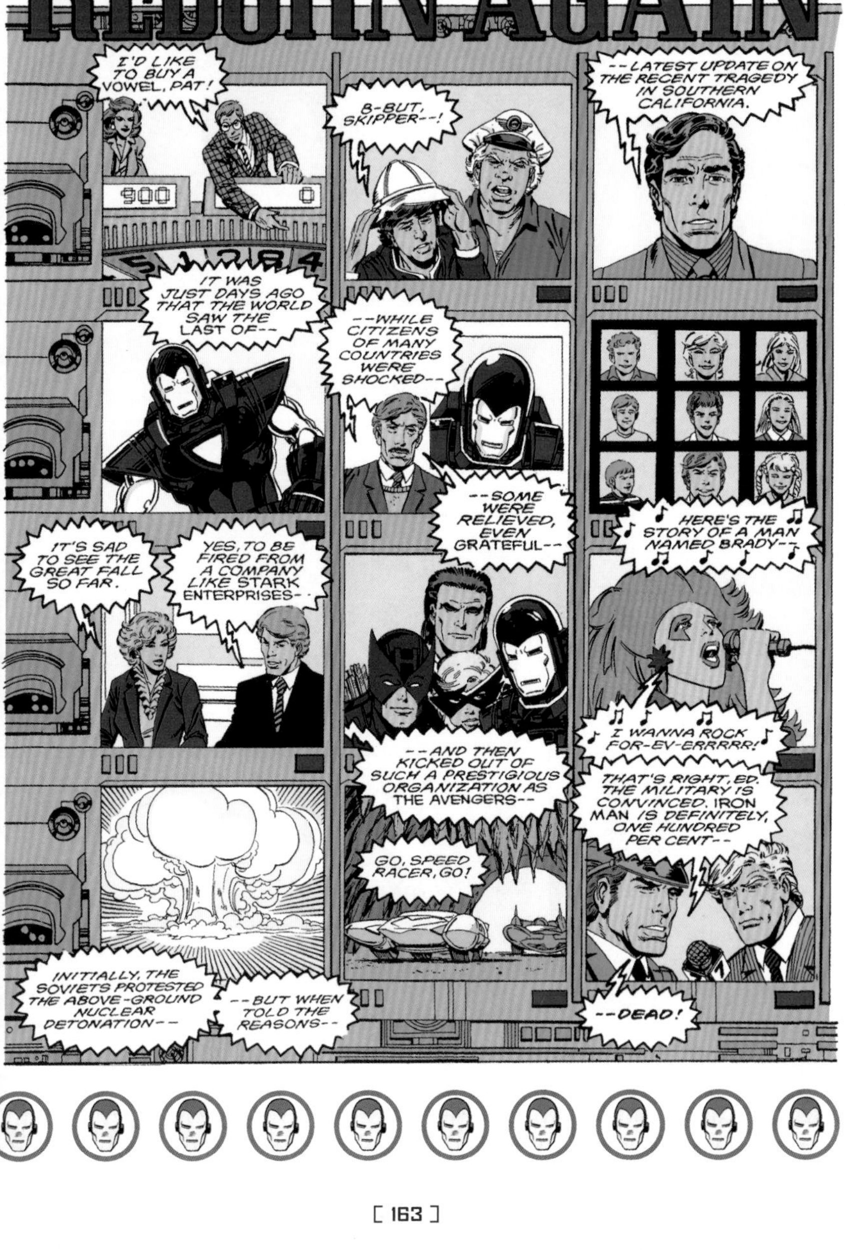

I'D LIKE TO BUY A VOWEL, PAT!
900
0
B-BUT, SKIPPER--!
--LATEST UPDATE ON THE RECENT TRAGEDY IN SOUTHERN CALIFORNIA.
IT WAS JUST DAYS AGO THAT THE WORLD SAW THE LAST OF--
--WHILE CITIZENS OF MANY COUNTRIES WERE SHOCKED--
--SOME WERE RELIEVED, EVEN GRATEFUL--
HERE'S THE STORY OF A MAN NAMED BRADY--
IT'S SAD TO SEE THE GREAT FALL SO FAR.
YES, TO BE FIRED FROM A COMPANY LIKE STARK ENTERPRISES--
--AND THEN KICKED OUT OF SUCH A PRESTIGIOUS ORGANIZATION AS THE AVENGERS--
I WANNA ROCK FOR-EV-ERRRRR!
THAT'S RIGHT, ED. THE MILITARY IS CONVINCED. IRON MAN IS DEFINITELY, ONE HUNDRED PER CENT--
GO, SPEED RACER, GO!
INITIALLY, THE SOVIETS PROTESTED THE ABOVE-GROUND NUCLEAR DETONATION--
--BUT WHEN TOLD THE REASONS--
--DEAD!

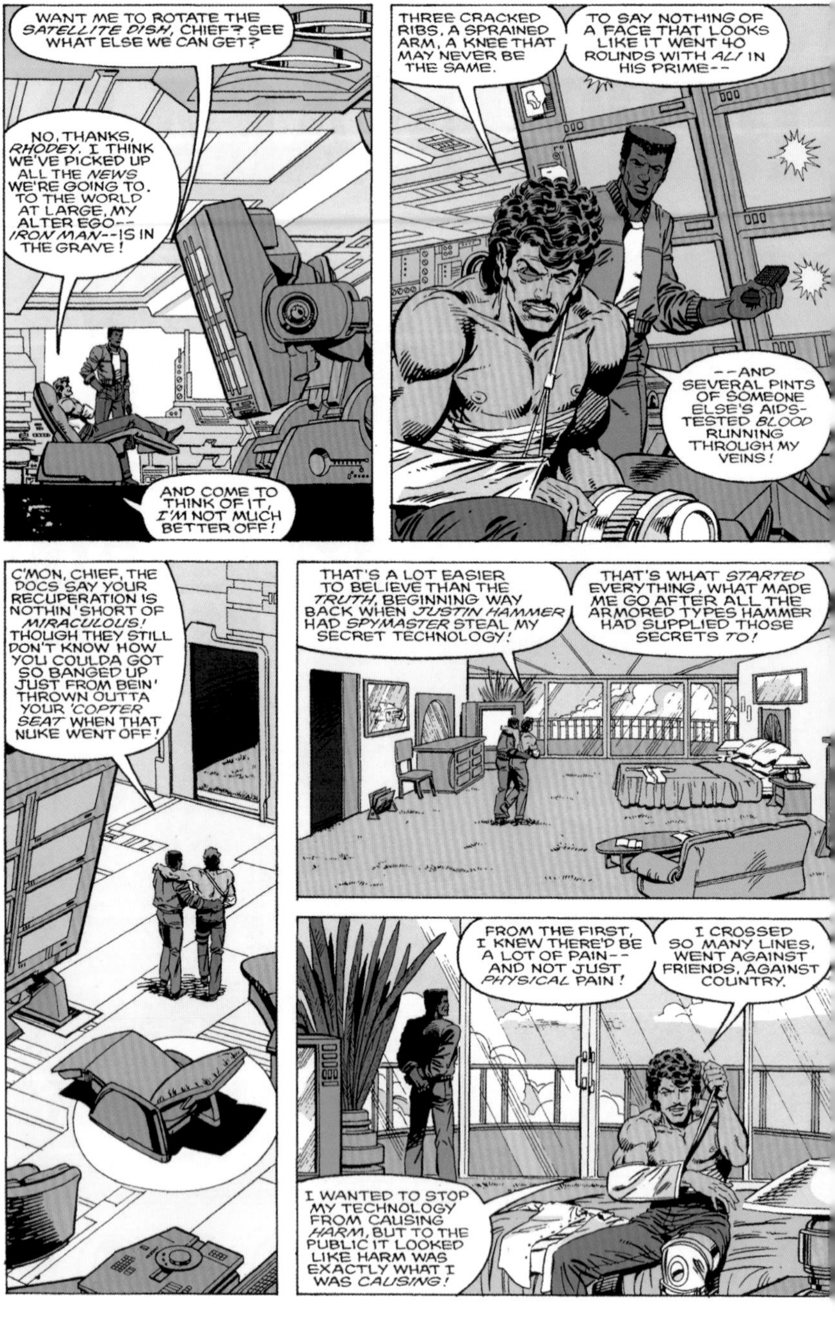

WANT ME TO ROTATE THE SATELLITE DISH, CHIEF? SEE WHAT ELSE WE CAN GET?
NO, THANKS, RHODEY. I THINK WE'VE PICKED UP ALL THE NEWS WE'RE GOING TO. TO THE WORLD AT LARGE, MY ALTER EGO-- IRON MAN--IS IN THE GRAVE!
AND COME TO THINK OF IT, I'M NOT MUCH BETTER OFF!
THREE CRACKED RIBS, A SPRAINED ARM, A KNEE THAT MAY NEVER BE THE SAME.
TO SAY NOTHING OF A FACE THAT LOOKS LIKE IT WENT 40 ROUNDS WITH ALI IN HIS PRIME--
--AND SEVERAL PINTS OF SOMEONE ELSE'S AIDS-TESTED BLOOD RUNNING THROUGH MY VEINS!
C'MON, CHIEF, THE DOCS SAY YOUR RECUPERATION IS NOTHIN' SHORT OF MIRACULOUS! THOUGH THEY STILL DON'T KNOW HOW YOU COULDA GOT SO BANGED UP JUST FROM BEIN' THROWN OUTTA YOUR 'COPTER SEAT WHEN THAT NUKE WENT OFF!
THAT'S A LOT EASIER TO BELIEVE THAN THE TRUTH, BEGINNING WAY BACK WHEN JUSTIN HAMMER HAD SPYMASTER STEAL MY SECRET TECHNOLOGY!
THAT'S WHAT STARTED EVERYTHING, WHAT MADE ME GO AFTER ALL THE ARMORED TYPES HAMMER HAD SUPPLIED THOSE SECRETS TO!
FROM THE FIRST, I KNEW THERE'D BE A LOT OF PAIN-- AND NOT JUST PHYSICAL PAIN!
I CROSSED SO MANY LINES, WENT AGAINST FRIENDS, AGAINST COUNTRY.
I WANTED TO STOP MY TECHNOLOGY FROM CAUSING HARM, BUT TO THE PUBLIC IT LOOKED LIKE HARM WAS EXACTLY WHAT I WAS CAUSING!

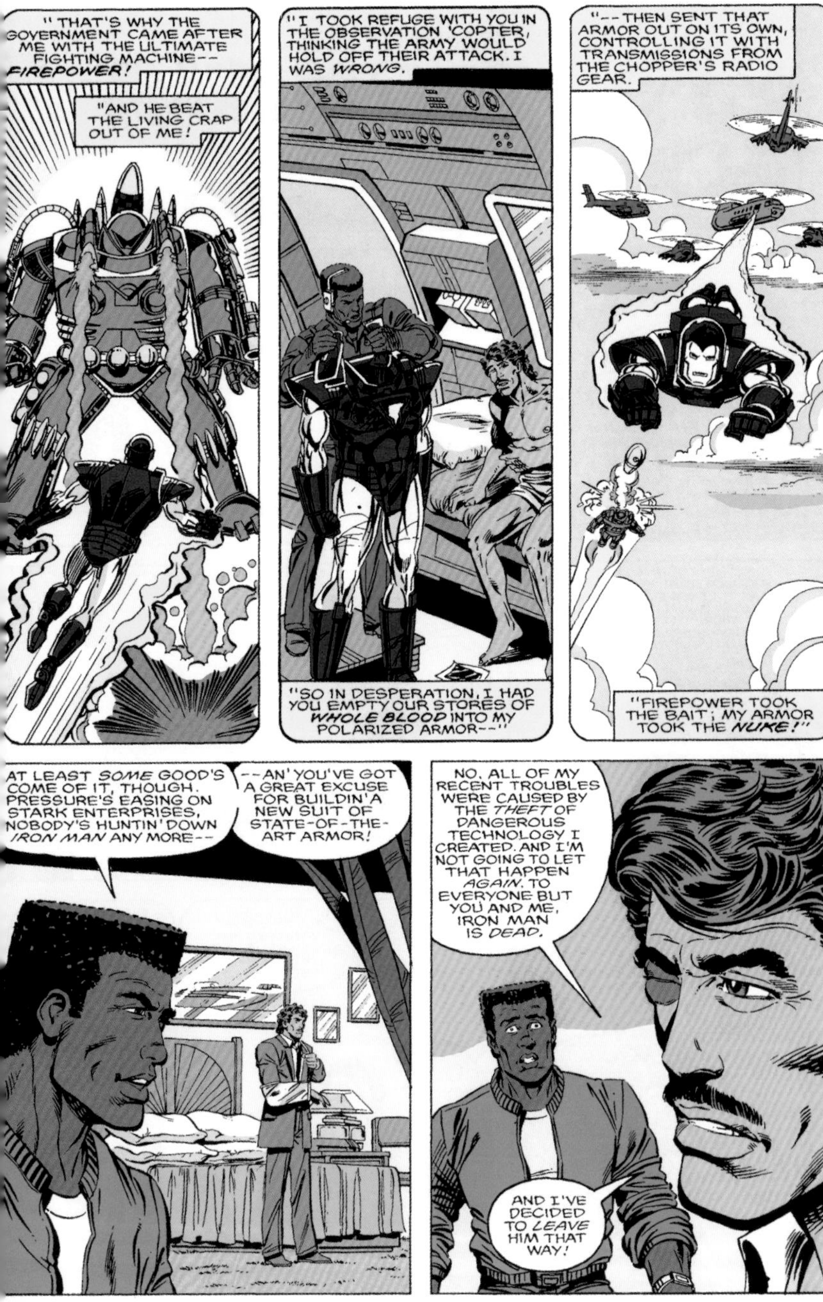
"THAT'S WHY THE GOVERNMENT CAME AFTER ME WITH THE ULTIMATE FIGHTING MACHINE-- FIREPOWER!
"AND HE BEAT THE LIVING CRAP OUT OF ME!
"I TOOK REFUGE WITH YOU IN THE OBSERVATION 'COPTER, THINKING THE ARMY WOULD HOLD OFF THEIR ATTACK. I WAS WRONG.
"SO IN DESPERATION, I HAD YOU EMPTY OUR STORES OF WHOLE BLOOD INTO MY POLARIZED ARMOR--"
"--THEN SENT THAT ARMOR OUT ON ITS OWN, CONTROLLING IT WITH TRANSMISSIONS FROM THE CHOPPER'S RADIO GEAR.
"FIREPOWER TOOK THE BAIT; MY ARMOR TOOK THE NUKE!"
AT LEAST SOME GOOD'S COME OF IT, THOUGH. PRESSURE'S EASING ON STARK ENTERPRISES, NOBODY'S HUNTIN' DOWN IRON MAN ANY MORE--
--AN' YOU'VE GOT A GREAT EXCUSE FOR BUILDIN' A NEW SUIT OF STATE-OF-THE-ART ARMOR!
NO, ALL OF MY RECENT TROUBLES WERE CAUSED BY THE THEFT OF DANGEROUS TECHNOLOGY I CREATED. AND I'M NOT GOING TO LET THAT HAPPEN AGAIN. TO EVERYONE BUT YOU AND ME, IRON MAN IS DEAD.
AND I'VE DECIDED TO LEAVE HIM THAT WAY!

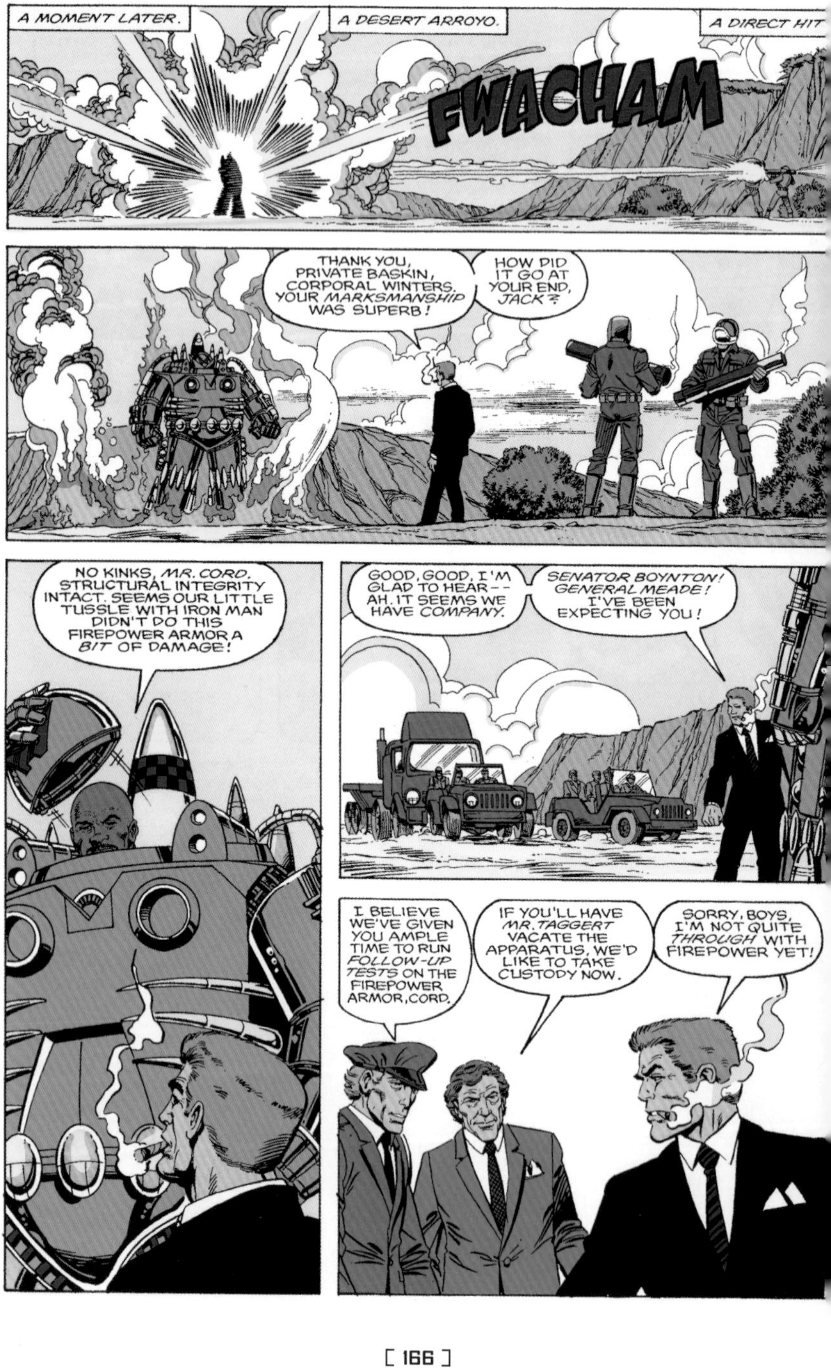
A MOMENT LATER.
A DESERT ARROYO.
A DIRECT HIT
FWACHAM
THANK YOU, PRIVATE BASKIN, CORPORAL WINTERS. YOUR MARKSMANSHIP WAS SUPERB!
HOW DID IT GO AT YOUR END, JACK?
NO KINKS, MR. CORD. STRUCTURAL INTEGRITY INTACT. SEEMS OUR LITTLE TUSSLE WITH IRON MAN DIDN'T DO THIS FIREPOWER ARMOR A BIT OF DAMAGE!
GOOD, GOOD, I'M GLAD TO HEAR-- AH. IT SEEMS WE HAVE COMPANY.
SENATOR BOYNTON! GENERAL MEADE! I'VE BEEN EXPECTING YOU!
I BELIEVE WE'VE GIVEN YOU AMPLE TIME TO RUN FOLLOW-UP TESTS ON THE FIREPOWER ARMOR, CORD.
IF YOU'LL HAVE MR. TAGGERT VACATE THE APPARATUS, WE'D LIKE TO TAKE CUSTODY NOW.
SORRY, BOYS, I'M NOT QUITE THROUGH WITH FIREPOWER YET!

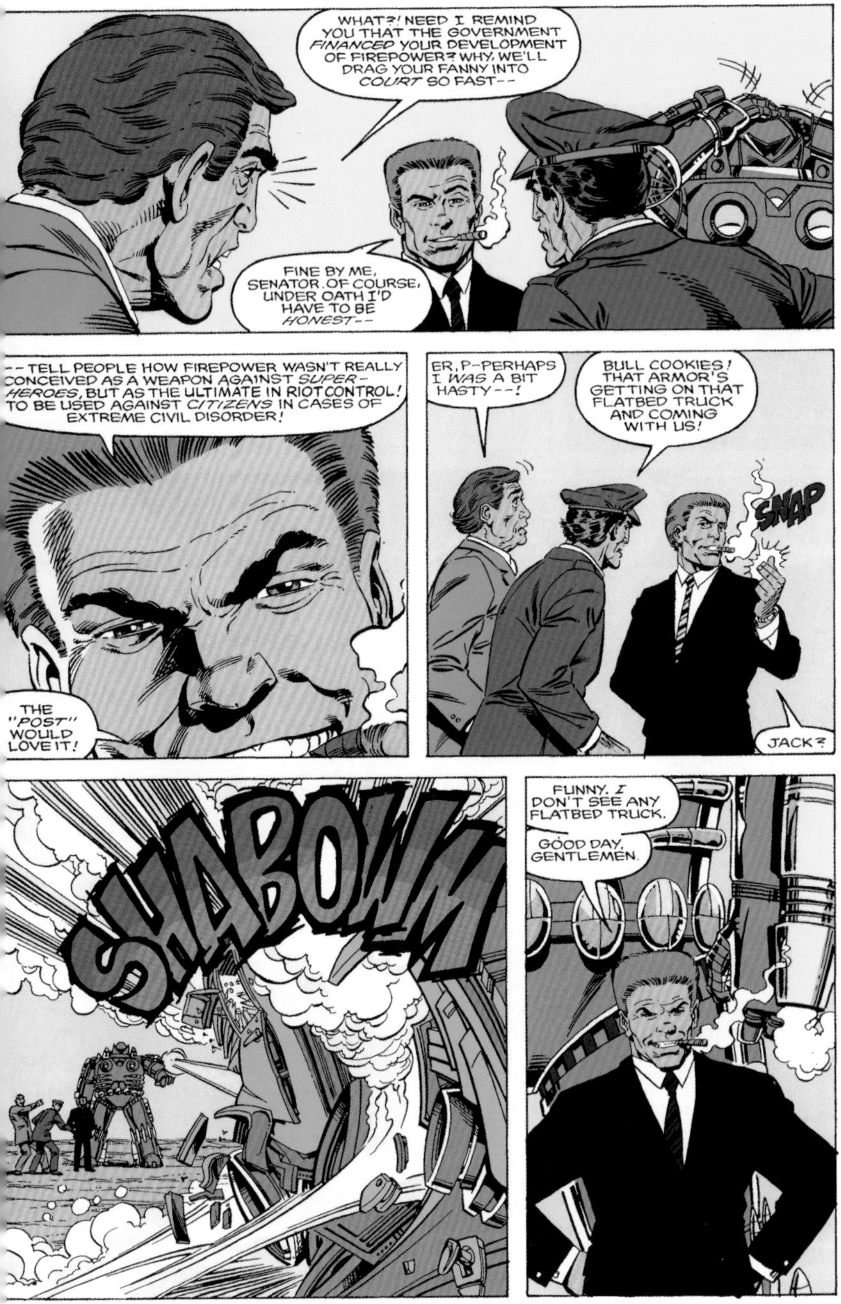
WHAT?! NEED I REMIND YOU THAT THE GOVERNMENT *FINANCED* YOUR DEVELOPMENT OF FIREPOWER? WHY, WE'LL DRAG YOUR FANNY INTO *COURT* SO FAST--
FINE BY ME, SENATOR. OF COURSE, UNDER OATH I'D HAVE TO BE *HONEST*--
--TELL PEOPLE HOW FIREPOWER WASN'T REALLY CONCEIVED AS A WEAPON AGAINST *SUPER-HEROES*, BUT AS THE ULTIMATE IN RIOT CONTROL! TO BE USED AGAINST *CITIZENS* IN CASES OF EXTREME CIVIL DISORDER!
THE "*POST*" WOULD LOVE IT!
ER, P-PERHAPS I *WAS* A BIT HASTY--!
BULL COOKIES! THAT ARMOR'S GETTING ON THAT FLATBED TRUCK AND COMING WITH US!
SNAP
JACK?
SHABOOM
FUNNY. *I* DON'T SEE ANY FLATBED TRUCK.
GOOD DAY, GENTLEMEN.

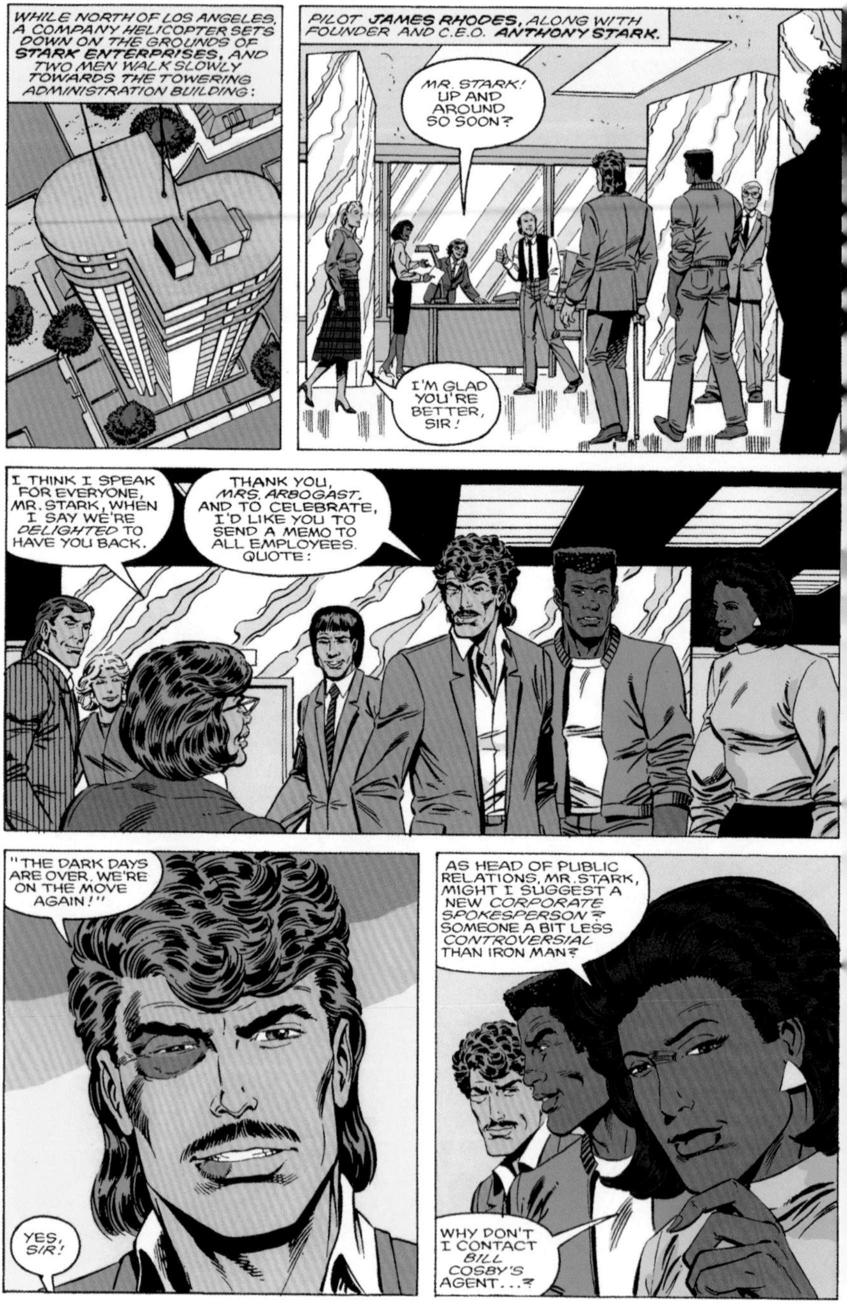

WHILE NORTH OF LOS ANGELES, A COMPANY HELICOPTER SETS DOWN ON THE GROUNDS OF STARK ENTERPRISES, AND TWO MEN WALK SLOWLY TOWARDS THE TOWERING ADMINISTRATION BUILDING:
PILOT JAMES RHODES, ALONG WITH FOUNDER AND C.E.O. ANTHONY STARK.
MR. STARK! UP AND AROUND SO SOON?
I'M GLAD YOU'RE BETTER, SIR!
I THINK I SPEAK FOR EVERYONE, MR. STARK, WHEN I SAY WE'RE DELIGHTED TO HAVE YOU BACK.
THANK YOU, MRS. ARBOGAST. AND TO CELEBRATE, I'D LIKE YOU TO SEND A MEMO TO ALL EMPLOYEES. QUOTE:
"THE DARK DAYS ARE OVER. WE'RE ON THE MOVE AGAIN!"
YES, SIR!
AS HEAD OF PUBLIC RELATIONS, MR. STARK, MIGHT I SUGGEST A NEW CORPORATE SPOKESPERSON? SOMEONE A BIT LESS CONTROVERSIAL THAN IRON MAN?
WHY DON'T I CONTACT BILL COSBY'S AGENT...?

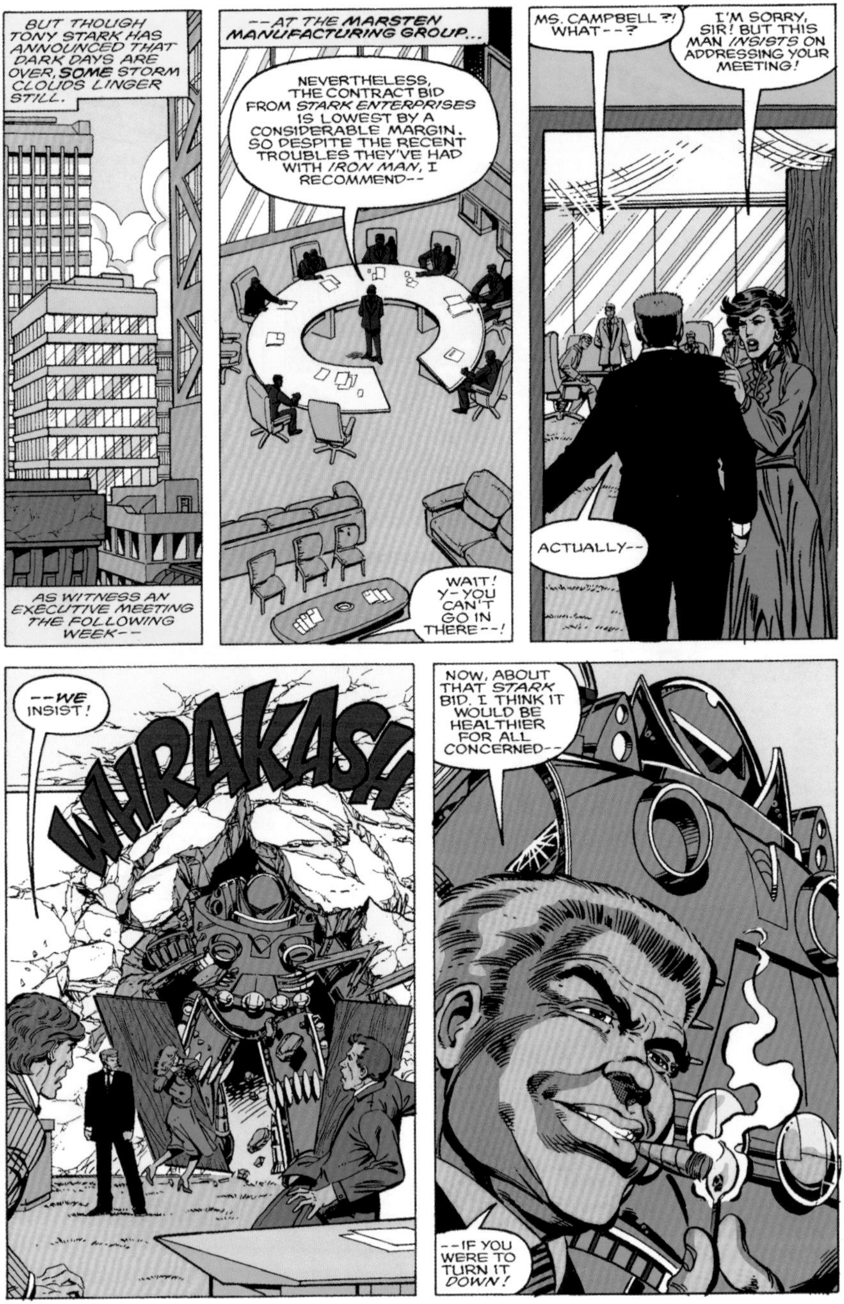
BUT THOUGH TONY STARK HAS ANNOUNCED THAT DARK DAYS ARE OVER, SOME STORM CLOUDS LINGER STILL.
AS WITNESS AN EXECUTIVE MEETING THE FOLLOWING WEEK--
--AT THE MARSTEN MANUFACTURING GROUP...
NEVERTHELESS, THE CONTRACT BID FROM STARK ENTERPRISES IS LOWEST BY A CONSIDERABLE MARGIN. SO DESPITE THE RECENT TROUBLES THEY'VE HAD WITH IRON MAN, I RECOMMEND--
WAIT! Y-YOU CAN'T GO IN THERE--!
MS. CAMPBELL?! WHAT--?
I'M SORRY, SIR! BUT THIS MAN INSISTS ON ADDRESSING YOUR MEETING!
ACTUALLY--
--WE INSIST!
WHRAKASH
NOW, ABOUT THAT STARK BID. I THINK IT WOULD BE HEALTHIER FOR ALL CONCERNED--
--IF YOU WERE TO TURN IT DOWN!

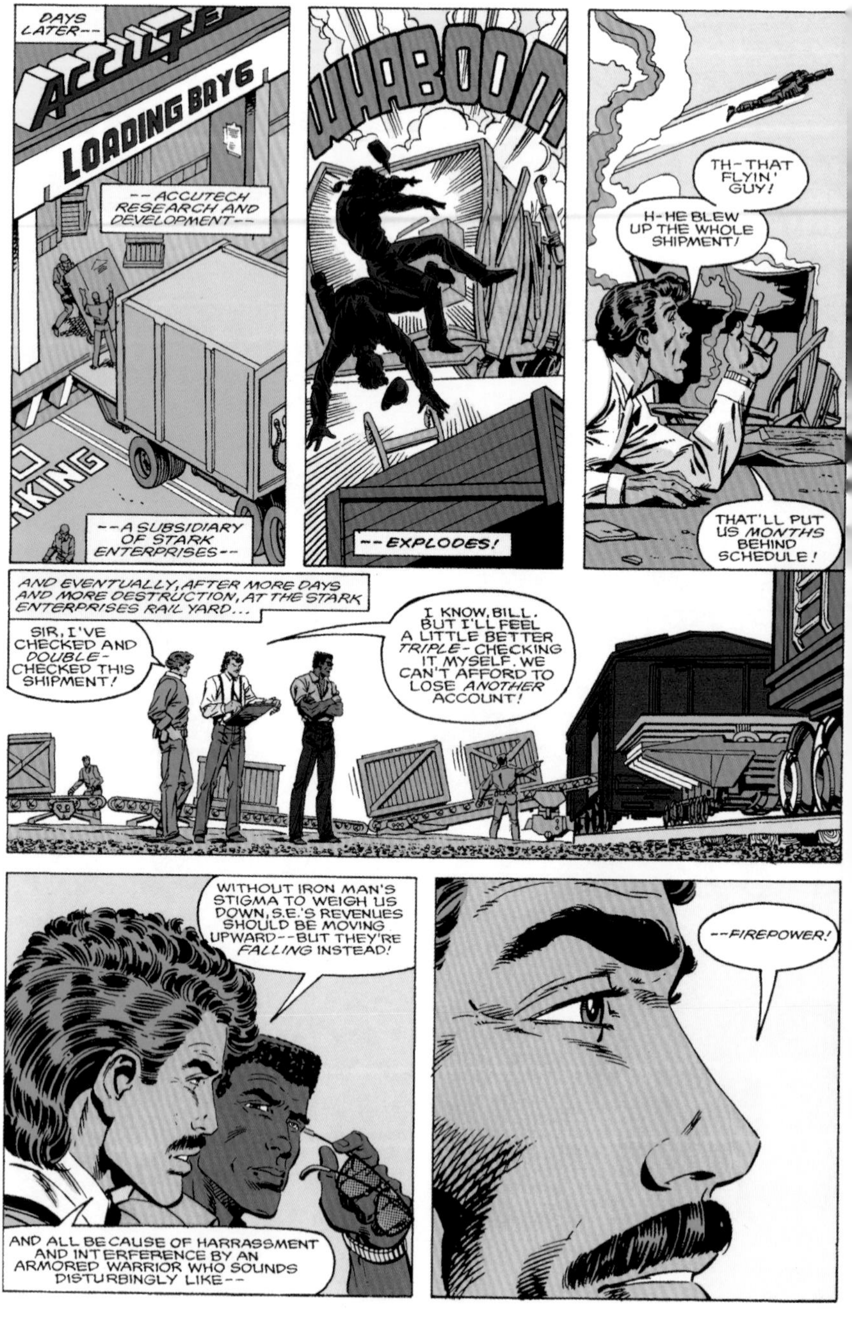
DAYS LATER--
ACCUTECH
LOADING BAYS
--ACCUTECH RESEARCH AND DEVELOPMENT--
--A SUBSIDIARY OF STARK ENTERPRISES--
WHABOOM
--EXPLODES!
TH-THAT FLYIN' GUY!
H-HE BLEW UP THE WHOLE SHIPMENT!
THAT'LL PUT US MONTHS BEHIND SCHEDULE!
AND EVENTUALLY, AFTER MORE DAYS AND MORE DESTRUCTION, AT THE STARK ENTERPRISES RAIL YARD...
SIR, I'VE CHECKED AND DOUBLE-CHECKED THIS SHIPMENT!
I KNOW, BILL. BUT I'LL FEEL A LITTLE BETTER TRIPLE-CHECKING IT MYSELF. WE CAN'T AFFORD TO LOSE ANOTHER ACCOUNT!
WITHOUT IRON MAN'S STIGMA TO WEIGH US DOWN, S.E.'S REVENUES SHOULD BE MOVING UPWARD--BUT THEY'RE FALLING INSTEAD!
AND ALL BECAUSE OF HARRASSMENT AND INTERFERENCE BY AN ARMORED WARRIOR WHO SOUNDS DISTURBINGLY LIKE--
--FIREPOWER!

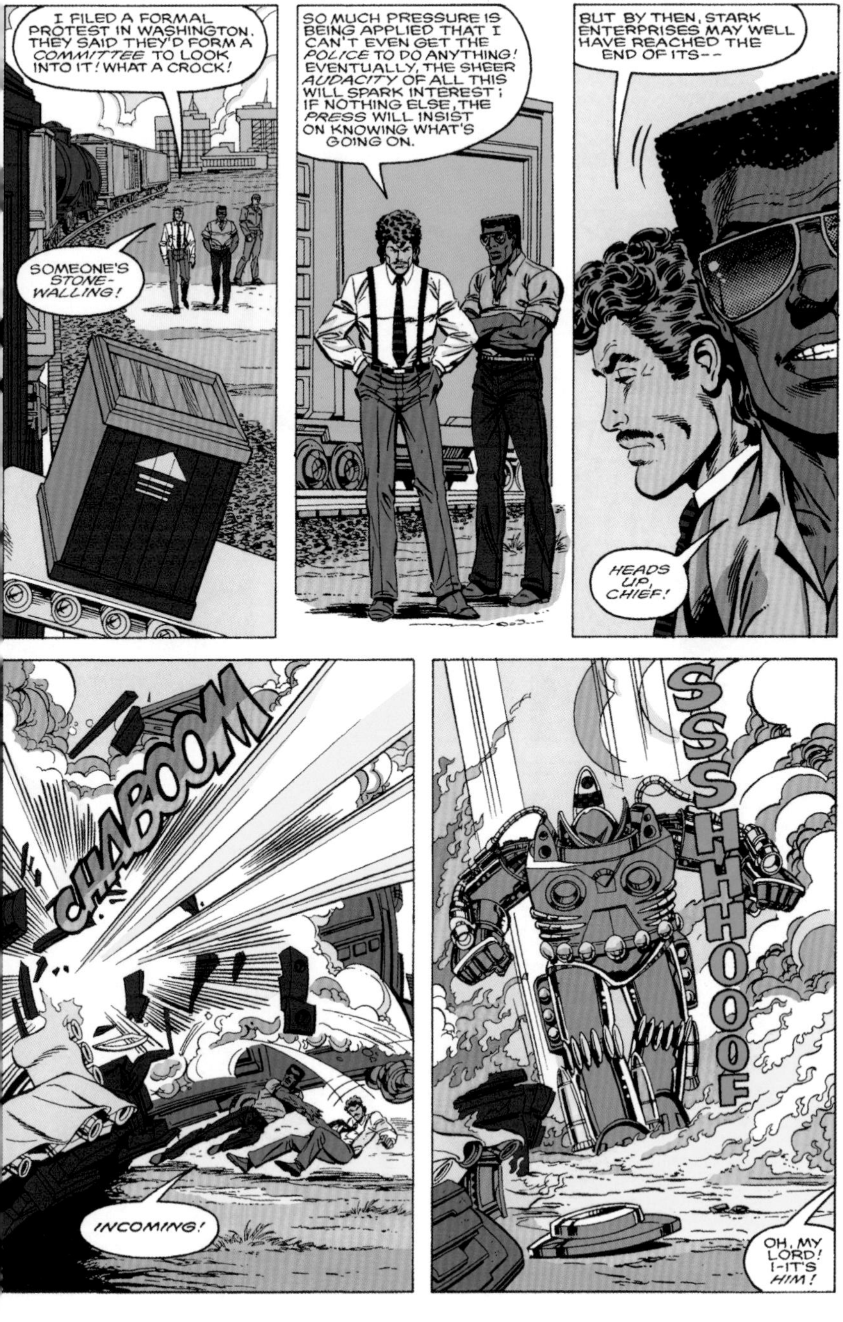
I FILED A FORMAL PROTEST IN WASHINGTON. THEY SAID THEY'D FORM A COMMITTEE TO LOOK INTO IT! WHAT A CROCK!
SOMEONE'S STONE-WALLING!
SO MUCH PRESSURE IS BEING APPLIED THAT I CAN'T EVEN GET THE POLICE TO DO ANYTHING! EVENTUALLY, THE SHEER AUDACITY OF ALL THIS WILL SPARK INTEREST; IF NOTHING ELSE, THE PRESS WILL INSIST ON KNOWING WHAT'S GOING ON.
BUT BY THEN, STARK ENTERPRISES MAY WELL HAVE REACHED THE END OF ITS--
HEADS UP, CHIEF!
CHABOOM
INCOMING!
SSSHHHHOOOOF
OH, MY LORD! I-IT'S HIM!

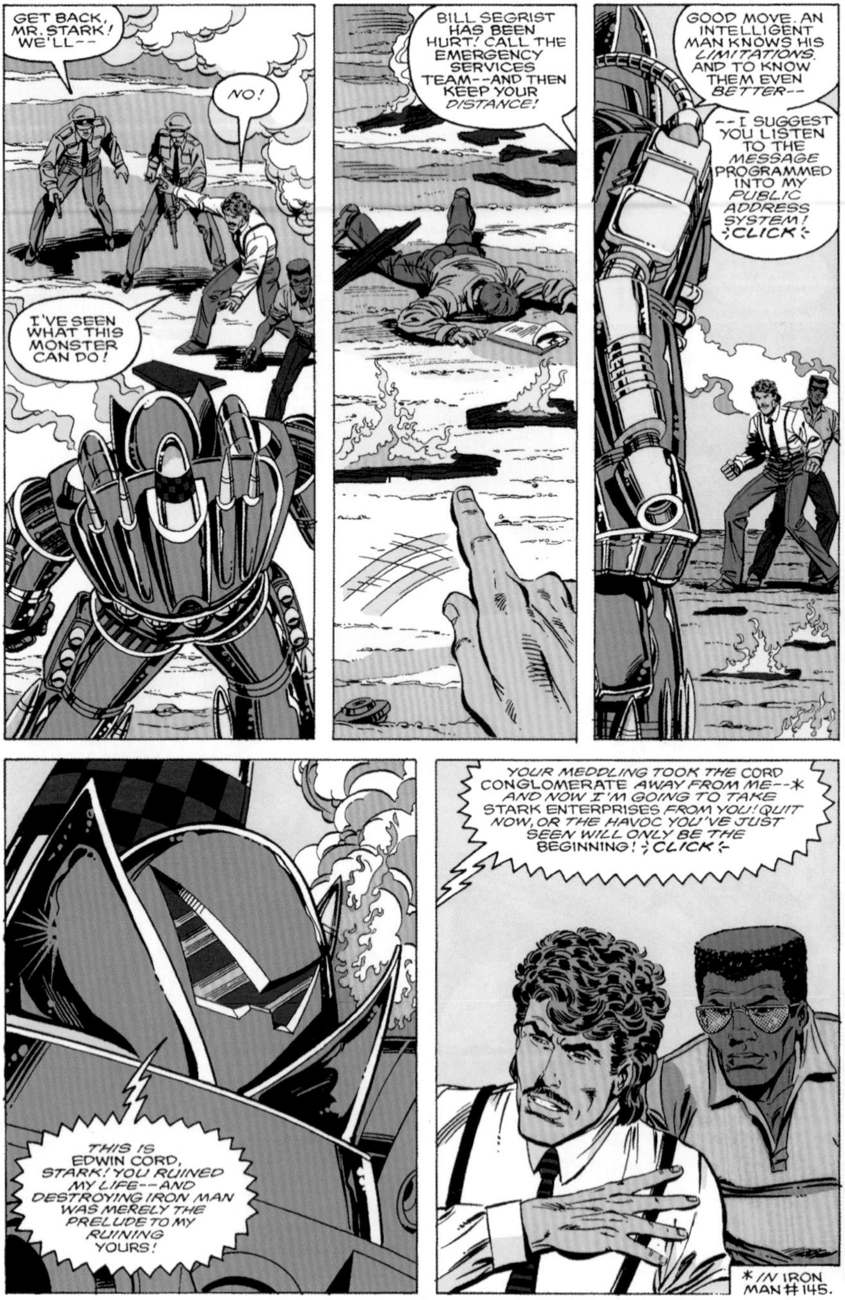
GET BACK, MR. STARK! WE'LL--
NO!
I'VE SEEN WHAT THIS MONSTER CAN DO!
BILL SEGRIST HAS BEEN HURT! CALL THE EMERGENCY SERVICES TEAM--AND THEN KEEP YOUR DISTANCE!
GOOD MOVE. AN INTELLIGENT MAN KNOWS HIS LIMITATIONS. AND TO KNOW THEM EVEN BETTER--
--I SUGGEST YOU LISTEN TO THE MESSAGE PROGRAMMED INTO MY PUBLIC ADDRESS SYSTEM! ;CLICK;
THIS IS EDWIN CORD, STARK! YOU RUINED MY LIFE--AND DESTROYING IRON MAN WAS MERELY THE PRELUDE TO MY RUINING YOURS!
YOUR MEDDLING TOOK THE CORD CONGLOMERATE AWAY FROM ME--* AND NOW I'M GOING TO TAKE STARK ENTERPRISES FROM YOU! QUIT NOW, OR THE HAVOC YOU'VE JUST SEEN WILL ONLY BE THE BEGINNING! ;CLICK;
*IN IRON MAN #145.

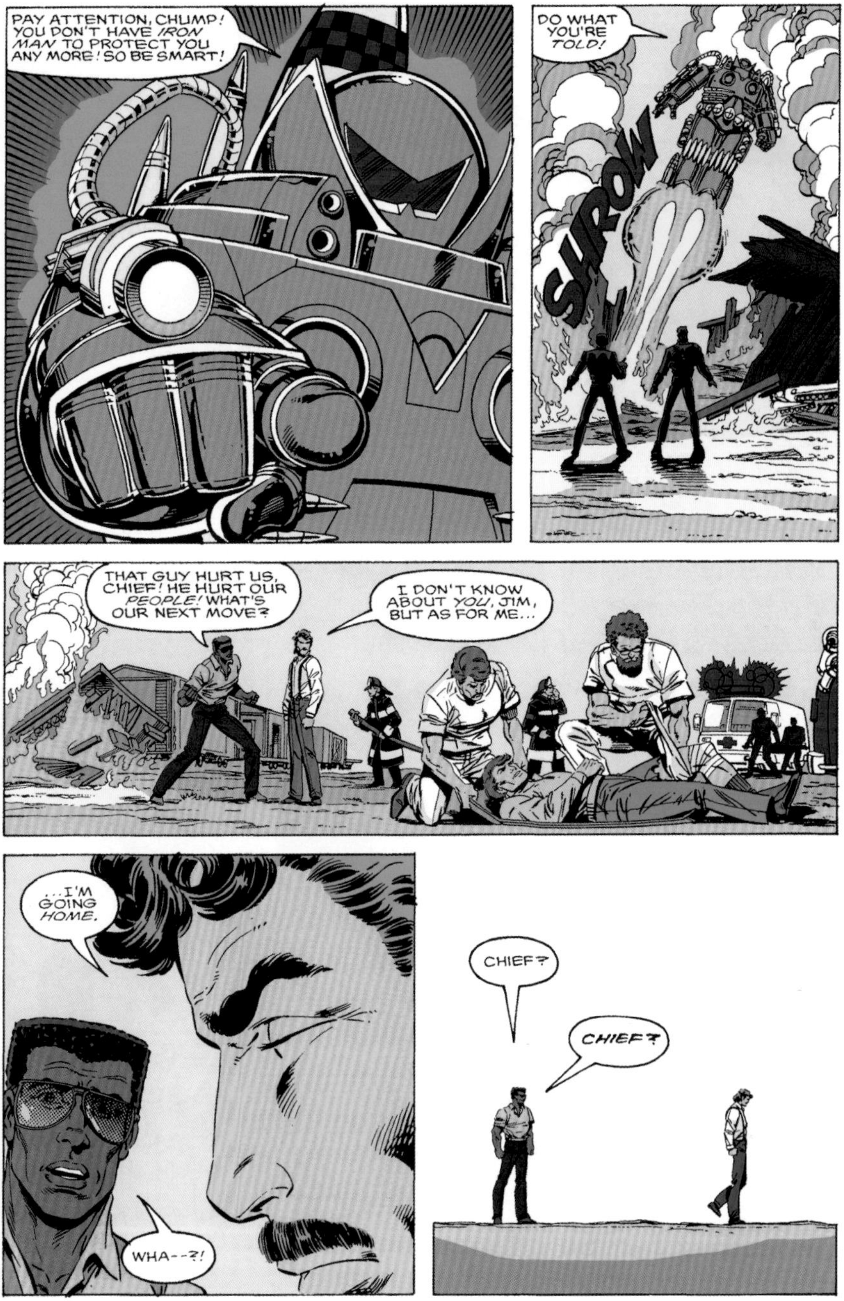
PAY ATTENTION, CHUMP! YOU DON'T HAVE IRON MAN TO PROTECT YOU ANY MORE! SO BE SMART!
DO WHAT YOU'RE TOLD!
SHROW
THAT GUY HURT US, CHIEF! HE HURT OUR PEOPLE! WHAT'S OUR NEXT MOVE?
I DON'T KNOW ABOUT YOU, JIM, BUT AS FOR ME...
...I'M GOING HOME.
WHA--?!
CHIEF?
CHIEF?

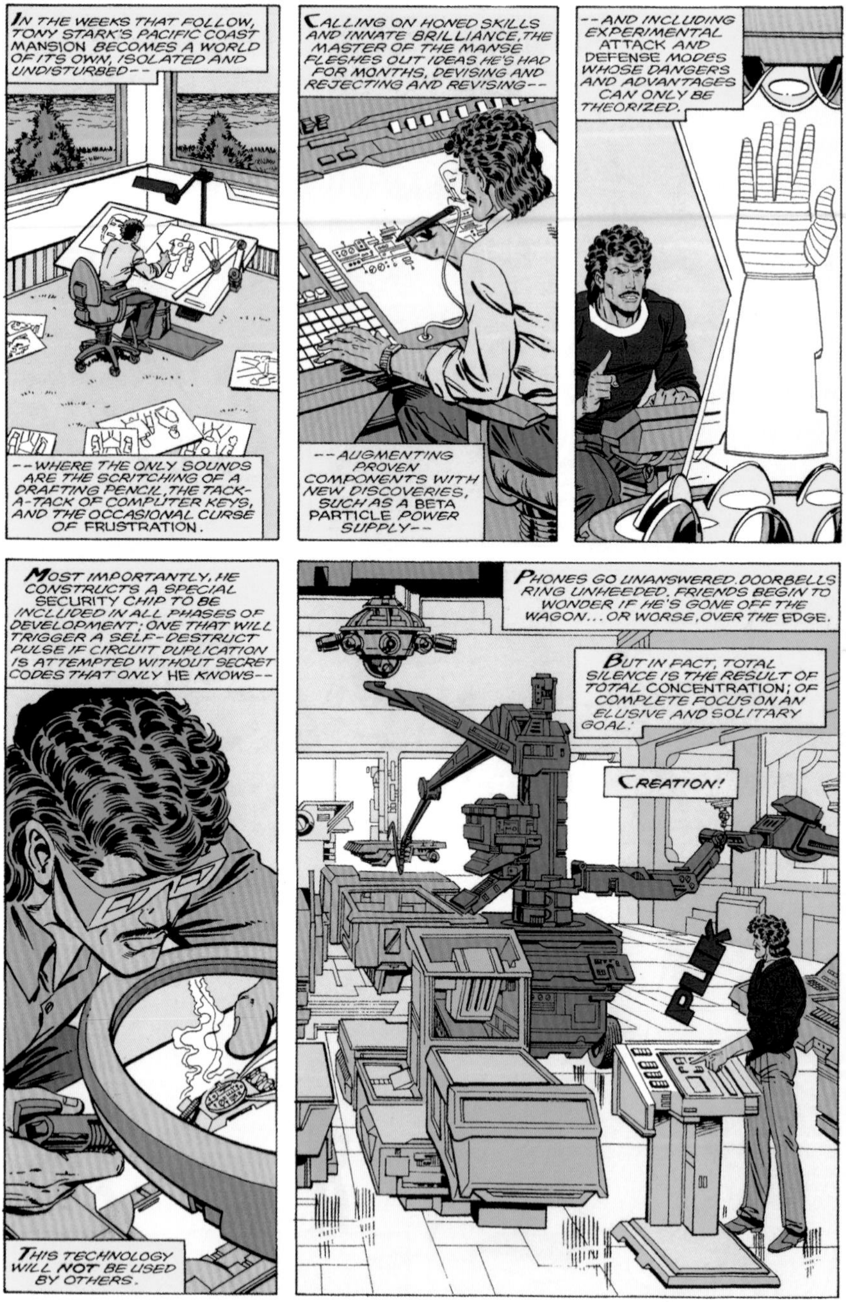
IN THE WEEKS THAT FOLLOW, TONY STARK'S PACIFIC COAST MANSION BECOMES A WORLD OF ITS OWN, ISOLATED AND UNDISTURBED--
--WHERE THE ONLY SOUNDS ARE THE SCRITCHING OF A DRAFTING PENCIL, THE TACK-A-TACK OF COMPUTER KEYS, AND THE OCCASIONAL CURSE OF FRUSTRATION.
CALLING ON HONED SKILLS AND INNATE BRILLIANCE, THE MASTER OF THE MANSE FLESHES OUT IDEAS HE'S HAD FOR MONTHS, DEVISING AND REJECTING AND REVISING--
--AUGMENTING PROVEN COMPONENTS WITH NEW DISCOVERIES, SUCH AS A BETA PARTICLE POWER SUPPLY--
--AND INCLUDING EXPERIMENTAL ATTACK AND DEFENSE MODES WHOSE DANGERS AND ADVANTAGES CAN ONLY BE THEORIZED.
MOST IMPORTANTLY, HE CONSTRUCTS A SPECIAL SECURITY CHIP TO BE INCLUDED IN ALL PHASES OF DEVELOPMENT; ONE THAT WILL TRIGGER A SELF-DESTRUCT PULSE IF CIRCUIT DUPLICATION IS ATTEMPTED WITHOUT SECRET CODES THAT ONLY HE KNOWS--
THIS TECHNOLOGY WILL NOT BE USED BY OTHERS.
PHONES GO UNANSWERED. DOORBELLS RING UNHEEDED. FRIENDS BEGIN TO WONDER IF HE'S GONE OFF THE WAGON... OR WORSE, OVER THE EDGE.
BUT IN FACT, TOTAL SILENCE IS THE RESULT OF TOTAL CONCENTRATION; OF COMPLETE FOCUS ON AN ELUSIVE AND SOLITARY GOAL:
CREATION!
PLIK

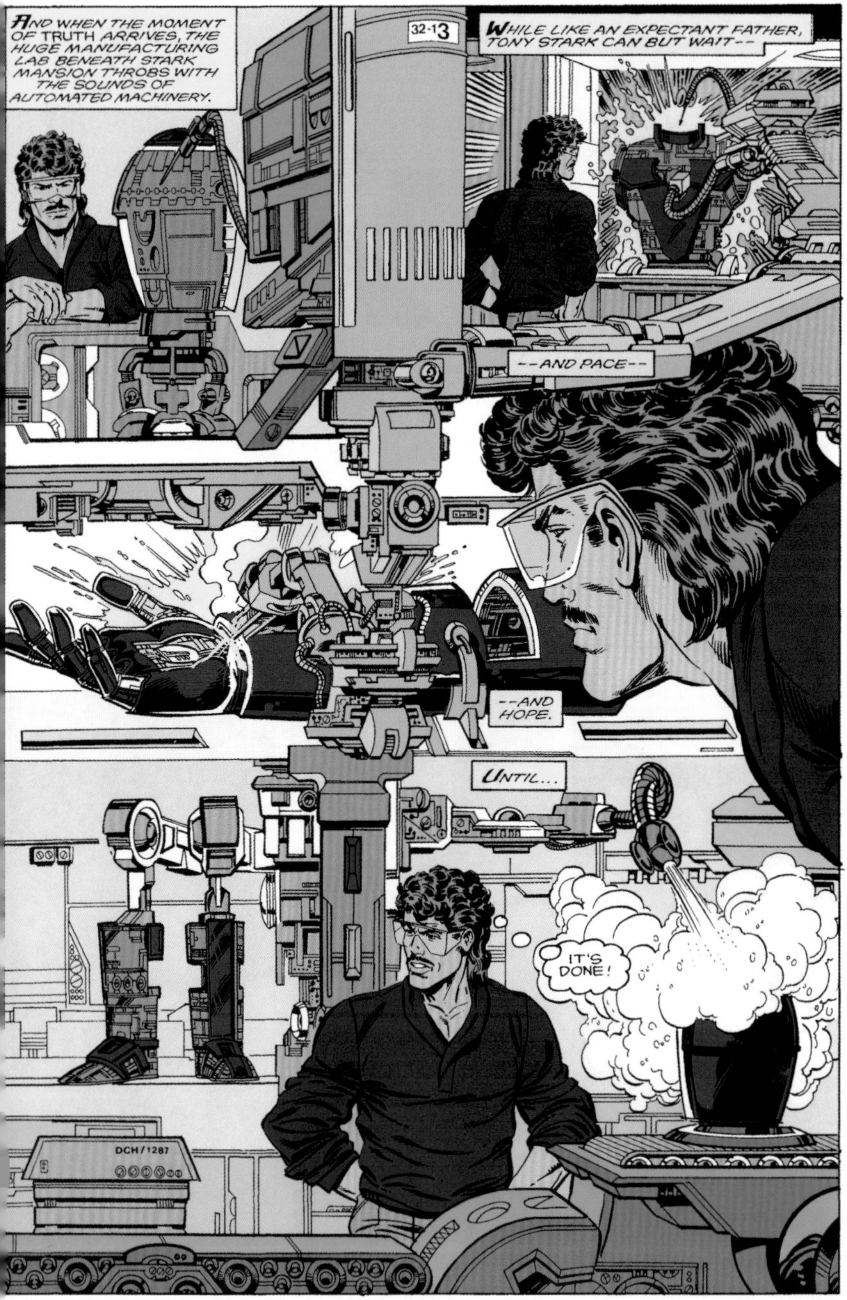
AND WHEN THE MOMENT OF TRUTH ARRIVES, THE HUGE MANUFACTURING LAB BENEATH STARK MANSION THROBS WITH THE SOUNDS OF AUTOMATED MACHINERY.
32-13
WHILE LIKE AN EXPECTANT FATHER, TONY STARK CAN BUT WAIT--
--AND PACE--
--AND HOPE.
UNTIL...
IT'S DONE!
DCH/1287

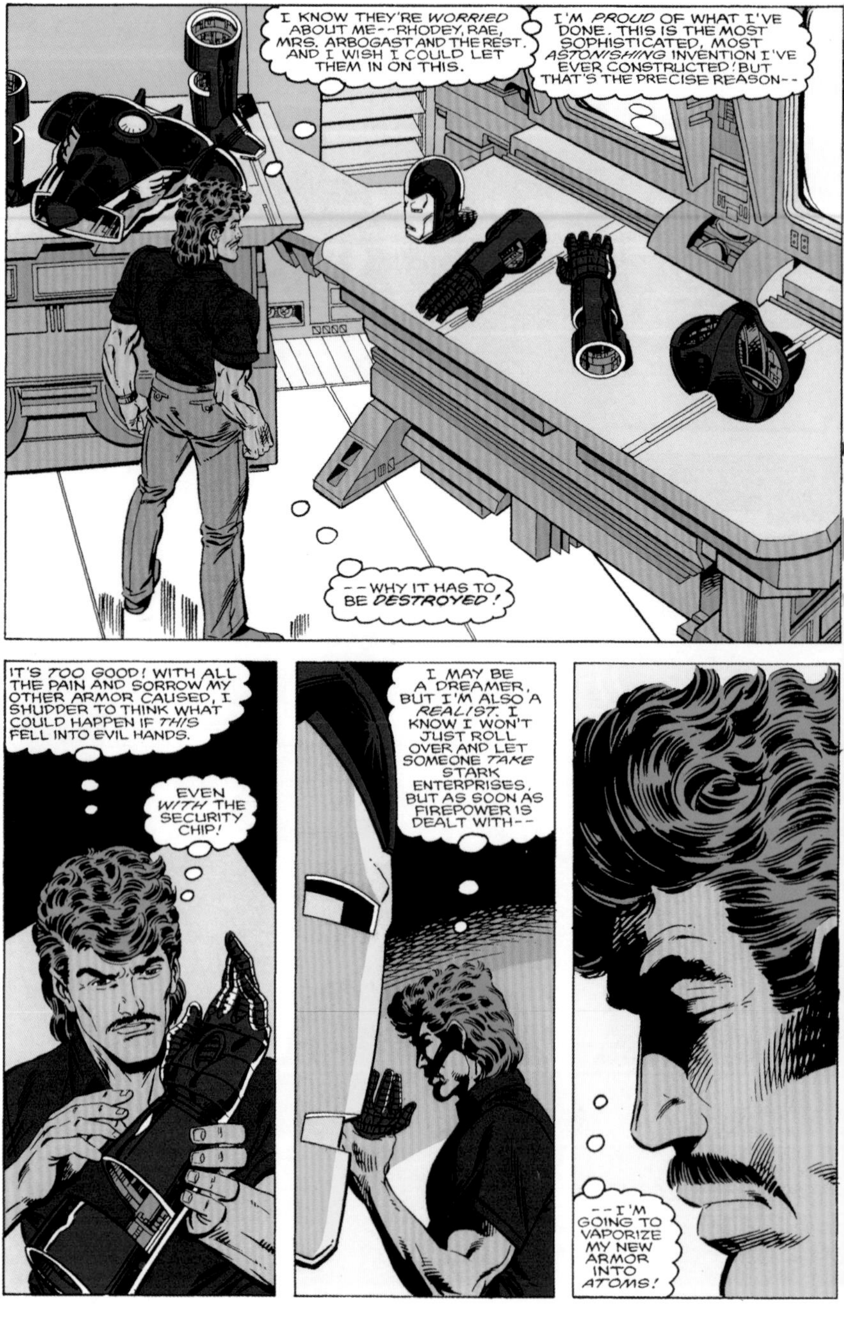
I KNOW THEY'RE *WORRIED* ABOUT ME--RHODEY, RAE, MRS. ARBOGAST AND THE REST. AND I WISH I COULD LET THEM IN ON THIS.
I'M *PROUD* OF WHAT I'VE DONE. THIS IS THE MOST SOPHISTICATED, MOST *ASTONISHING* INVENTION I'VE EVER CONSTRUCTED! BUT THAT'S THE PRECISE REASON--
--WHY IT HAS TO BE *DESTROYED*!
IT'S *TOO* GOOD! WITH ALL THE PAIN AND SORROW MY OTHER ARMOR CAUSED, I SHUDDER TO THINK WHAT COULD HAPPEN IF *THIS* FELL INTO EVIL HANDS.
EVEN *WITH* THE SECURITY CHIP!
I MAY BE A DREAMER, BUT I'M ALSO A *REALIST*. I KNOW I WON'T JUST ROLL OVER AND LET SOMEONE *TAKE* STARK ENTERPRISES. BUT AS SOON AS FIREPOWER IS DEALT WITH--
--I'M GOING TO VAPORIZE MY NEW ARMOR INTO *ATOMS*!

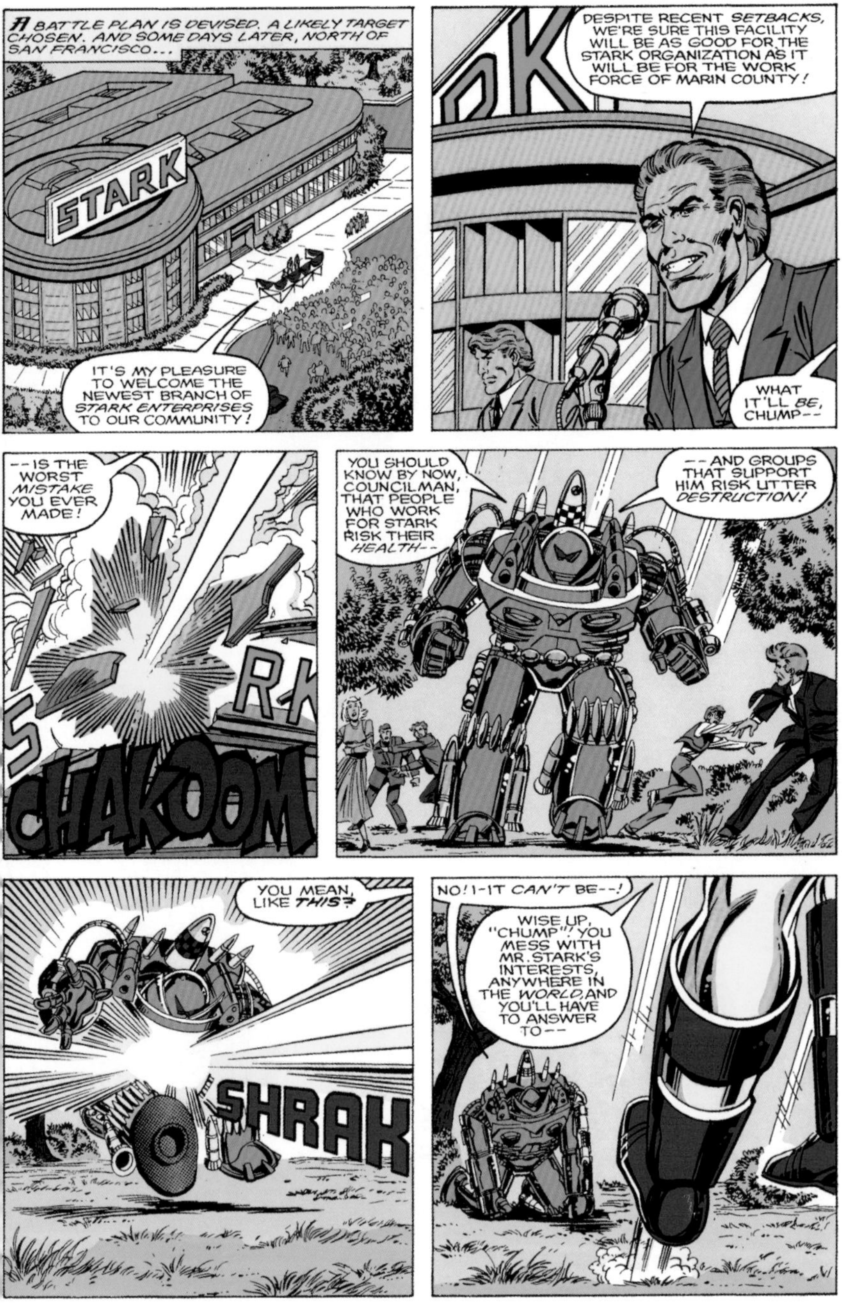
A BATTLE PLAN IS DEVISED. A LIKELY TARGET CHOSEN. AND SOME DAYS LATER, NORTH OF SAN FRANCISCO...
STARK
IT'S MY PLEASURE TO WELCOME THE NEWEST BRANCH OF STARK ENTERPRISES TO OUR COMMUNITY!
DESPITE RECENT SETBACKS, WE'RE SURE THIS FACILITY WILL BE AS GOOD FOR THE STARK ORGANIZATION AS IT WILL BE FOR THE WORK FORCE OF MARIN COUNTY!
WHAT IT'LL BE, CHUMP--
--IS THE WORST MISTAKE YOU EVER MADE!
CHAKOOM
YOU SHOULD KNOW BY NOW, COUNCILMAN, THAT PEOPLE WHO WORK FOR STARK RISK THEIR HEALTH--
--AND GROUPS THAT SUPPORT HIM RISK UTTER DESTRUCTION!
YOU MEAN, LIKE THIS?
SHRAK
NO! I-IT CAN'T BE--!
WISE UP, "CHUMP"! YOU MESS WITH MR. STARK'S INTERESTS, ANYWHERE IN THE WORLD, AND YOU'LL HAVE TO ANSWER TO--

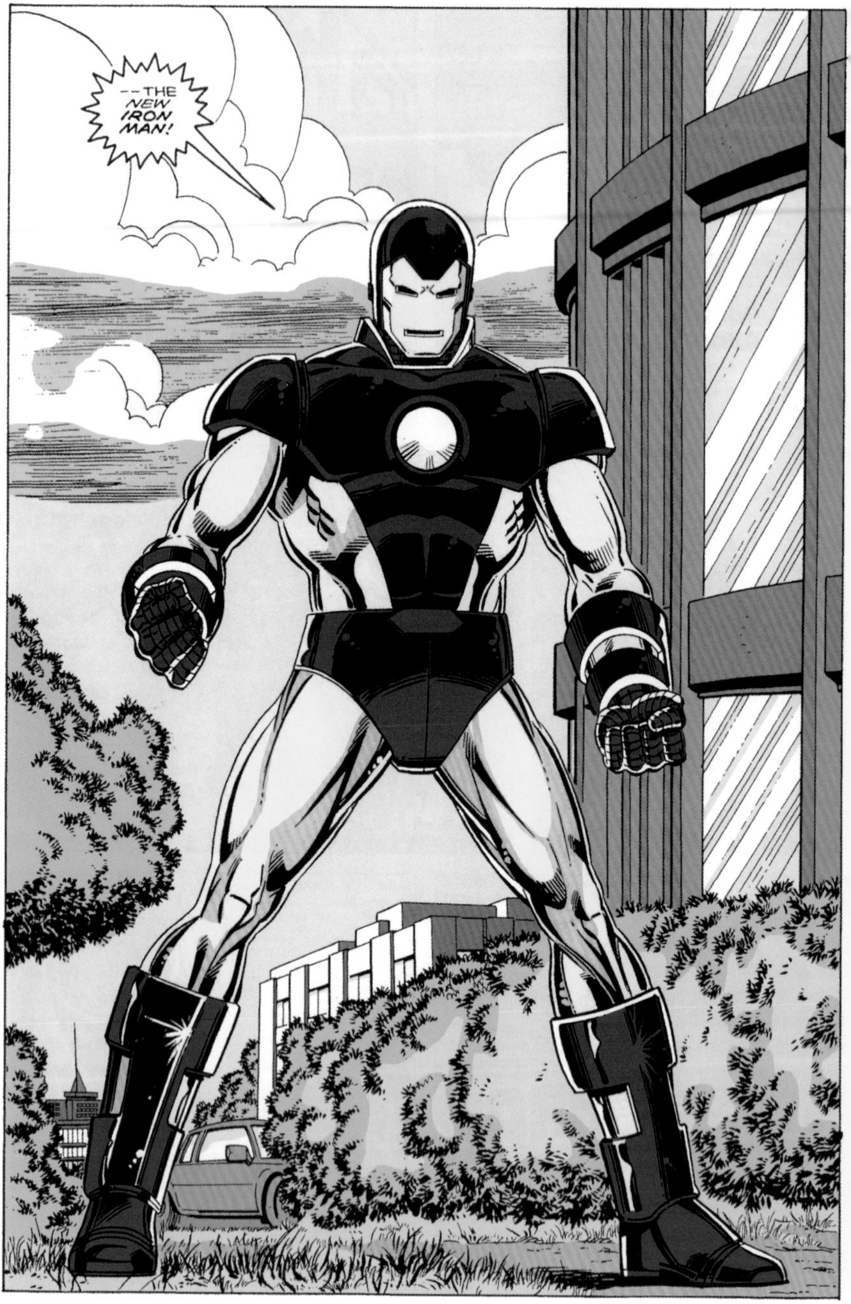
--THE NEW IRON MAN!

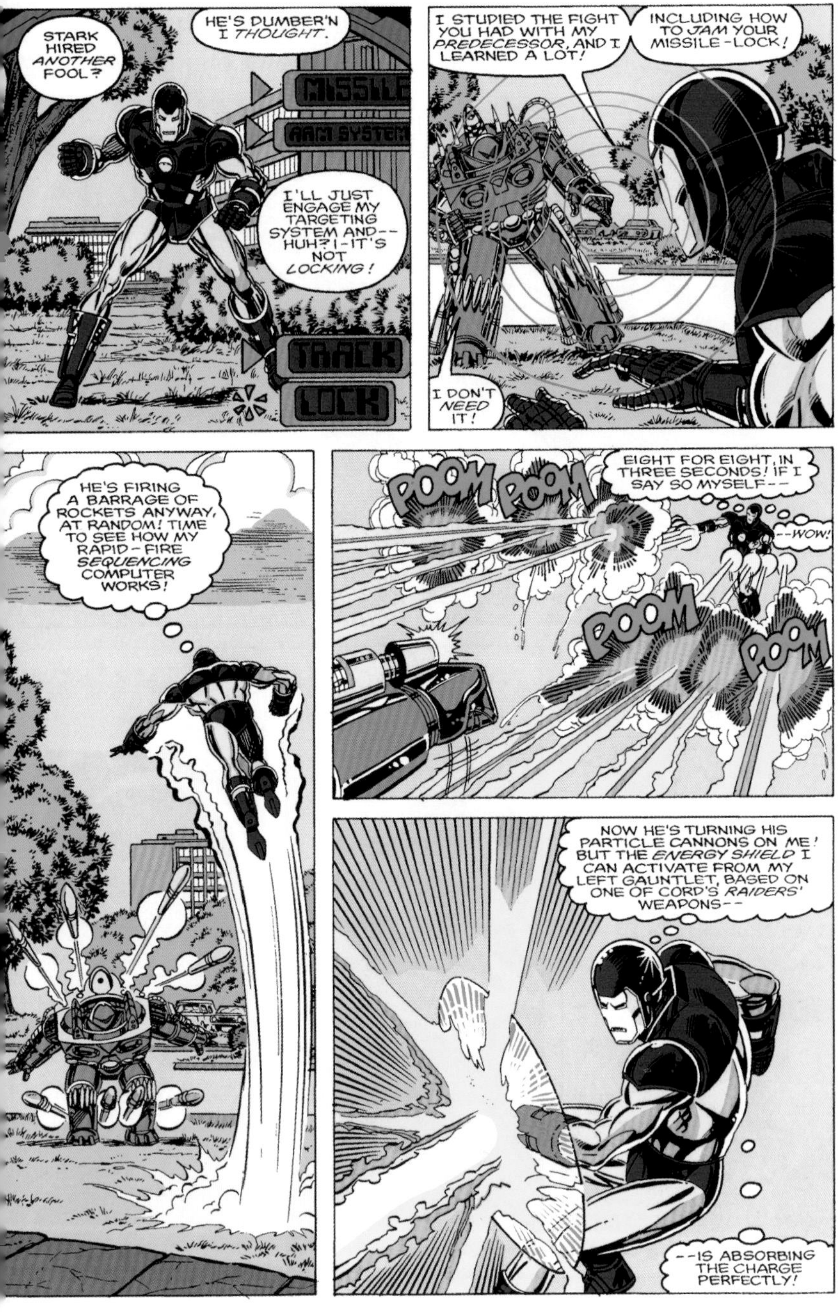
STARK HIRED ANOTHER FOOL?
HE'S DUMBER'N I THOUGHT.
MISSILE
ARM SYSTEM
I'LL JUST ENGAGE MY TARGETING SYSTEM AND-- HUH?! I-IT'S NOT LOCKING!
TRACK
LOCK
I STUDIED THE FIGHT YOU HAD WITH MY PREDECESSOR, AND I LEARNED A LOT!
INCLUDING HOW TO JAM YOUR MISSILE-LOCK!
I DON'T NEED IT!
HE'S FIRING A BARRAGE OF ROCKETS ANYWAY, AT RANDOM! TIME TO SEE HOW MY RAPID-FIRE SEQUENCING COMPUTER WORKS!
POOM POOM
EIGHT FOR EIGHT, IN THREE SECONDS! IF I SAY SO MYSELF--
--WOW!
POOM
POOM
NOW HE'S TURNING HIS PARTICLE CANNONS ON ME! BUT THE ENERGY SHIELD I CAN ACTIVATE FROM MY LEFT GAUNTLET, BASED ON ONE OF CORD'S RAIDERS' WEAPONS--
--IS ABSORBING THE CHARGE PERFECTLY!

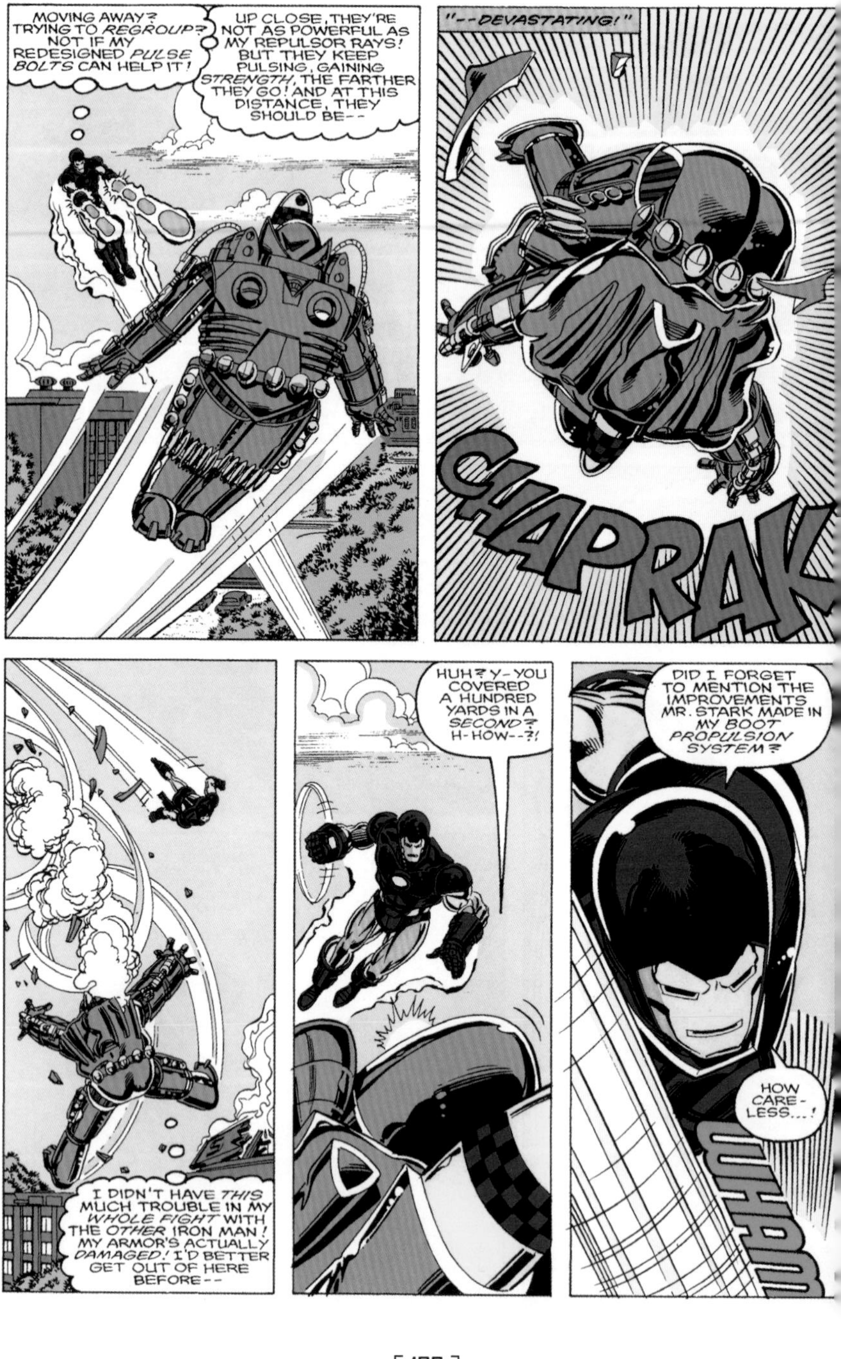
MOVING AWAY? TRYING TO REGROUP? NOT IF MY REDESIGNED PULSE BOLTS CAN HELP IT!
UP CLOSE, THEY'RE NOT AS POWERFUL AS MY REPULSOR RAYS! BUT THEY KEEP PULSING, GAINING STRENGTH, THE FARTHER THEY GO! AND AT THIS DISTANCE, THEY SHOULD BE--
"--DEVASTATING!"
CHAPRAK
I DIDN'T HAVE THIS MUCH TROUBLE IN MY WHOLE FIGHT WITH THE OTHER IRON MAN! MY ARMOR'S ACTUALLY DAMAGED! I'D BETTER GET OUT OF HERE BEFORE--
HUH? Y-YOU COVERED A HUNDRED YARDS IN A SECOND? H-HOW--?!
DID I FORGET TO MENTION THE IMPROVEMENTS MR. STARK MADE IN MY BOOT PROPULSION SYSTEM?
HOW CARE-LESS...!
WHAM

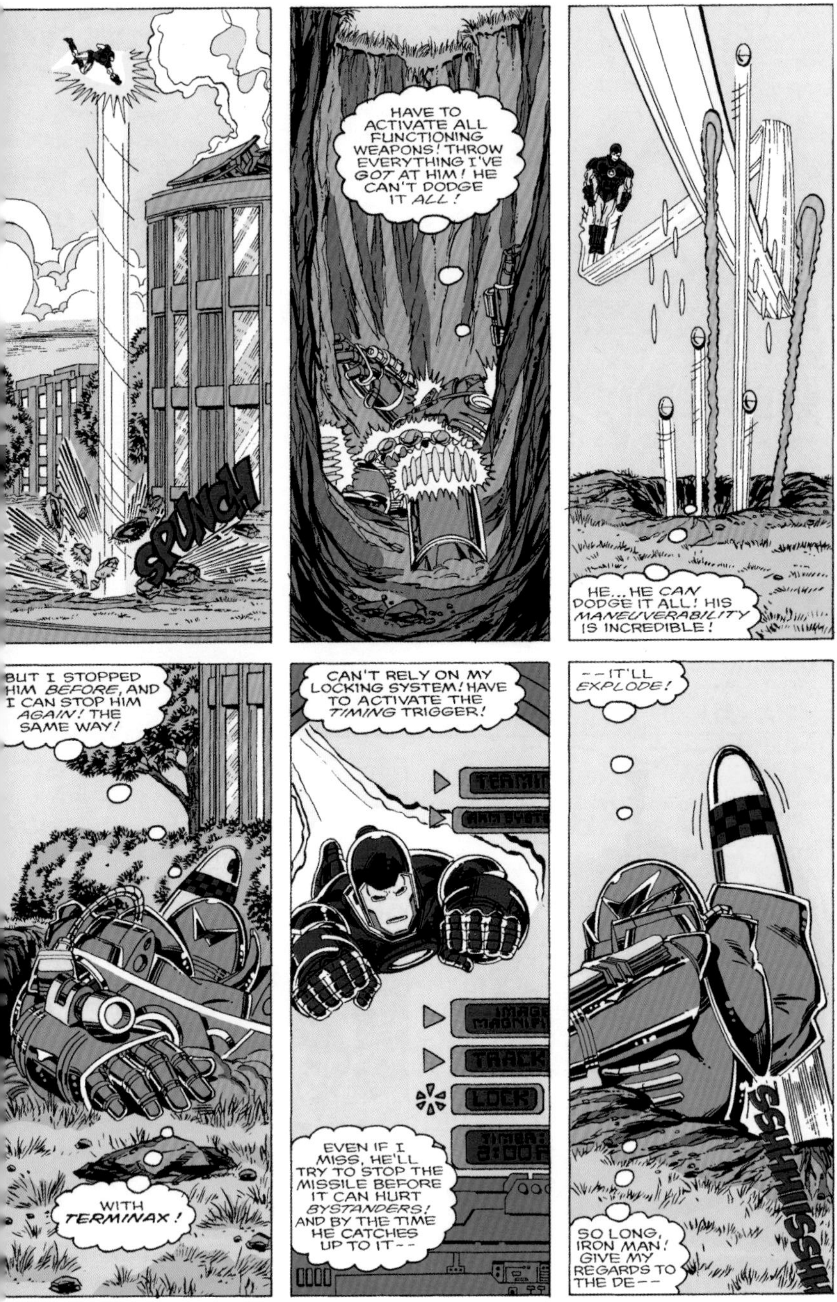
SPUNCH
HAVE TO ACTIVATE ALL FUNCTIONING WEAPONS! THROW EVERYTHING I'VE GOT AT HIM! HE CAN'T DODGE IT ALL!
HE... HE CAN DODGE IT ALL! HIS MANEUVERABILITY IS INCREDIBLE!
BUT I STOPPED HIM BEFORE, AND I CAN STOP HIM AGAIN! THE SAME WAY!
WITH TERMINAX!
CAN'T RELY ON MY LOCKING SYSTEM! HAVE TO ACTIVATE THE TIMING TRIGGER!
TRACK
LOCK
EVEN IF I MISS, HE'LL TRY TO STOP THE MISSILE BEFORE IT CAN HURT BYSTANDERS! AND BY THE TIME HE CATCHES UP TO IT--
--IT'LL EXPLODE!
SSHHHISSSHH
SO LONG, IRON MAN! GIVE MY REGARDS TO THE DE--

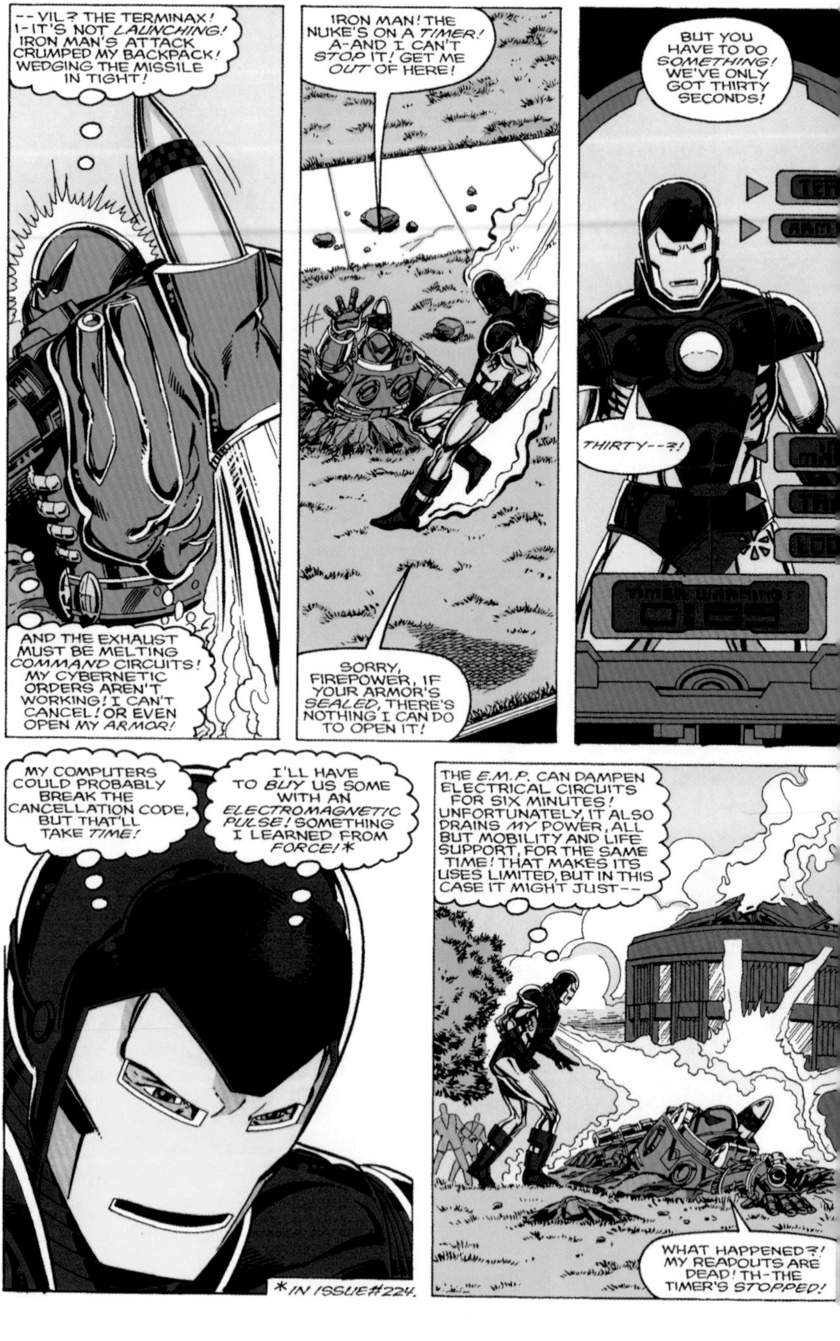
--VIL? THE TERMINAX! I-IT'S NOT LAUNCHING! IRON MAN'S ATTACK CRUMPED MY BACKPACK! WEDGING THE MISSILE IN TIGHT!
AND THE EXHAUST MUST BE MELTING COMMAND CIRCUITS! MY CYBERNETIC ORDERS AREN'T WORKING! I CAN'T CANCEL! OR EVEN OPEN MY ARMOR!
IRON MAN! THE NUKE'S ON A TIMER! A-AND I CAN'T STOP IT! GET ME OUT OF HERE!
SORRY, FIREPOWER, IF YOUR ARMOR'S SEALED, THERE'S NOTHING I CAN DO TO OPEN IT!
BUT YOU HAVE TO DO SOMETHING! WE'VE ONLY GOT THIRTY SECONDS!
THIRTY--?!
MY COMPUTERS COULD PROBABLY BREAK THE CANCELLATION CODE, BUT THAT'LL TAKE TIME!
I'LL HAVE TO BUY US SOME WITH AN ELECTROMAGNETIC PULSE! SOMETHING I LEARNED FROM FORCE!*
*IN ISSUE #224.
THE E.M.P. CAN DAMPEN ELECTRICAL CIRCUITS FOR SIX MINUTES! UNFORTUNATELY, IT ALSO DRAINS MY POWER, ALL BUT MOBILITY AND LIFE SUPPORT, FOR THE SAME TIME! THAT MAKES ITS USES LIMITED, BUT IN THIS CASE IT MIGHT JUST--
WHAT HAPPENED?! MY READOUTS ARE DEAD! TH-THE TIMER'S STOPPED!

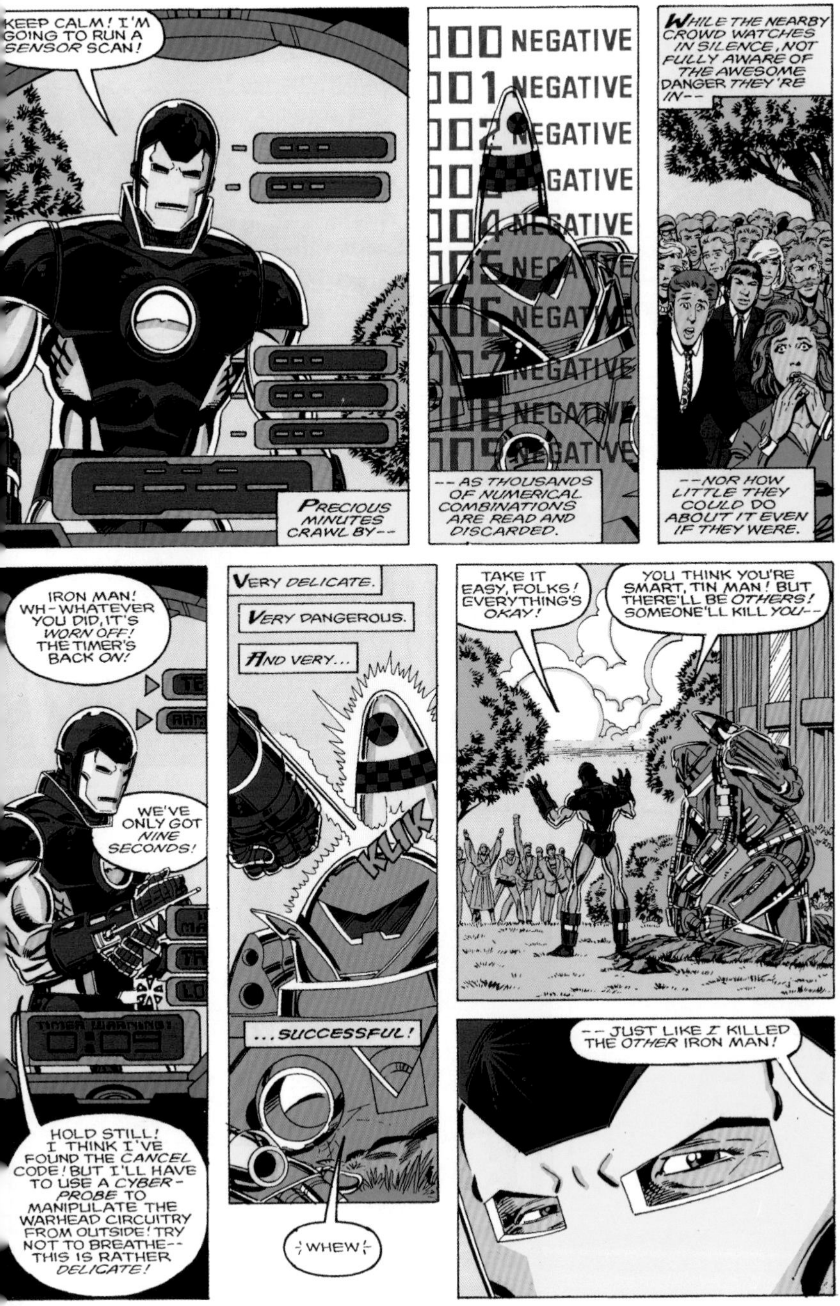
KEEP CALM! I'M GOING TO RUN A SENSOR SCAN!
PRECIOUS MINUTES CRAWL BY--
000 NEGATIVE
001 NEGATIVE
002 NEGATIVE
--AS THOUSANDS OF NUMERICAL COMBINATIONS ARE READ AND DISCARDED.
WHILE THE NEARBY CROWD WATCHES IN SILENCE, NOT FULLY AWARE OF THE AWESOME DANGER THEY'RE IN--
--NOR HOW LITTLE THEY COULD DO ABOUT IT EVEN IF THEY WERE.
IRON MAN! WH-WHATEVER YOU DID, IT'S WORN OFF! THE TIMER'S BACK ON!
WE'VE ONLY GOT NINE SECONDS!
TIMER WARNING!
0:05
HOLD STILL! I THINK I'VE FOUND THE CANCEL CODE! BUT I'LL HAVE TO USE A CYBER-PROBE TO MANIPULATE THE WARHEAD CIRCUITRY FROM OUTSIDE! TRY NOT TO BREATHE-- THIS IS RATHER DELICATE!
VERY DELICATE.
VERY DANGEROUS.
AND VERY...
KLIK
...SUCCESSFUL!
WHEW
TAKE IT EASY, FOLKS! EVERYTHING'S OKAY!
YOU THINK YOU'RE SMART, TIN MAN! BUT THERE'LL BE OTHERS! SOMEONE'LL KILL YOU--
--JUST LIKE I KILLED THE OTHER IRON MAN!

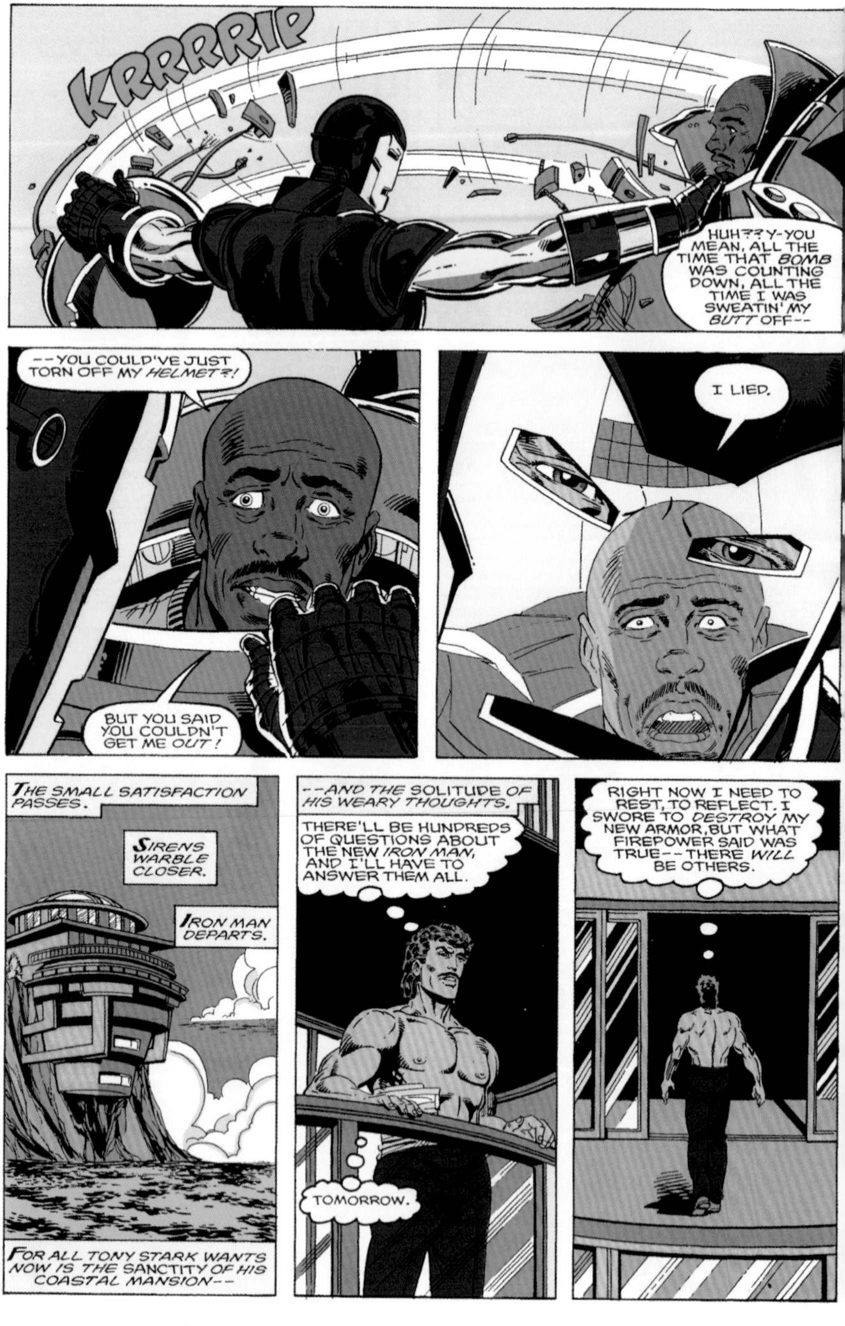
KRRRRIP
HUH?? Y-YOU MEAN, ALL THE TIME THAT BOMB WAS COUNTING DOWN, ALL THE TIME I WAS SWEATIN' MY BUTT OFF--
--YOU COULD'VE JUST TORN OFF MY HELMET?!
BUT YOU SAID YOU COULDN'T GET ME OUT!
I LIED.
THE SMALL SATISFACTION PASSES.
SIRENS WARBLE CLOSER.
IRON MAN DEPARTS.
FOR ALL TONY STARK WANTS NOW IS THE SANCTITY OF HIS COASTAL MANSION--
--AND THE SOLITUDE OF HIS WEARY THOUGHTS.
THERE'LL BE HUNDREDS OF QUESTIONS ABOUT THE NEW IRON MAN, AND I'LL HAVE TO ANSWER THEM ALL.
TOMORROW.
RIGHT NOW I NEED TO REST, TO REFLECT. I SWORE TO DESTROY MY NEW ARMOR, BUT WHAT FIREPOWER SAID WAS TRUE-- THERE WILL BE OTHERS.

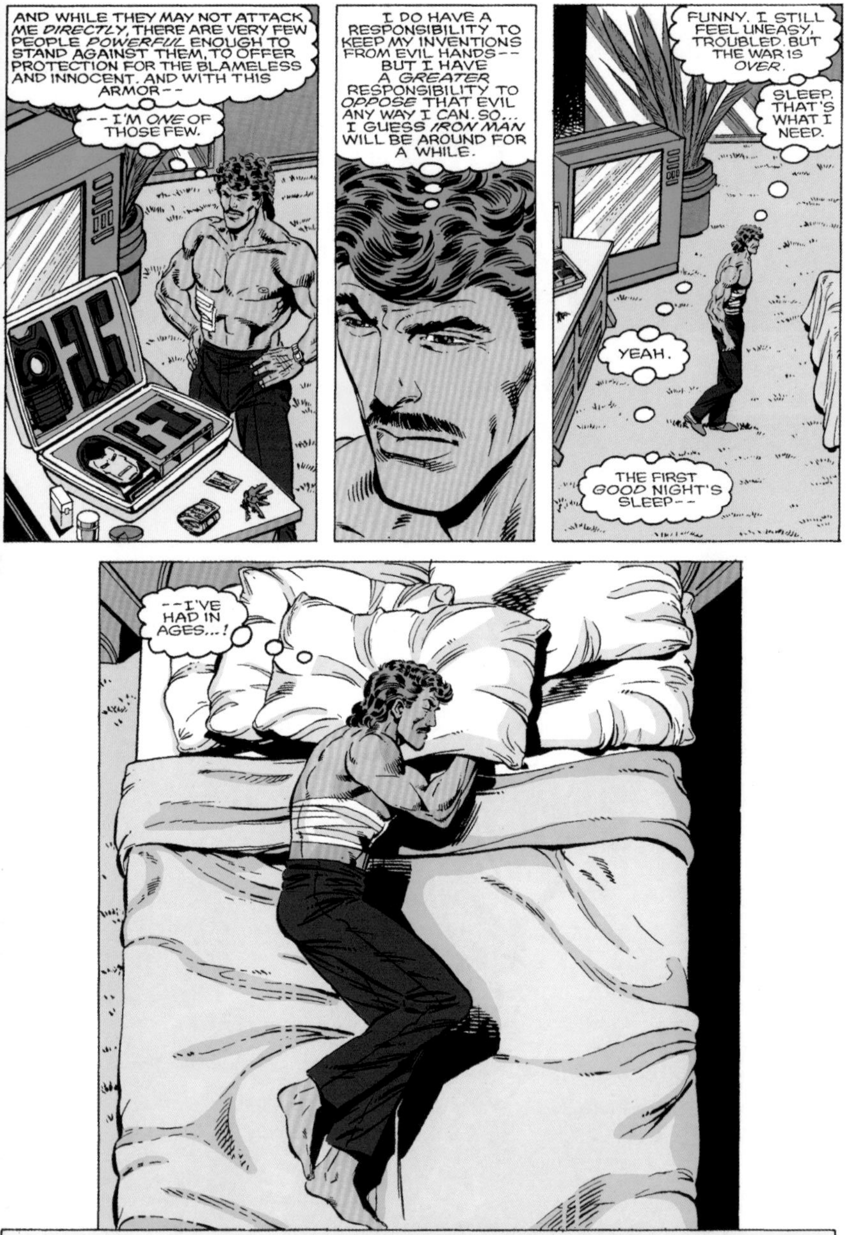
AND WHILE THEY MAY NOT ATTACK ME DIRECTLY, THERE ARE VERY FEW PEOPLE POWERFUL ENOUGH TO STAND AGAINST THEM, TO OFFER PROTECTION FOR THE BLAMELESS AND INNOCENT. AND WITH THIS ARMOR--
--I'M ONE OF THOSE FEW.
I DO HAVE A RESPONSIBILITY TO KEEP MY INVENTIONS FROM EVIL HANDS-- BUT I HAVE A GREATER RESPONSIBILITY TO OPPOSE THAT EVIL ANY WAY I CAN. SO... I GUESS IRON MAN WILL BE AROUND FOR A WHILE.
FUNNY. I STILL FEEL UNEASY, TROUBLED. BUT THE WAR IS OVER.
SLEEP. THAT'S WHAT I NEED.
YEAH.
THE FIRST GOOD NIGHT'S SLEEP--
--I'VE HAD IN AGES...!
THE STARK WARS SAGA WAS BROUGHT TO YOU BY:
DAVID MICHELINIE PLOT/SCRIPT • DOC BRIGHT BREAKDOWNS • BOB LAYTON PLOT/FINISHES • JANICE CHIANG LETTERS • BOB SHAREN COLORS • MARK GRUENWALD EDITOR • TOM DeFALCO EDITOR IN CHIEF

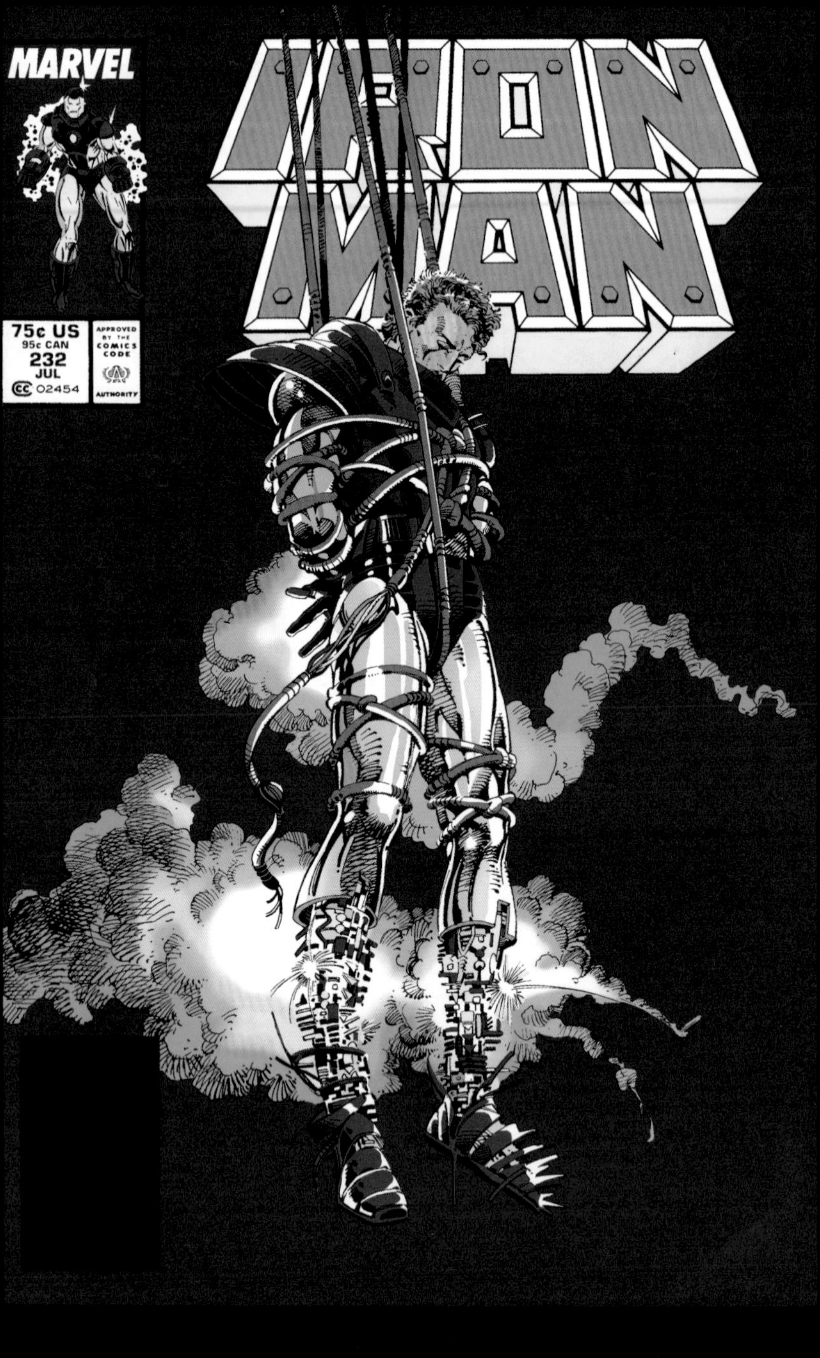
MARVEL
IRON MAN
75¢ US
95¢ CAN
232
JUL
CC 02454
APPROVED BY THE COMICS CODE AUTHORITY

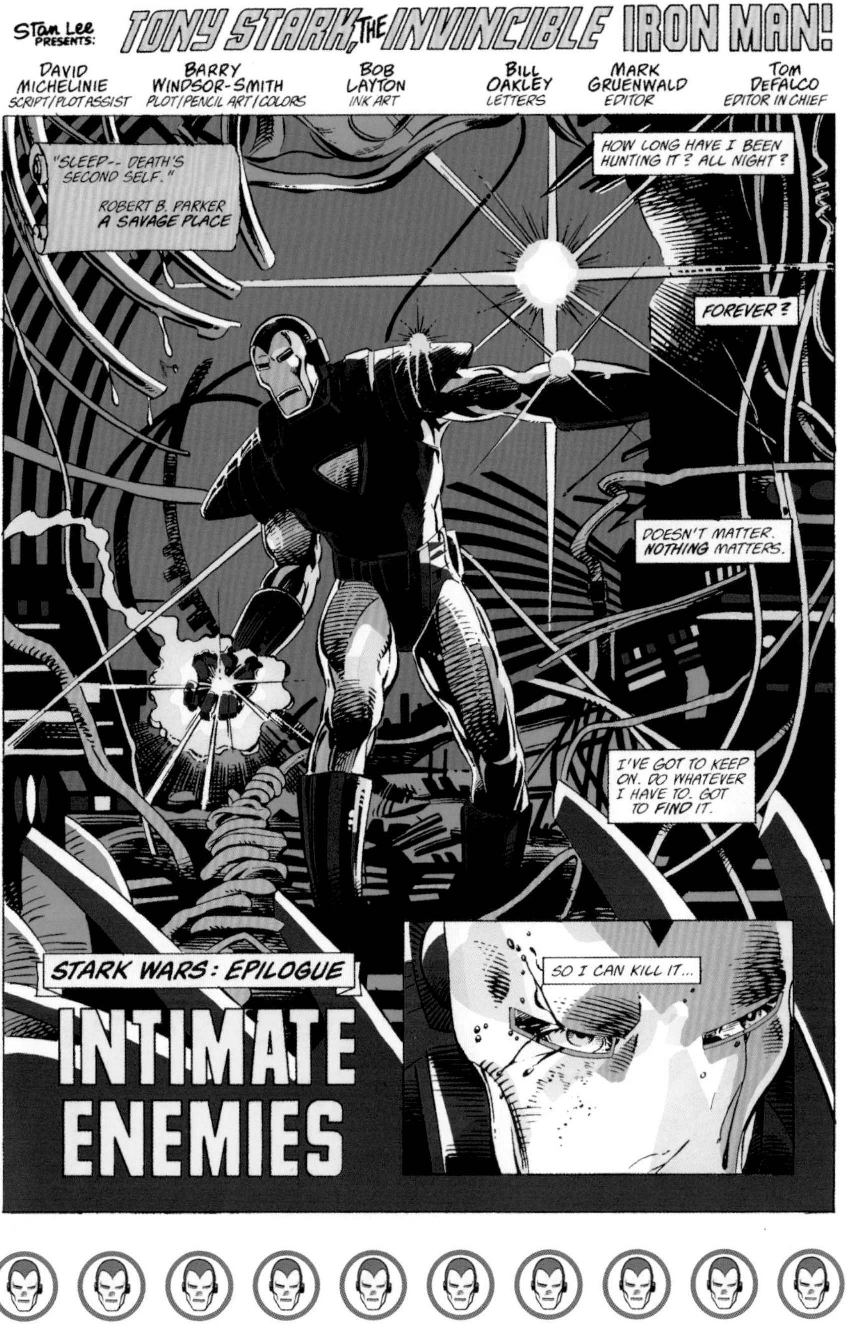

STAN LEE PRESENTS:
TONY STARK, THE INVINCIBLE IRON MAN!
DAVID MICHELINIE SCRIPT/PLOT ASSIST
BARRY WINDSOR-SMITH PLOT/PENCIL ART/COLORS
BOB LAYTON INK ART
BILL OAKLEY LETTERS
MARK GRUENWALD EDITOR
TOM DEFALCO EDITOR IN CHIEF
"SLEEP-- DEATH'S SECOND SELF." ROBERT B. PARKER A SAVAGE PLACE
HOW LONG HAVE I BEEN HUNTING IT? ALL NIGHT?
FOREVER?
DOESN'T MATTER. NOTHING MATTERS.
I'VE GOT TO KEEP ON. DO WHATEVER I HAVE TO. GOT TO FIND IT.
STARK WARS: EPILOGUE
INTIMATE ENEMIES
SO I CAN KILL IT...

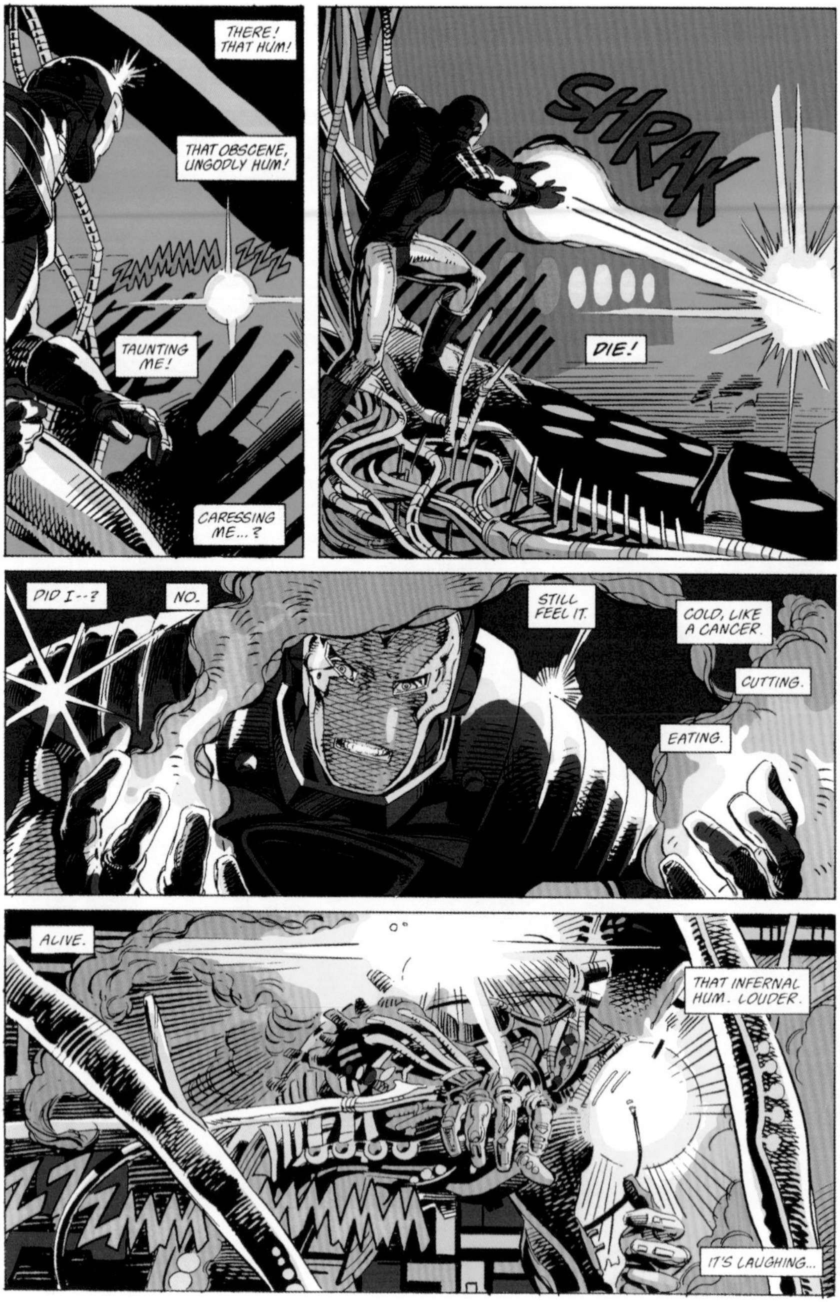
THERE! THAT HUM!
THAT OBSCENE, UNGODLY HUM!
ZMMMM ZZZ
TAUNTING ME!
CARESSING ME...?
SHRAK
DIE!
DID I--?
NO.
STILL FEEL IT.
COLD, LIKE A CANCER.
CUTTING.
EATING.
ALIVE.
THAT INFERNAL HUM. LOUDER.
IT'S LAUGHING...

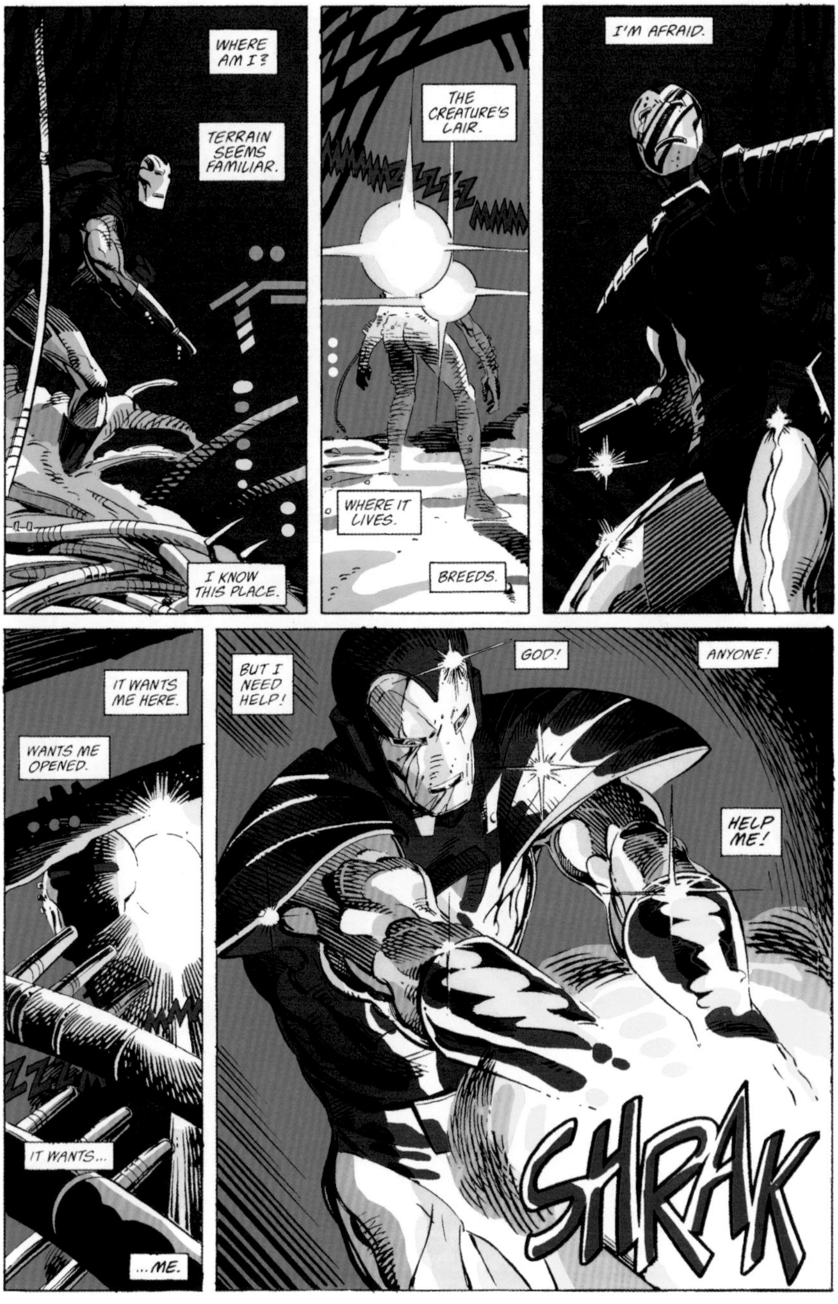
WHERE AM I?
TERRAIN SEEMS FAMILIAR.
I KNOW THIS PLACE.
THE CREATURE'S LAIR.
WHERE IT LIVES.
BREEDS.
I'M AFRAID.
IT WANTS ME HERE.
WANTS ME OPENED.
IT WANTS...
...ME.
BUT I NEED HELP!
GOD!
ANYONE!
HELP ME!
SHRAK

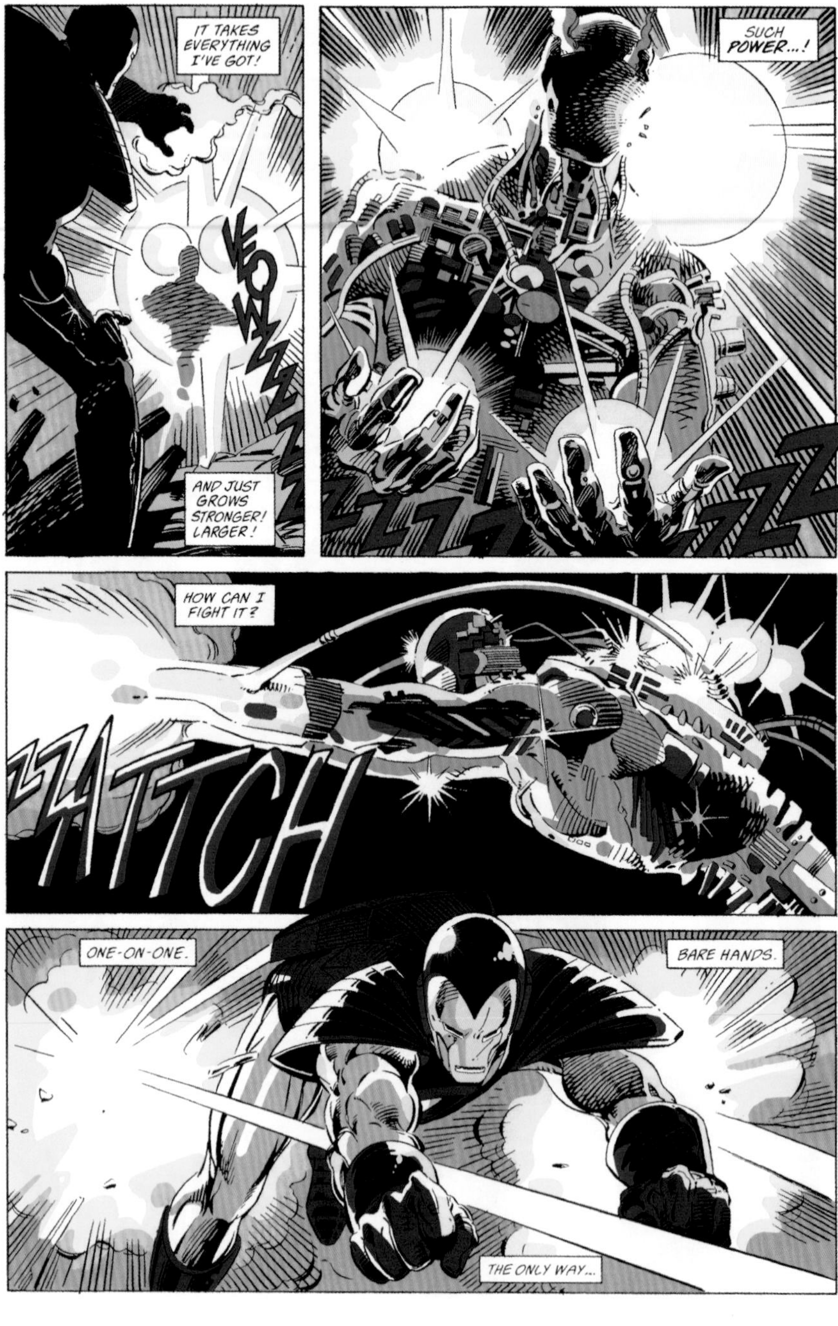
IT TAKES EVERYTHING I'VE GOT!
VEOWWZZZ
AND JUST GROWS STRONGER! LARGER!
SUCH POWER...!
ZZZ
HOW CAN I FIGHT IT?
ZZATTCH
ONE-ON-ONE.
BARE HANDS.
THE ONLY WAY...

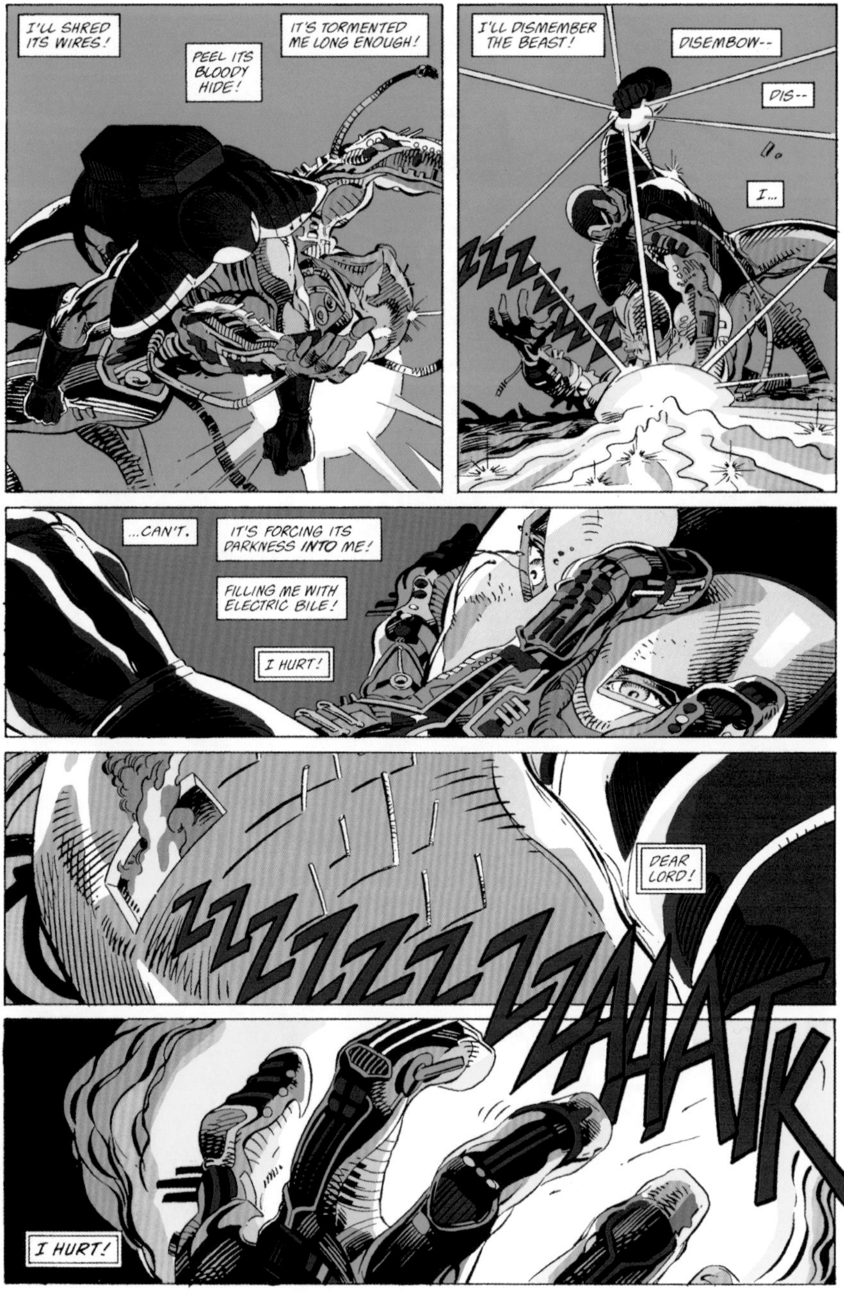
I'LL SHRED ITS WIRES!
PEEL ITS BLOODY HIDE!
IT'S TORMENTED ME LONG ENOUGH!
I'LL DISMEMBER THE BEAST!
DISEMBOW--
DIS--
I...
...CAN'T.
IT'S FORCING ITS DARKNESS INTO ME!
FILLING ME WITH ELECTRIC BILE!
I HURT!
DEAR LORD!
ZZZZZZZZZZAAATK
I HURT!

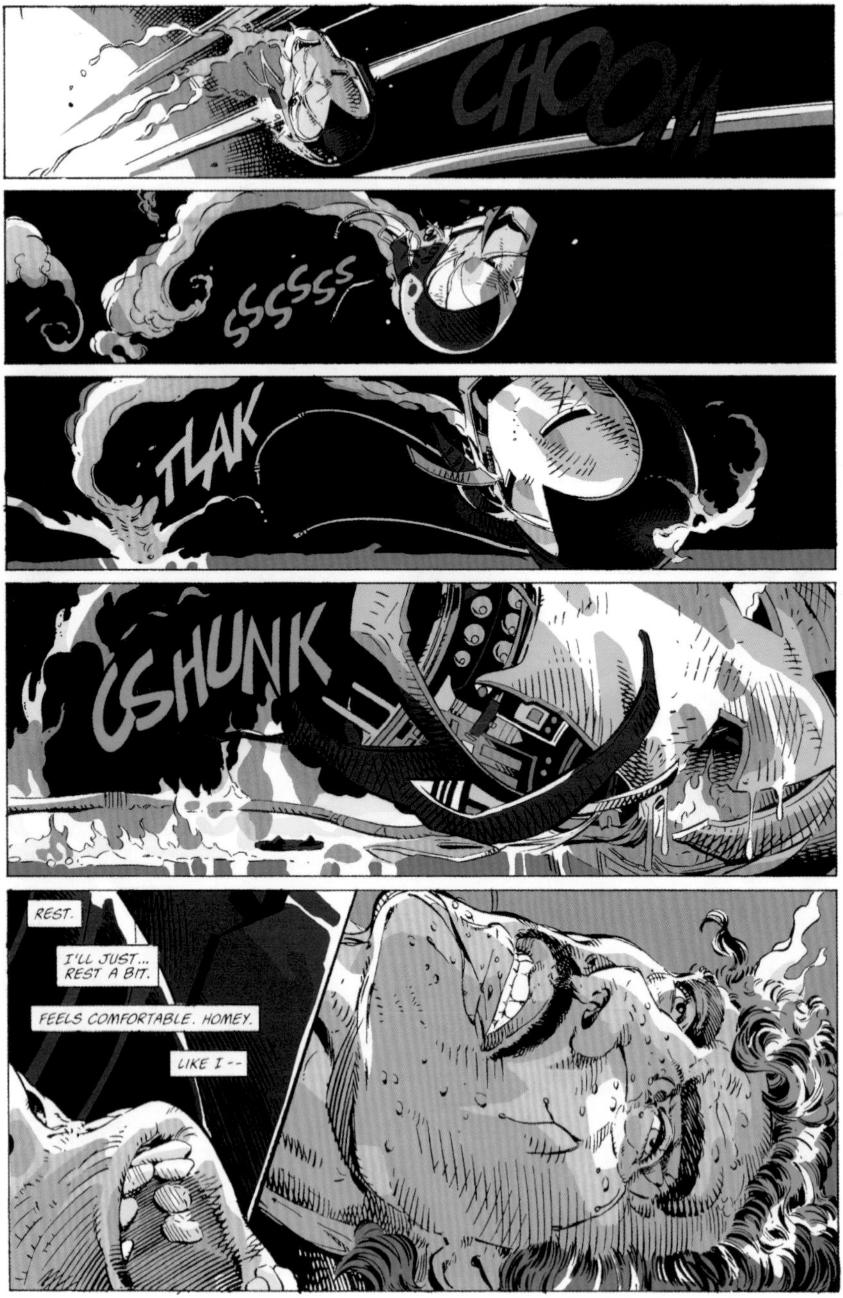
CHOOM
SSSSSS
TLAK
CSHUNK
REST.
I'LL JUST... REST A BIT.
FEELS COMFORTABLE. HOMEY.
LIKE I --

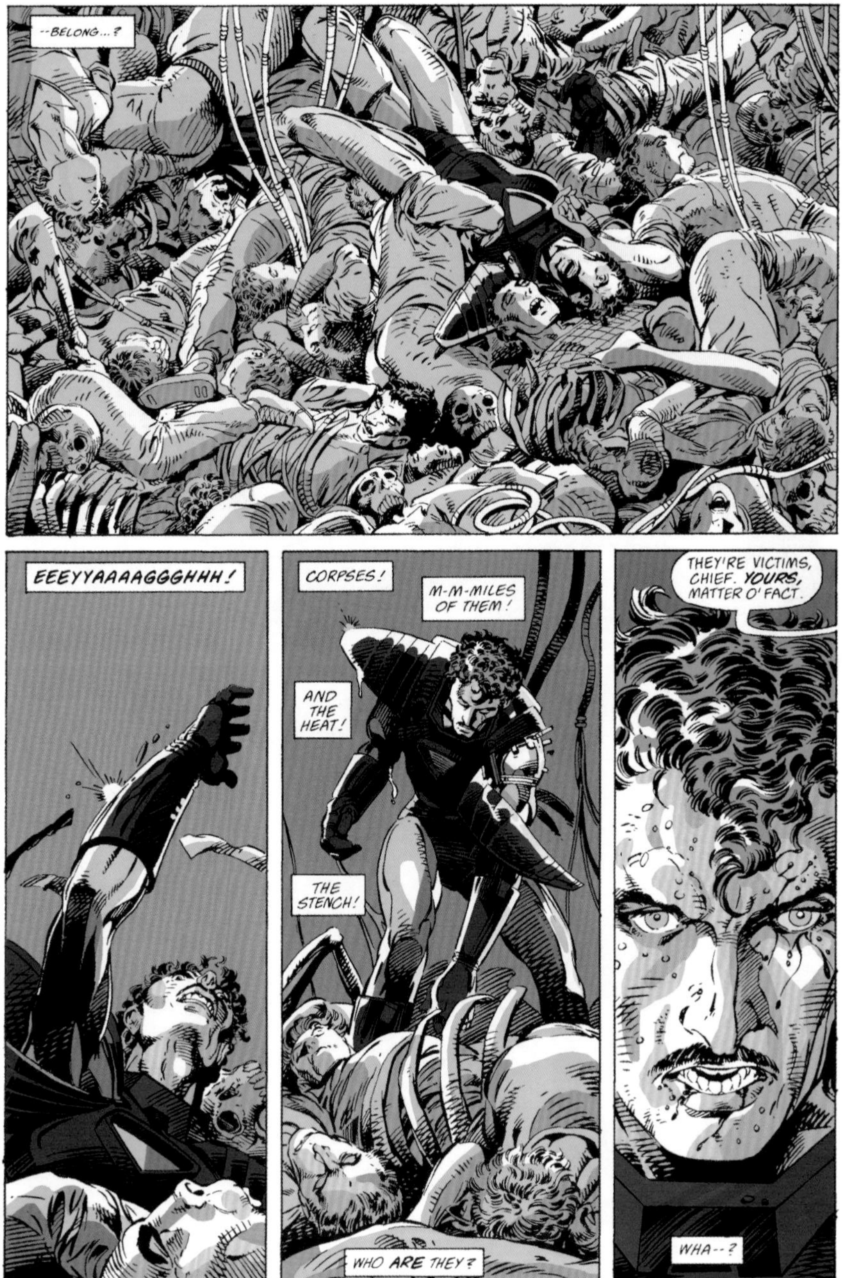
--BELONG...?
EEEYYAAAAGGGHHH!
CORPSES!
M-M-MILES OF THEM!
AND THE HEAT!
THE STENCH!
WHO ARE THEY?
THEY'RE VICTIMS, CHIEF. YOURS, MATTER O' FACT.
WHA--?

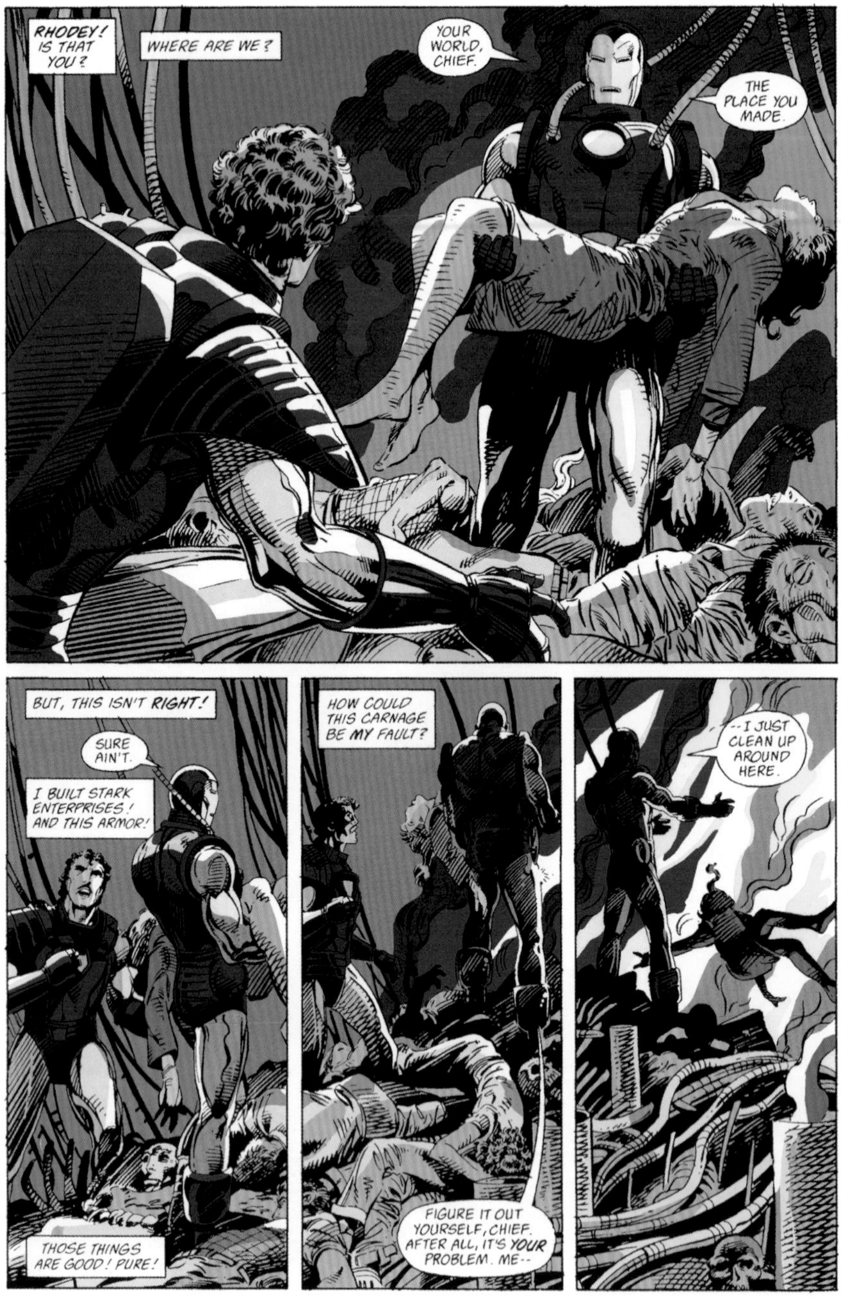
RHODEY! IS THAT YOU?
WHERE ARE WE?
YOUR WORLD, CHIEF.
THE PLACE YOU MADE.
BUT, THIS ISN'T RIGHT!
SURE AIN'T.
I BUILT STARK ENTERPRISES! AND THIS ARMOR!
THOSE THINGS ARE GOOD! PURE!
HOW COULD THIS CARNAGE BE MY FAULT?
FIGURE IT OUT YOURSELF, CHIEF. AFTER ALL, IT'S YOUR PROBLEM. ME--
--I JUST CLEAN UP AROUND HERE.

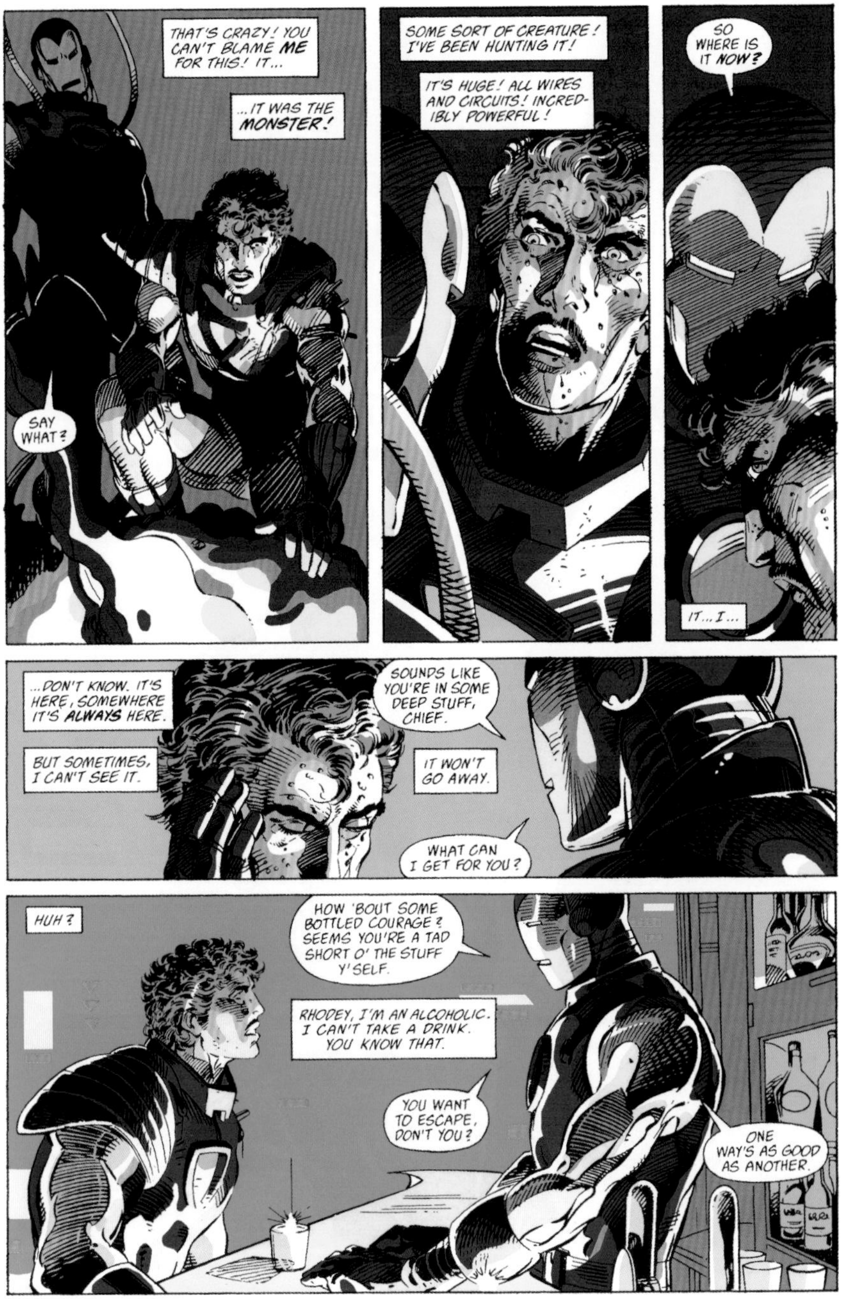
THAT'S CRAZY! YOU CAN'T BLAME **ME** FOR THIS! IT...
...IT WAS THE **MONSTER!**
SAY WHAT?
SOME SORT OF CREATURE! I'VE BEEN HUNTING IT!
IT'S HUGE! ALL WIRES AND CIRCUITS! INCREDIBLY POWERFUL!
SO WHERE IS IT **NOW?**
IT... I...
...DON'T KNOW. IT'S HERE, SOMEWHERE IT'S **ALWAYS** HERE.
BUT SOMETIMES, I CAN'T SEE IT.
SOUNDS LIKE YOU'RE IN SOME DEEP STUFF, CHIEF.
IT WON'T GO AWAY.
WHAT CAN I GET FOR YOU?
HUH?
HOW 'BOUT SOME BOTTLED COURAGE? SEEMS YOU'RE A TAD SHORT O' THE STUFF Y'SELF.
RHODEY, I'M AN ALCOHOLIC. I CAN'T TAKE A DRINK. YOU KNOW THAT.
YOU WANT TO ESCAPE, DON'T YOU?
ONE WAY'S AS GOOD AS ANOTHER.

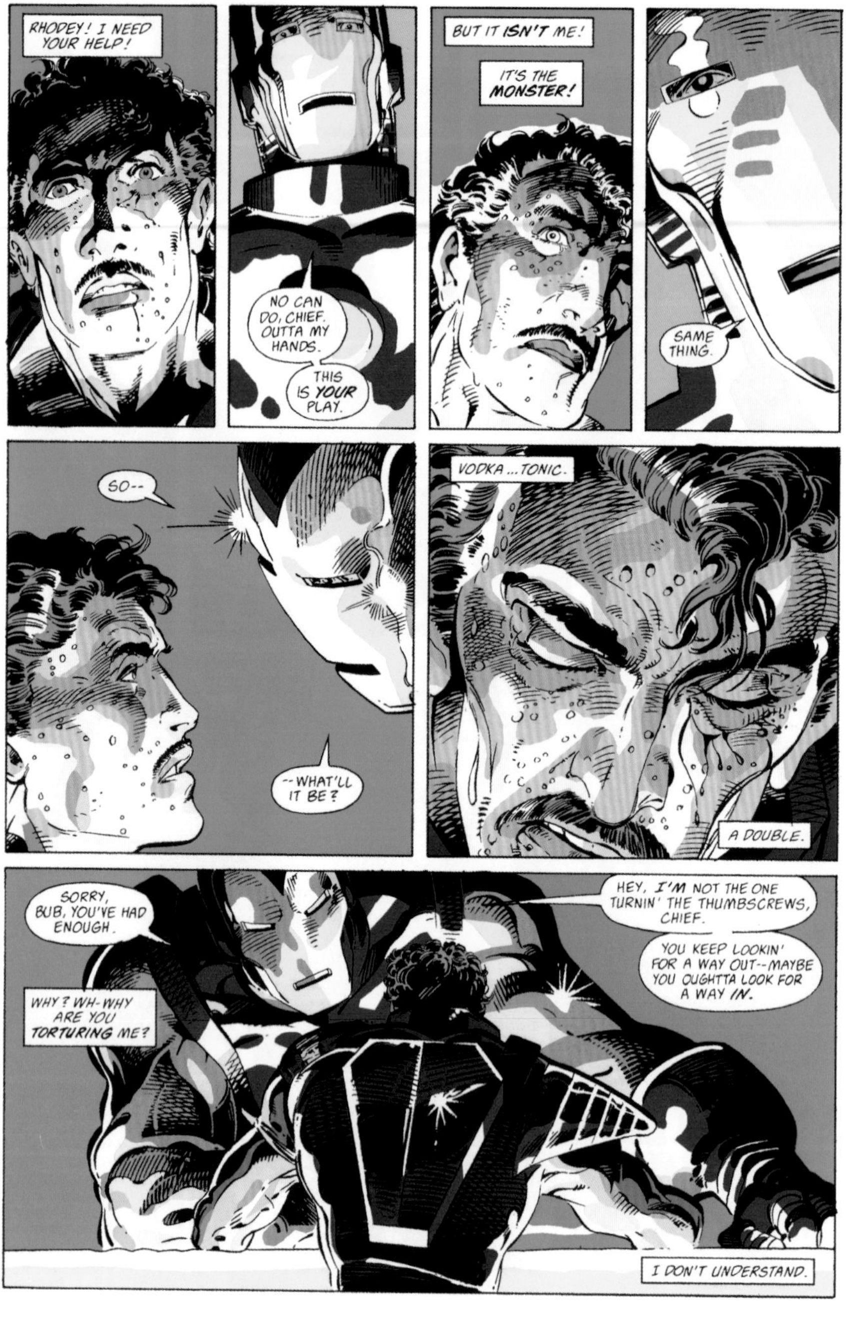
RHODEY! I NEED YOUR HELP!
NO CAN DO, CHIEF. OUTTA MY HANDS.
THIS IS YOUR PLAY.
BUT IT ISN'T ME!
IT'S THE MONSTER!
SAME THING.
SO--
--WHAT'LL IT BE?
VODKA...TONIC.
A DOUBLE.
SORRY, BUB, YOU'VE HAD ENOUGH.
WHY? WH-WHY ARE YOU TORTURING ME?
HEY, I'M NOT THE ONE TURNIN' THE THUMBSCREWS, CHIEF.
YOU KEEP LOOKIN' FOR A WAY OUT--MAYBE YOU OUGHTTA LOOK FOR A WAY IN.
I DON'T UNDERSTAND.

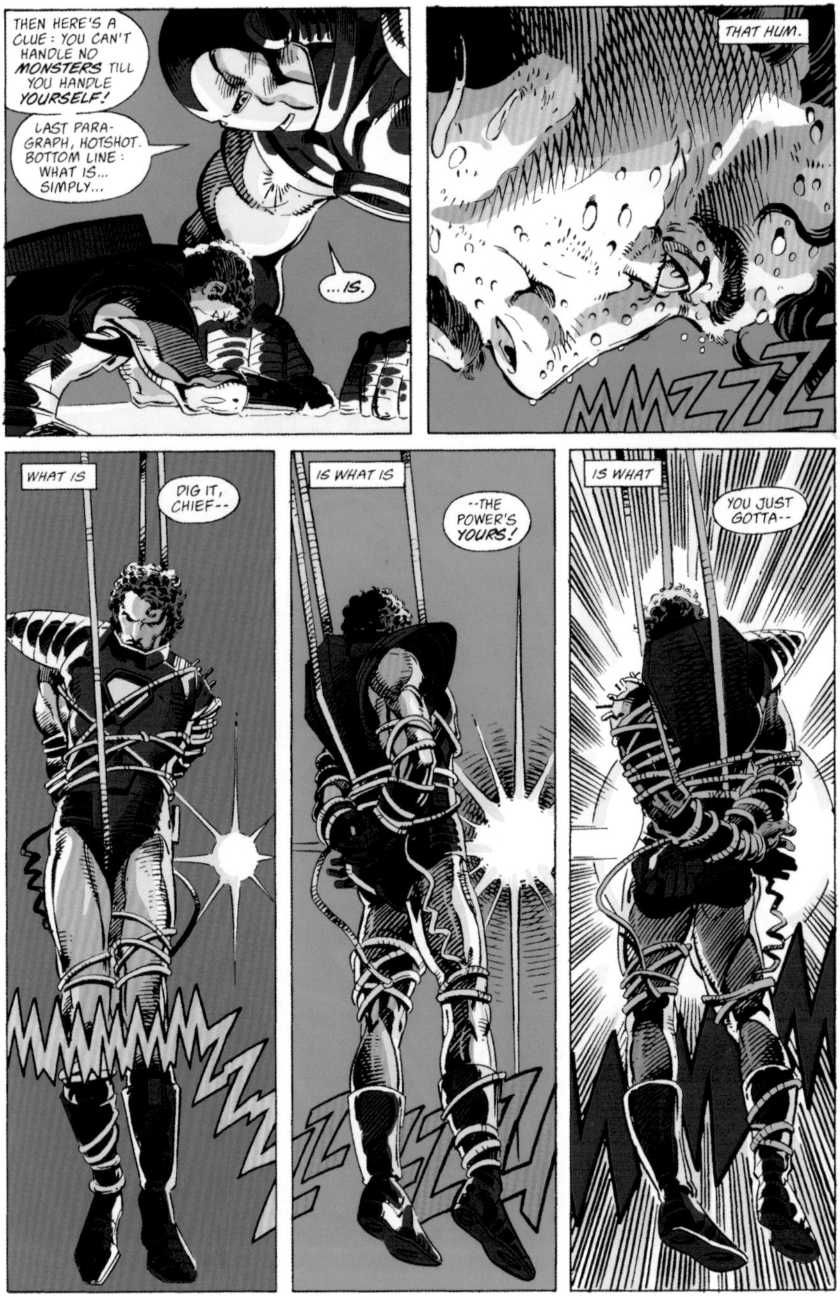
THEN HERE'S A CLUE: YOU CAN'T HANDLE NO MONSTERS TILL YOU HANDLE YOURSELF!
LAST PARAGRAPH, HOTSHOT. BOTTOM LINE: WHAT IS... SIMPLY...
...IS.
THAT HUM.
MMMZZZ
WHAT IS
DIG IT, CHIEF--
IS WHAT IS
--THE POWER'S YOURS!
IS WHAT
YOU JUST GOTTA--

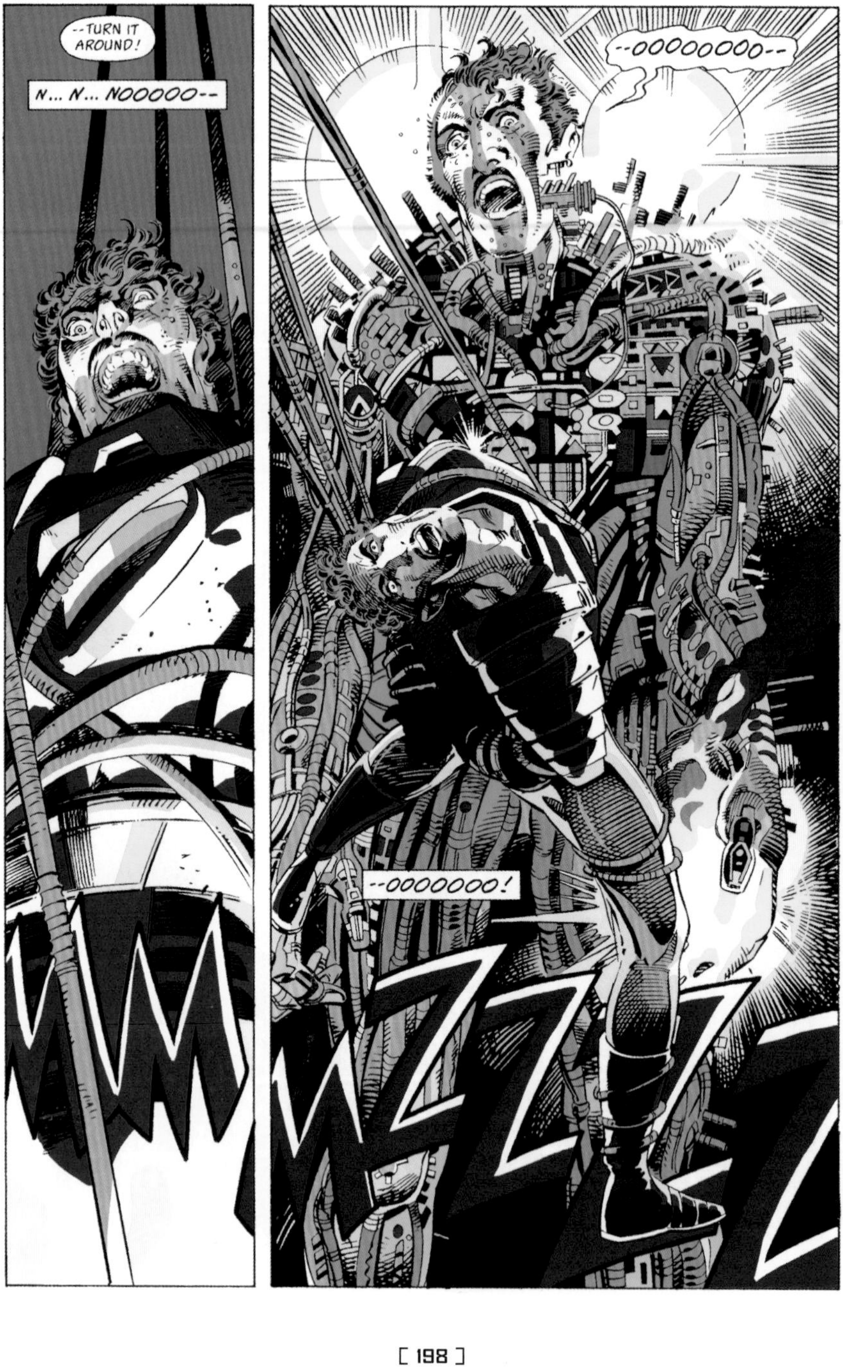
--TURN IT AROUND!
N... N... NOOOOO--
--OOOOOOOO--
--OOOOOOO!

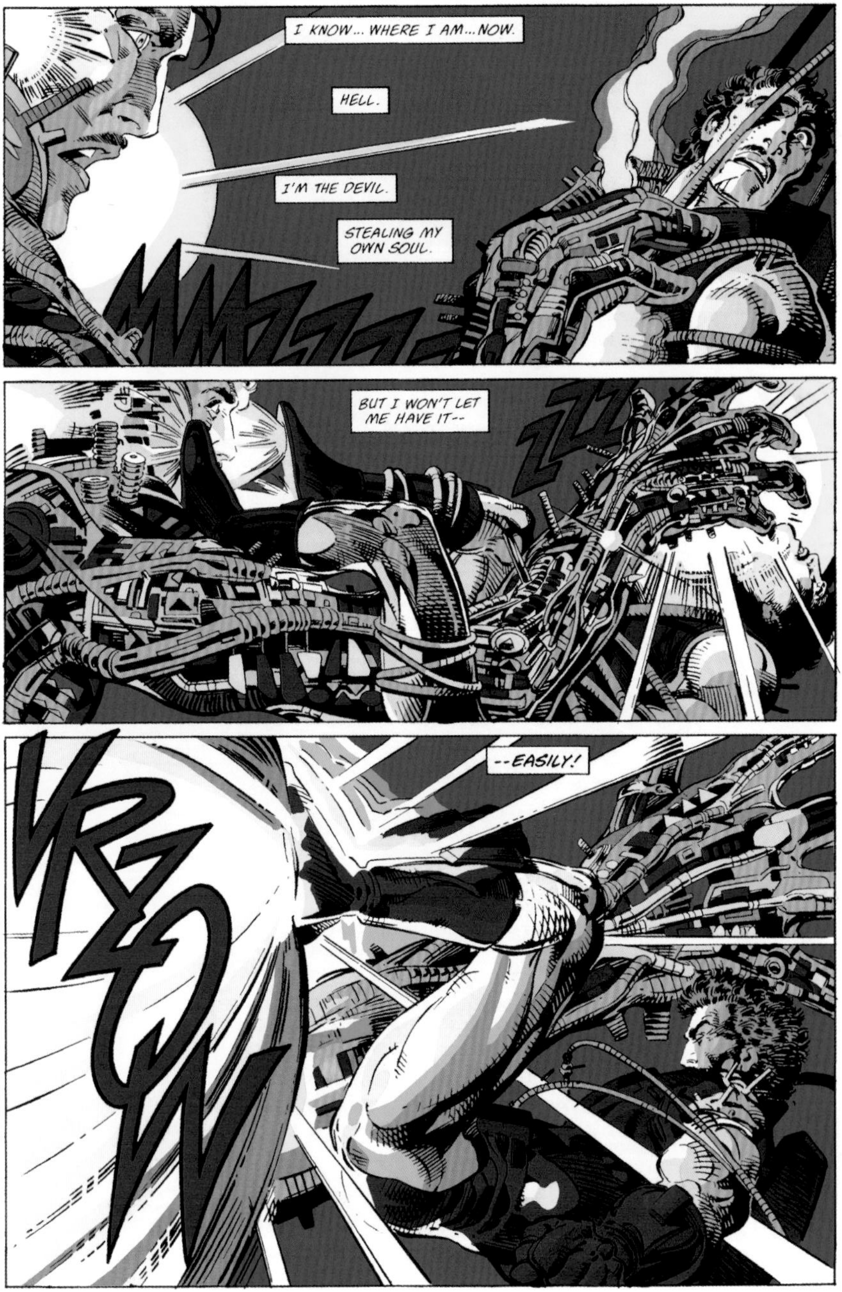
I KNOW... WHERE I AM... NOW.
HELL.
I'M THE DEVIL.
STEALING MY OWN SOUL.
MMMZZZZZ
BUT I WON'T LET ME HAVE IT--
ZZZ
--EASILY!
VRZOW

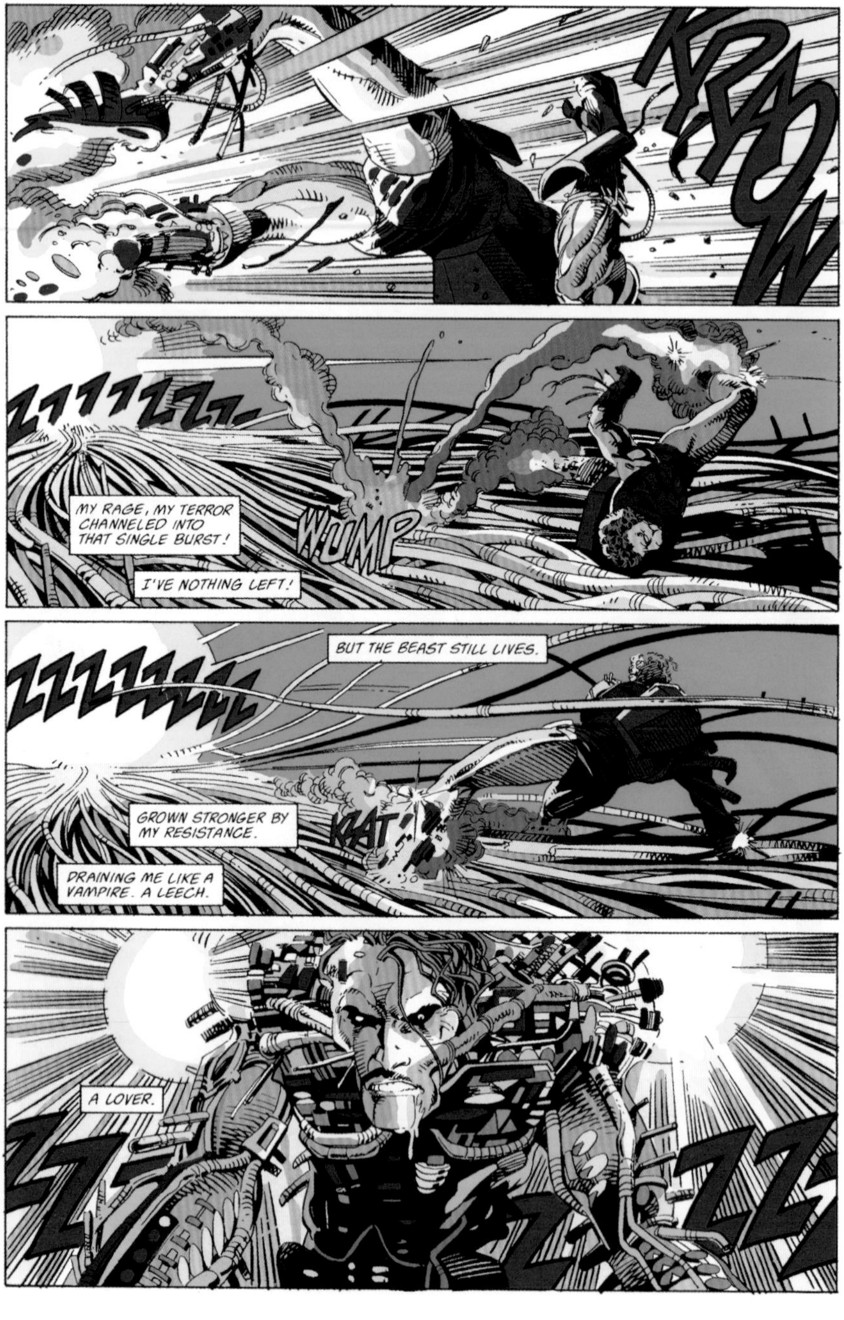
KRAOW
ZZZZZZZ
MY RAGE, MY TERROR CHANNELED INTO THAT SINGLE BURST!
WUMP
I'VE NOTHING LEFT!
BUT THE BEAST STILL LIVES.
ZZZZZZZZZ
GROWN STRONGER BY MY RESISTANCE.
KRAT
DRAINING ME LIKE A VAMPIRE. A LEECH.
A LOVER.
ZZZ
ZZZ

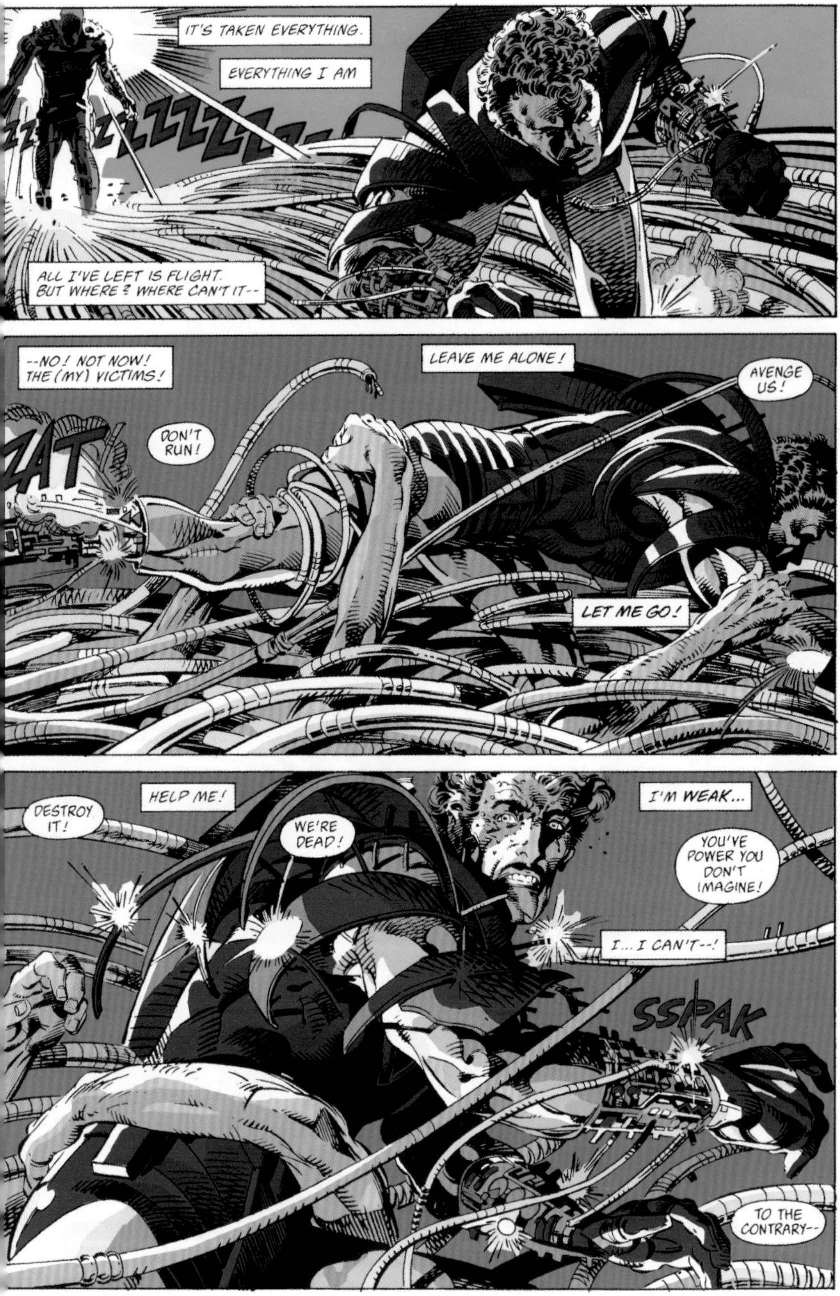

IT'S TAKEN EVERYTHING.
EVERYTHING I AM
ZZZZZZZZZ
ALL I'VE LEFT IS FLIGHT. BUT WHERE? WHERE CAN'T IT--
--NO! NOT NOW! THE (MY) VICTIMS!
LEAVE ME ALONE!
AVENGE US!
ZAT
DON'T RUN!
LET ME GO!
HELP ME!
DESTROY IT!
WE'RE DEAD!
I'M WEAK...
YOU'VE POWER YOU DON'T IMAGINE!
I... I CAN'T--!
SSPAK
TO THE CONTRARY--

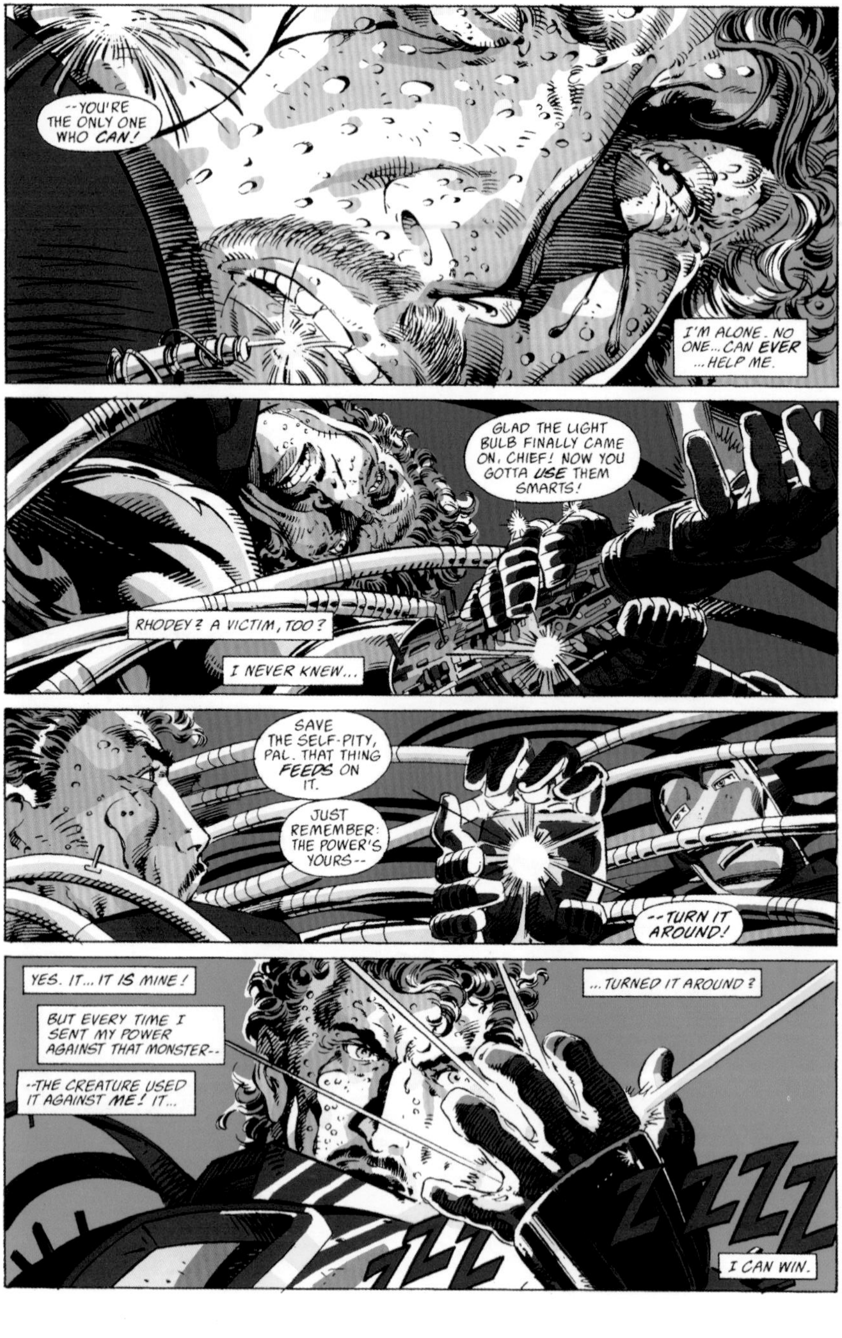
--YOU'RE THE ONLY ONE WHO CAN!
I'M ALONE. NO ONE... CAN EVER ...HELP ME.
GLAD THE LIGHT BULB FINALLY CAME ON, CHIEF! NOW YOU GOTTA USE THEM SMARTS!
RHODEY? A VICTIM, TOO?
I NEVER KNEW...
SAVE THE SELF-PITY, PAL. THAT THING FEEDS ON IT.
JUST REMEMBER: THE POWER'S YOURS--
--TURN IT AROUND!
YES. IT... IT IS MINE!
BUT EVERY TIME I SENT MY POWER AGAINST THAT MONSTER--
--THE CREATURE USED IT AGAINST ME! IT...
...TURNED IT AROUND?
ZZZ
ZZZZ
I CAN WIN.

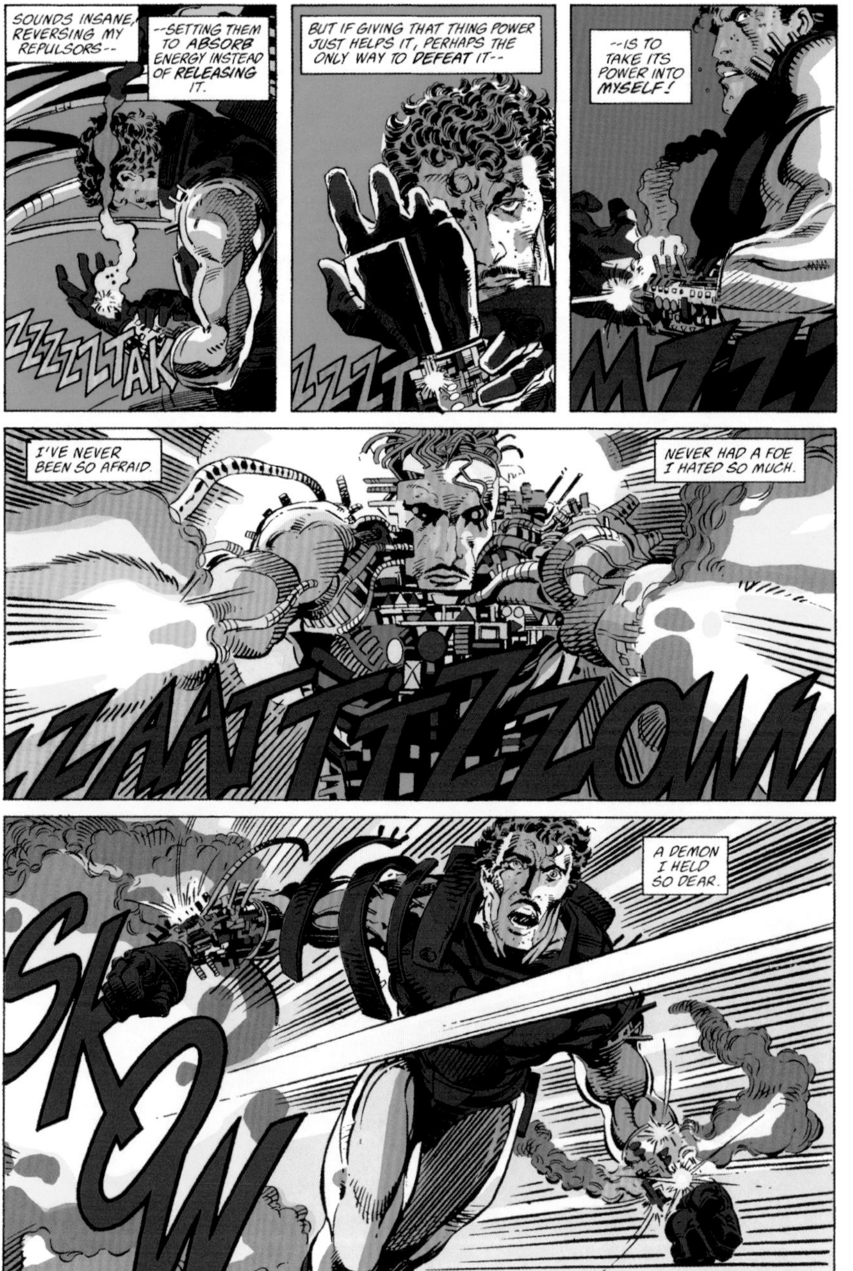
SOUNDS INSANE, REVERSING MY REPULSORS--
--SETTING THEM TO ABSORB ENERGY INSTEAD OF RELEASING IT.
ZZZZZTAK
BUT IF GIVING THAT THING POWER JUST HELPS IT, PERHAPS THE ONLY WAY TO DEFEAT IT--
--IS TO TAKE ITS POWER INTO MYSELF!
I'VE NEVER BEEN SO AFRAID.
NEVER HAD A FOE I HATED SO MUCH.
ZZAATTTZZOWW
A DEMON I HELD SO DEAR.

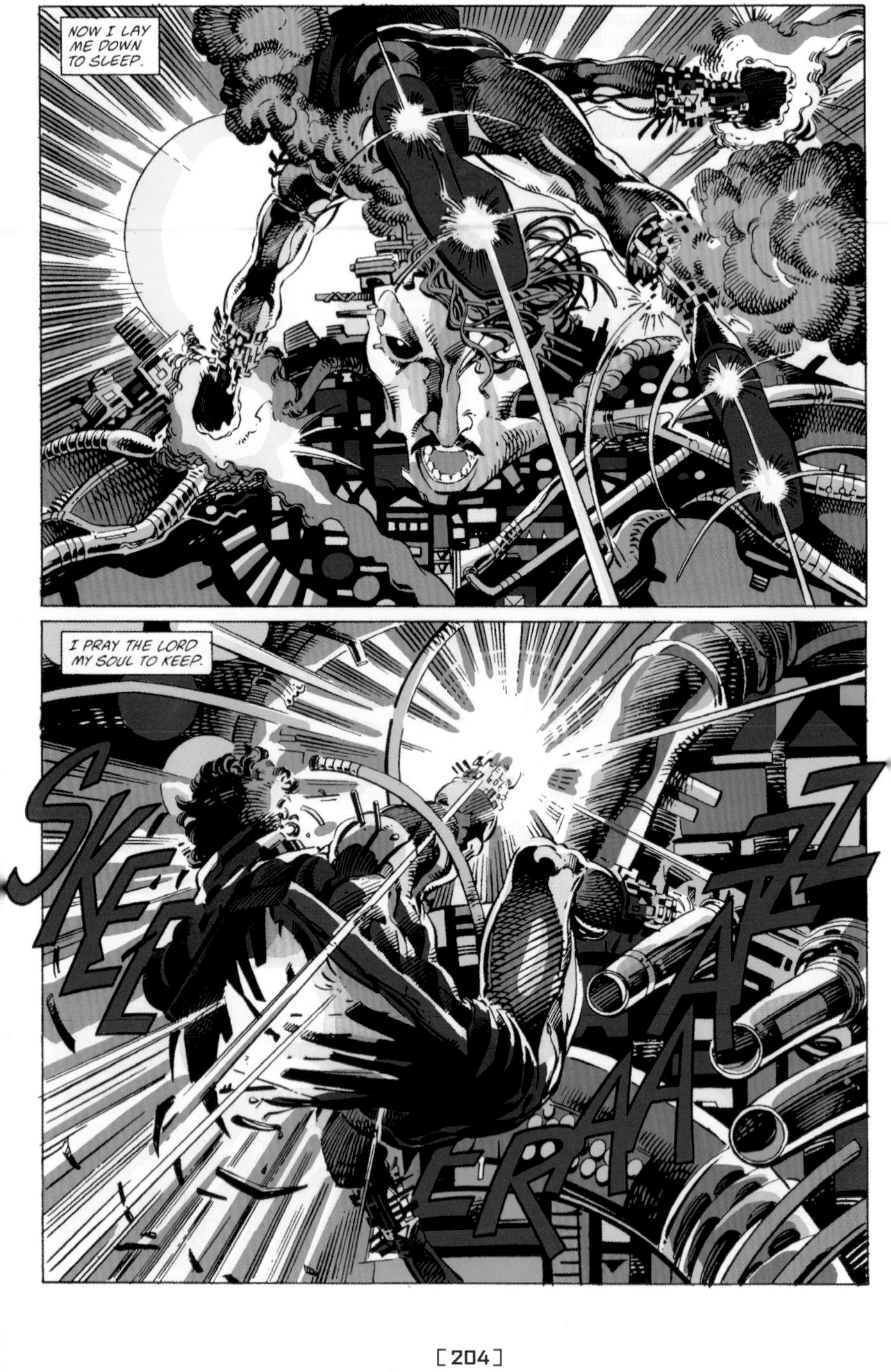

NOW I LAY ME DOWN TO SLEEP.
I PRAY THE LORD MY SOUL TO KEEP.

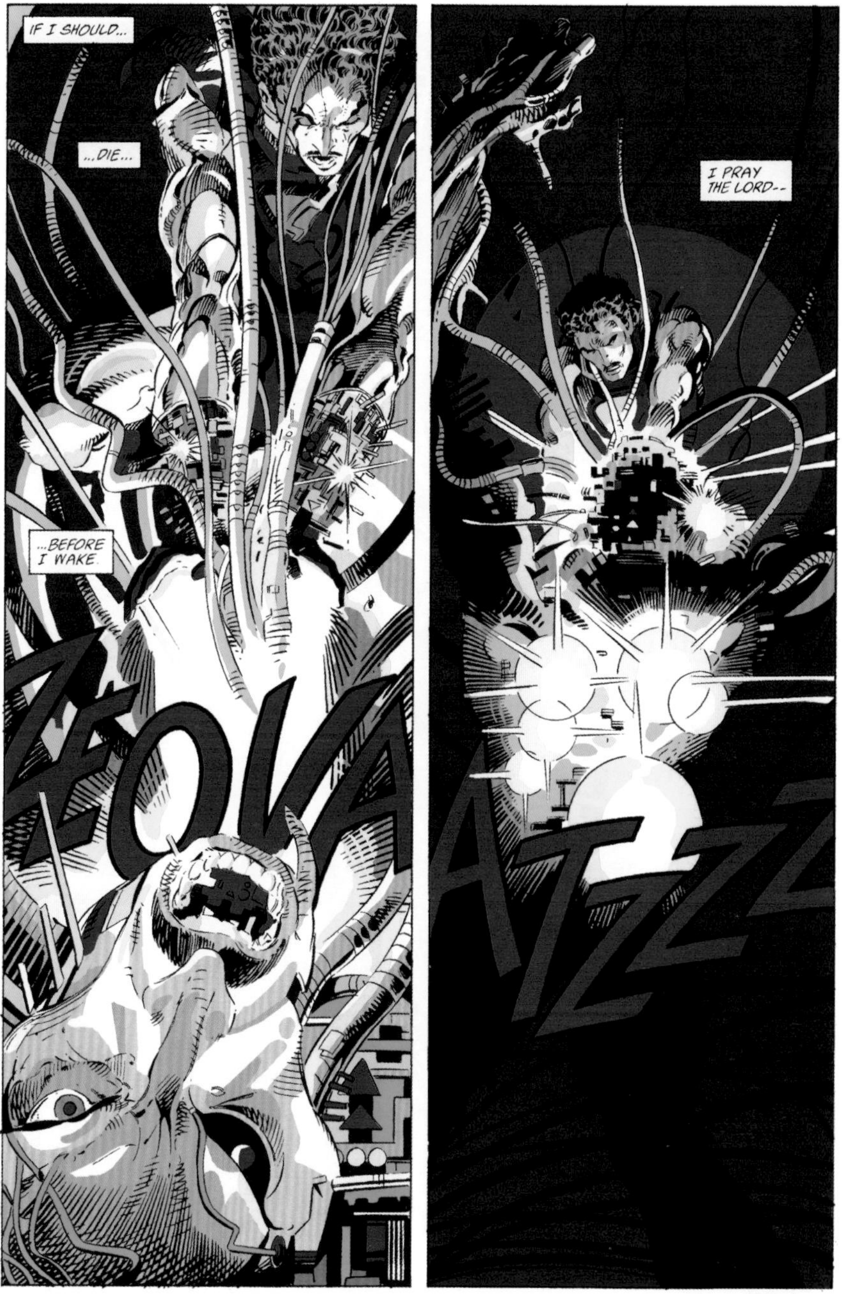
IF I SHOULD...
...DIE...
...BEFORE I WAKE.
ZOVA
I PRAY THE LORD--
ATZZZ

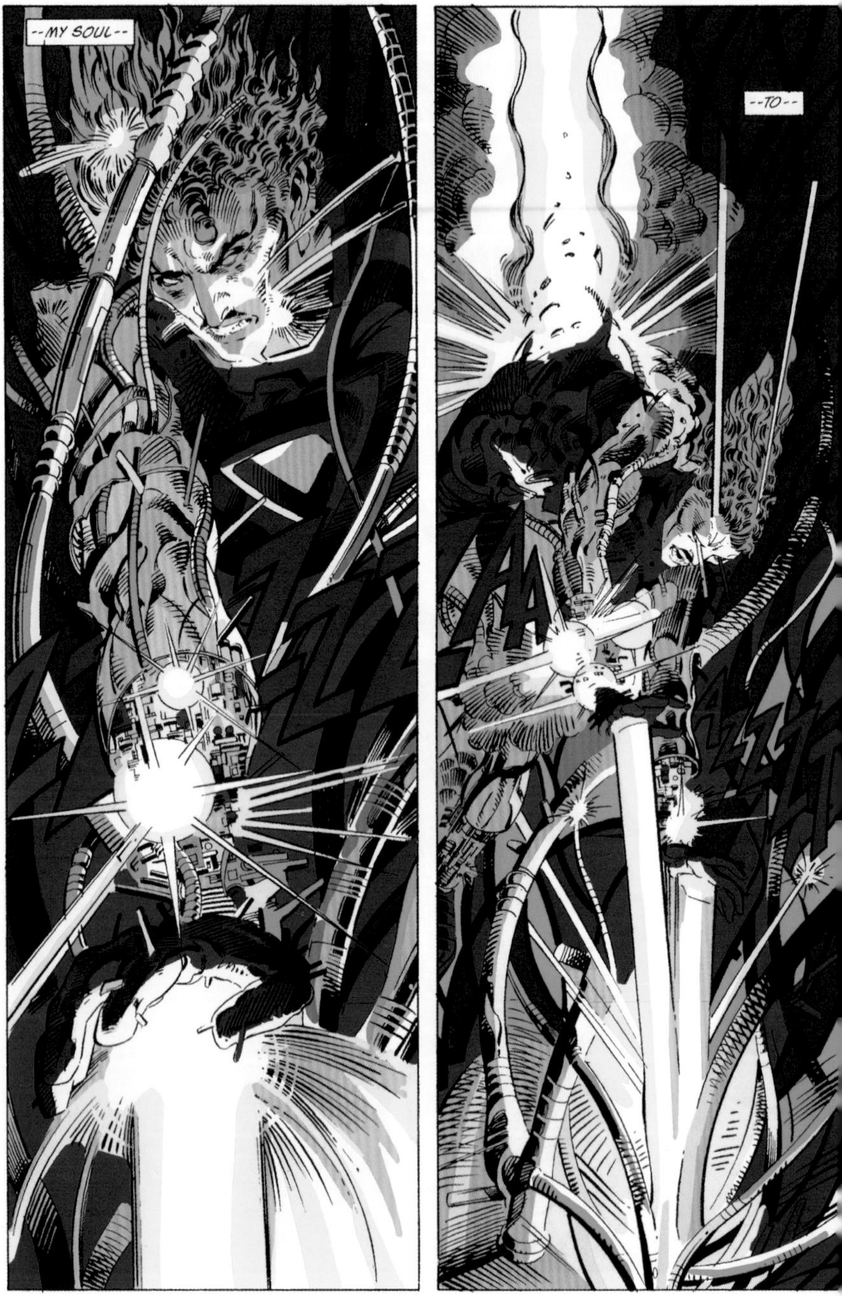
--MY SOUL--
--TO--

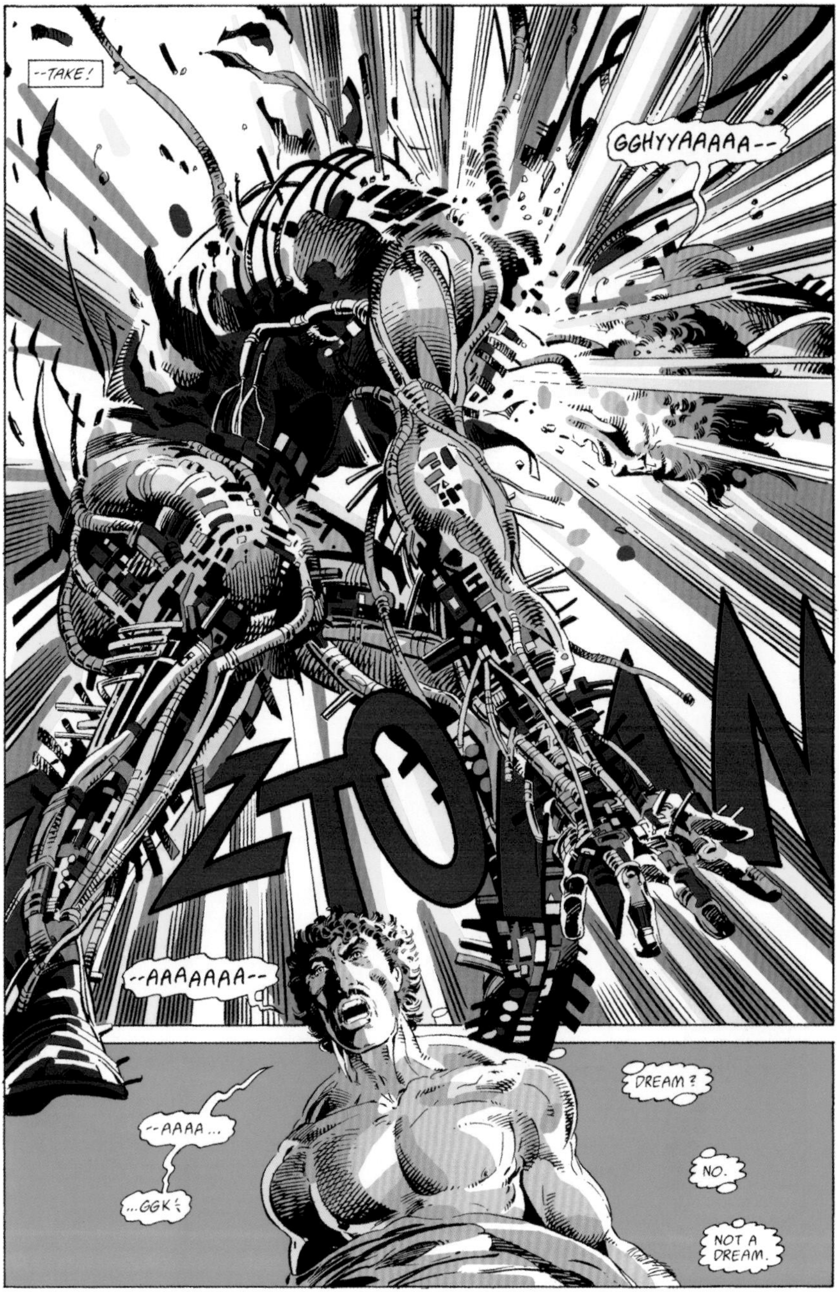
--TAKE!
GGHYYAAAAA--
ZTOM
--AAAAAAA--
--AAAA...
...GGK!
DREAM?
NO.
NOT A DREAM.

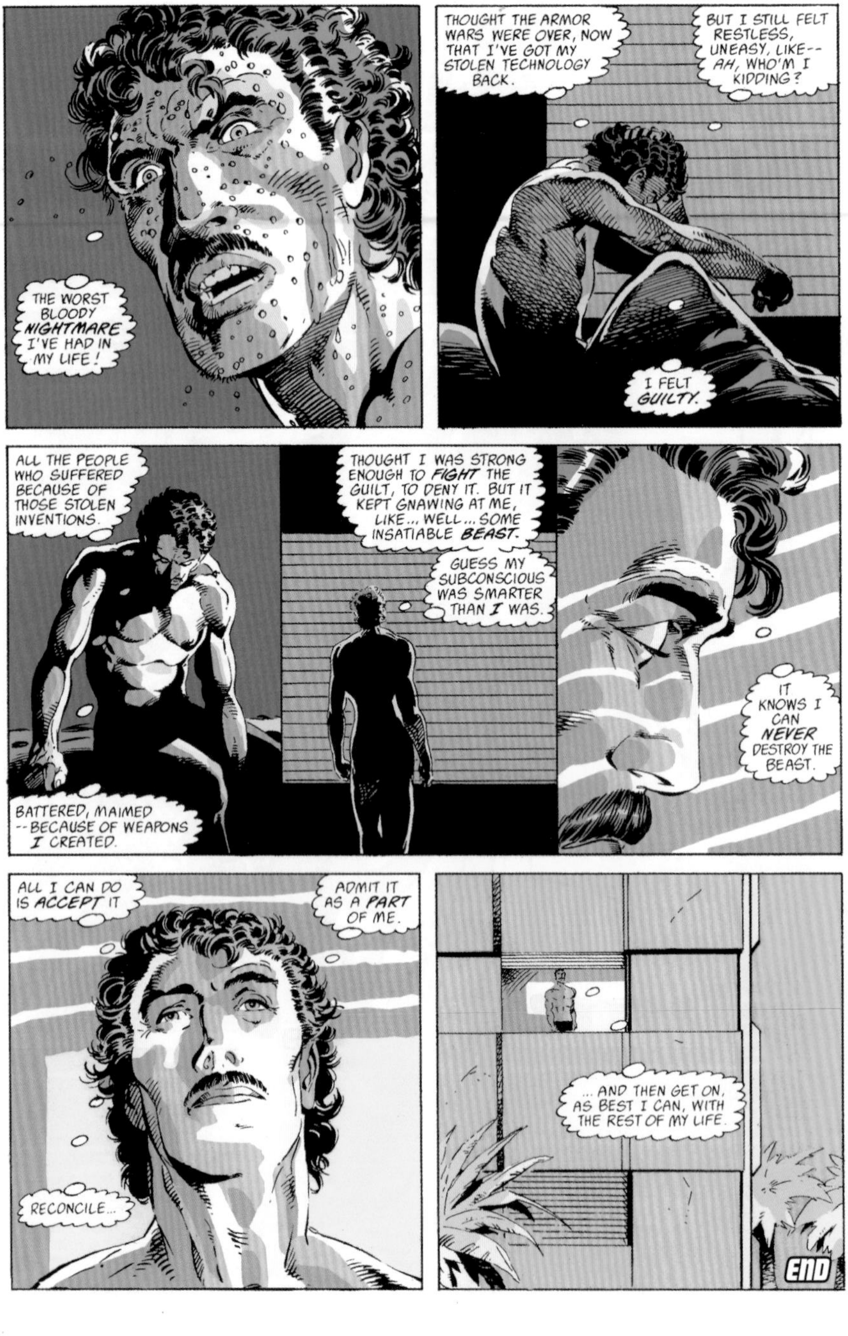
THE WORST BLOODY NIGHTMARE I'VE HAD IN MY LIFE!
THOUGHT THE ARMOR WARS WERE OVER, NOW THAT I'VE GOT MY STOLEN TECHNOLOGY BACK.
BUT I STILL FELT RESTLESS, UNEASY, LIKE-- AH, WHO'M I KIDDING?
I FELT GUILTY.
ALL THE PEOPLE WHO SUFFERED BECAUSE OF THOSE STOLEN INVENTIONS.
BATTERED, MAIMED --BECAUSE OF WEAPONS I CREATED.
THOUGHT I WAS STRONG ENOUGH TO FIGHT THE GUILT, TO DENY IT. BUT IT KEPT GNAWING AT ME, LIKE... WELL... SOME INSATIABLE BEAST.
GUESS MY SUBCONSCIOUS WAS SMARTER THAN I WAS.
IT KNOWS I CAN NEVER DESTROY THE BEAST.
ALL I CAN DO IS ACCEPT IT
ADMIT IT AS A PART OF ME.
RECONCILE...
... AND THEN GET ON, AS BEST I CAN, WITH THE REST OF MY LIFE.
END

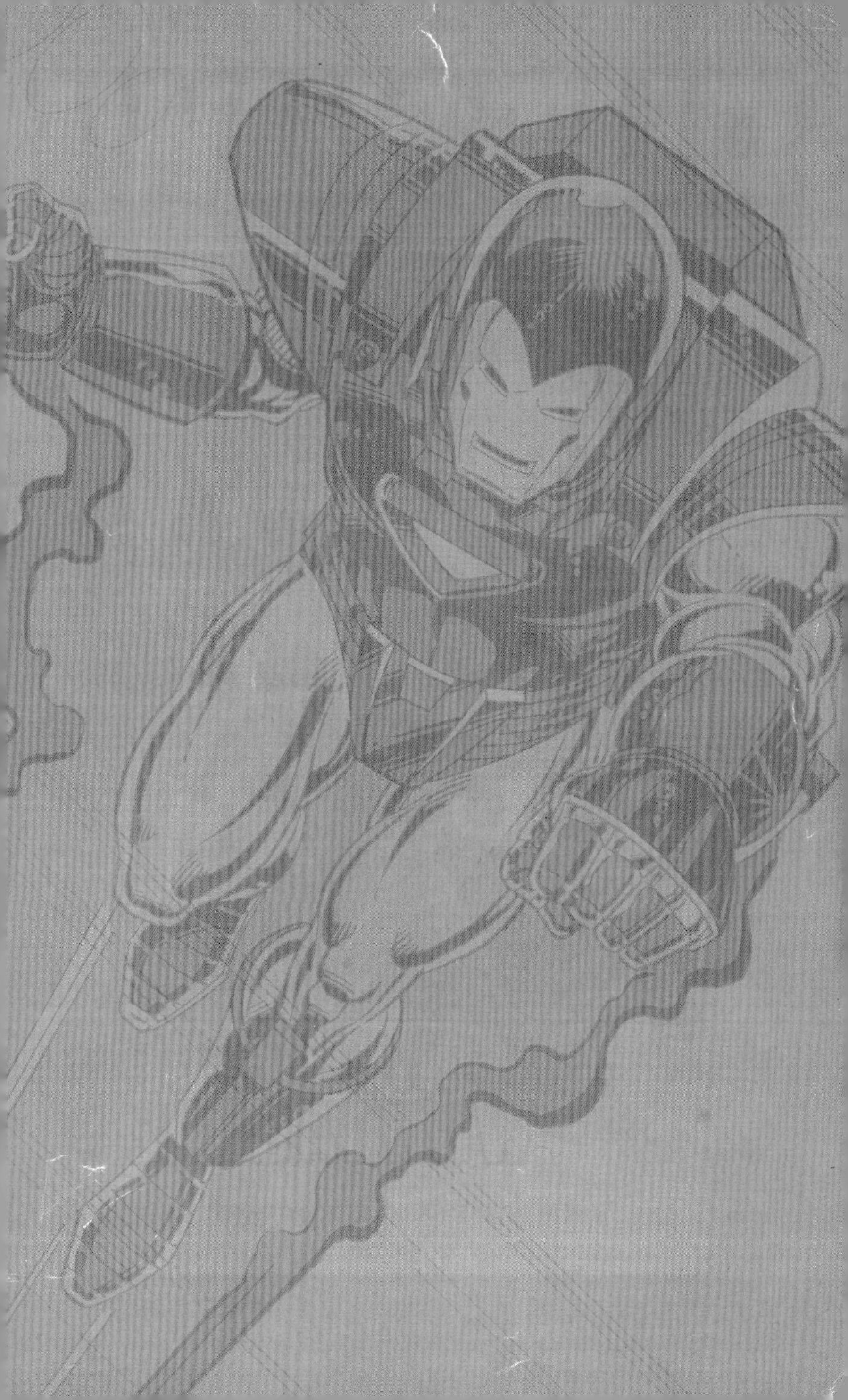

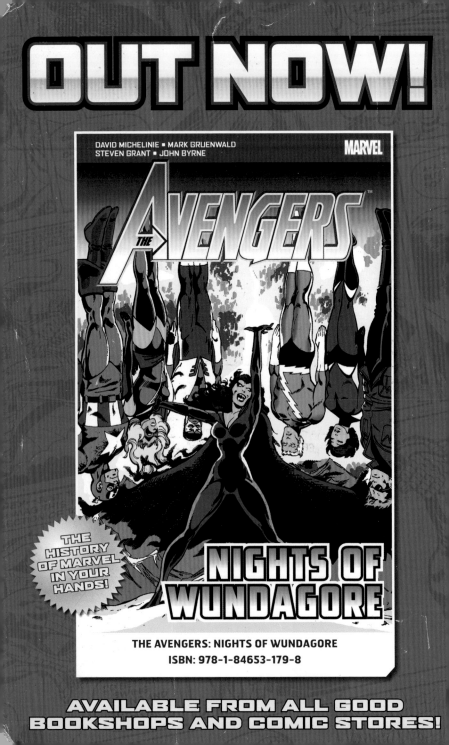